Errata:

Cover illustration: Reconstruction by Mark Gridley
showing the building of the Iron Age defences at Taplow

Plate 1.1. Copyright GeoPerspectives

Translations by Markus Dylewski, Nathalie Haudecoeur-Wilks and Magali Bailliot

From Bronze Age enclosure to Anglo-Saxon settlement

Archaeological excavations at Taplow hillfort, Buckinghamshire, 1999-2005

by Tim Allen, Chris Hayden and Hugo Lamdin-Whymark

with contributions by
Roger Ainslie, Leigh Allen, Edward Biddulph, Paul Blinkhorn, Matthew Canti, Dana Challinor, Kate Cramp, Emily Edwards, Emma-Jane Evans, Rowena Gale, Peter Hacking, Elias Kupfermann, Peter Marshall, Peter Northover, Adrian Parker, Mark Robinson, Jean-Luc Schwenninger, Ruth Shaffrey and Roberta Tomber

Illustrations by
Julia Moxham, Magdalena Wachnik, Jeff Wallis, Lucy Martin, Amy Hemingway, Sarah Lucas and Georgina Slater

Oxford Archaeology
Thames Valley Landscapes Monograph No 30
2009

The publication of this volume has been generously funded by English Heritage

Published for Oxford Archaeology by Oxford University School of Archaeology as part of the Thames Valley Landscapes Monograph series

Designed by Oxford Archaeology Graphics Office

Edited by Alan Hardy and Tim Allen

This book is part of a series of monographs about the Thames Valley Landscapes – which can be bought from all good bookshops and internet bookshops.

For more information visit **thehumanjourney.net**

© 2009 The Oxford Archaeological Unit Ltd

Figures 1.1 and 1.2 are reproduced from the Ordnance Survey on behalf of the controller of Her Majesty's Stationery Office, © Crown Copyright, AL100005569

ISBN-13: 978-1-905905-09-6

Typeset by Production Line, Oxford
Printed in Great Britain by Information Press, Eynsham, Oxford

Contents

List of Figures xi
List of Plates xv
List of Tables xvii
Summary xxi
Acknowledgements xxiv

CHAPTER 1: THE PROJECT 1
    INTRODUCTION 1
    LOCATION, GEOLOGY, GEOGRAPHY AND TOPOGRAPHY 1
    SITE LOCATION AND PROJECT BACKGROUND 1
    RESEARCH AIMS OF THE PROJECT 4
    ARCHAEOLOGICAL BACKGROUND 5
        Palaeolithic and Mesolithic 5
        Neolithic to early Bronze Age 5
        Middle and late Bronze Age 5
        Iron Age 5
        Roman 5
        Anglo-Saxon 7
        Medieval 8
        Post-medieval 8
    PRELIMINARY FIELDWORK 8
        The 1998 archaeological evaluation 8
        The Taplow Court Archaeological Survey Team (TCAST) trenches ... 8
        The main excavations 1999-2005 9
    EXCAVATION METHODOLOGY AND LIMITATIONS 9
        General 9
        Maps and aerial photographs 11
        Geophysical survey 12
    THE STRUCTURE OF THIS REPORT 13
        Conventions used in this report 14

CHAPTER 2: CHRONOLOGY 15
    INTRODUCTION 15
    LIMITATIONS OF THE EVIDENCE 15

CHAPTER 3: BEFORE THE HILLFORT: FROM THE MESOLITHIC TO THE MIDDLE BRONZE AGE 23
    INTRODUCTION 23
    FLINT DISTRIBUTIONS 23
        Mesolithic activity 23
        Mesolithic and Neolithic flint in tree-throw holes 23

    Early Bronze Age activity 28
        The early Bronze Age hollows (1119) 28
        Finds in the early Bronze Age hollows and other early Bronze Age finds 29
        Pit 133 and other evidence of early Bronze Age activity 32
        An undated ditch (1114) and a possible continuation (1079) 32
        Subsoil layers, rampart deposits and ditch 1114 in the south-western part of the site 32
    Middle Bronze Age activity 33

CHAPTER 4: THE LATE BRONZE AGE HILLFORT 35

    INTRODUCTION 35
    LATE BRONZE AGE DEFENCES 35
    The stratigraphic evidence 35
    Posthole rows 1107 and 1108 35
        The stratigraphic relationships and dating evidence for posthole row 1107 35
        The stratigraphic relationships and dating evidence for posthole row 1108 39
        The dimensions and spacing of posthole rows 1107 and 1108 39
        Other finds associated with postholes rows 1107 and 1108 41
        The possible structure or structures associated with posthole rows 1107 and 1108 41
    Palisade trench 1106 41
        The form of the palisade associated with trench 1106 45
        Finds and other dating evidence associated with palisade trench 1106 46
    Posthole rows within the hillfort (935, 1132 and 1133) 47
        Finds and other dating evidence associated with posthole rows 935, 1132 and 1133 47
        Posthole row 1132 47
        The interpretation of posthole rows 935, 1132 and 1133 49
    The V-profiled ditch (574) and its rampart 50
        The V-profiled ditch 574 and its fills 50
        Finds from the V-profiled ditch (574) 54
        Rampart (1120) associated with the V-profiled ditch 56
        The extent and character of the rampart 1120 57
        The entrance 58
    Posthole row 1104 58
        Dating evidence and other finds associated with posthole row 1104 62
    Activity within the hillfort 63
        Posthole group and possible roundhouse 1117, four-post structures FP1-3 and the
        occupation layer (1121 and 1123) 63
        Dating evidence and other finds from posthole group 1117 63
        Finds associated with occupation layer within the hillfort and around posthole group
        1117, including the decorated late Bronze Age bracelet 63
        Relationship of the occupation deposit to the posthole circle 1117 65
        Posthole group and possible roundhouse 1134, and possible four-post structures FP4-7 67
        Finds associated with posthole group and possible roundhouse 1134 69
    Activity outside the hillfort 70
        Pit 3032 and residual late Bronze Age pottery in the outer ditch 70
    The standstill layer (1102) 71
        The formation of the standstill layer 71

CHAPTER 5: THE EARLY-MIDDLE IRON AGE HILLFORT 73

    INTRODUCTION 73
    THE U-PROFILED DITCH (460) 73

THE RAMPART	75
The chalk kerb (925) and posthole row 1104	78
The timber rampart structure	80
Sediments	83
The form of the rampart	83
DESTRUCTION OF THE HILLFORT DEFENCES	85
The burning of the rampart	85
The lower fills of the U-profiled ditch (460)	87
Finds from the lower fills of the U-profiled ditch (460) and its rampart	90
THE ENTRANCE	92
Pit 1016	92
Posthole row and foundation trench 987	94
Gully 647 and associated features	94
The hornwork (1118)	95
The entrance structure	95
THE OUTER DITCH (3050)	95
Evidence for activity within the early-middle Iron Age hillfort	99

CHAPTER 6: LATE IRON AGE AND ROMAN ACTIVITY AND ANGLO-SAXON OCCUPATION 101

EVIDENCE FOR LATE IRON AGE AND ROMAN ACTIVITY	101
THE ANGLO-SAXON EVIDENCE	101
Inhumation 105 and other human remains	101
The condition of the hillfort in the Anglo-Saxon period	101
Anglo-Saxon finds in the top of the U-profiled and outer ditches (460 and 3050), including the possibly eastern Mediterranean sherd	104
Other Anglo-Saxon finds: tree-throw hole 3030 and the TCAST trenches	105
Foundation trench 846	105

CHAPTER 7: ARTEFACTS 109

FLINT *by Kate Cramp and Hugo Lamdin-Whymark*	109
Methodology	109
Condition	109
Raw materials	109
The assemblage	111
Mesolithic	111
Neolithic	111
Tree-throw hole 813	111
Tree-throw hole 816	113
Tree-throw hole 914	113
Early Bronze Age	115
Hollow 578	115
Later Bronze Age	118
Discussion	118
PREHISTORIC POTTERY *by Emily Edwards*	119
Methodology	119
Condition	119
Summary of provenance and dating	119
Fabrics	120
Sources of raw materials	122

  Forms 122
   Decoration and surface treatment 123
 Pottery by groups 123
  The early Bronze Age hollows (1119) 124
  The V-profiled ditch (574) 124
  The occupation layer (1121 and 1123) 124
  The standstill layer (1102) 125
  The rampart gravels (1100 and 1112) 126
  The posthole rows (935, 1104, 1107 and 1108) and the palisade trench (1106) 126
  The U-profiled ditch (460) 126
  The possible roundhouse (1117) and surrounding postholes 126
  Other discrete features 126
 Pottery recovered by TCAST 126
 Discussion 128
LATE IRON AGE AND ROMAN POTTERY *by Edward Biddulph* 134
 Wares 134
 Vessels 135
  Condition and chronology 136
 Roman pottery from the hillfort 136
ANGLO-SAXON POTTERY *by Paul Blinkhorn* 136
 Methodology 136
 Fabrics 136
 Anglo-Saxon pottery from the main excavation 136
  Fabrics 137
  Chronology 137
  Vessel forms 138
 Anglo-Saxon pottery from the TCAST trenches 138
  Chronology 138
 Discussion 138
 Catalogue of illustrated Anglo-Saxon pottery 139
 The possibly eastern Mediterranean late Roman sherd *by Roberta Tomber* 139
METALWORK 140
 The bronze bracelet 140
 Analysis of the bronze bracelet *by Peter Northover* 140
  The metal 141
  Conclusions 141
 Other metalwork *by Leigh Allen* 141
  Copper alloy objects 141
  Iron objects 142
  Lead objects 142
FIRED CLAY *by Emily Edwards* 143
 Introduction 143
 Methodology 143
  Condition 143
  Fabrics 143
  Range and variety of material 144
  Provenance 144
 Fired clay by category (excluding amorphous fragments) 144
  Loomweights 144
  Oven or hearth clay 145
  Other objects 145
 Discussion 145

WORKED STONE *by Ruth Shaffrey* 145
   Introduction 145
   Description 145
   Catalogue 146

CHAPTER 8: ENVIRONMENTAL EVIDENCE 147

   HUMAN SKELETAL REMAINS *by Peter Hacking* 147
      Introduction 147
      Methodology 147
      Results 147
         Grave 105, skeleton 107 147
         The U-profiled ditch (460), cut 376, layer 214 147
   ANIMAL BONE *by Emma-Jayne Evans* 147
      Methodology 147
      Results 147
      Discussion 149
   CHARRED PLANT REMAINS (excluding charcoal) *by Mark Robinson* 149
      Introduction 149
      Methodology 150
         Mesolithic 150
         Earlier Neolithic tree-throw hole 497 150
         Early Bronze Age hollows (1119) 150
         Middle Bronze Age 150
         Posthole row 1104 150
         Late Bronze Age posthole circle 1117 150
         Anglo-Saxon fills of the U-profiled ditch (460) 150
         Anglo-Saxon fills of the outer defensive ditch (3050) 151
      Discussion 151
   CHARCOAL *by Rowena Gale* 151
      Methodology 153
      Results 153
      Discussion 153
         Early Bronze Age hollows (1119) 153
         Early-middle Iron Age rampart gravels (1100) 154
      The timber structure (1113) *by Dana Challinor* 154
         Anglo-Saxon deposits in the U-profiled ditch (460) 154
      Environmental evidence 154
   PHYTOLITHS AND POLLEN *by Adrian G Parker* 155
      Methodology 155
      Results and discussion 158
         The V-profiled ditch (574) 158
         The U-profiled ditch (460) 158
         Conclusions 159
      Deposits and site formation processes *by M G Canti* 159
         Introduction 159
         Dark feature fills and deposits (1100, 1120 and 1123) 159
         Reddened fills (1100) 161

CHAPTER 9: ABSOLUTE DATES 165

   INTRODUCTION 165

OPTICALLY STIMULATED LUMINESCENCE DATES *by Jean-Luc Schwenninger* 165
    Methodology 165
    Results 165
RADIOCARBON DATES AND BAYESIAN MODELLING *by P Marshall, D Hamilton, T Allen,*
C Bronk Ramsey, G Cook, J-L Schwenninger and C Hayden 167
    Introduction 167
    Methodology 167
    Results 168
        Calibration 168
        Stable isotopes 168
    Interpretative methodology 169
        Objectives and sampling strategy 169
        The sequence 172
    Results 174
    Conclusions 175
    Discussion of the radiocarbon and OSL dates *by Chris Hayden* 175
        Chronological summary of late Bronze Age and Iron Age defences 175
        Durations and hiatuses 176
        The period over which the V-profiled ditch (574) was filled and became stable 177
        The interval between the stabilisation of the V-profiled ditch and the cutting of the
        U-profiled ditch 178

CHAPTER 10: GEOPHYSICAL SURVEY 179

    INTRODUCTION 179
    Methodology 179
    Results 179
        The northern area 179
        The churchyard 183
        The southern area 183
        The extent of the hillfort defences 183

CHAPTER 11: DISCUSSION 185

    INTRODUCTION 185
    THE SITE CHRONOLOGY 185
    The Mesolithic 185
    The Neolithic 186
    The early Bronze Age 187
    The middle Bronze Age 188
    The late Bronze Age 190
        Recurrence without transmission 190
        Possible middle Bronze Age precursors 191
        Taplow in relation to other late Bronze Age enclosures 191
        Activity within the enclosure 196
        Taplow Court in relation to boundaries in other contexts: field systems and
        territorial boundaries 197
        Taplow Court in relation to other late Bronze Age settlements: longevity ... 197
        Taplow Court in relation to weapons and warfare: defence 198
        Violence and cosmology 198
        Taplow Court in relation to other late Bronze Age settlements: similarities and
        differences 199

    Taplow Court in relation to the Thames: metalwork and human remains 199
    The abandonment of the late Bronze Age enclosure 201
The early-middle Iron Age 201
    The defences 201
    The early Iron Age hiatus 202
    The significance of re-use 203
    The extent of the Iron Age hillfort 203
    Taplow Court and other local hillforts 204
    Internal features 204
    Taplow Court in relation to local Iron Age settlement 204
    The burnt rampart and entrance features 205
    Multivallation 205
The Anglo-Saxon period 205
    The Taplow Mound 205
    Status and occupation: the finds from the hillfort ditches 206
    The eastern Mediterranean sherd and connections with Kent 206
    Anglo-Saxon re-use of the hillfort 206
    Taplow and the wider Anglo-Saxon context 207

BIBLIOGRAPHY 209

INDEX 219

List of Figures

CHAPTER 1
1.1 Site location plan 2
1.2 Geology and contours 3
1.3 Map of the area around Taplow showing excavated archaeological sites and selected cropmarks and findspots 6
1.4 Overall site plan showing each phase of fieldwork 9

CHAPTER 2
2.1 Overall phase plan of main excavation area 16
2.2 Main excavation area in relation to Wessex evaluation trenches and showing the location of major sections 18
2.3 Schematic section summarising main stratigraphic information and phasing 20

CHAPTER 3
3.1 Mesolithic to middle Bronze Age features: overall plan 24
3.2 Worked flint: distribution (total number of pieces) 25
3.3 Burnt, unworked flint: distribution (total number of pieces) 26
3.4 Sections of tree-throw holes which contained Mesolithic/early Neolithic flint (816 and 497) 28
3.5 The early Bronze Age hollows (1119): plan 29
3.6 The early Bronze Age hollows (1119): sections 30

CHAPTER 4
4.1 Late Bronze Age features: overall plan 36
4.2 Detailed plan of posthole rows 1107 and 1108: plan and sections 37
4.3 Section 273, showing palisade trench 1106 and rampart deposits 38
4.4 Schematic reconstructions of the defences in the Late Bronze Age 42
4.5 Detailed plan of palisade trench 1106 and selected sections 43
4.6 Detailed plan of posthole rows 935, 1108A and B, 1132, 1132A and 1133 and selected sections 48
4.7 The V-profiled ditch (574): plan 51
4.8 The V-profiled ditch (574): sections 227, 125 and 123 52
4.9 The V-profiled ditch (574): section 229 53
4.10 Detailed plan of posthole row 1104 highlighting those containing charcoal, and selected sections 59
4.11 Section 230 60
4.12 Summary of quantities of pottery (weight, g) by fabric in major features 62
4.13 Summary of proportions of pottery (quantified by weight) by fabric groups in major features 62
4.14 Posthole group 1117, possible roundhouse and four-post structures FP 1-3: plan and sections 64
4.15 Posthole group 1134, possible roundhouse and four-post structures FP4-7: plan and sections 68

CHAPTER 5
5.1 Early-middle Iron Age features: overall plan 74
5.2 The U-profiled ditch (460): sections 219 and 46 76
5.3 The U-profiled ditch (460): sections 1 and 37 77

5.4	The chalk kerb (925): plans and sections 236 and 279	79
5.5	Selected plans of charred timbers (1113) within areas of burnt rampart	81
5.6	Schematic reconstructions of the Iron Age defences associated with the U-profiled ditch	84
5.7	The entrance to the early-middle Iron Age hillfort: plan and sections	93
5.8	The outer ditch (3050): section 314	94
5.9	Schematic reconstruction of the Iron Age multivallate defences	98

CHAPTER 6

6.1	Anglo-Saxon features and finds: overall plan	102
6.2	Inhumation 105: plan	103
6.3	Detailed plan and sections of post-in-trench structure 846 and Wessex Archaeology Trench 6	106

CHAPTER 7

7.1	Selected worked flint	112
7.2	Length and breadth of complete flints from (A) tree-throw hole 497 (B) tree-throw hole 813 (C) tree-throw hole 816 (D) tree-throw hole 914 (E) pit 578 and (F) pit 700.	114
7.3	Selected late Bronze Age pottery from the main excavations	129
7.4	Late Bronze Age gritted base from the V-profiled ditch	130
7.5	Selected late Bronze Age and Iron Age pottery from the main excavations	131
7.6	Selected Bronze Age pottery from the TCAST trenches	132
7.7	Selected late Bronze Age and early Iron Age pottery from the TCAST trenches	133
7.8	Selected Anglo-Saxon pottery	139

CHAPTER 8

8.1	Particle size analyses of the feature fill (644) and related deposits (889, 890) in the interior	160
8.2	Sub 1 mm particle size analyses of the feature fill (644) and related deposits (889 and 890) in the interior	161

CHAPTER 9

9.1	Location of samples for absolute dating	166
9.2	Probability distribution of single grain data obtained for sample X074	167
9.3	Probability distributions of dates from Taplow Court. Each distribution represents the relative probability that an event occurred at a particular time. These distributions are the result of simple radiocarbon calibration (Stuiver and Reimer 1993)	168
9.4	Probability distributions of dates from Taplow Court: each distribution represents the relative probability that an event occurs at a particular time. For each of the radiocarbon/OSL dates two distributions have been plotted, one in outline, which is the result of simple calibration, and a solid one, which is based on the chronological model used. The other distributions correspond to aspects of the model.	172
9.5	Probability distributions of dates from Taplow Court: V-profiled ditch 574, posthole row 935, posthole group 1134 and roundhouse 1117. Each distribution represents the relative probability that an event occurred at a particular time	173
9.6	Probability distributions of dates from Taplow Court: burnt rampart 1113 and pit 1016. Each distribution represents the relative probability that an event occurred at a particular time	174

CHAPTER 10

10.1	The areas investigated by geophysical surveys	180
10.2	Resistivity survey of the northern area in relation to the excavated defensive ditches	181
10.3	Magnetometer survey of the northern area in relation to the excavated defensive ditches	182

Figures

CHAPTER 11

11.1 Plan showing conjectural extents of the late Bronze Age hilltop enclosure and of the early-middle and later Iron Age hillforts in relation to local archaeological discoveries, together with an extract from the 2nd edn 6" OS map of 1899 showing the supposed southern banks 189

11.2 Plans of comparative late Bronze Age hilltop enclosures in Southern England 192

11.3 Map of major Bronze Age and Iron Age defended and riverine sites in the Upper and Middle Thames valley. 194

List of Plates

CHAPTER 1
1.1   Aerial view of Taplow Court from the north. The excavations, in progress, are at the bottom left 4
1.2   View of the Taplow Mound in the graveyard of the former church south of Taplow Court (from the east) 7
1.3   Oblique aerial photograph of the Plessey buildings and area to the north taken in 1956 (Cambridge University Collection, TH 86) 12

CHAPTER 2
2.1   The northern end of the U-profiled ditch (460) from the north. Posthole row 1104 runs to the right of the ditch. Burnt gravel patches mark the location of the V-profiled ditch across which several sections have been cut 15
2.2   Looking north along the U-profiled ditch towards the terminal, with post-row 1104 and one of the burnt patches within the gravel rampart to the left 17
2.3   The excavation from the south. The V-profiled ditch (574, section 125) is at the bottom right. Posthole rows 1107 and 1108, with palisade trench 1106 between them, can be made out on the left 17

CHAPTER 3
3.1   The early Bronze Age hollows (1119). Postholes forming part of posthole rows 1108 and 1107, and sections across palisade trench 1106 run across the middle of the picture 28
3.2   Detail showing a cluster of struck flint within one of the early Bronze Age hollows 29

CHAPTER 4
4.1   Palisade trench 1106, sections 175 and 158. To the right lie postholes forming part of posthole row 1107 44
4.2   Detail of the palisade 1106 in section, showing the post-pipe abutted by the rampart soil 1120 44
4.3   The V-profiled ditch (574): section 125 50
4.4   The V-profiled ditch (574): section 123 54
4.5   Posthole row 1104 between the Bronze Age and Iron Age ditches, showing postholes on the very lip of the U-profiled ditch 60

CHAPTER 5
5.1   The U-profiled ditch (460) from the south 73
5.2   Charred timbers (783) and fire-reddened gravel from the rampart associated with the U-profiled ditch (460), with dark soil (644) in the background 75
5.3   The chalk kerb (925): below it lies a posthole forming part of posthole row 1104 78
5.4   Charred timbers (1113) and fire-reddened gravel (1000) from the rampart associated with the U-profiled ditch 80
5.5   Section 227 across the V-profiled ditch, showing the standstill layer cut by posthole 912, and the remains of the charred upright continuing through the burnt gravel rampart above 82
5.6   Fire reddened gravel (1100) in the rampart associated with the U-profiled ditch (460) 86
5.7   View of curving palisade trench 987 at the entrance, showing the burnt post-pipes and chalk in the top, looking west. 92
5.8   The outer ditch (3050) in 2005 evaluation Trench 1 97

CHAPTER 6
6.1 Anglo-Saxon inhumation 107, in grave 105 103
6.2 Burning in posthole 717/719 at the entrance to the Iron Age hillfort 104
6.3 Foundation trench 846 107

CHAPTER 7
7.1 The sherd possibly from an imported, eastern Mediterranean vessel 140
7.2 X-ray of Bronze Age bracelet fragment 140
7.3 The Anglo-Saxon spiral-headed pin 142
7.4 Fragments of fired clay from a cylindrical loomweight 144

CHAPTER 8
8.1 The dark type fill (644) 160
8.2 Reddened material (645) – one of the three samples tested 162
8.3 Reddening of the selected contexts at different temperatures and for different durations 162

CHAPTER 11
11.1 Taplow Court from the south, across the recently cut Jubilee River 200

List of Tables

CHAPTER 2
2.1   Chronological summary 19

CHAPTER 3
3.1   Summary of finds in tree-throw holes 27
3.2   Summary of finds in the early Bronze Age hollows (1119) and pit 133 31

CHAPTER 4
4.1   Summary of dimensions of postholes in rows, structures and other groups 38
4.2   Summary of finds in posthole rows 1107 and 1108 40
4.3   Summary of finds in palisade trench 1106 46
4.4   Summary of finds in posthole rows 935 and 1132 49
4.5   Summary of finds in the V-profiled ditch (574), the standstill layer (1102) and the rampart associated with the U-profiled ditch (460) 55
4.6   Summary of finds in posthole row 1104 61
4.7   Summary of finds in posthole group and roundhouse 1117 65
4.8   Summary of finds in the occupation layers (1121 and 1123) within the hillfort 66
4.9   Dimensions of possible four-post structures and their postholes 67
4.10 Summary of finds from posthole group and possible roundhouse 1134 69
4.11 Summary of finds in pit 3032 70

CHAPTER 5
5.1a Summary of finds in the U-profiled ditch (460): section 219, cut 713. The double line marks the boundary between prehistoric and Anglo-Saxon deposits; the dashed lines mark the deposits containing the clearest evidence for fire, related to the burning of the associated rampart 88
5.1b Summary of finds in the U-profiled ditch (460): section 1, cut 102 89
5.1c Summary of finds in the U-profiled ditch (460): section 46, cut 238 90
5.1d Summary of finds in the U-profiled ditch (460): section 37, cut 376 91
5.2   Summary of finds from features associated with the entrance to the early-middle Iron Age hillfort 94
5.3   Summary of finds in the outer ditch (3050). The double line marks the boundary between prehistoric and Anglo-Saxon deposits 97
5.4   Summary of sand-tempered pottery within the hillfort 99

CHAPTER 6
6.1   Summary of finds in foundation trench 846 105

CHAPTER 7
7.1   Summary of flint by type 110
7.2   Catalogue of flint illustrated in Figure 7.1 111–2
7.3   Flint by type from tree-throw holes 497, 813, 816 and 914 113
7.4   Flint by type from the early Bronze Age intercutting pits (group 1119) and tree-throw hole 899 116
7.5   Flint by type from the main stratigraphic groups 117

7.6	Quantities of pottery from the main excavation by phase. Codes: EBA: early Bronze Age; MBA: middle Bronze Age; LBA: late Bronze Age; LBAEIA: late Bronze Age to early Iron Age; EIA: early Iron Age; MIA: middle Iron Age; IA: Iron Age; IND: indeterminate; EPREH: early prehistoric; LPREH: late prehistoric; PREH: prehistoric	119
7.7	Fabric descriptions against % of total sherd count	120
7.8	Summary of the number of sherds and decorated sherds, and weight and proportions of ceramic fabrics in the ditches and ramparts (excluding Saxon pottery). Contexts are shown in stratigraphic order with the earliest at the bottom. The four sections cut through the U=profiled ditch (460) are shown separately with the fills within each section in stratigraphic order.	121
7.9	Late Prehistoric Vessel Forms at Taplow	123
7.10	Types of decoration noted within the Taplow assemblage	123
7.11	Summary of pottery in posthole-rows, trench 1106 and subsoil layers	125
7.12	Summary of pottery associated with features within the hillfort	127
7.13	Quantification by sherd count of pottery from TCAST Trenches 1 to 3	127
7.14	Summary quantification of assemblages from TCAST Trenches 4 and 5	127
7.15	Catalogue of illustrated prehistoric pottery from the main excavation	128
7.16	Catalogue of illustrated prehistoric pottery from the TCAST trenches	130
7.17	Quantification of LIA and Roman pottery from the TCAST excavations by trench	134
7.18	Quantification of LIA and Roman pottery from the TCAST excavations by ware	134
7.19	Quantification of the TCAST pottery by EVE arranged by vessel class	135
7.20	Occurrence of Anglo-Saxon pottery in the main excavation by number and weight (in g) of sherds per context by fabric type. E/MS = early-middle Saxon	137
7.21	Occurrence of Anglo-Saxon pottery in the TCAST trenches by number and weight (in g) of sherds per context by fabric type	138
7.22	Early/middle Saxon pottery occurrence in both the main and TCAST excavations by number of sherds per fabric type	139
7.23	Analysis of the bracelet	140
7.24.	Summary of metal objects other than the bronze bracelet. CA = copper alloy; Fe = iron; Pb	142
7.25	Summary of fired clay. Type Codes: A – amorphous; LW – loomweight; TLW – Triangular loomweight; PLW – Pyramidal Loomweight; ALW – Annular loomweight,; CLW – cylindrical loomweight; O – Object; HO – Hearth or oven	143

CHAPTER 8

8.1	Condition of the hand-collected and sieved animal bone	148
8.2	Total number of animal bones identified to species and phase	148
8.3	Summary of charred plant remains (excluding charcoal)	152–3
8.4	Summary of analysed charcoal (excluding the burnt rampart timbers 1113). Key: h = heartwood; r = roundwood (diameter <20mm); s = sapwood (diameter unknown). The number of fragments identified is indicated	155
8.5	Summary of phytolith analysis	156–7

CHAPTER 9

9.1	Summary of OSL samples and dating results featuring the multi grain age estimates in addition to the revised single grain date for sample X074 (in bold characters). Gamma dose rates are based on in-situ gamma-ray spectroscopy measurements. Beta dose rate values were calculated using the concentrations of uranium, thorium and potassium as determined by neutron activation analysis (NAA). Corrections were made in the age calculation for the water content of the sediment samples using the correction factors of Aitken (1985). The contribution of cosmic radiation was calculated as a function of latitude, altitude, burial depth and average overburden density according to the formulae of Prescott and Hutton (1994). Further details regarding individual samples may be found in the site archive.	167
9.2	Summary of radiocarbon determinations	170–1
9.3	Summary of modelled absolute dates (dates given as minus are cal BC; others as cal AD)	176–7

Tables

CHAPTER 11
11.1 Summary of the density of worked flint in tree-throw holes and on the site as a whole 186
11.2 Summary of the composition of worked flint from tree-throw holes, features and layers 186

Summary

Recent excavations at Taplow Court (at NGR SU 907 823), undertaken in advance of the construction of a Conference Hall for the owners Soka Gakkai International-UK, have revealed a long sequence of activity stretching from the Mesolithic to the Anglo-Saxon period.

Mesolithic struck flints and charred hazelnuts, and early Neolithic flints, were found in a small number of tree-throw holes. A group of intercutting hollows or shallow pits of early Bronze Age date included sherds of Collared Urn and worked flint, rare evidence of domestic activity of this period. There were also finds of the middle Bronze Age, although no features of that phase were confirmed.

In the late Bronze Age, a defensible hilltop enclosure, just over 1 ha in area, was constructed on the site. The enclosure, probably first established in the 11th century BC, had a complex sequence of defences including a pair of posthole rows possibly indicating a timber palisade backed by a raised walkway, a trench-built palisade, a ditch and rampart and further posthole-lines outside the ditch. Only a limited area of the interior was examined, but it contained a series of parallel fence lines, one probable roundhouse and up to six possible four-post structures, with occupation extending into the 9th century BC.

There followed a probable hiatus in activity represented by a very slow-forming deposit – termed in this report the 'standstill' layer – in the upper part of the ditch. Subsequently a larger U-profiled hillfort ditch was constructed in the early Iron Age, probably in the 5th century BC, the spoil being dumped over the previous ditch to form a timber-laced rampart. Another internal roundhouse may be middle Iron Age in date. Soon after its construction the rampart was destroyed in places by fire, and remains of the charred timbers within the rampart have revealed some details of the ramparts construction. In contrast, the associated ditch remained open into the Saxon period.

A third and even larger V-profiled ditch was found outside the second ditch. Although the date of construction of this outer ditch is uncertain, it too remained open into the Saxon period, suggesting that the hillfort was multivallate in its later stages.

The abandoned hillfort was re-occupied in the Saxon period, probably in the late 6th or early 7th century AD, at roughly the same time as the rich burial within the Taplow Mound. No evidence for reconstruction of the hillfort was found but considerable quantities of domestic material were deposited within the surviving Iron Age hillfort ditches. Amongst the domestic debris was a sherd probably from an eastern Mediterranean amphora, the first from Buckinghamshire, and an indicator of high status. A fragmentary early Anglo-Saxon inhumation associated with a knife was found in the entrance to the hillfort. The ditches were finally infilled in the 11th-12th century AD.

Zusammenfassung

Neuerliche Ausgrabungen in Taplow Court (Koordinaten SU907823) im Vorfeld der Errichtung einer Konferenzsaal (*Butsuma*) im Auftrag der Eigentümer, Soka Gakkai International-UK, haben eine lang anhaltende Aktivität, welche vom Mesolithikum bis zur angelsächsischen Periode reichte, nachgewiesen.

Mesolithische beschlagene Feuersteine und verkohlte Haselnüsse, sowie Frühneolithische Feuersteine wurden in einer kleinen Anzahl Baumumwürfen gefunden. Eine Gruppe sich untereinander schneidender ausgehöhlter oder flacher Gruben der Frühen Bronzezeit, enthielten Scherben von Kragenurnen sowie bearbeitete Feuersteine, diese sind somit seltene Nachweise domestischer Aktivität aus dieser Zeit.

Zwar konnten keine Befunde der Mittleren Bronzezeit eindeutig nachgewiesen werden, doch einige Funde dieser Periode wurden sichergestellt.

In der Späten Bronzezeit wurde im Untersuchungsgebiet eine befestigte Höhenanlage auf einer Fläche von über einem Hektar angelegt.

Die Verteidigungsanlage, vermutlich genutzt seit dem 11ten Jahrhundert vor unserer Zeitrechnung, bestand aus einer komplexen Sequenz unterschiedlicher Strukturen, darunter zwei Reihen Pfostenlöcher – wobei es sich wahrscheinlich um eine Holzpalisade mit anschließendem erhöhtem Gang handelt, einer Grabenpalisade, einem weiteren Graben mit anschließendem Wall und einigen Pfostenlochreihen außerhalb des Grabens.

Nur Teile des Inneren der Anlage wurden untersucht, diese enthielten einige parallele Zaunreihen, wahrscheinlich ein Rundhaus und bis zu sechs mögliche Strukturen mit jeweils vier Pfostenlöchern, welche bis ins 9. vorchristliche Jahrhundert genutzt wurden.

Dieser Phase folgte möglicherweise ein Hiatus, beschrieben durch eine sich nur sehr langsam formenden Schicht im oberen Bereich des Grabens – welche in diesem Bericht als „Stillstand" Schicht bezeichnet wird.

In dessen Folge wurde in der frühen Eisenzeit eine große U-förmige Wallburg angelegt, wahrscheinlich im 5. Jahrhundert v. Chr. Der Aushub dieser Anlage wurde über den vorangegangenen Graben geschichtet und formte damit einen mit Holz überdeckten Wall.

Ein weiteres Rundhaus im Inneren der Anlage stammt vermutlich aus der mittleren Eisenzeit. Nur kurz nach dessen Errichtung wurde der Wall teilweise durch Feuer zerstört. Teile der verkohlten Hölzer im Wall konnten einige detaillierte Informationen über den Aufbau des Walls liefern. Im Gegenzug blieb der dazugehörige Graben bis zur Zeit der Sachsen offen.

Ein dritter noch größerer V-förmiger Graben wurde außerhalb des zweiten Grabens angefunden. Obwohl nicht sicher gesagt werden kann, wann dieser Graben errichtet wurde, ist klar, dass er bis in die Sachsenzeit offen blieb, was suggeriert, dass die Wallburg in ihrer späteren Zeit durch Mehrfachgräben, bzw. Wälle abgesichert war.

Die verlassene Höhenanlage wurde in der Sachsenzeit im späten 6. oder frühen 7. Jahrhundert n. Chr. wieder in Benutz genommen – ungefähr zur selben Zeit aus der die reiche Bestattung im Inneren des Taplow Grabhügels stammt. Es gibt keine Anzeichen für die Wiedererrichtung der Höhenanlage doch wurde eine große Anzahl Siedlungsmaterial in den erhaltenen eisenzeitlichen Gräben deponiert. Unter anderem wurde eine Amphorenscherbe aus vermutlich mediterranem Kontext in diesem Material entdeckt, welche damit die erste Scherbe dieser Art ist, die in Buckinghamshire gefunden wurde und somit auf einen hohen Status der Anlage hinweist.

Eine fragmentierte früh angelsächsische Bestattung mit einem Messer als Grabbeigabe wurde im Eingang der Höhenanlage gefunden. Die Gräben wurden schließlich im 11. bis 12. Jahrhundert n. Chr. verfüllt.

Résumé

De récentes fouilles archéologiques à Taplow Court (à NGR SU 907823/Buckinghamshire) menées sur l'emprise du projet de construction d'un centre de conférence (Butsuma) appartenant à Soka Gakkai International-UK, ont permis de mettre au jour les vestiges d'une occupation allant du Mésolithique à la période anglo-saxonne.

Les éléments les plus précoces consistent en du mobilier lithique du Mésolithique et du néolithique ainsi que des restes de noisettes carbonisés découverts dans quelques chablis. La présence de tessons d'une urne (de type Collared Urn) et de silex travaillé dans un réseau de cavités ou de fosses peu profondes du Bronze ancien, constitue les indices rares d'une activité domestique. Du mobilier du Bronze Moyen a aussi été mis au jour bien qu'aucune structure de cette phase n'ait été confirmée.

Au Bronze récent, une enceinte fortifiée ceignant un peu plus d'un hectare fut édifiée sur le site. Cette enceinte, probablement établie au XIème siècle av. J.-C., comportait une série complexe de défenses dont deux rangées de trous de poteaux indiquant probablement une palissade en bois renforcée par un passage surélevé, doublée d'une clôture fossoyée, d'un fossé défensif de profil en « V », d'un rempart et d'une série d'alignements de trous de poteaux extérieurs au fossé. Seule une portion a été analysée à l'intérieur de l'enceinte mais la fouille de celle-ci a toutefois révélé une série de clôtures parallèles, un bâtiment circulaire et peut-être six structures à quatre poteaux, attestant une occupation jusqu'au IXe siècle av. J.-C.

L'activité anthropique du site est également marquée par un hiatus clairement perceptible, un comblement très lent, évoqué dans cette publication comme « standstill layer » - dans la partie supérieure du fossé. Par la suite, une enceinte fortifiée plus profonde caractérisée par son profil en « U » fut édifiée, probablement au Vème siècle av. J.-C., les remblais de laquelle ont comblé l'ancien fossé et ont ainsi formé un rempart en bois. Un autre bâtiment circulaire intérieur pourrait dater du second Age du Fer. Peu après son achèvement, le rempart fut partiellement détruit par le feu, comme l'attestent les restes de bois carbonisés découverts au sein du rempart et qui permettent de documenter la construction de ce rempart. En contraste, le fossé associé demeure ouvert jusqu'à la période anglo-saxonne.

Un troisième fossé encore plus vaste de profil en « V » a été découvert à l'extérieur du deuxième. Bien que la date de construction de ce fossé extérieur demeure incertaine, il reste lui aussi ouvert jusqu'à la période anglo-saxonne, suggérant que l'enceinte était dotée d'un système de fossés multiples vers la fin de l'Age du Fer.

L'enceinte abandonnée fut réinvestie à la période anglo-saxonne, probablement au Ve et VI siècle ap. J.-C., approximativement au même moment que la riche sépulture du monticule de « Taplow Mound ». Si aucun élément de construction n'a été observé, les fossés de la fortification ont livré une abondance de vestiges domestiques dont un tesson d'amphore de Méditerranée orientale, unique exemplaire jamais découvert à ce jour dans le Buckinghamshire qui atteste le statut privilégié des occupants du site. Une inhumation fragmentée de la période anglo-saxonne et un couteau ont été mis au jour à l'entrée de la fortification. Les fossés de l'enceinte furent finalement comblés au XI et XIIèmes siècles.

Acknowledgements

We would like to thank Soka Gakkai International-UK for funding the excavations and the post-excavation assessment, and English Heritage for funding the post-excavation analysis and publication. SGI-UK also kindly allowed geophysical surveys north and south of Taplow Court, which helped put the excavations into context. English Heritage gave permission for geophysical survey of St. Nicholas Church within the Scheduled Area.

Tim Allen would like to thank Sean Cook, who supervised the 1999 excavation, and Mike Farley and Julia Wise of Buckinghamshire County Council for their advice and support in formulating an excavation strategy. During the fieldwork John Maloney of AOC acted as archaeological consultant to SGI-UK, and we would like to thank James Lichfield, who had the unenviable task of dealing with the unexpected significance of the archaeological discoveries within an already agreed construction programme, for his understanding and patience.

Much invaluable help has been received from local archaeologists and in particular Geoff Fairclough and Elias Kupfermann of the Taplow Court Archaeological Survey Team. For the geophysical surveys we would particularly like to thank Roger Ainslie and the many members of the Marlow Archaeological Society who volunteered in carrying out the resistivity surveys. We are also very grateful to Angela Bolger, archivist at Taplow Court, for her interest and for the loan of the pottery from the TCAST trenches to record and include within this report.

Emily Edwards would like to thank Stuart Needham for advice on the pottery.

Chris Hayden would like to thank the many colleagues at OA who have assisted with his numerous queries, and in particular Leo Webley for discussion concerning the late Bronze Age enclosure at Fairfield Park and the late Bronze Age enclosure at Castle Hill, Little Wittenham, Oxfordshire.

The authors would like to thank all of the specialist contributors listed at the front of the report, and also the illustrators, Julia Moxham and Magdalena Wachnik. Tim Allen would especially like to thank Alan Hardy, who, in addition to copy-editing the report, suggested how the report might be shortened, and carried out the consequent reordering and renumbering of the tables and figures.

Oxford Archaeology would like to thank the following for their significant contribution to the project during and after fieldwork: Robert Bailey, Michelle Bailey, Dan Bashford, William Bedford, J Bennett, Rosie Burton, Gaylynne Carter, Sharon Cook, Jodie Ford, Rose Grant, T Jenkins, Steve Kelly, Mike Kershaw, Steve Laurie-lynch, Darko Maricevic, Penny Middleton, Jim Mumford, Andy Norton, Andrew Parkinson, Mark Peters, Mercedes Planas, Kay Proctor, Christopher, Richardson, Emma Sanderson, M Sutherland.

Chapter 1 – The Project

INTRODUCTION

Taplow Court is an imposing Victorian country house in Buckinghamshire owned by the Buddhist organisation Sokka Gakkai International-UK, and is situated on the western outskirts of the village of Taplow overlooking the river Thames. This volume presents the results of archaeological survey and excavation within the grounds undertaken by Oxford Archaeology between 1999 and 2005 in advance of development. The excavations revealed a long sequence of prehistoric activity and later occupation in the Saxon period. The early development of the site is described and interpreted in the context of the stratigraphic, artefactual, ecofactual and geophysical evidence, and is considered in the context of the economic and social dynamics of this region of the Thames Valley.

LOCATION, GEOLOGY, GEOGRAPHY AND TOPOGRAPHY

Taplow Court is in the county of Buckinghamshire some 40 km west of London, England (Fig. 1.1). It sits upon a projecting spur of the Burnham Plateau on the east bank of the Thames, and from its elevation of c 65 m OD overlooks the river and its valley floor (Fig. 1.2). On the west and south sides the ground drops steeply from the plateau to the river Thames, but slopes more gently to the east. To the north the plateau is interrupted by a natural gully, defining an area approximately 6 ha in extent.

The underlying geology is Black Park terrace gravel over Upper Chalk (British Geological Survey, 1: 50,000 Solid and Drift series, Sheet 255). The Black Park gravels represent mixed deposits of poorly sorted, unconsolidated flint gravels interleaved with moderately sorted loose sand. The gravels formed a deposit over 4 m thick, with chalk not encountered during the excavation of any archaeological features. During construction of the Conference Hall Upper Chalk was encountered c 5-6 m below the current ground surface.

Currently Taplow Court consists of an imposing Victorian house surrounded by formal gardens, tree-lined walks, walled enclosures and ancillary buildings, bounded on the west by the steep edge of the plateau, surrounded to the north and south by paddocks and fields, and bounded on the east by the Clivedon Road and beyond that by Taplow village. South of the main Victorian edifice is a walled enclosure containing the graveyard of the former estate church of St. Nicholas, demolished in the mid-19th century Also within the enclosure is the Taplow Mound, a large barrow containing a princely Saxon burial, at the very south end of the spur overlooking the Middle Thames valley. The barrow was partly excavated in the late 19th century, and is now a Scheduled Monument (SM 19050).

SITE LOCATION AND PROJECT BACKGROUND

The site is situated towards the north end of the Taplow Court Estate, Cliveden Road, Taplow, Buckinghamshire, centred upon NGR SU 907 823 (Fig. 1.1; Plate 1.1).The archaeological works were initiated by a planning application by Soka Gakkai International (SGI-UK), the owners of the Taplow Court Estate, to redevelop a series of extensive single story industrial workshops erected in the 1950s-1960s by the British Telecommunications Research Company/Plessey Electronics and construct a 500-seat conference hall.

An archaeological desktop study and an evaluation by trenching was carried out by Wessex Archaeology following the specification set out in a Brief supplied by Mike Farley, Buckinghamshire County Archaeologist, and a Project Design written by Wessex Archaeology (1998). Wessex Archaeology's evaluation comprised 12 trenches (see Fig. 1.4), but this was carried out while the Plessey buildings were still standing, restricting access to much of the site.

Planning permission was granted in 1999 with a condition requiring the excavation of the footprint of the Conference Hall, and a watching brief on the demolition of the existing buildings and any new services. AOC Archaeology acted as consultants to SGI-UK, and Oxford Archaeology (OA) were appointed to carry out the work. The excavations were directed by Tim Allen. Sean Cook supervised the excavation in 1999, Hugo Lamdin-Whymark the further work in 2000 and Darco Maricevic the further evaluation in 2005. Once the site had been stripped it was apparent that the 1998 evaluation had not adequately characterised the archaeology, which comprised significant elements of two phases of hillfort defences and a small area of the hillfort's interior. As excavation proceeded, a strategy for dealing with this was devised by OA and AOC acting for SGI-UK, and by representatives from the Buckinghamshire Archaeological Services department.

Due to the unexpected scale and complexity of the discoveries the cost of the archaeological fieldwork far exceeded the expectations of SGI-UK, on whose behalf John Maloney (formerly of AOC) and Tim Allen approached English Heritage for PPG16-

From Bronze Age enclosure to Anglo-Saxon settlement

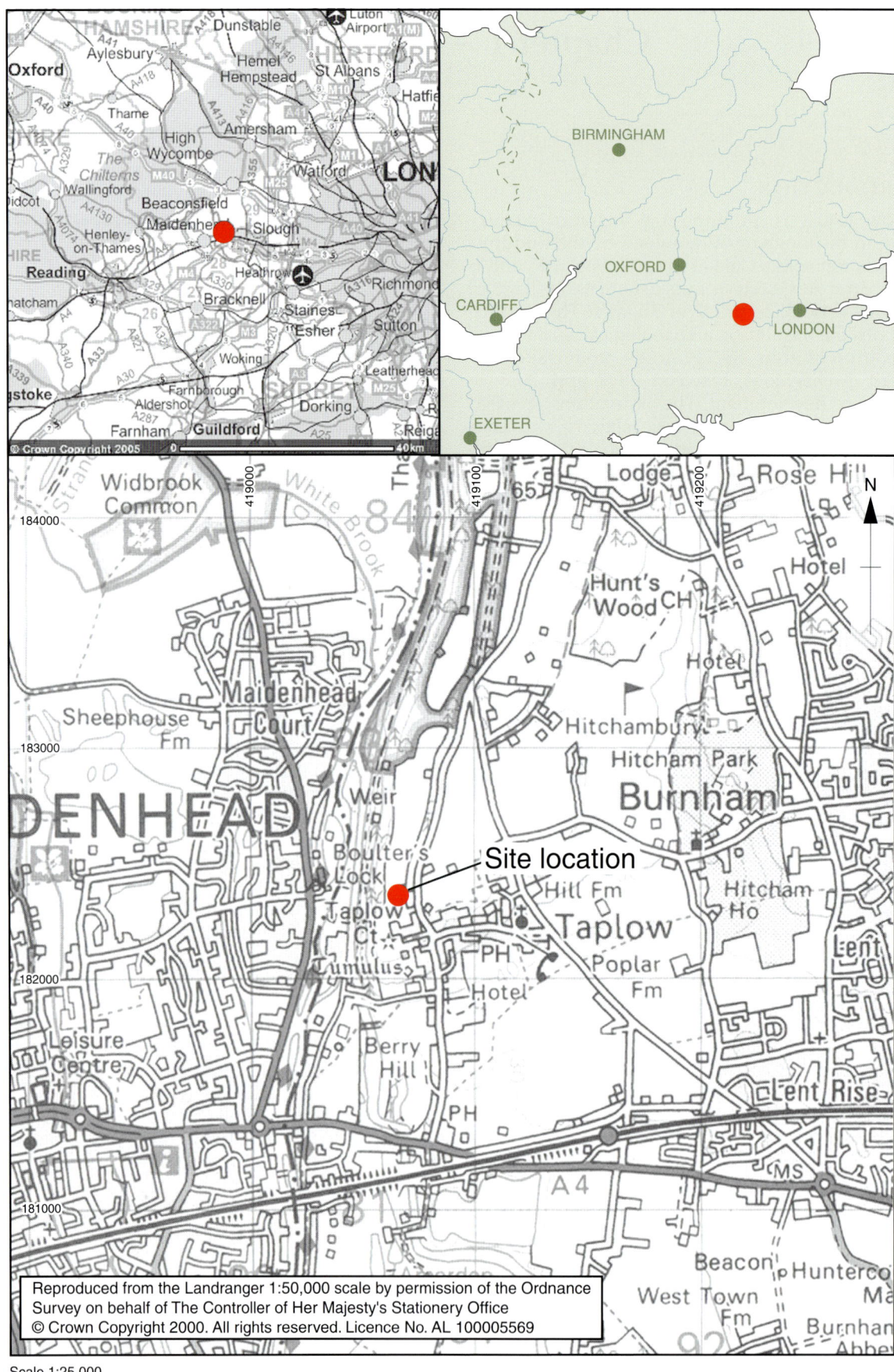

Fig. 1.1   Site location plan

Chapter 1

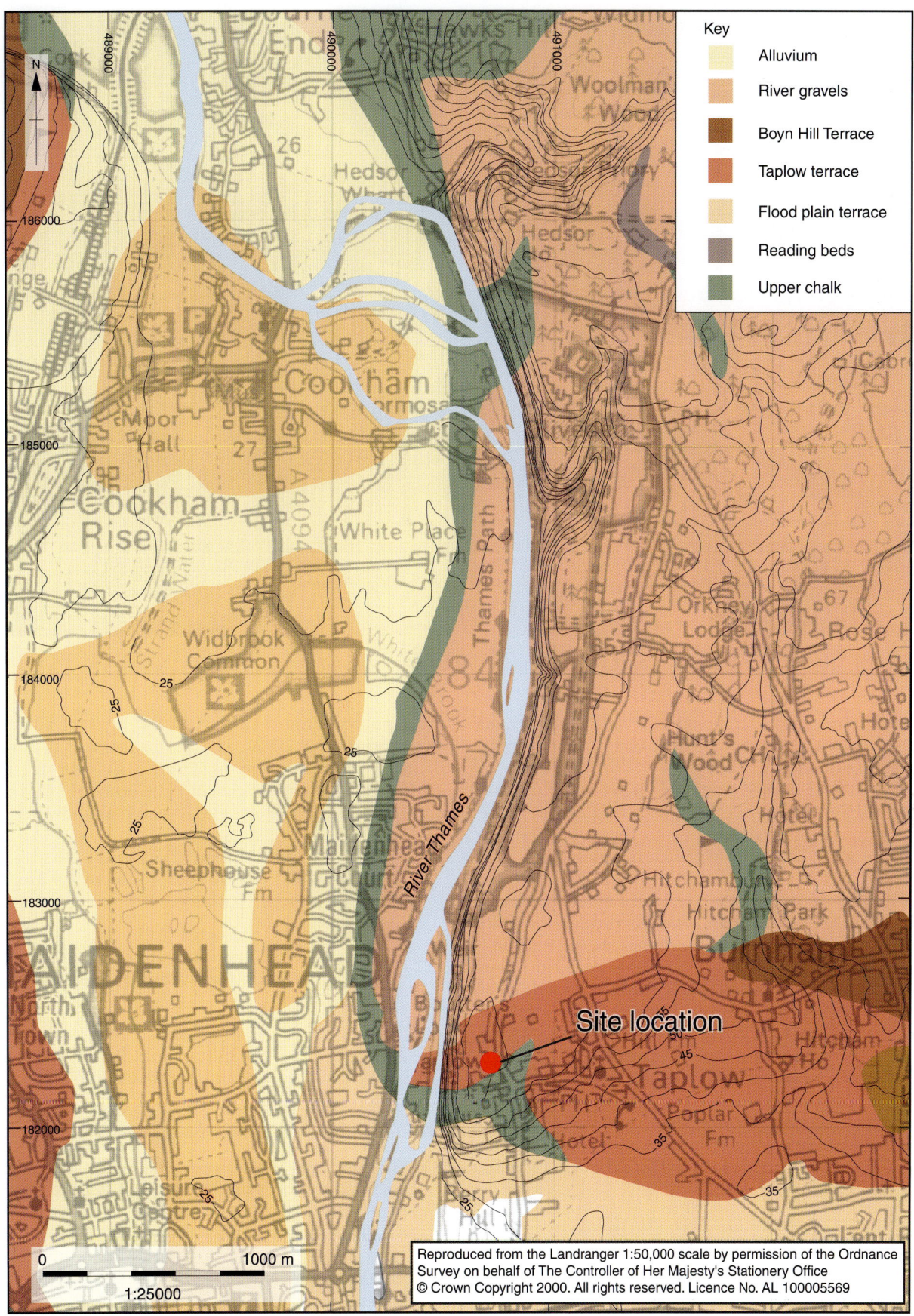

Fig. 1.2   Geology and contours

Plate 1.1   Aerial view of Taplow Court from the north. The excavations, in progress, are at the bottom left

assisted funding for the post-excavation assessment and analysis of the results. English Heritage commissioned a Project Design, on the basis of which it was agreed that SGI-UK would fund the post-excavation assessment, with English Heritage funding the analysis leading to the publication of this report. The post-excavation assessment was carried out by Hugo-Lamdin Whymark, and the post-excavation analysis by Chris Hayden, under the direction of Tim Allen, who also edited the draft publication report and co-authored the discussion.

During the post-excavation assessment Tim Allen and Elias Kupfermann, who had directed local society excavations south of Taplow Court, devised a joint strategy for a geophysical survey of the north and south ends of the Taplow Court complex, which was carried out through the voluntary efforts of Roger Ainslie (magnetometer survey) and the Marlow Archaeological Society (resistivity survey) concurrently with the post-excavation analysis. The results of these surveys can be found in Chapter 10.

RESEARCH AIMS OF THE PROJECT

Due to the exceptional circumstance of this project the original fieldwork aims were insufficient to deal with the results of the excavation. Revised aims were devised as excavation proceeded to take account of emerging results, and once excavation had been completed the revised aims were set out in the Updated Project Design in the light of all the discoveries (OA 2002). The revised research aims focus on various aspects of the early use of the hilltop and the chronological development, decline and reuse of the hillfort. The research aims were:

- To characterise Mesolithic and Neolithic activity on the hilltop and its relationship to local and regional patterns

- To establish the character of the pre-enclosure use of the hillfort, and in particular, the character, duration and extent of early Bronze Age activity

- To establish the date and range of later Bronze Age activity on the hilltop and characterise the activity in the local and regional context

- To consider the transition between the late Bronze Age and early Iron Age enclosures

- To date and characterise the early Iron Age occupation and establish its significance in its local and regional context. Furthermore, to establish the duration of the activity on the hilltop and to determine if the hillfort was abandoned when the structure was destroyed by fire

- To establish the character of Roman activity in the vicinity of the hillfort

- To determine the extent and character of the Saxon activity on the hilltop and determine the relationship of this activity to the princely burial in the Taplow Mound.

ARCHAEOLOGICAL BACKGROUND

Taplow Court is situated in an area rich in archaeological discoveries spanning the Palaeolithic to post-medieval periods. A summary of discoveries made in the vicinity of Taplow was prepared by Scrimgeour and Farley in 1987, but has not been published. Their work forms the basis for the following summary with the addition of information on more recent excavations, notably those along the Maidenhead, Windsor and Eton Flood Alleviation Scheme (the Jubilee River) and on the Eton Rowing Course (Allen *et al.* in prep; Foreman *et al.* 2002).

Figure 1.3 shows most of the sites and findspots described below; for a detailed view of those closest to the site see Figure 11.1. The summary background given below is not comprehensive, so does not include all of the sites and findspots on Figure 1.3, some of which were discovered after the project began. For further discussion of these sites see Chapter 11.

Palaeolithic and Mesolithic

Taplow has been a focus of activity over a considerable period of time. A single Palaeolithic blade and Mesolithic flints have been recorded as stray finds in the vicinity of Taplow and during the excavation of the Taplow Mound (Buckinghamshire Sites and Monuments Record 1542, hereafter Bucks SMR).

Neolithic to early Bronze Age

Considerable Neolithic to early Bronze Age activity has been identified at Taplow Court and in the surrounding area. Worked flint of Neolithic date comprising two cores, two scrapers and a flake are recorded as from Taplow Court (Bucks SMR 1034), and another flint scraper was recovered from Ten Acre Field to the east (Bucks SMR 1561). Excavations by Oxford Archaeology at Taplow Mill Site 2, *c* 500 m to the south of Taplow Court, investigated layers, tree-throw holes and a pit from which over 1500 flints of late Neolithic/early Bronze Age date were recovered. In addition excavations at Taplow Mill site 1, some 700 m to the south of Taplow Court revealed four pits, three of which contained middle Neolithic Peterborough ware (Allen *et al.* 2004, 92). Ring ditches were excavated at Marsh Lane East (Site 2) some 2 km to the south-east, and more at the Eton Rowing Course south of that (Allen *et al.* 2000), where Beaker and early Bronze Age settlement was also found (Allen *et al.* 2004, 98 and fig. 9.11).

Middle and late Bronze Age

Significant numbers of Bronze Age metal objects have been dredged from the river Thames immediately below the site. This material consists predominantly of weapons of late middle Bronze Age and late Bronze Age date, and much of it had been destroyed or ritually 'killed' (York 2002, 83-4). Excavations just over 2 km to the south-east at Marsh Lane East (Site 1) revealed middle Bronze Age ditches and cremations (Foreman 1998, 28), while a little further south-east pits and cremations were found at Cippenham (Ford 2003). Further south at the Eton Rowing Course and across the Thames at Weir Bank Stud Farm, Bray, extensive systems of enclosures have been identified and excavated (Allen 2000; Barnes *et al.* 1995). A group of late Bronze Age pits was found at Lot's Hole (Foreman 1998), and ditches south of Eton Wick (Ford 1993). Some 2 km to the north-west of Taplow Court, on the other side of the Thames, late Bronze Age settlement has been found at Widbrook Common (Catherall and Foreman 2000, 22).

Iron Age

Two findspots of Iron Age material are recorded at Taplow Court (see Fig. 11.1). Iron Age pottery was found during the excavation of the Taplow Mound in 1883 (Bucks SMR 1542), and two spindlewhorls of Kimmeridge shale may also be of this date (Bucks SMR 4639). James Rutland, the excavator of the mound, believed it to be sited within an Iron Age hillfort, and had recorded a ditch which he thought to be the inner ditch of this hillfort running north-south beneath the former church (Scrimgeour and Farley 1987, 5). Linear earthworks, possibly defining the south and west sides of an enclosure with a double bank and ditch, are shown on the Second Edition 6" OS map (1899; Bucks SMR 1544) at the southern end of the promontory (see Fig. 11.1). The date of these features is, however, unproven.

Early Iron Age ditches and other features were found at Lake End Road West, north of Dorney Court (Foreman 1998, 29), and waterlogged timber structures in a palaeochannel of the Thames at the Eton Rowing Course (Allen and Welsh 1997; Allen and Welsh 1998). An early-middle Iron Age unenclosed settlement was also found at the Eton Rowing Course (Allen and Welsh 1997, 29), and middle and late Iron Age enclosed settlements at the Eton Rowing Course, at Cippenham and at Agars Plough to the east of Eton (Allen and Welsh 1998; Ford 2003; Catherall and Foreman 2000, 22).

Roman

A considerable quantity of Romano-British pottery was recovered during the excavation the Taplow Mound (Bucks SMR 1542), and pottery was also recovered from the surrounding graveyard (Bucks SMR 5639). To the east of Taplow Court Romano-

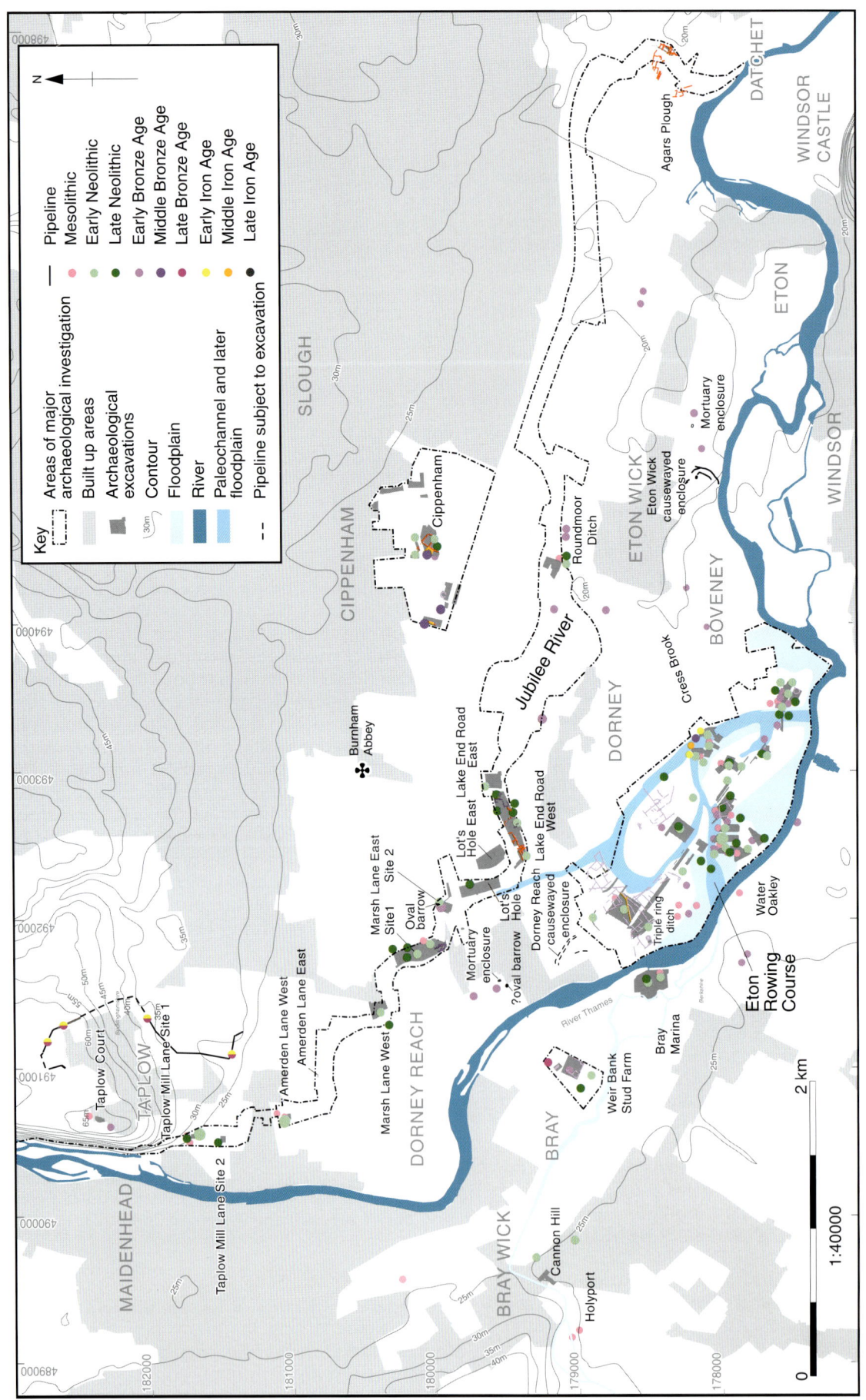

Fig. 1.3 Map of the area around Taplow showing excavated archaeological sites and selected cropmarks and findspots

British pottery and other finds including clay, daub, slag, and a Hod Hill-type bronze brooch were found on Ten Acre Field during groundworks carried out between 1954 and 1956, but there is no record of any associated features (Bucks SMR 1561).

Rectilinear cropmarks are known about 1 km to the north-east (SMR 5307) and to the south-east (SMR 4551), which may be of Roman date. A Roman rural settlement was excavated at Lake End Road West (Foreman 1998, 29), while the enclosed farmsteads at Cippenham and at the Eton Rowing Course both continued in the early Roman period. Other cropmark sites of probable Roman date are known north-east of Dorney and north of Dorney Reach next to the M4 (Carstairs 1986, fig. 2 Sites E and possibly A). Across the river a Roman villa was excavated at Cox Green, Maidenhead (Ford 1987b, 92), and a Late Roman cemetery was found adjacent to Bray Marina (Stanley 1972, 12-13).

Anglo-Saxon

The Taplow Mound (Bucks SMR 1542, National Monuments No. 19050) stands within the churchyard just south of Taplow Court, some 160 m south of the excavations reported upon here (Plate 1.2). Partial excavation of the mound in 1882 (Rutland 1885; Geake 1997, 146; Stocker *et al.* 1995) revealed a poorly preserved skeleton associated with an extremely rich assemblage of grave goods: clothing represented by gold braid, a large gold buckle inlaid with garnets and two clasps; weaponry consisting of two shields, a sword and three spearheads; a varied collection of vessels and cups, including a 'Coptic' bowl, a bronze cauldron in which two large decorated drinking horns were found – two further horns was found elsewhere – two bronze and iron-bound buckets, four glass claw-beakers and the silver rims of two wooden cups; as well as a lyre and gaming pieces. The burial dates from the late 6th century or the first half of the 7th century AD. The mound was reconstituted after its excavation, and now stands 4 m tall and 21 m wide (Stocker *et al.* 1995, 441). On the basis of the grave goods it has been suggested that the burial was that of a Kentish prince, or at least an ally to a Kentish king (Hawkes 1986; Welch 1992, 96).

Lord Desborough described the discovery of the foundations of an Anglo-Saxon church in close proximity to the medieval church of St. Nicholas, which lay east of the barrow (Scrimgeour and Farley 1987, 7). A geophysical survey and record of parchmarks was undertaken by Stocker and Went in the north east corner of the churchyard at Taplow Court in 1995. The survey recorded the buried remains of a multi-period church, and the results were interpreted as indicating an original Saxon church of national importance (National Monument No. 19050) adjacent to the burial mound. This church was thought likely to be of 8th- or 9th-century date, and together with the burial mound was taken to represent important evidence for the continued use of the site from pagan times through to the establishment of Christianity (see also Kidd

Plate 1.2   View of the Taplow Mound in the graveyard of the former church south of Taplow Court (from the east)

2004). A second geophysical survey of the church carried out by the Marlow Archaeological Society in 2005 is illustrated later in this report (see Chapter 10); their interpretation of the survey findings did not confirm the early, Saxon church (Kupfermann 2006).

An iron knife and a skull are recorded as coming from 'Bapsey', probably either Bapsey Pond or the adjacent field to the south of Taplow Court house. Bapsey Pond is connected by tradition to St. Birinus who is said to have baptised converts there (Page 1925, 240), but whether the knife and skull derive from an Anglo-Saxon or earlier burial is unclear.

A Saxon inhumation burial was found nearly 2 km to the south-east at Hitcham (Foreman *et al.* 2002, 13 and fig. 2.2), and early Saxon finds were found on cobbling overlying the Late Roman cemetery at Bray (Bates and Stanley unpublished). A large middle Saxon site has recently been excavated some 3.5 km to the south-east at Lake End Road West close to Dorney, while a 7th-century female burial was found on the Eton Rowing Course (Foreman *et al.* 2002).

Medieval

Taplow Manor is recorded in Domesday. In AD 1197 the Manor of Taplow became the property of Merton Priory, and a monastic grange was established, and remained so until the Dissolution, but the location of the medieval manorial buildings is not known. The most important ecclesiastical site in the vicinity is Burnham Abbey, some 3 km to the south-east (Fig. 1.4). Geophysical surveys in 1995 and again in 2005 south of Taplow Court revealed evidence for foundations related to the expanded medieval and post-medieval church of St. Nicholas, which lay east of the Taplow Mound, and was not demolished until 1852. The only surviving illustration of the church shows Early English ornament, suggesting a later 12th- or early 13th-century date (Scrimgeour and Farley 1987, 7; Kupfermann 2006). Possibly the church was built when the grange was first established.

The medieval manorial buildings are likely to lie close by. The first trench dug by a local amateur group, the Taplow Court Archaeological Survey Team (hereafter TCAST) in 1996, found a chalk block wall 1.5 m wide and over 1 m deep below the lawn west of Taplow Court, associated with 12th-/13th-century pottery (Fairclough and Kupfermann 2003; see also Fig. 10.1). This may well belong to the medieval grange, though insufficient was exposed to establish its function.

Post-medieval

The earliest mention of a manorial building at Taplow Court is that leased to Henry Guilford in 1614, and burned down in 1616 (Page 1925, 242). It seems likely that the house was rebuilt soon after this as in 1637 it was in the possession of Thomas Hampson, whose family carried out work on the house. It was this house that was sold to Lord Orkney in 1700. However, the earliest illustration of Taplow Court (of *c* 1800) shows a building of the late 18th century, perhaps a total rebuild of the manor house that had already been 'Gothicised' by Lord Orkney and its subsequent owner, Pascoe Grenfell (Scrimgeour and Farley 1987, 13-15). A wall of 'Tudor' bricks probably belonging to the building leased to Guilford was found during excavations for a lift shaft in 2007 (OA 2007).

PRELIMINARY FIELDWORK

The 1998 archaeological evaluation

The archaeological evaluation, undertaken by Wessex Archaeology (1998), comprised a preliminary desk-based study and twelve evaluation trenches (Fig. 1.4). The field evaluation was carried out while the Plessey buildings were still standing, restricting access to much of the site.

Three phases of activity were identified in the evaluation: Mesolithic, late Bronze Age and post-medieval. A concentration of fresh Mesolithic flint was found in Wessex Archaeology Trench 1, and although not *in situ*, suggested that a focus of activity had existed nearby. Late Bronze Age pottery was recovered in quite large quantities from a feature tentatively identified as a ditch in Wessex Archaeology Trench 12. A number of features – including a group of large postholes (Wessex Archaeology Trench 3) and a gully (Wessex Archaeology Trench 6) – could not be dated, although it was suggested that they were prehistoric. No Roman, Anglo-Saxon or medieval remains were found. Large ditches were found in Wessex Archaeology Trenches 3 and 4, and were interpreted as 17th-century landscape features, although it is now clear that these were prehistoric hillfort ditches. Wessex Archaeology Trench 5 lay entirely within a third large deep feature that was undated; this corresponds to the third outer hillfort ditch. In the walled enclosure south of the excavations Wessex Archaeology Trench 8 exposed a post-medieval ditch that may have formed part of a 17th-century walled garden associated with Taplow Court.

The Taplow Court Archaeological Survey Team (TCAST) trenches

Shortly before the main excavations and watching briefs took place, a local archaeological society – the Taplow Court Archaeological Survey Team (TCAST) excavated five small trenches: one on the lawn west of the Victorian building, one south of the churchyard and three within the churchyard adjacent to the Taplow Mound but outside the scheduled area (see also Fig. 10.1). Although these small trenches did not allow a clear understanding of the features uncovered they did recover a significant assemblage of

Chapter 1

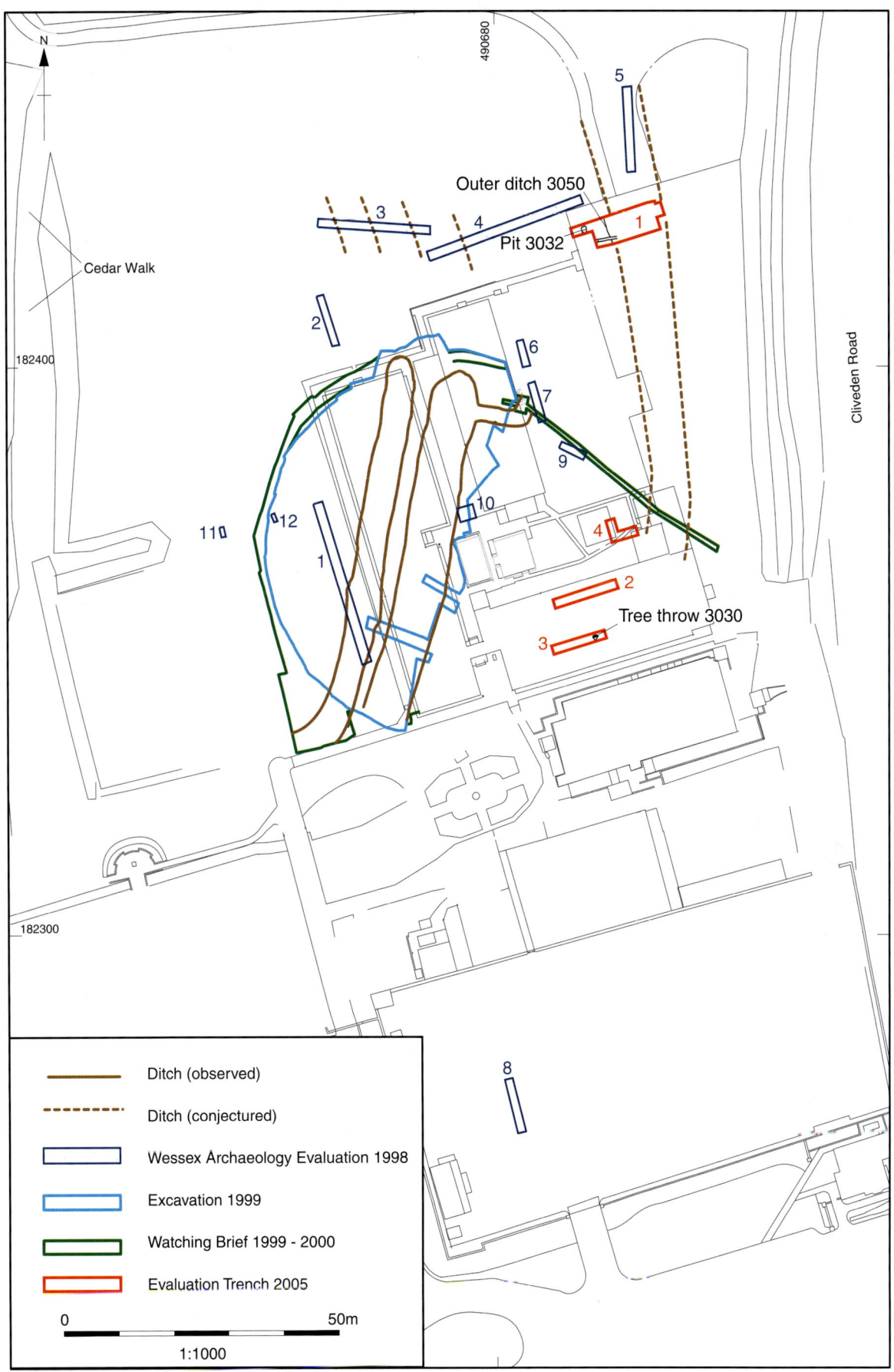

Fig. 1.4 Overall site plan showing each phase of fieldwork

prehistoric, Roman, Saxon and medieval pottery, as well as some struck flint. The work was directed by Elias Kupfermann, and the results were written up, though not published, by Geoff Fairclough (Fairclough 2001; Fairclough 2003, Fairclough and Kupfermann 2003).

The main excavations 1999-2005

Fieldwork in and around the area where the Conference Hall was to be built was carried out by OA in three phases (Fig. 1.4). The main excavation in the area of the Conference Hall was carried out in 1999. Over the winter of 1999-2000 a small area surrounding this main area on its western side and a long service trench extending to the east were subject to further excavation during a watching brief (Allen and Lamdin-Whymark 2000). In 2005, a second phase of excavations was carried out in relation to the construction of an accommodation block proposed as the second phase of development of this area. This involved four further evaluation trenches to the east and north-east of the main excavation (Allen *et al.* 2006).

EXCAVATION METHODOLOGY AND LIMITATIONS

General

The area of proposed development included the site of the previous single-storey buildings. These buildings were demolished under archaeological supervision to monitor subsurface disturbance. The single-storey buildings truncated the archaeological deposits to the surface of (or into) the natural gravel, so the overlying building debris was removed to the surface of the gravel using a 360° mechanical excavator under archaeological supervision. The stripped archaeological horizons, and the surface of the natural, were cleaned by hand.

The 1999 excavation was undertaken by OA in the expectation of a short season of work dealing principally with large but shallow late or post-medieval ditches and limited numbers of prehistoric features. Once the main area was stripped, one large ditch was immediately apparent (see Plate 2.1), with one or more lines of postholes immediately to the west, but the initial excavation slots showed that this was U-profiled, ie vertical-sided and flat-bottomed, and more than 2.5 m deep, and finds suggested that it was prehistoric. Some way to the west was a parallel palisade slot with lines of postholes either side, with a band of coarse and apparently natural gravel between them and the ditch, and with patches of charcoal and burnt gravel suggesting tree-holes at intervals (see Plates 2.1 and 2.2). West of this was a spread of postholes. The whole was clearly much more significant than had been expected.

The excavation strategy, and the results, need to be understood within the context of the funding and time constraints. Sampling of the postholes was begun, and with the assistance of Mike Farley acting for Buckinghamshire County Council, a strategy for controlled hand-excavation of a length of the U-profiled ditch was agreed, the aim of which was to record in detail the filling of the ditch and its chronology. Neither the latest fill, which was removed by machine under archaeological supervision, nor the primary silts on either side of the ditch, which were left *in situ*, were included. A complex succession of gullies and postholes belonging to the hillfort entrance lay at the very north edge of the excavation, but excavation here was hindered by considerable damage caused by services and foundations associated with the Plessey buildings.

Investigation of the supposed tree-throw holes showed that the burnt gravel extended to a depth of as much as 1 m, and that some of the burnt patches included parallel lengths of charred timber, suggesting that these were not roots, but deliberately placed timbers. It was only when the excavations through these burnt gravel areas were deepened that it was realised that the gravel was redeposited, and lay in the top of another large ditch parallel to the first. The original three-week excavation eventually expanded to 14 weeks with a significantly larger team than anticipated, and both the costs and the duration of the works were putting the construction programme at risk. Because of this, it was not possible to carry out a similarly large-scale investigation of the earlier ditch, although three slots through the ditch were bottomed, and a length of the standstill phase silt layer below the rampart was exposed.

West of the ditches almost all of the postholes within the southern part of the interior were excavated. In the northern part of the interior, however, truncation during the construction of the Plessey buildings had been deeper, and the survival of archaeological features appeared less coherent, only a few postholes being visible after stripping. The north-west part of the site was therefore not regarded as a high priority, and there was only time to remove the redeposited gravel and silt left by construction at the very end of the excavation, and to plan the other postholes that were revealed continuing the lines of postholes either side of the palisade slot. The existence of several continuous lines of postholes found just within the western edge of the 1999 excavation was only fully appreciated during this final hand-stripping, and as a result very little excavation in this area was carried out.

Examination and recording of the section around the south-western perimeter of the 1999 excavation (see Fig. 2.2, section 229) showed that a sequence of stratified deposits survived here, the edges of which had been removed during the initial machine stripping before they were recognised. A baulk west of the U-profiled ditch consisting of gravel and clay lumps some 0.2 m high had been left within the main excavation in case it represented surviving rampart from the U-profiled ditch, but this was more likely redeposited material from the construction of the Plessey buildings, and was subsequently removed by machine under archaeological supervision without discovering anything significant, or recovering any finds.

Sections in the south-west part of the site allowed the establishment of a number of relationships between features that were entirely separate in plan. In particular, two of the posthole-rows and a palisade trench between them were all overlain by a dark soil, which was overlapped by a slow-forming clay layer in the top of the V-profiled ditch, and this in turn was overlain by the gravel from the excavation of the U-profiled ditch. In the interior the archaeological features were mainly overlain by a thick and very dark (almost black) deposit containing many finds. This was interpreted as an occupation horizon within the interior, much mixed from later cultivation.

Knowing that preservation was considerably better outside the area associated with the Plessey buildings, a targeted Watching Brief was carried out on the excavation of two successive narrow strips around the curving west side of the main excavations (WB1999 and WB2000). These areas were stripped under close archaeological supervision to the archaeological horizon below the mixed dark subsoil, which allowed the planning and recording of the stratigraphy, the tracing of posthole lines that continued into this area, and the further investigation of relationships between the major feature groups. Despite this, however, time for excavation was limited, and only a small proportion of the revealed features could be investigated. A watching brief maintained upon the eventual removal of the V-profiled ditch at the south end provided some further limited observations.

A watching brief maintained upon the excavation of a service trench east of the main excavations revealed another large ditch, which it was suspected might relate to a deep but undated feature found further north within the Wessex Archaeology evaluation (Trench 5). A further phase of construction was planned at Taplow Court, and in 2005 SGI-UK asked Oxford Archaeology to evaluate an alternative location for this, and to examine a gap between the previous trenches. Confirmation as to whether there was a third major ditch was a key aim of this evaluation, and this was proven (2005 evaluation Trench 1). The other evaluation trenches were laid out to examine the area immediately east of the Conference Hall (the site of the 1999 excavations), and the trenches were limited to the area of a complementary semicircle for the proposed building, and were not extended to look for the continuation of the ditch.

Bearing these limitations in mind, all intersections of all linear features were hand-excavated. Longitudinal sections were excavated through palisade slots as appropriate. Artefact concentrations were assessed on site to see if *in situ* activity was represented, and where this was identified – ie in a group of early Bronze Age pits – each artefact was numbered individually, and their position was recorded in three-dimensions using a total station. Otherwise, an appropriate sampling grid was employed to recover the finds by areas within context.

A full record was made of all excavated features and deposits using single context recording techniques on standard OA record sheets (Wilkinson 1992). Plans were drawn of all excavated features and significant deposits (including of all the layers within a 6 m length of the U-profiled ditch) at 1:50 or other appropriate scale. Sections of all excavated features were drawn at 1:20 or more detailed scale as appropriate. A photographic record in colour and black and white was made of all archaeological features. Human remains were lifted under Home Office licence No. A1784.

The *in situ* charred timbers of the rampart were assessed on site by Damian Goodburn, who advised on their excavation and sampling. Dr M Canti and Dr N Linford (Centre for Archaeology) also visited the site during the excavation to advise and sample burnt fills surrounding the charred timbers of the rampart. The environmental sampling strategy was devised by Dr Mark Robinson and was managed on a day to day basis by Dana Challinor. Dr Alex Bayliss of the Centre for Archaeology visited the site to advise on sampling for scientific dating, and as a result samples for radiocarbon dating and other scientific dating techniques were taken as appropriate. Dr E Rhodes of the Research Laboratory for Archaeology at Oxford visited the excavation to collect samples for magnetic and OSL dating.

Maps and aerial photographs

The aerial photographs available for the area surrounding Taplow include vertical pictures produced by the military aerial reconnaissance of 1936-47 and the Buckingham County Council survey (*Fairey Photographic Survey 1979*). There is also an oblique picture obtained from the Cambridge University Collection (TH 86) taken on the 14th of June 1956.

The marks observed on the verticals were all very ephemeral and unclear and more likely to be related to natural geological variation rather than archaeological remains. Aerial photograph 2631 (*Fairey Photographic Survey 1979*) shows a clear curvilinear mark of quite considerable size, *c* 1 km south of the excavation. However this appears to have been of recent origin as there is no sign of it on any of the earlier pictures of the same area. The oblique picture from the Cambridge University Collection (TH86) shows the Plessey buildings under construction in 1956. No earthworks or cropmarks of the ditches are clearly visible. However, *c* 200 m NNE of the excavation there appears to be a cropmark indicating a subcircular enclosure, *c* 50 m in diameter, with internal features (Plate1.3).

Geophysical survey

Two phases of geophysical survey were carried out in relation to the excavations described here. The first survey, in 2005, consisted of a resistivity survey carried by the Marlow Archaeological Society and magnetometer survey by Roger Ainslie in three areas (Fig. 10.1). The largest area lay immediately north of the main excavation. The other two areas lay to the south of Taplow Court, and consisted of a square to the east of the Taplow Mound (where the earlier geophysical and parchmark survey had previously identified an Anglo-Saxon church) and a north-south transect south of the churchyard in the area where the Second Edition 6" OS map (1899) had recorded the existence of a double bank and ditch. Subsequently, in 2006, the area of the northern survey was extended to the north and west. The results of these surveys are presented in Chapter 10.

Plate 1.3   Oblique aerial photograph of the Plessey buildings and area to the north taken in 1956 (Cambridge University Collection, TH 86)

THE STRUCTURE OF THIS REPORT

The chronology of the site in general, and the late Bronze Age evidence in particular, has important implications for its significance, but in some aspects has been difficult to bring to a clear resolution. Complexities in some aspects of the evidence are introduced in Chapter 2, and are then dealt with at relevant points in the succeeding chapters, which provide an interpretative description of the site phase by phase. Specialist reports on particular categories of finds, the absolute dates and other analyses follow, together with the results of geophysical surveys. The final chapter provides a more wide-ranging discussion of the interpretation and significance of the discoveries.

Conventions used in this report

The radiocarbon dates are listed at 2 standard deviations (2σ – 95% confidence) in Table 9.1, but the radiocarbon dates used for the Bayesian modelling were ranged at 1σ (68% confidence). Optical Stimulated Luminescence (OSL) dates are quoted at 1σ and 2σ in Table 9.3, but again the ranges used for the Bayesian modelling were at 1s only.

Chapter 2 – Chronology

INTRODUCTION

Alongside the more limited (primarily artefactual) evidence for Mesolithic, Neolithic, early and middle Bronze Age and Anglo-Saxon activity, the most striking finds at Taplow consisted of a series of posthole rows, some forming palisades, and hillfort ditches and ramparts, dating from the late Bronze Age and Iron Age (Fig. 2.1; Plates 2.1 and 2.2). At least six rows of postholes (from west to east: 1132, 1133, 935, 1108, 1107 and 1104), and one substantial trench (1106), defined probably late Bronze Age palisades or fences (Plate 2.3). Two hillfort ditches – one V-profiled (574) dating to the late Bronze Age, the other U-profiled (460) and dug in the early-middle Iron Age – were found crossing the main area of excavation, as well as in evaluation trenches to the north. The interior of the hillfort lay to the west, between the ditches and the edge of the escarpment less than 100 m distant. During the watching brief, traces of a third, outer hillfort ditch (3050) were found to the east of the other ditches, and this was confirmed by further evaluation in 2005.

The location of all the major sections excavated to examine the large, mostly linear, features across the site is depicted in Figure 2.2. Particularly in the southern part of the site, some of these sections also included preserved soils.

Preserved soils (1120), representing traces of the rampart associated with the V-profiled ditch (574), or of the soil buried below the rampart, were found overlying the subsoil (1005) to the west of ditch (574) at the south end of the site. These soils were overlain by the edge of a slow-forming standstill layer (1102) in the top of the earlier V-profiled ditch (574), and this in turn was overlain by the rampart (1100, 1112 and 1113) associated with the early-middle Iron Age U-profiled ditch (460), which was subsequently burnt.

A summary of the overall chronology of the site is presented in Table 2.1, correlating (as far as is possible) the principal stratigraphic elements with the scientific dating, associated dominant pottery fabrics, and metalwork, set against Needham's established periodisation of the Bronze Age.

LIMITATIONS OF THE EVIDENCE

The archaeological features revealed by the excavations are of very considerable significance, and in conjunction with the associated finds and other sites, indicate a site with a long history of regional importance. It is however important to state at the outset the limitations of what was achieved by these excavations, and to make clear the considerable further potential that the site still contains.

Three main sources of evidence have been used to establish the chronology of the features: stratigraphy, artefactual evidence (mainly pottery) and absolute dates derived from radiocarbon and optically stimulated luminescence (OSL) determinations.

A number of key stratigraphic relationships between major features were recovered from the better-preserved stratigraphy at the southern end of the site. It must however be remembered that relationships established by individual postholes at one end of a line need not necessarily hold good of

Plate 2.1 The northern end of the U-profiled ditch (460) from the north. Posthole row 1104 runs to the right of the ditch. Burnt gravel patches mark the location of the V-profiled ditch across which several sections have been cut

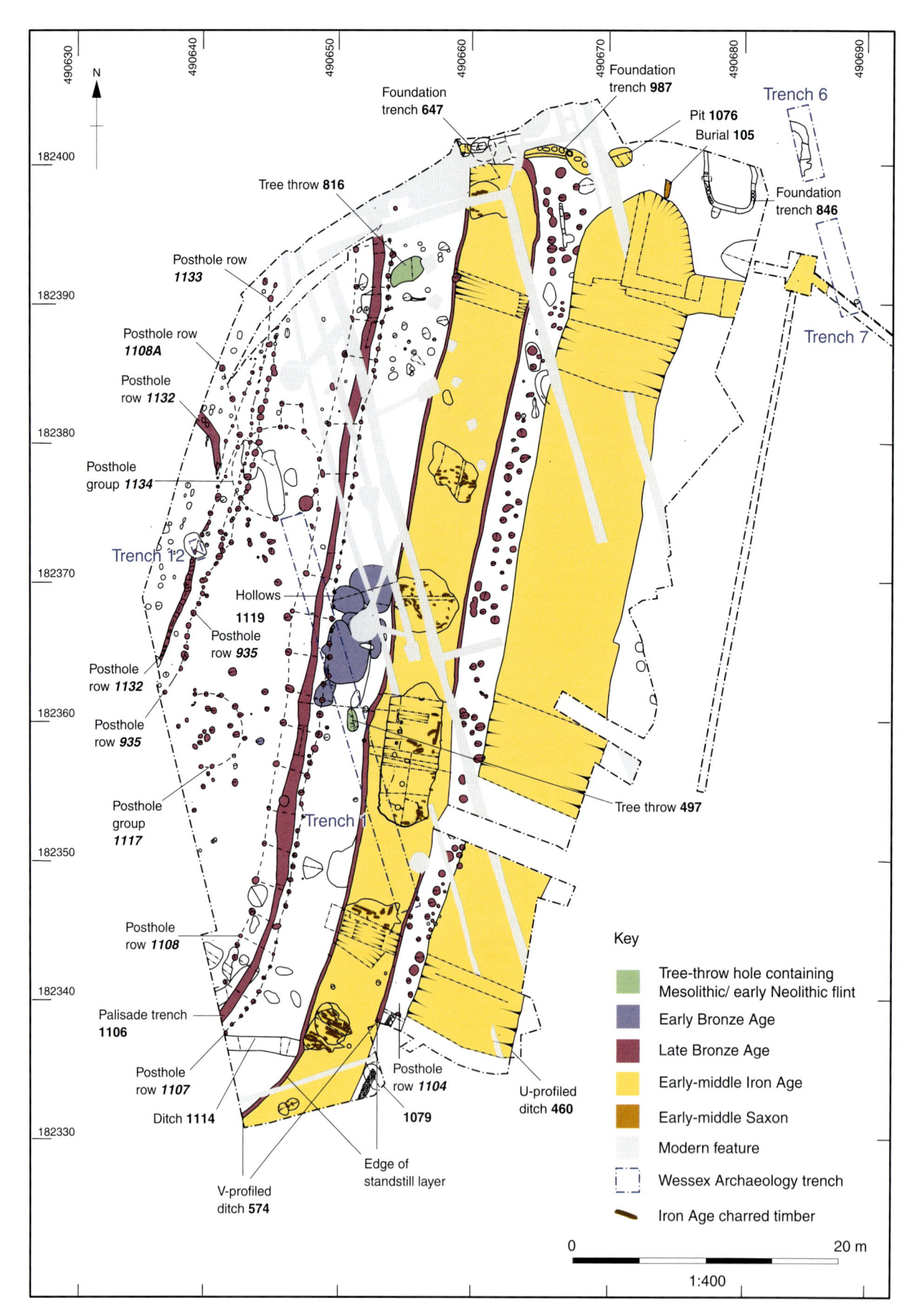

From Bronze Age enclosure to Anglo-Saxon settlement

Fig. 2.1   Overall phase plan of main excavation area

Plate 2.2   Looking north along the U-profiled ditch towards the terminal, with post-row 1104 and one of the burnt patches within the gravel rampart to the left.

Plate 2.3   The excavation from the south. The V-profiled ditch (574, section 125) is at the bottom right. Posthole rows 1107 and 1108, with palisade trench 1106 between them, can be made out on the left

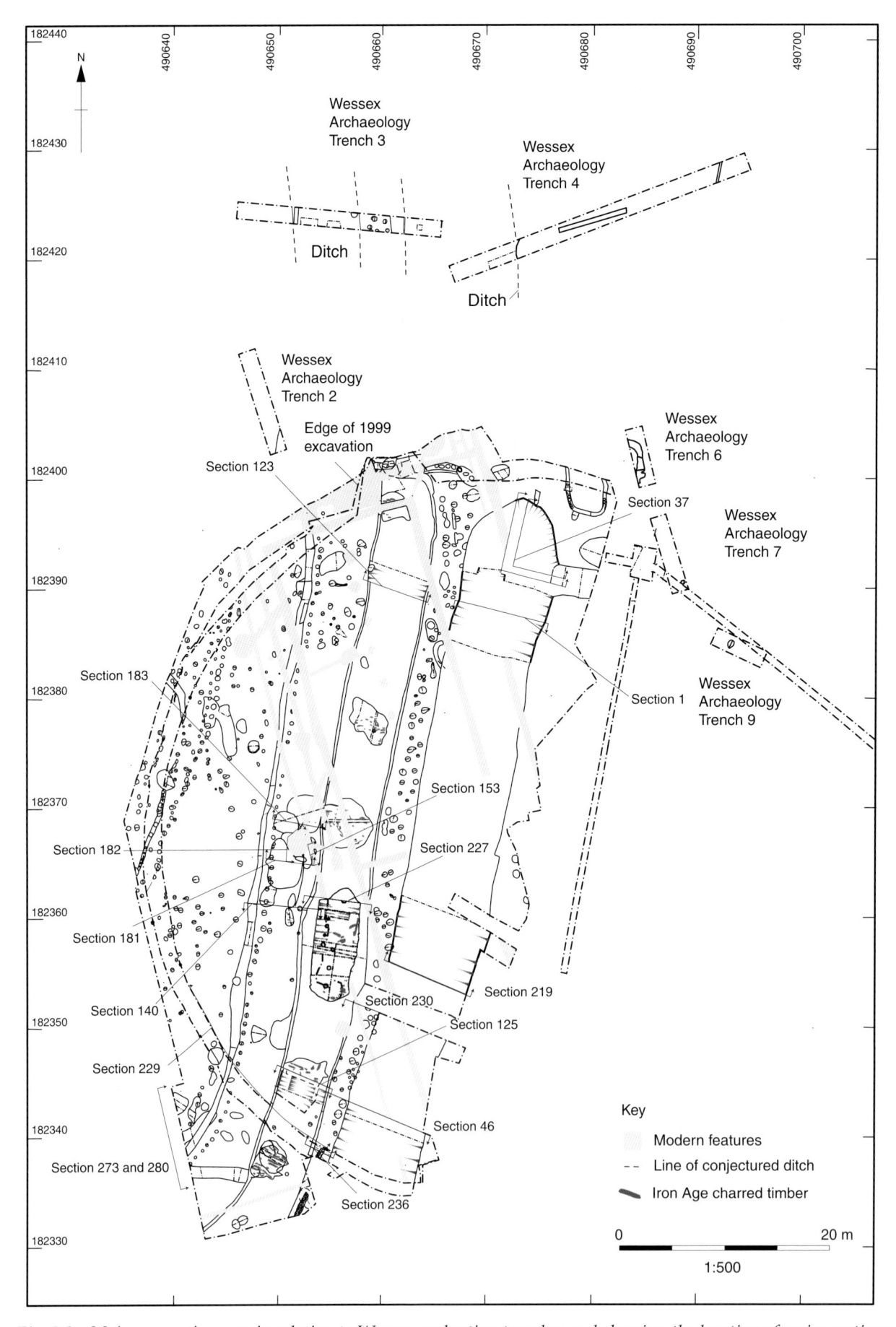

Fig. 2.2 Main excavation area in relation to Wessex evaluation trenches and showing the location of major sections

Table 2.1: Chronological summary

Period	¹⁴C and OSL date range 95.4% probability	¹⁴C and OSL date range 68.2% probability	Features and finds	Dominant pottery fabrics	Needham (1996) period	Metalwork (Needham 1996)
Mesolithic and Neolithic	?		Tree-throw holes; residual artefacts	-	-	-
Early Bronze Age	1740-1520 cal BC	1690-1610 cal BC	Hollows 1119 and residual finds	Grog-tempered	Period 4	MA VI
Middle Bronze Age	1450-1120 cal BC	1430-1210 cal BC	Residual and stray artefacts; possibly posthole-row 1132	Fine flint-tempered	Period 5	Acton Park 2 Taunton
						Penard
Late Bronze Age	1130-930 cal BC	1120-980 cal BC	Posthole-rows 1107 and 1108;	(Uncertain - probably flint-tempered)	Period 6	Wilburton
	1130-750 cal BC	1120-800 cal BC	Possibly palisade trench 1106 and posthole-row 1104			
	1020-890 cal BC	1005-1020 cal BC	Posthole-row 935; ? posthole-rows 1132 and 1133			
	1050-700 cal BC	980-800 cal BC	V-profiled ditch (574) Occupation soils 1121 and 1123	Flint-tempered	Period 7	Ewart Park Bracelet frag
	970-810 cal BC	910-830 cal BC	Posthole group 1134 (including ? roundhouse and 4-posters)			
	930-790 cal BC (or middle Iron Age)	900-800 cal BC (or middle Iron Age)	Posthole group 1117 (including ? roundhouse) Upper fills of V-profiled ditch	Biconical bowl		
Late Bronze Age/ early Iron Age	940-490 cal BC;	860-580 cal BC	Standstill layer (1102, upper fill of V-profiled ditch 574)	Flint and sand tempered	Period 7-Period 8 transition	
Early Iron Age	?		Stray pottery from TCAST excavations	Sand-tempered	Period 8	Llyn Fawr
Early-middle Iron Age	510-390 cal BC	480-400 cal BC	U-profiled ditch (460) and rampart (1100, 1112 and 1113), entrance pit 1016; ? Outer ditch (3050)	Sand-tempered	-	
Anglo-Saxon	cal AD 550-680	cal AD 590-670	Inhumation 105; burial in Taplow mound; Saxon deposits in U-profiled; and outer ditches (460 and 3050)	Sand-tempered and chaff-tempered	-	
	post-cal AD 700		Continued deposition in the U-profiled ditch (460)		-	

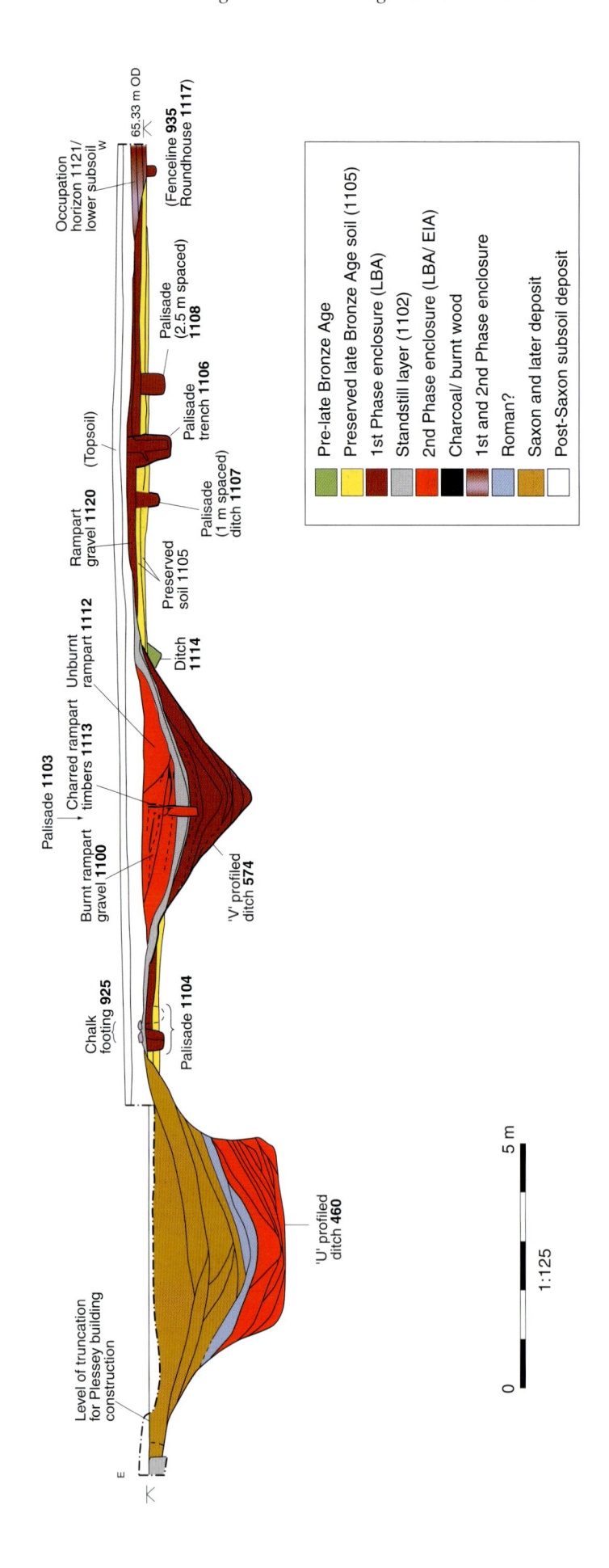

From Bronze Age enclosure to Anglo-Saxon settlement

Fig. 2.3 Schematic section summarising main stratigraphic information and phasing

all others along the line, for which no stratigraphic relationships survived. The lines of postholes are not so regular that they could not include later repairs, or, due to the density of activity, include unassociated features that happen to coincide with their alignment.

Secondly, as a result of the constraints on excavation, sampling of the earlier V-profiled ditch was limited, and finds from below the upcast gravel rampart of the later ditch were few (23 sherds from the main fills and 73 from the stand-still layer). Even less work was possible on the outermost hillfort ditch (3050), only the later fills of which produced any artefactual evidence. Sampling of the posthole rows was also limited, and biased towards certain parts of their length. Sufficient of the palisade trench was excavated to understand its character, but few finds were retrieved. Excavation of the U-profiled ditch was more extensive, and finds were more numerous (100 prehistoric sherds, though only 59 came from the prehistoric fills of the ditch).

Although excavation of the strips west of the main excavation in 1999 and 2000 allowed the sampling of preserved stratigraphic horizons, and indeed some of the most significant finds from the excavation came from these deposits, they were only examined in a very narrow strip, which did not allow full interpretation of their derivation and taphonomy. The majority of the finds from the excavations came from the occupation soils in the interior, which had been disturbed and mixed by later cultivation. Securely stratified groups of pottery are therefore not generally large.

In addition, due to the limited sampling, material for radiocarbon dating from these elements of the site was not always abundant, or of the highest integrity. Bone was not well-preserved in these acidic soils, and suitable bone samples were limited to the later deposits. Charcoal was the main material to be dated, and with such a long sequence of activity on the site, some residuality and intrusiveness was to be expected, and did in fact occur.

In the case of the hillfort ditches and their ramparts, the three strands of chronological evidence – stratigraphy, artefactual evidence and absolute dating – are generally consistent, and the sequence of development is thus reasonably clear. A schematic representation of the principal stratigraphy is shown in Figure 2.3, compiled from the relevant sections, and showing the preferred interpretative phasing. However, in the case of other features – and particularly the posthole rows – these three strands of evidence sometimes contradict each other or otherwise fail to give a clear picture of the chronology, and a degree of subjective judgement is involved in suggesting a date. Despite these caveats, the excavations have provided the framework of a very long-lived and pivotal site in the history of the Middle Thames region.

Chapter 3 – Before the hillfort: from the Mesolithic to the middle Bronze Age

INTRODUCTION

The most significant features representing activity predating the late Bronze Age defences (Fig. 3.1) were a few tree-throw holes (497, 816, 813 and 914) containing possibly *in situ* Mesolithic or earlier Neolithic worked flint, a group of intercut hollows (1119) containing sherds from Collared Urns and further worked flint, and a small ditch (1114) in the south-east corner of the site which, although it contained no artefacts, must, on stratigraphic grounds, predate the late Bronze Age defences (Fig. 3.1). A small number of other tree-throw holes are also stratigraphically earlier than the late Bronze Age activity. A number of residual artefacts, mostly worked flint, also provide evidence for activity predating the late Bronze Age.

The most intriguing of the residual finds are a few sherds of pottery and fragments of cylindrical loomweights that, like some of the radiocarbon dates, can be assigned to the middle Bronze Age. However, no features can be dated confidently to this period, and it does not appear that a focus of middle Bronze Age settlement existed within the excavated area.

FLINT DISTRIBUTIONS

Worked flint dating from the earlier Mesolithic to the late Bronze Age was found scattered across the site, much of it residual (Fig. 3.2). There were also a few concentrations of Mesolithic or earlier Neolithic flint in tree-throw holes (497, 816, 813 and 914) that may have remained *in situ* (see Fig. 3.1). A significant assemblage of earlier Neolithic or Mesolithic flintwork was also recovered from one of the early Bronze Age hollows (578), within group 1119 and very close to tree-throw hole 497. In addition the assemblage recovered by Wessex Archaeology from the subsoil overlying both 497 and the western edge of the early Bronze Age hollows contained a significant proportion of blades attributed in their evaluation report to the Mesolithic (WA 1998), as well as a smaller number of Bronze Age pieces. It seems therefore that there was a focus of Mesolithic, early Neolithic and early Bronze Age activity in this part of the site.

While the distribution of the burnt, unworked flint appears to follow a similar pattern (Fig.3.3), there was almost none at all in the early Bronze Age hollows, so it is possible that it relates to later Bronze Age activity.

Mesolithic activity

The few diagnostically Mesolithic artefacts were all residual in later contexts and were spread thinly across the site: two microburins and a microlith from sections of the palisade trench (1106) near to the early Bronze Age hollows (1119); a microlith from a posthole (362) probably forming part of palisade 1104; and a microburin and a complete tranchet axe from the recent cultivation soil (103). Both microliths were broad-blade types, perhaps suggesting an earlier Mesolithic date. A larger assemblage of struck flint, including blades and blade cores attributed to the Mesolithic was found in WA Trench 1, above, and possibly within, tree-throw hole 497 and the early Bronze Age hollows (Wessex Archaeology 1998).

Further evidence for Mesolithic activity was provided by a radiocarbon determination on a clearly residual charred hazelnut shell from posthole 537 in palisade 1104. This gave a date range in the early Mesolithic of 8560-8290 cal BC (SUERC-4969: 9220±40 BP).

Mesolithic and Neolithic flint in tree-throw holes

The only possibly *in situ* flint assemblages were groups of probably earlier Neolithic flint in two tree-throw holes (497 and 816; see Figs 3.1 and 3.4) and smaller groups of Mesolithic or earlier Neolithic flint in two others (813 and 914; Fig. 3.1).

The flint from these features is discussed by Cramp and Lamdin-Whymark below (Chapter 7). It was generally in a fresh condition, and refits found within tree-throw holes 497 and 816 suggest that the flints had remained more or less *in situ* (ie were deposited into the tree-throw hole whilst it was open or were redeposited only by the fall of the tree itself). In tree-throw hole 816 two refitting snapped fragments of a blade were found in different layers, suggesting that if the finds had not been redeposited, the feature had filled over a relatively short period.

Flakes dominated the two larger assemblages (497: 74 pieces; 816: 95 pieces; Table 3.1), but blades, bladelets and blade-like flakes occurred in proportions which suggest an earlier Neolithic date (20% in 497 and 37% in 816). Some of the retouched blades in tree-throw hole 497 may, however, have been residual Mesolithic pieces, a possibility strengthened by the Mesolithic blades and blade cores found above this feature in WA Trench 1.

Fig. 3.1 Mesolithic to middle Bronze Age features: overall plan

Chapter 3

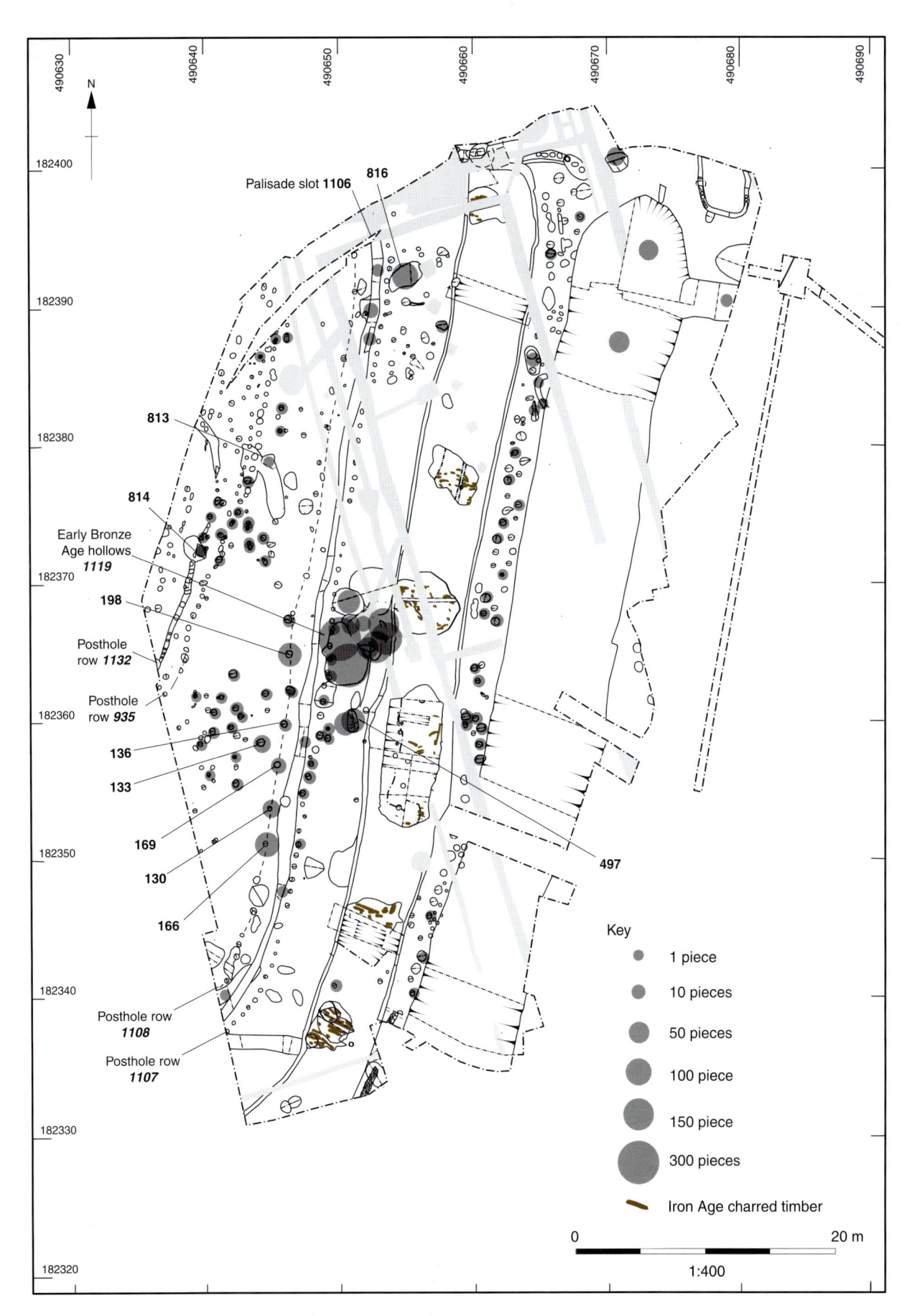

Fig. 3.2 Worked flint: distribution (total number of pieces)

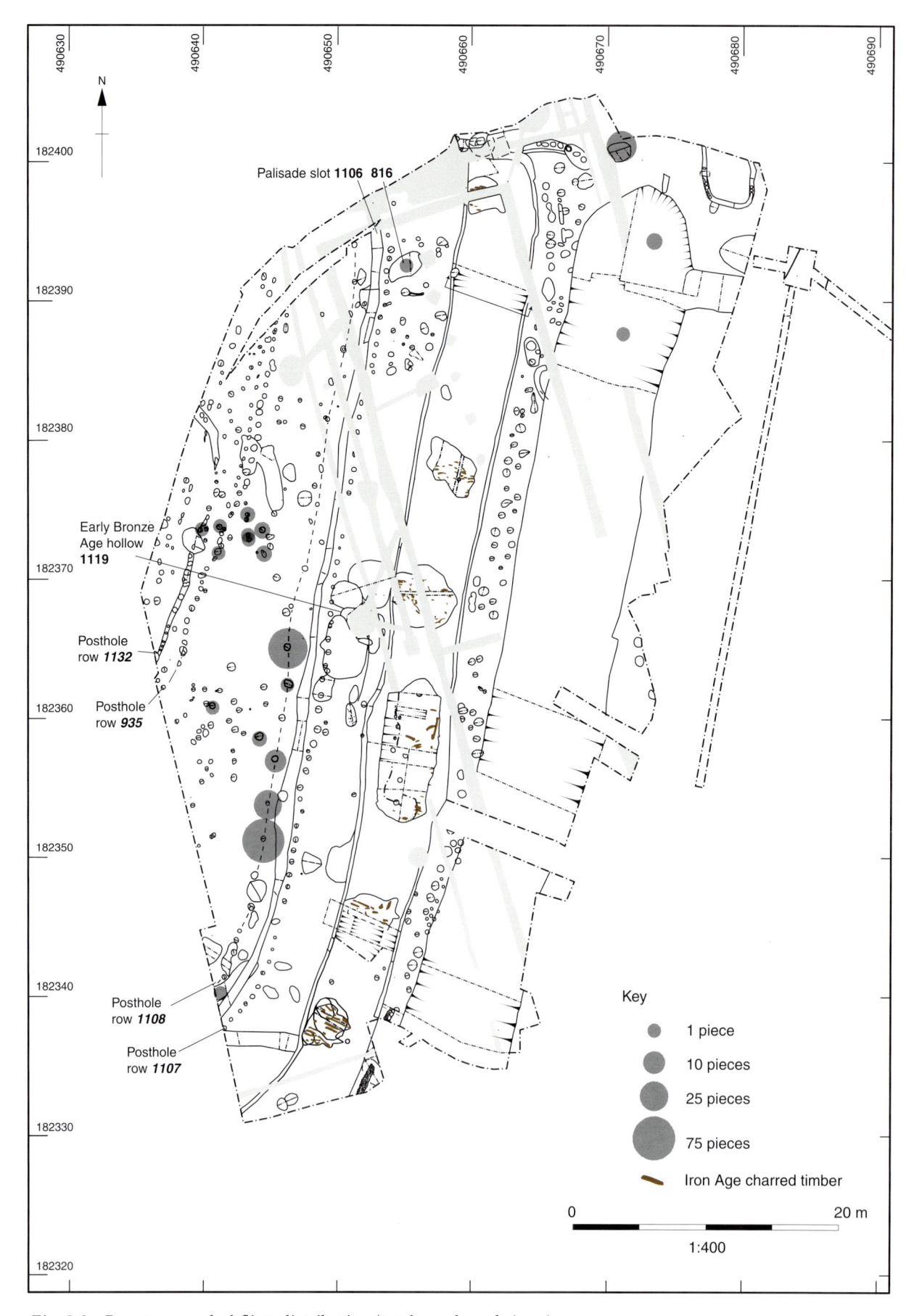

Fig. 3.3 Burnt, unworked flint: distribution (total number of pieces)

Both of these tree-throw holes contained appreciable numbers of cores, but relatively little knapping waste. They also both contained relatively few retouched pieces.

Although in the two smaller assemblages flakes and blades occurred in equal or nearly equal proportions, neither contained chronologically diagnostic artefacts, and neither assemblage was large enough (813: 13 pieces; 914: 3 pieces) to indicate more than a broad Mesolithic to earlier Neolithic date. Both also contained flake cores. The only other finds from these features were 20 charred hazelnut shells (not dated) in tree-throw hole 497.

The tree-throw holes themselves were all more or less oval or D-shaped in plan, and irregular in profile (see Fig. 3.4). They varied from 1.6 m – 3.1 m across, but were all relatively shallow, only 0.30 m - 0.54 m deep. Their width was 3.6-8.6 times their depth (mean = 5.5), which is similar to the ranges found for tree-throw holes at other sites (*cf.* Hayden and Stafford 2006; Hayden 2006). Their fills consisted of orange-brown or grey-brown silty sands similar to those filling many of the other features.

Their stratigraphic position is consistent with their early date: tree-throw hole 813 was cut by posthole row 935, tree-throw hole 914 by palisade 1132, and tree-throw hole 497 seemed to underlie the orange-brown subsoil (1105) that was cut by many of the later features on the site. As the flint may have been redeposited by the tree-throws, however, the features can only be dated between the earlier Neolithic and the late Bronze Age.

A sizeable assemblage of Mesolithic or early Neolithic struck flint, consisting of finely struck blades, was also found in hollow 578, one of a group of shallow broad pits (1119) in the centre of the site. Although its stratigraphic relationship to the other pits was uncertain, the dark fill of this hollow was very similar to those of the other pits, and like them it contained small fragments of early Bronze Age pottery. It is therefore likely that the struck flint is residual, although the number of blades, and their fresh condition, suggests that a Neolithic feature or activity area may have been disturbed by the excavation of this pit in the early Bronze Age.

Table 3.1: Summary of finds in tree-throw holes

Pit	Layer	Pottery	Flake	Chips and waste flakes	Blade, bladelet and blade-like flake	Cores	Retouched pieces	Axe	Microlith	Other worked flint	Burnt unworked flint	Charred plant remains and charcoal	Animal bone
497	467		40	8	11	7	7			1			
816	817		38	9	27	4	1			4	1		
816	819		8		4								
813	814		6		4	1			1	1			
801	584		2	1									
899	900		9		1								
914	915		1		1								
371	372		2										
1078	1077										1		
1001	1002	EBA 1/4											
1003	1004	MIA 1/8											
497	498											Hazel nut shell 20	
3030	3033											Rye + Barley ++ Oats + Cereal indet. ++ Bean + Pea + Weeds ++ Beech charcoal + Oak charcoal +	Cattle 2 phalanges

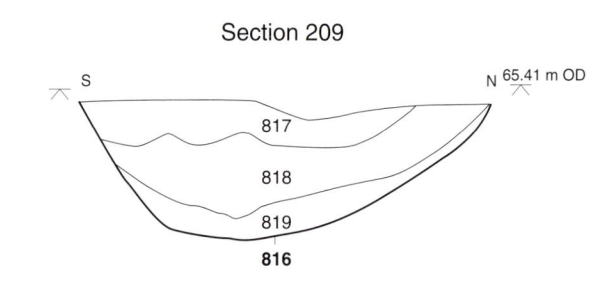

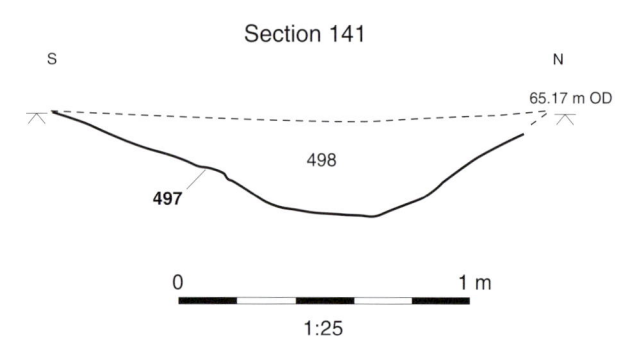

Fig. 3.4 Sections of tree-throw holes which contained Mesolithic/early Neolithic flint (816 and 497)

Early Bronze Age activity

The early Bronze Age hollows (1119)

A group of six shallow hollows (1119) containing sherds of Collared Urn, worked flint and fired clay were found near the centre of the excavation (Figs 3.1 and 3.5; Plate 3.1). Tree-throw hole (899), which contained a small assemblage of technologically comparable flint, lay 25 m to the north-east, anda small pit (133), 6.5 m to the south-west, contained two sherds of early Bronze Age pottery and a little worked flint. These may belong to the same phase.

The hollows were rather irregular ovoid features in plan, and more or less bowl-shaped in section (Figs 3.5 and 3.6). They ranged in width from 1.3 to 4.8 m, and were all shallow, between 0.12 and 0.40 m deep, with an average width to depth ratio of 11.2 (range 3.3 – 22.5), even higher than that for the tree-throw holes. However, they lacked features distinctive of tree-throw holes.

The largest hollow 642 was the latest, and cut the edges of those to the south (631) and north (703), while 703 cut 702, and 702 cut 700. Hollow 578 had an uncertain relationship with the others (due to modern truncation), but also contained early Bronze Age pottery. They were all filled with orange- or yellow-brown sandy silts, with the exception of

Plate 3.1 The early Bronze Age hollows (1119). Postholes forming part of posthole rows 1108 and 1107, and sections across palisade trench 1106 run across the middle of the picture

Chapter 3

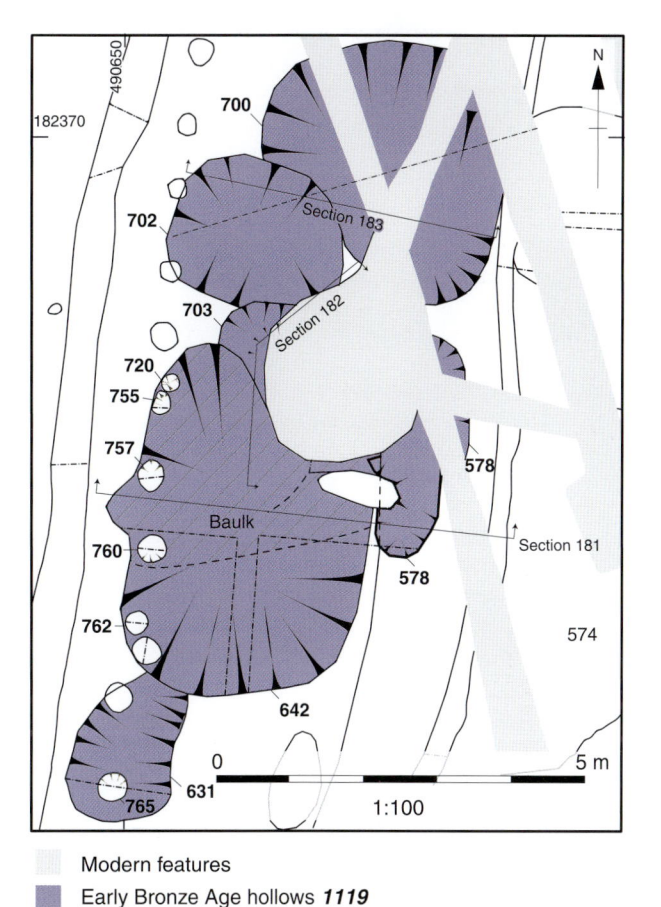

darker black-brown deposits (706 and 533) in hollows 703 and 642 respectively, from which the charcoal and charred cereal grains came.

Finds in the early Bronze Age hollows and other early Bronze Age finds

The concentration of early Bronze Age pottery and of flint – including refitting pieces – suggests that the finds in these hollows had remained more or less *in situ* (Plate 3.2). A few early Bronze Age sherds were found in features close to the hollows (posthole 185 in the hillfort interior, cut 597 of palisade trench 1106, directly adjacent to the hollows, and pit 133 just to the south-west) or, in two cases (tree-throw hole 1001 and cut 993 through the V-profiled ditch), near to the southern edge of the excavation. The wider distribution of flint, which may include further early Bronze Age pieces, has already been discussed.

Not all of the finds in the early Bronze Age hollows (Table 3.2) were deposited 'fresh'. The potsherds, mostly in grog-tempered fabrics and including sherds from Collared Urns, are mostly small (mean weight = 4.2 g) and in some cases abraded. In contrast, the flint, which consists largely of broad, thick flakes, is in good condition (including the finely struck blades in hollow 578 that may be residual Mesolithic or earlier Neolithic

Fig. 3.5 (left) The early Bronze Age hollows (1119): plan

Plate 3.2 Detail showing a cluster of struck flint within one of the early Bronze Age hollows

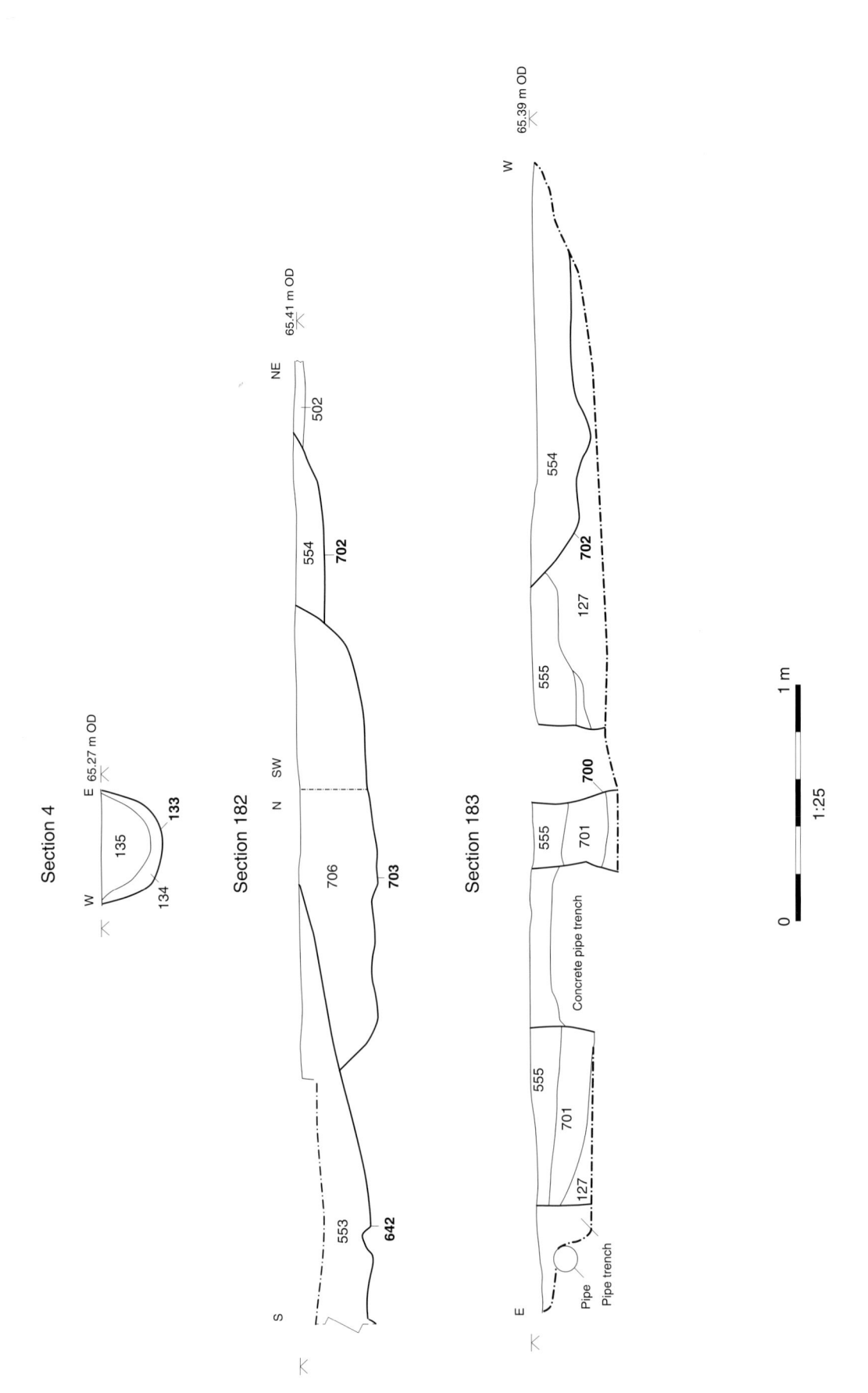

Fig. 3.6 The early Bronze Age hollows (1119): sections

Table 3.2: Summary of finds in the early Bronze Age hollows (1119) and pit 133

Hollow	Layer	EBA pot (no. of sherds/weight (g))	Mean sherd weight (g)	Other pot (no. of sherds/weight (g))	Flake	Chips and waste flakes	Blade, bladelet and blade-like flake	Cores	Retouched pieces	Axe	Other worked flint	Burnt unworked flint	Fired clay (no. frags/weight (g))	Charred plant remains	Charcoal	Other finds
578	550=643	Grog 1/10, Sand 1/3	10.0, 3.0	-	144	10	32	6	5	1	4	-	4/7	-	-	-
642	551=552-557	Sand and flint 2/5	2.5	-	78	8	17	5	5	-	1	-	2/3	-	-	-
642	553	Grog 17/65, Sand and flint 1/2, Sand 8/35	3.8, 2.0, 4.4	-	145	26	13	11	1	-	4	-	16/8 2*	Wheat - 3, Barley - 2	Field Maple - 3, Ash - 1, Hawthorn/apple - 15, Blackthorn - 16, Oak - 20, Coniferous	Burnt quartzite pebble; Burnt frag worked sandstone
631	556	-	-	-	-	-	-	-	-	-	-	-	-	-	-	-
703	706	Grog 1/3	3.0	Flint and sand 3/5, Sand and flint 1/1	22	3	3	-	-	-	1	-	-	-	-	-
702	554	Grog 2/3, Coarse flint 1/4, Sand 2/2	1.5, 4.0, 1.0	-	45	6	6	4	1	-	3	-	-	-	-	Frag greensand
700	555=722	Grog 4/36, Sand and flint 1/4, Sand 1/6	9.0, 4.0, 6.0	-	164	59	8	9	7	-	9	-	-	-	-	Burnt frag red sandstone
700	701	-	-	-	3	-	-	-	-	-	-	-	-	-	-	-
133	135	untempered 2/23	11.5	-	21	1	-	-	-	-	-	2	-	-	-	-
133	134	-	-	-	2	-	-	-	-	-	-	-	-	-	-	Quartzite hammerstone

*including shaped piece
+ = 1-5 pieces; ++++ = over 100 frags

pieces). The hollows also contained appreciable numbers of cores and a few retouched pieces, especially scrapers, as well as a flaked axe.

A sample taken from hollow 642 contained a few grains of charred wheat and barley as well as charcoal from several species of trees and shrubs (Table 3.2). A radiocarbon date (OxA-14268, 3356±55 BP: 1740-1530 cal BC) was obtained from *Maloideae* charcoal from this hollow, consistent with the Collared Urn pottery.

A few fragments of fired clay, mostly amorphous, were also found in three of the hollows. One piece from hollow 642 looked like the corner of an object with a smoothed interior surface, but not enough of it survived to suggest its original form.

The other finds included fragments of stone, one of which showed signs of having been worked, and a few, probably intrusive, small sherds of flint and sand-tempered pot from deposit 706 within hollow 703.

During the excavation three of the hollows (631, 642 and 702) were recorded as cutting a group of nine postholes (765, 587, 585, 757, 720, 755, 760, 762 and 831 – see Fig. 3.5) in posthole row 1107, and one of the hollows was also recorded as cutting the edge of the V-profiled ditch (574). Were these stratigraphic relationships accepted, it would imply that the hollows dated from the late Bronze Age or later and that the early Bronze Age finds they contained were residual. Given the apparently *in situ* concentration of early Bronze Age finds and the corresponding early Bronze Age radiocarbon date, however, it seems more likely that the pits were cut in the early Bronze Age. The relationship between the hollows and the edge of the V-profiled ditch could only be observed in a small area, much of which had been destroyed by recent pipe trenches. In retrospect it seems likely that the edge of the V-profiled ditch cut the pits, or was misidentified and lay further to the east, not actually reaching the hollows. The fills of the postholes in row 1107 were almost all orange-brown sandy silts, very similar in colour, texture and inclusions to the fills of the early Bronze Age hollows, and may therefore not have been recognised as distinct from them.

Pit 133 and other evidence of early Bronze Age activity

Pit 133 lay 6.5 m to the south-west of the hollows (1119). It was a small, circular pit, bowl-shaped in profile and measuring 0.62 m across and 0.26 m deep (Fig. 3.1; Fig. 3.6). It contained two sherds of early Bronze Age pottery, 23 flint flakes and a quartzite hammerstone. It was filled with orange sandy silt fills which contained a little burnt flint.

One further indication of early Bronze Age activity is provided by a radiocarbon date (1870-1610 cal BC; SUERC-4967) which was obtained from probably residual *Alnus/Corylus* charcoal from the post-pipe (200) in a posthole (198) belonging to palisade 1108 which lay close to the early Bronze Age hollows. A small quantity of early Bronze Age pottery was also found in the TCAST trenches to the south of the main excavation.

An undated ditch (1114) and a possible continuation (1079)

An undated ditch (1114) was traced for 10 m east-west across the south-east corner of the main excavation (Fig. 3.1). The ditch was shallow V-shaped in profile, 1.35 m wide and 0.45 m deep (see Fig. 4.3, section 273). It was filled with two layers of orange-brown silty sands containing 5% – 20% gravel, and contained no finds.

The ditch was overlain by the upper fills of the V-profiled ditch (Fig. 3.1). The relationship was not further investigated, so the ditch may have been earlier than, or contemporary with, the early use of the V-profiled ditch. In the west edge of the excavation, however, this ditch was apparently overlain by subsoil layer 1105, which was cut by the V-profiled ditch, suggesting that ditch (1114) was earlier than the cutting of the V-profiled ditch (see Fig. 4.3).

East of the V-profiled ditch in the very south-east corner of the excavation, feature 1079 was discovered during the watching brief below the standstill layer (here numbered 1074) and the underlying fill (1075) within the top of the V-profiled ditch (Fig. 3.1; see also Fig. 5.4, section 279). This feature displayed a possible north-west terminus, extending south-east beyond the edge of the excavation. In profile it was rounded, 0.5 m wide, and survived 0.30 m deep below the ditch. The ditch fill (1080) was a dark orange-brown silty sand with 15% gravel, yielding no finds. This could have been a tree-throw hole, but had similar dimensions to ditch 1114, and could have been related to it, perhaps a continuation.

Subsoil layers, rampart deposits and ditch 1114 in the south-western part of the site

Subsoil layer 1105 lay directly above the natural yellow sand and gravels (127), and consisted of orange-brown sandy silt deposits These can be seen depicted as layers 1023 (see Fig. 4.3, section 273), and 891 and 928 (see Fig. 4.9, section 229).

Ditch 1114, and later postholes of both rows 1107 and 1108, were not observed until this layer was removed. The similarity of the fills of these features to layer 1105, and the parallel alignment of posthole rows 1107 and 1108 to that of palisade 1106, which cut soil 1105, may mean that these features were simply not observed cutting this buried soil. Alternatively, the truncation of these features at the top of the gravel may indicate an episode of ploughing or other disturbance of the orange-brown sandy silts. In some places grey- or brown-yellow sandy deposits containing high proportions of gravel (see context 892 in Fig. 4.9, section 229) and 503 in section 140 (NI) were recorded as distinct layers at the interface between the natural gravel

(127) and the silts (1105), possibly indicating an episode of ploughing followed by worm-sorting.

Middle Bronze Age activity

The evidence for middle Bronze Age activity is confined to artefacts and to radiocarbon dates. The artefacts consist of a few sherds of pottery and fragments of cylindrical loomweights. The three sherds were all thick, and made in flint-tempered fabrics. One (36 g) came from a posthole (1052) in posthole row 1108, and the other two (11 g – one with an applied cordon) came from one of the middle fills (863) of the V-profiled ditch (574: cut 865, see Fig. 4.8, section 227). Two fragments of cylindrical loomweights were found, one (37 g) in the 'occupation' layer (1123) within the hillfort and the other (26 g) in the modern subsoil (1122) above. Such loomweights are usually dated to the middle Bronze Age, but have also been found at the late Bronze Age ringwork at Carshalton (Adkins and Needham 1985) and at other late Bronze Age sites (eg Pingewood; Johnson and Bowden 1985).

Two radiocarbon dates fall into the middle Bronze Age. One of the dates (OxA-14358: 3120±30 BP; 1450-1310 cal BC) was obtained from charred grains of *Triticum* from a post-pipe in posthole 279 which formed part of posthole row 1132; the other (SUERC-4970: 3020±40 BP; 1410-1120 cal BC) from the fill (571) of the step on the western side of palisade trench 1106. Neither posthole row 1132 or palisade trench 1106 are securely dated, but what evidence there is (see Chapter 4) suggests that they date from the late Bronze Age, implying that the dated material was residual.

The combination of pottery, possibly weaving equipment, charred grain and charcoal indicates domestic occupation, but is too limited in quantity to suggest that the excavated area included the focus of this middle Bronze Age activity. Perhaps the most plausible suggestion is that any such settlement lay nearby, and the undated early ditch (1144) at the south end of the excavation, which has more the appearance of a field or enclosure boundary ditch than a barrow or monument ditch, may have been associated.

Chapter 4 – The late Bronze Age hillfort

INTRODUCTION

The earliest defensive barrier identified at Taplow Court was erected during the late Bronze Age, and from the number and complexity of the posthole rows that were found, may have marked the start of a sequence of activity that lasted for several hundred years (Fig. 4.1).

Stratigraphically the earliest posthole rows were 1107 and 1108, which may even have been parts of a single structure. They were probably replaced by an adjacent palisade constructed within a continuous foundation trench (1106). This was in turn replaced by a V-profiled ditch (574) to the east, whose upcast probably formed a simple dump rampart. The posthole rows which lie within the later hillfort defences (935, 1132 and 1133) may possibly have belonged to another phase of hilltop defence, but more likely represented a long-lived internal boundary fence within the late Bronze Age enclosure. Some of the postholes within the hillfort also seem to belong to the later part of the late Bronze Age, and would probably have been contemporary with the later phases of the enclosure. Part of posthole row 1104 may have predated the V-profiled ditch (574), or may have formed an external and associated defence.

Evidence for activity after the 9th century BC is slight. Although considerable quantities of pottery probably dating from the period 860-580 BC were found in the standstill layer, there is little other evidence for activity in this period in the area of the main excavation. Early Iron Age pottery has, however, been found further down the slope to the south in the TCAST trenches. The area of the main excavation does not appear to have been reoccupied until the 5th century BC.

LATE BRONZE AGE DEFENCES

The stratigraphic evidence

As described previously (Chapter 1), the northern part of the site had suffered from more severe disturbance than the southern, where a series of subsoil layers survived over the natural gravel in the southern part of the site, providing the most useful stratigraphic evidence (particularly in relation to the posthole rows).

The most informative sections were recorded in three areas (see Fig. 2.2): at the edge of the excavation in its south-western corner, section 273 (see Fig. 4.3), slightly to the north of this, near to the edge of the first phase of excavations, sections 229/236 (Fig. 4.9) and slightly further north, section 230 (Fig. 4.11); near the centre of the excavation, around the early Bronze Age hollows (1119), sections 182 and 183 (see Fig. 3.6); and across the adjacent part of the V-profiled ditch and rampart, section 227 (Fig. 4.8).

Posthole rows 1107 and 1108

Two rows of postholes ran parallel to the V-profiled ditch on the west, and lay either side of a palisade trench 1106 (described below). One row (1107), consisting of closely spaced postholes, lay to the east of the trench, the other (posthole row 1108), consisting of widely spaced postholes, lay to the west. The two rows ran parallel to one another, and it is possible that these two rows of postholes were related, and together formed part of a single structure. The chronological evidence related to them is contradictory, but the most plausible interpretation suggests that both date from the late Bronze Age, and predated the V-profiled ditch (574) and its rampart.

The stratigraphic relationships and dating evidence for posthole row 1107

In the south-western corner of the site, three of the postholes in this row (1063, 1065 and 1067, see Fig. 4.2) seemed to be covered by the lowest, orange-brown subsoil layer (group 1105, recorded as layer 1023 in Fig. 4.3, section 273) above which lay the darker brown buried soil/rampart deposits (1120, recorded here as 992).

Beyond this corner of the excavation, the stratigraphic relationships of the postholes in this row were generally uninformative: most cut the natural gravel (127) and lay below the subsoil which covered most of the site. However, near the centre of the main excavation, a sequence of nine of the postholes (765, 587, 585, 757, 720, 755, 760, 762 and 831) in this posthole row seemed to have been cut by three hollows (631, 642 and 702; part of group 1119) which contained over 50 sherds of early Bronze Age pottery and a large number of struck flints in fresh condition that were probably contemporary. Posthole 500 in posthole row 1107 contained a sherd of sand and flint-tempered pottery weighing 23 g, and posthole 506 a fragment of sand-tempered pottery weighing 1 g. Two radiocarbon dates were obtained from *Alnus/Corylus* and *Maloideae* charcoal from postholes (506 and 510) in this row; both gave results falling in the early-middle Saxon period (SUERC 5150: 1305±35 BP, cal AD 650-780 and OxA-14297: 1258±24 BP, cal AD 670-810, both 94% confidence).

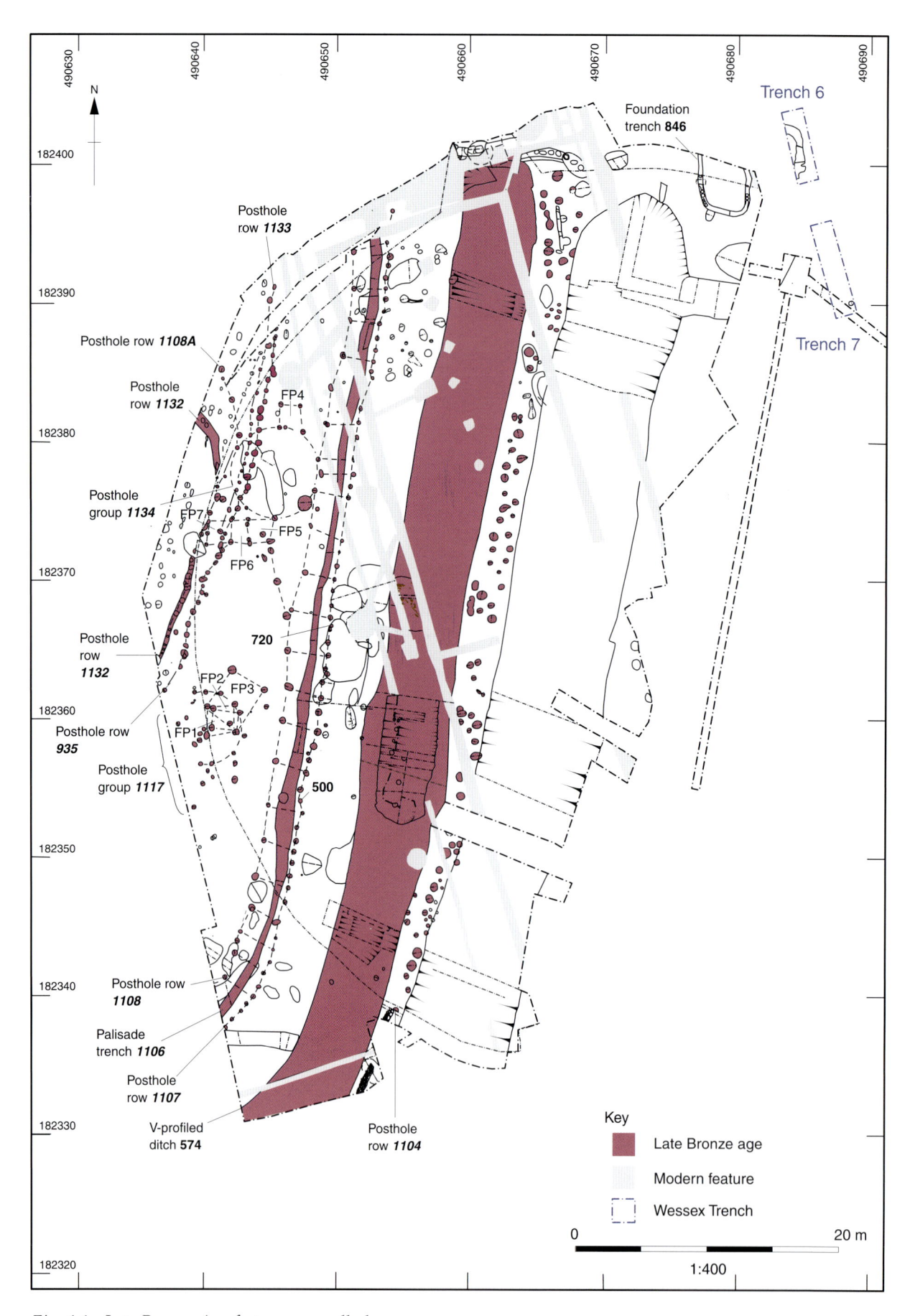

From Bronze Age enclosure to Anglo-Saxon settlement

Fig. 4.1 Late Bronze Age features: overall plan

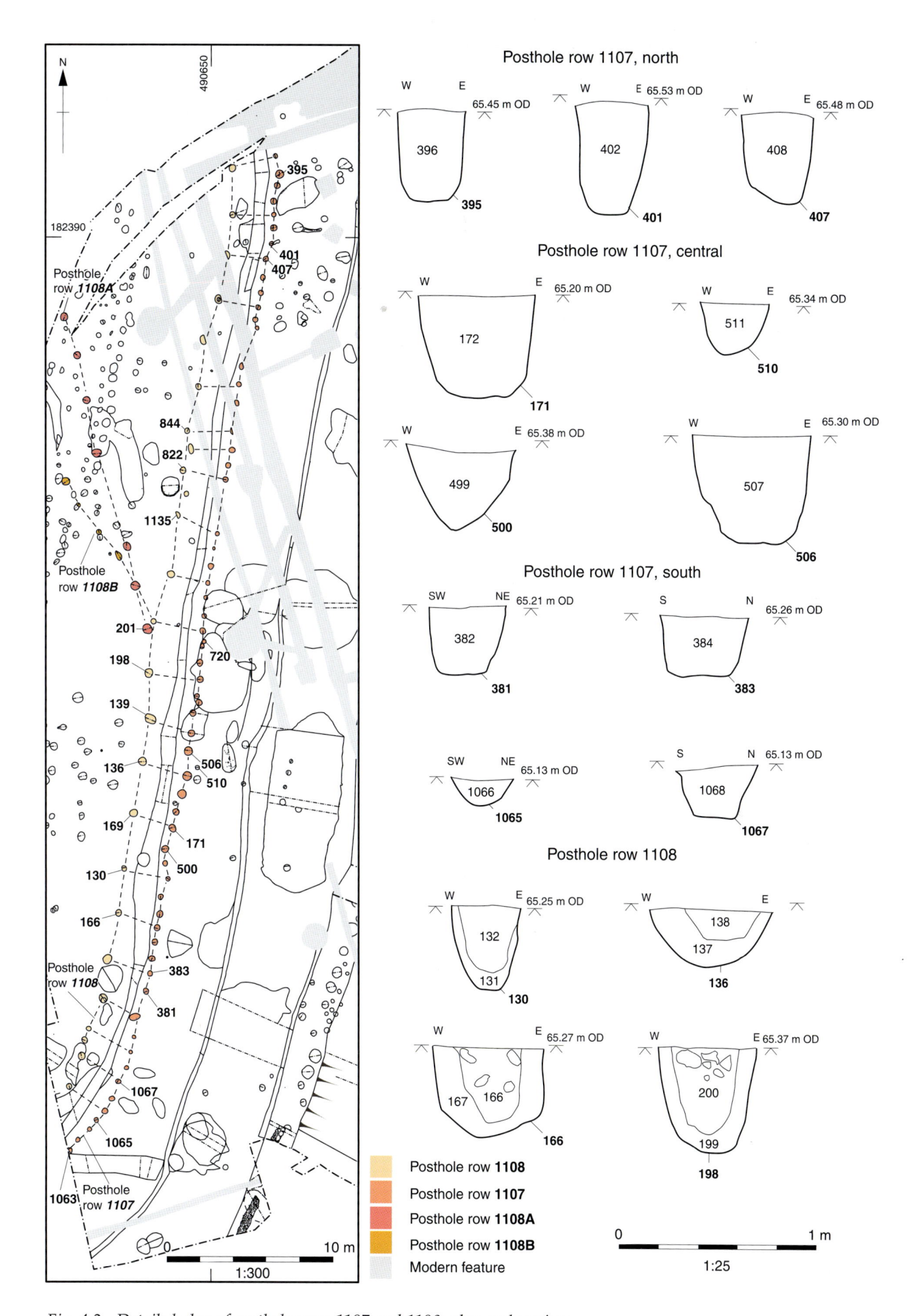

Fig. 4.2 *Detailed plan of postholes rows 1107 and 1108: plan and sections*

From Bronze Age enclosure to Anglo-Saxon settlement

Fig. 4.3 Section 273, showing palisade trench 1106 and rampart deposits

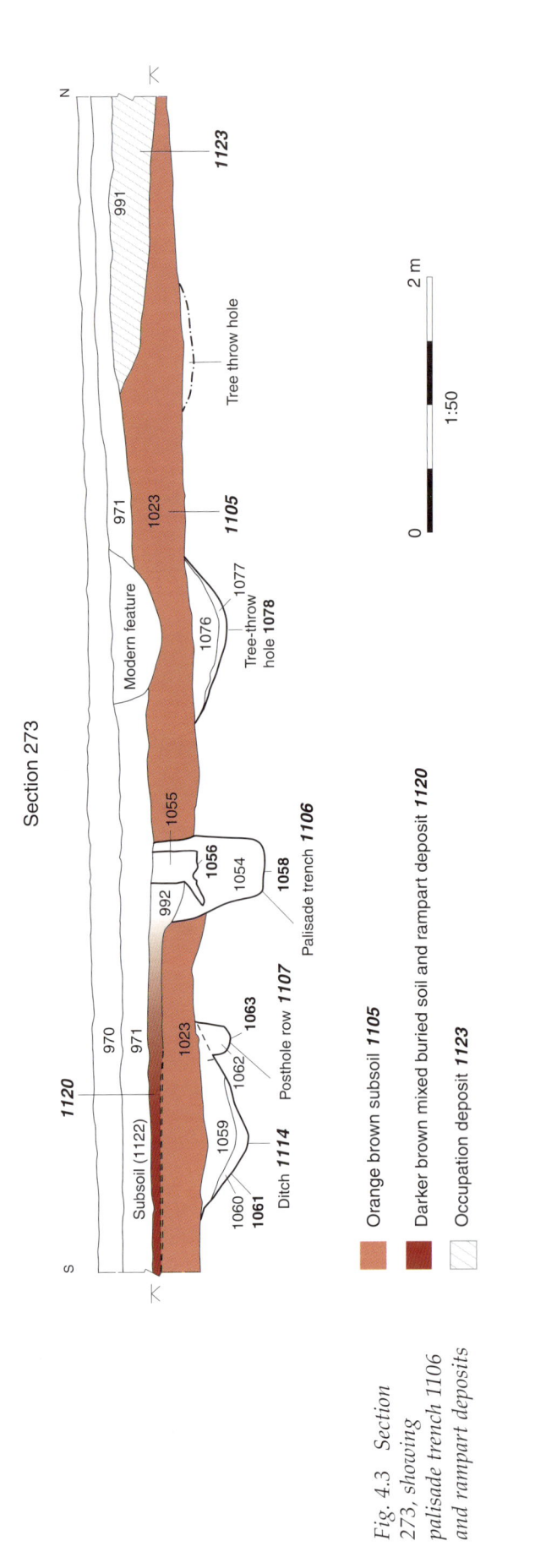

Table 4.1. Summary of dimensions of postholes in rows, structures and other groups

Posthole row	Width					Depth					Spacing			
	Mean	sd	min	max	no.	Mean	sd	min	max	no.	Mean	sd	min	max
1107	0.31	0.07	0.18	0.50	64	0.31	0.09	0.12	0.58	31	0.95	0.15	0.69	1.45
north	0.29	0.04	0.18	0.35	28	0.37	0.03	0.34	0.42	5	-	-	-	-
central	0.38	0.06	0.29	0.5	16	0.33	0.10	0.20	0.58	16	-	-	-	-
south	0.27	0.04	0.20	0.35	20	0.25	0.07	0.12	0.35	10	-	-	-	-
1108	0.46	0.09	0.33	0.69	21	0.30	0.06	0.21	0.41	16	-	-	-	-
Between 1107 and 1108	-	-	-	-	-	-	-	-	-	-	3.1	0.24	2.6	3.6
1106 postpipes	0.35	0.07	0.22	0.48	13	0.52	0.13	0.34	0.74	13	3.0	0.24	2.7	3.5
1104*	0.48	0.16	0.16	0.83	101	0.29	0.09	0.10	0.53	54	0.65	0.42	0.09	1.96
935	0.40	0.09	0.26	0.63	35	0.23	0.09	0.08	0.38	14	0.33	0.19	0.00	0.76
1132	0.32	0.10	0.15	0.49	14	0.24	0.09	0.12	0.44	10	0.45	0.26	0.12	0.97
1133	0.28	0.04	0.23	0.38	12	0.25	-	0.18	0.32	2	0.64	0.26	0.24	1.20
1117 roundhouse	0.35	0.04	0.29	0.46	12	0.21	0.10	0.06	0.35	10	-	-	-	-
1117 other postholes	0.40	0.13	0.15	0.63	22	0.21	0.07	0.07	0.38	18	-	-	-	-
1134 roundhouse	0.35	0.07	0.22	0.45	11	0.27	0.10	0.14	0.44	8	-	-	-	-
1134 other postholes	0.38	0.13	0.16	0.63	31	0.23	0.05	0.16	0.35	20	-	-	-	-

* spacing estimated on the most regular alignments of the larger postholes

As argued above, the fills of the postholes in row 1107 were almost all orange-brown sandy silts, very similar in colour, texture and inclusions to both the orange-brown subsoil layer (group 1105) and to the fills of the early Bronze Age hollows, and may therefore not have been recognised as distinct from them. The orange-brown posthole fills were, however, distinct from the darker brown buried soil/rampart deposits (1120) which overlay the orange-brown subsoil (1105), and suggests that the posthole row predated the construction of the rampart.

This stratigraphic evidence implies that the radiocarbon dates must have derived from intrusive material, or that the postholes from which the dated material came did not belong to the row. One of these postholes (510; Fig. 4.2) actually lay slightly to the east of the main alignment of the row (1107). However, the other (506) lay quite precisely on the alignment. Posthole 506 contained a fragment of sand-tempered pottery, which, given the Saxon date obtained from charcoal, is also probably intrusive. The sand and flint-tempered sherd from posthole 500 was a larger sherd whose fabric, although more characteristic of the late Bronze Age-early Iron Age, also occurs in the fills of the V-profiled ditch, and so is compatible with a date in the earlier part of the late Bronze Age.

The stratigraphic relationships and dating evidence for posthole row 1108

As was the case for posthole row 1107, the fills of the postholes in posthole row 1108 were often orange-brown sandy silts similar to the orange-brown subsoil layer (1105). In this case, however, only one of the postholes in this row (1069) was recorded as being sealed by the orange-brown subsoil (group 1105, recorded here as 1023), while two others (postholes 1049 and 1052) were planned as cutting through it. Again, the postholes did not appear through the darker brown rampart deposits (1120; recorded as 992 in section 273; Fig. 4.3) that lay above the orange-brown subsoil. Stratigraphically, therefore, this posthole row is similar to posthole row 1107.

Away from the southern corner of the site, the postholes were truncated to the level of the natural gravel (127), and were covered by the post-medieval subsoil or by deposits related to the Plessey buildings.

The only pottery associated with this posthole row was a single thick flint-tempered sherd (36 g) in posthole 1052 that is most likely of Middle Bronze Age date, although it could be late Bronze Age. There were two dates obtained from posthole row 1108, one – 1870-1610 cal BC – in the early Bronze Age (SUERC-4967: 3415±35 BP), the other – 1130-930 cal. BC – in the late Bronze Age (OxA-14924: 2851±26 BP). The first date, which was obtained on *Alnus/Corylus* charcoal from posthole 198, probably derives from residual early Bronze Age material. The other radiocarbon date was on *Quercus* sapwood charcoal from the post-pipe of posthole 166.

The radiocarbon and ceramic evidence from posthole row 1108 is thus generally consistent with the stratigraphy in suggesting a late Bronze Age date, preceding the cutting of the V-profiled ditch (574) and the construction of its rampart. The evidence from posthole row 1107 is more problematic, but stratigraphically it belongs early in the sequence, in a similar stratigraphic position in the sequence to posthole row 1108.

The dimensions and spacing of posthole rows 1107 and 1108

Posthole row 1107 ran just east of north-south, curving slightly to the west at the southern end of the excavation. At the north end there was considerable damage from 20th-century buildings, but a lone (unnumbered) posthole on the same alignment (see Fig. 4.1) probably indicates that row 1107 was continuing on the same alignment. Nevertheless, this posthole still lay short of the line of the entrance through the V-profiled ditch, so if this posthole row led to a corresponding entrance it would have lain beyond the northern edge of the excavation.

The postholes in this row were closely spaced, lying on average just 0.95 m apart. The spacing was reasonably consistent (standard deviation = 0.15, although the range = 0.69 m – 1.45 m; Table 4.1). On average the (truncated) postholes were 0.31 m wide and 0.31 m deep. There were, however, differences in the diameters of the postholes – and hence presumably also of the posts – along its length. The postholes in the middle (from around posthole 500 to posthole 720) were larger (mean diameter 0.38 m) than those to the north and south (mean diameters 0.28 m and 0.27 m respectively). An ANOVA (Analysis of Variance, combining statistical tests to reduce error) of the diameters of the three groups of postholes suggests that the central postholes were significantly larger than the others (F = 30; F crit = 3; p = 8x10-10). It is possible that the posthole width increased incrementally toward the middle of the revealed posthole row, in the area of postholes 720-500. There were also significant differences in the depths of the excavated postholes in these three groups (31 out of a total of 64), but contrary to expectation it was the northern group (believed to have suffered most truncation) that was the deepest (northern group mean depth = 0.37 m; central group = 0.32 m; southern group = 0.25 m; F = 4.3; F crit = 3.3; p = 0.02). At the south edge of the excavation postholes of row 1107 were recorded as overlain by layer 1105 (section 273) and the dark soil 1120 over that. As argued above, the postholes were probably simply not seen cutting through similar soil 1105, and the depth of the posthole would therefore have been c 0.5 m.

The postholes in posthole row 1108 were much more widely spaced than those in posthole row

1107; on average they were 3.1 m apart (Table 4.1). Although the pattern is partially obscured at the northern end of the excavation, the spacing was quite regular (sd = 0.24; range = 2.61 m-3.6 m). It is possible that postholes 822 and 844 assigned to group 1134 (Fig. 4.1; Fig. 4.15), and a further unexcavated posthole 1135 (not recognised at the end of WA Trench 1), actually belong with posthole row 1108, evening out the spacing in the northern part of the row (see Fig. 4.2). The posthole row ran parallel to posthole row 1107, on average 3.0 m to the west of it (sd = 0.24; range = 2.7 m-3.5 m), thus defining approximately square areas to the west of posthole row 1107. The (truncated) postholes were larger than those in posthole row 1107, measuring, on average, 0.46 m across, and surviving 0.30 m deep (Table 4.1).

In plan, there is a group of regularly spaced large postholes in the central part of the row (from posthole 169 to 201), which diverges from its line at posthole 201 (where there is a smaller posthole adjacent continuing the line of the row), and continues in a north-north-westerly direction (posthole row 1108A, see Fig. 4.2). This line is very clear as far as a group of three closely spaced postholes (including 224 and 232), after which there is a gap before the row continues with postholes 833, 952 and 1047 into the edge of the excavation (see Fig. 4.6). The gap in the row may have been filled by large posthole 802 or the large unexcavated posthole adjacent, although either or both of these may have belonged to posthole row 935. Alternatively the gap may have been left to accommodate possible roundhouse 1134 (see Figs 4.1 and 4.15).

Whatever the detailed arrangements of this posthole row, it suggests either that posthole row 1108 was from the start intended to enclose a V-shaped area in the northern part of the site, or may have been constructed in two parts, row 1108A perhaps being added at some point. Another smaller line of postholes beginning adjacent to posthole 202 can tentatively be traced north-westwards ending adjacent to posthole 472 in row 1132 (see Fig. 4.6, row 1108B). If genuine, this would suggest another phase of division of the site along this general line, perhaps linking to the change in alignment of posthole row 1132 (see below).

The postholes in both rows 1107 and 1108 varied from quite regular, vertical-sided and flat-based

Table 4.2: Summary of finds in posthole rows 1107 and 1108

Cut	Context	Pottery (weight g)	Flake	Chips and waste flakes	Blade, bladelet and blade-like flake	Core	Retouched peices	Other worked flint	Burnt unworked flint	Other finds
1107										
171	172		4		1	1				
391	392			1						
493	494		1		1					
500	499	23	1							
504	505								1	
506	507	1								Oak roundwood charcoal
508	509		1							
510	511		2							Hammerstone 1
585	586		1	1						
720	721		1							
765	766		1							
760	761		1	1						
1108										
130	132								27	
136	138		3				1	1		Processor - quartz sandstone
139	141								1	
142	144		1							Heat-fractured red sandstone pebble
166	168		1						75	
169	170		3		1				12	
198	200	65	1		1				63	
201	203		4	1						
1052	1053	36								

features to irregular bowl-shaped features. Curiously, although post-pipes were found in most of the excavated postholes in row 1108, none were found in row 1107. The postholes in row 1108 were not deeper than those in row 1107, and there is no obvious explanation for this pattern except to suggest that the posts in row 1107 were removed while those in row 1108 were not. However, the posts in row 1108 were probably the larger and hence perhaps the most likely to be reused. Furthermore, there were no clear indications, such as disturbance to one edge of the posthole (Reynolds 1995) in either row to suggest that any posts had been removed. The postholes were mostly filled with orange brown sandy silts containing small proportions of gravel. The post-pipes in row 1108 were usually darker, although there was considerable variation.

Other finds associated with postholes rows 1107 and 1108

There were few finds from either of these posthole rows, and these consisted mostly of undiagnostic worked flint, usually flakes (see Fig. 3.2 and Table 4.2). Most of the flint came from posthole row 1108, and a large proportion was found in postholes near to, and to the south of, the early Bronze Age hollows (1119). It is tempting to regard this flint as derived from early Bronze Age activity; however, the distribution of worked flint in the posthole rows also roughly corresponded to that of burnt unworked flint (see Fig. 3.3), and since there was almost no burnt unworked flint in the early Bronze Age hollows, the distribution may be unrelated to the hollows, and be of middle or late Bronze Age activity. In contrast to posthole row 1108, there was very little burnt unworked flint in posthole row 1107. The other finds consisted of fragments of stone including a processor made from a quartz sandstone pebble, and a little oak charcoal. The processor may have been used to sharpen small tools or for grinding or mixing small quantities of material (see Shaffrey below, Chapter 7).

The possible structure or structures associated with posthole rows 1107 and 1108

The rows ran parallel (Fig. 4.2), and might at one stage have been associated with each other, forming a structure like a box rampart between 2.7 m and 3.5 m wide (Fig. 4.4A). Several strands of evidence, namely the presence of post-pipes and of burnt flint in row 1108 but not in row 1107, and the fact that the matching of postholes between row 1108 and row 1107 is not exact, could be used to argue that the posts of the two rows were not contemporary, or at least were not constructed to form a single structure. With one row of postholes spaced much closer together than the other, it is not surprising that roughly corresponding postholes to those in 1108 can be found in row 1107, although exact matching of posts may not necessarily have been required. Despite question marks over their precise association, however, it is worthwhile to consider what form of structure the postholes of these two rows might represent.

The postholes in post row 1108 were all cut vertically and did not form sloping 'buttresses' for a palisade (represented by posthole row 1107) in front. It is tempting to see the posts in these rows as together having formed a box rampart, the upright posts retaining an earth-filled core. However, no trace of this earth fill was found, unless the dark brown silts (1120) that covered the postholes of both rows represent the spreading of this fill after the demolition of the structure. It is possible that the relatively close-spaced uprights of row 1107 would have had to be removed to allow the spreading of the earth fill, whereas the widely-spaced uprights of row 1108 could have been left, provided that any linking horizontals were removed. If there were such an earth-filled rampart, however, it is difficult to imagine why this was simply not left *in situ* and palisade 1106 constructed alongside, providing access to the rear of the later palisade top. If the two rows were associated, it is, therefore, more likely that the posts would have formed a hollow timber structure, without an earth fill. The posts in posthole row 1108 might perhaps have supported a raised walkway which was also attached to the posts of posthole row 1107.

Palisade trench 1106

Whatever the structure associated with posthole rows 1107 and 1108, it appears to have been succeeded, perhaps deliberately replaced, by a palisade constructed in foundation trench 1106 (Fig. 4.5; Plate 4.1). Palisade trench 1106 ran between posthole rows 1107 and 1108, following exactly the same line, but was stratigraphically later.

At the south end of the site an area of dark soil and gravel 992 (part of layer 1120 overlying subsoil 1105) was exposed. This showed that the palisade trench and its postholes were largely sealed by these darker brown sediments. However, the evidence of section 273 (Fig. 4.3) suggests that the gravelly deposit (992) abutted the post-pipe (1055) within the palisade trench (1106: recorded as 1058) and covered the cut (1058) of the palisade trench (Plate 4.2). This would imply that the digging of the palisade trench predated the deposition of soil (992), and that the post within posthole 1055 was still standing when this occurred. This suggests that palisade trench 1106, unlike posthole rows 1107 and 1108 to either side, went out of use not long before this soil was deposited.

In section 229, the only other section where soils survived above the gravel (see Fig. 4.5), the post-pipe 377 was again abutted by layers 890 and 893 on the west, although the relationship on the east was largely removed by a later pit 884 cutting the top of

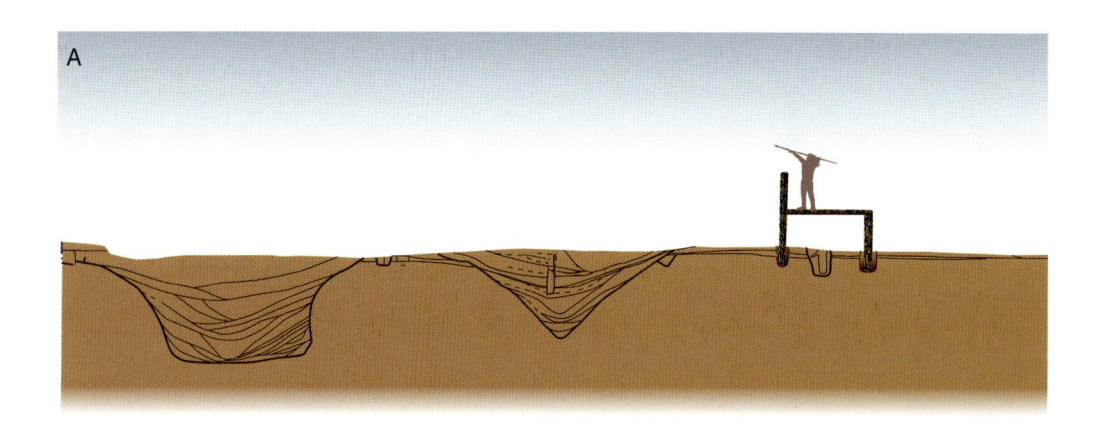

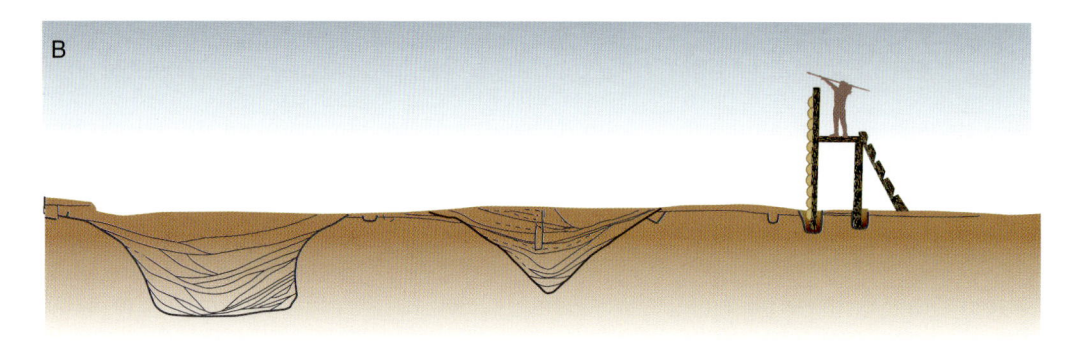

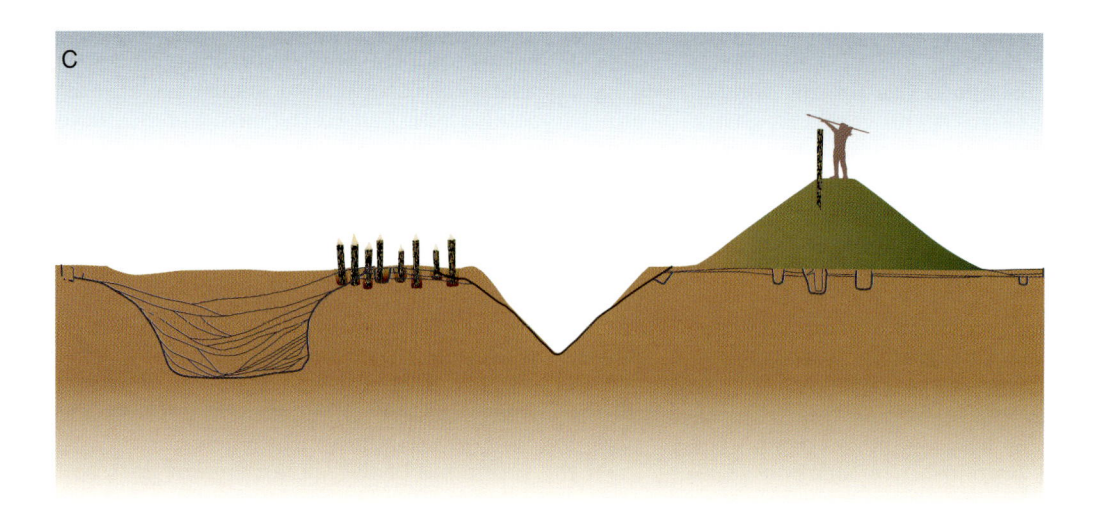

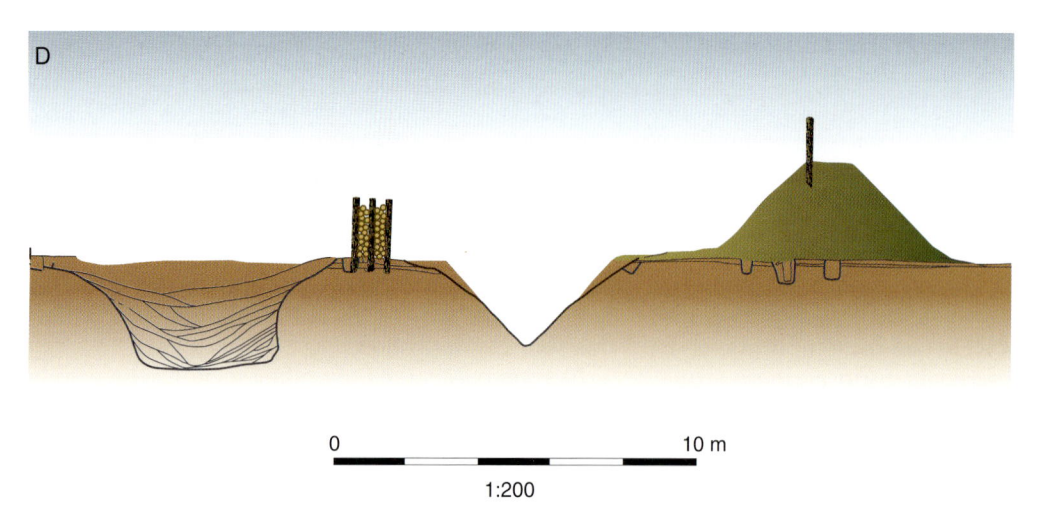

Fig. 4.4
Schematic
reconstructions of
the defences in the
Late Bronze Age

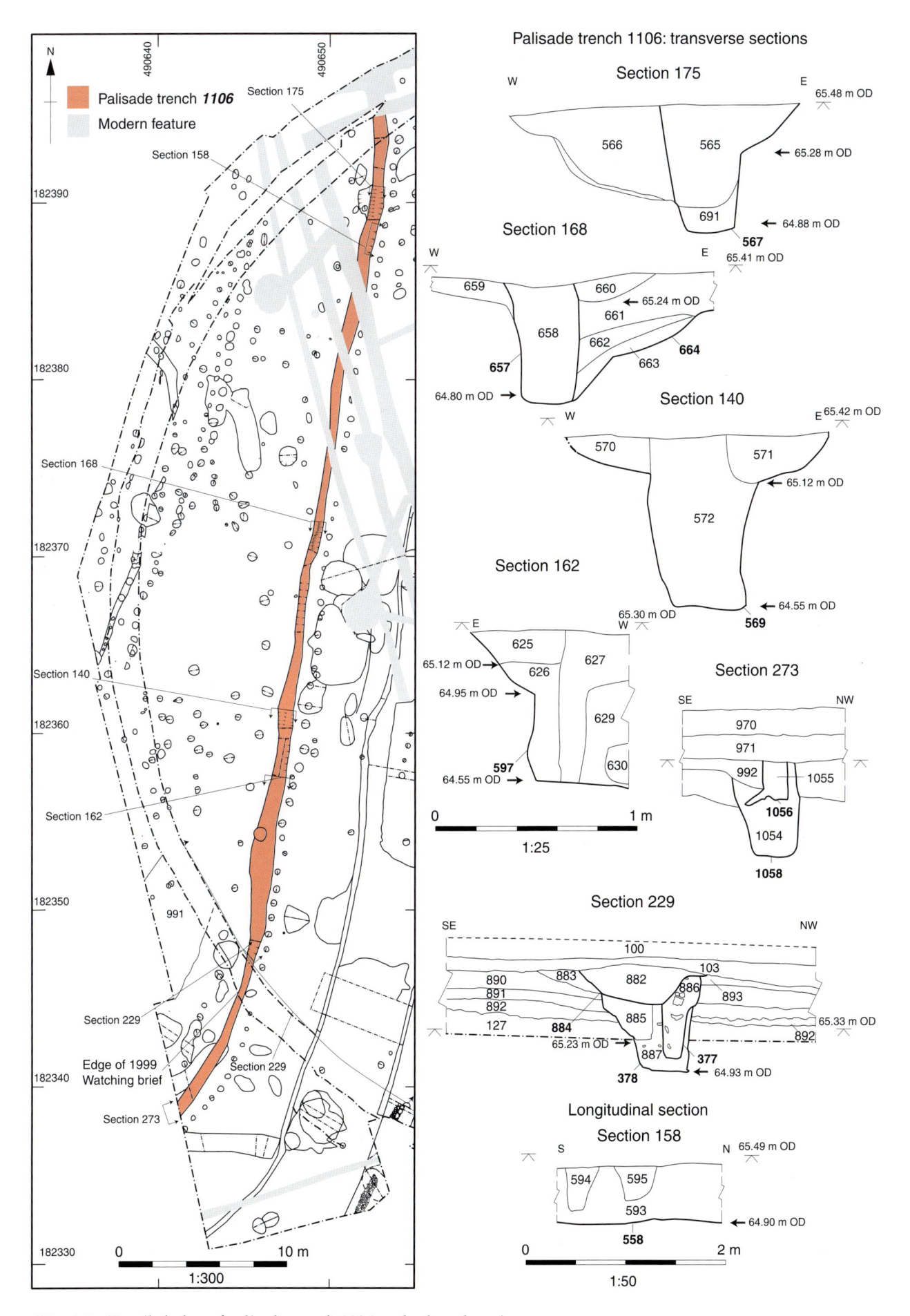

Fig. 4.5 Detailed plan of palisade trench 1106 and selected sections

Plate 4.1 Palisade trench 1106, sections 175 and 158. To the right lie postholes forming part of posthole row 1107

Plate 4.2 Detail of the palisade 1106 in section, showing the post-pipe abutted by the rampart soil 1120

the palisade trench. What little survived suggested that a step on the east side of the palisade trench filled with a similar dark soil (885), was abutted by the rampart soil (870), although it would be unwise to base too much on such slender evidence.

To dig the palisade trench any structure that might have linked rows 1107 and 1108 would have had to be dismantled, and at least one row of posts removed. This might explain the absence of post-pipes in row 1107. It is possible that row 1108 was left standing, and may have continued to provide a rampart walk for the new palisade (see Fig. 4.4B), allowing layer 1120 to be deposited or reworked subsequently.

The sections cut across palisade trench 1106 in the southern part of the site (where it was best-preserved) show that the trench had a flat base, and survived from 0.55 m to 0.80 m deep, being deepest in sections 273 and 229 at the south end (Fig. 4.5). This was at least in part due to better preservation of the stratigraphy at this end of the site, as in terms of level above OD the bottom of the palisade trench was deepest in sections 162 and 140, rising by as much as 0.3 m to the north and south. It may not be coincidence that this also corresponds to the part of posthole row 1107 where the postholes were larger (see Fig. 4.2).

Post-pipes were visible in a number of cross-sections. Two longitudinal sections cut along the middle of this trench suggest that posts were placed at intervals of 0.6 m along the trench (eg. Fig. 4.5, section 158). Their width, on average, was 0.35 m, similar to that of the post-pipes in most of the posthole rows (Table 4.1). This would suggest that in trench 1106 the gaps between the posts were about the same width as the width of the posts themselves. The post-pipes in longitudinal section 158 did not reach the bottom of the palisade trench, nor did the post-pipes in cross-sections 229 and 273, though that in section 162 did. This may indicate that the trench was dug to an even depth, and then backfilled as necessary to allow for variation in the length of the posts, ie that the tops of the posts were level. Alternatively, the apparent variation in the depth to which the posts were bedded may relate to the way in which they were excavated and recorded. Only excavation by spits in plan would have ensured that the exact positions, dimensions and angle of incline of the post-pipes was obtained, and in retrospect it was unfortunate that this method was not used. We cannot therefore be certain about the size and spacing of the posts, nor whether these were whole roundwood posts, or halved or otherwise split roundwood posts. The positions of the cross-sections and longitudinal sections may have cut obliquely across the post-pipes, and could have merely clipped them or missed them altogether.

The post-pipes that were recorded suggest that the posts were not always spaced centrally in the palisade trench, making oblique sections likely. The recorded width of the post-pipe in section 162, a mere 0.10 m, is a probable example of an oblique cut across the edge of a roundwood post-pipe, or the narrower part of a split roundwood post. If the sections or posts were not exactly vertical, post-pipes would appear wider at the top or the bottom, as indeed occurs in sections 229 and 158, and might have not been within the section at the bottom at all. We also need to bear in mind that roundwood posts would have irregularities along their length, like the possible branch-stub recorded in section 273. We can therefore only treat the recorded dimensions with caution.

The cross-sections show some variation in profile along the length of the trench. Whereas the western (inner) edge of the trench was generally more or less vertical, on the eastern (outer) edge there was a concave step, around 0.60 m from the top where it was least truncated, but elsewhere varying from 0.4 m to as little as 0.12 m deep. This was not the result of varying truncation of the palisade slot, as the bottom of this step was at different heights from the base of the trench along its length, and did not occur at a consistent height above OD (although there was some consistency within adjacent sections, see Fig. 4.5). In sections 140 and 162 there was also a step on the west, and a slight widening of the post-pipe was also evident in section 229.

Although the lower part of the trench was, on average, 0.40 m wide (sd = 0.10; range = 0.22 m – 0.52 m), because of the presence of this step the top was 0.90 m – 0.98 m wide where it was least truncated (and elsewhere 0.64 m – 0.76 m). The step was usually filled with brown silty clay similar to the fills of the post-pipes in the deeper part of the trench, and which contrasted with the lighter, more yellowish or orangey fills of the post-packing. In section 175, for instance, no distinction was made between them. In some sections the dark fill of the step was contiguous with the post-pipe, but in section 229 a thin band of grey-orange packing material ran vertically between the two. In section 162 the lower part of the eastern step fill was filled with the same material as the packing, although the upper part (layer 625) was darker, and the western step had the same fill as the post-pipe. The fills of the post-pipe and that of the eastern step were distinguished in sections 168 and 162, and in section 140 the fill of the step appeared to partially overlie that of the trench.

The form of the palisade associated with trench 1106

How the fills within the step should be interpreted is uncertain. One possibility is that the step housed a line of horizontal timbers providing additional support to the front of the palisade. The step was generally curved in profile, possibly indicating radially cut and untrimmed roundwood timbers. If so, these timbers would have been substantially larger than the recorded timber uprights, generally 0.5 m wide and, in the case of context 885 in section

229, 0.4 m deep. These timbers might have been braces for the palisade uprights (although no clear evidence was seen to suggest that the step held additional vertical or angled posts supporting the main posts in the deeper part of the trench), or may indicate that the front face of the palisade was formed of horizontal planking (Fig. 4.4B). Perhaps the strongest evidence that the step was part of the original plan is in section 162, where it was partly filled with the packing soil, perhaps to level up before a timber was laid. On this interpretation of the step on the east side of the palisade, the palisade would have been free-standing.

Alternatively, it is possible that the step was formed by a later cut, perhaps dug to retrieve or assist in cutting off the posts when the palisade went out of use. This interpretation might explain the virtual absence of a step in section 273, and its variable height from the base of the palisade in other sections.

Finds and other dating evidence associated with palisade trench 1106

The only finds other than worked flint were a fragment of amorphous fired clay, fragments of oak charcoal, a piece of burnt unworked flint, and three very small sherds of pottery: one probably a residual early Bronze Age fragment, one in a sand-tempered fabric which might be middle Iron Age, and another too small to be classified (Table 4.3). Most of the flint consisted of flakes, but there were also appreciable numbers of blades and cores, as well as two microburins and a microlith. As the presence of the microburins and microlith clearly indicates, much of this flint may have been residual, although it is possible that some dates from the late Bronze Age.

A single radiocarbon date (SUERC-4970: 3020±40 BP) was obtained from *Alnus/Corylus* charcoal from the fill (571) of the step on the eastern side of the palisade trench. The likelihood of this kind of context containing residual or intrusive material is high. The calibrated date range, 1410-1120 cal BC (94% confidence), is earlier than the range for the later date from the stratigraphically earlier posthole row 1108, and suggests that the charcoal was residual and derived from middle Bronze Age activity.

In conclusion, palisade trench (1106) appears to have been later than posthole rows 1108 and 1107, although since it follows their lines and runs so close to row (1107), it is unlikely that a considerable length of time elapsed between them. The parallel alignment of the ditch and palisade trench again argues for a close chronological relationship between them. While the palisade and the ditch are very closely aligned at the south and for most of the length of the excavated area, it is noticeable that the palisade turns westwards more at the north end than does the ditch, and it is particularly unfortunate that modern foundations and services had removed the further continuation of the palisade here.

Table 4.3. Summary of finds in palisade trench 1106

Cut	Context	Pottery (weight g)	Flake	Chips and waste flakes	Blade, bladelet and blade-like flake	Core	Retouched peices	Microburin	Microlith	Other worked flint	Burnt unworked flint	Other finds
377	378		2									
377	886				1	1						
564	562					1						
564	563		1		1							
567	565		8		3	1						
567	566		8									
569	571	4	9							1	1	Oak roundwood charcoal
569	911		15	9	4							Fired clay - amorphous 1/11
589	593		1		1					1		
589	595		1		1	1						
597	598	4	9		1	1				1		
597	604		2		2		1					
597	626		1					1				
597	627										1	
657	658		5	1		1	1					
657	660		14	2	1	1	2	1				

Posthole rows within the hillfort (935, 1132 and 1133)

Three rows of postholes (935, 1132 and 1133; Fig. 4.6) were found west of palisade 1106 and rows 1107 and 1108, running on a more easterly alignment, and so converging slightly with them towards the north. They may have formed further palisades or less substantial fences extending around the periphery of the hillfort.

The easternmost row (935) had the largest postholes (on average 0.40 m wide by 0.23 m deep; Table 4.1). The postholes of this row did not follow an exactly straight line, and the spacing of the postholes was also variable, with some clusters of two or more postholes very close together. A second row (1133) began immediately west of row 935 towards the centre of the excavated area, and ran north, parallel to row 935 and around 0.3 m from it for c 19 m to the north edge of the 1999 excavation. Row 1133 was constructed using smaller postholes, on average 0.28 m wide and 0.25 m deep (Table 4.1). The line of posthole row 935 was more erratic south of the end of row 1133, and contained a group of six very closely-spaced postholes just south of the end of row 1133, perhaps indicating that this part of row 935 contained postholes of both rows, ie that row 1133 continued south, re-using or incorporating part of row 935. There was a pair of intercutting postholes within this part of row 935, some of which may have belonged to other structures in Group 1117, or to another posthole row on a north-west alignment. At the south edge of the excavation there were two postholes alongside one another that could represent a resumption of row 1133.

At the southern end of the excavation a third posthole row (1132) ran parallel to row 935 around 1 m to the west of it. Row 1132 comprised postholes which were, on average, slightly smaller than those in row 935 – 0.32 m wide and 0.24 m deep (Table 4.1) – although at its very southern end the postholes were markedly smaller than those further north. Here the postholes were set within a shallow gully or palisade slot. This gully was only traced for around 8 m from the edge of the excavation, petering out at the edge of the WA Trench 12, where it was not observed. A row of substantial postholes continued on the same line for a further 5 m, but the row ended at a smaller posthole, adjacent to which the shallow slot, in which several postholes were planned but not excavated, continued north and then turned north-west into the edge of the excavation. A line of smaller and more widely-spaced postholes (row 1132A) also continued from the kink in the palisade slot north-eastwards, converging with rows 1133 and 935 at the north end of the 1999 excavation. It is possible that a short row of postholes on a north-west alignment (Fig. 4.6, Row 1108B) ran between posthole row 1108 and posthole row 1132, and was cut by posthole row 935. The association of these postholes is however uncertain, so cannot be used to phase the internal post-rows.

There was a short unexcavated gap between this and the surrounding strip dug in 2000, and it was uncertain to which (if any) of the posthole rows four further postholes found here belong. Further south there were a number of other postholes nearly 2 m west of row 1132, some of which may have belonged to yet another row parallel to it. Very few of these postholes were investigated.

The spacing of the postholes along all of these rows was rather irregular, but always close (centre to centre on average 0.33 m apart in row 953; 0.45 m apart in the palisade-row 1132; 0.85 m apart in the posthole row (1132A) continuing north from palisade-slot 1132, and 0.64 m apart in row 1133; Table 4.1). However, uncertainty concerning precisely which features belong to which posthole row encourages caution in considering these statistics.

The postholes in all of these rows were filled with dark orange- or grey-brown sandy silts. Post-pipes were recognised in only a small number of the postholes (921 and 249 in row 935; 1039, 956, 954 and 279 in row 1132; and 806 in row 1133), and were usually marked by deposits which were darker than the surrounding post-packing.

Finds and other dating evidence associated with posthole rows 935, 1132 and 1133

No finds were recovered from the postholes in row 1133; the only indication of its date is the fact that it begins immediately adjacent to row 935 halfway across the site, and runs north so close to it. Only three flint flakes were found in the postholes in row 1132 (Table 4.4). The number of finds associated with posthole row 935 was also small (Table 4.4). Posthole 243 contained small quantities of charred hazelnut shells, wheat and unidentified cereal, and posthole 249 further unidentified charred cereal and a small fragment of sheep/goat bone. A radiocarbon date (OxA-14357; 2803±27: 1020-890 cal BC) was obtained from some of the wheat in posthole 243. The remaining finds from posthole row 935 consisted of flint flakes, chips and blades, and two fragments of burnt unworked flint.

The only pottery associated with this posthole row was a single sherd of flint and sand tempered pot (18 g) from posthole or pit 967, which is consistent with the radiocarbon date. However, although it lay directly on the alignment of the posthole row feature 967, which had been burnt and contained large quantities of burnt stone and charcoal, appeared to cut another posthole, and may possibly have been a later feature, not associated with the row. Feature 967 was 0.52 m in diameter by 0.15 m deep, larger than the other postholes in this area, but was not the largest within the posthole row overall.

Posthole row 1132

Posts belonging to this row, the westernmost row within the excavation area, were cut into the top of tree-throw hole 914, which contained an assemblage

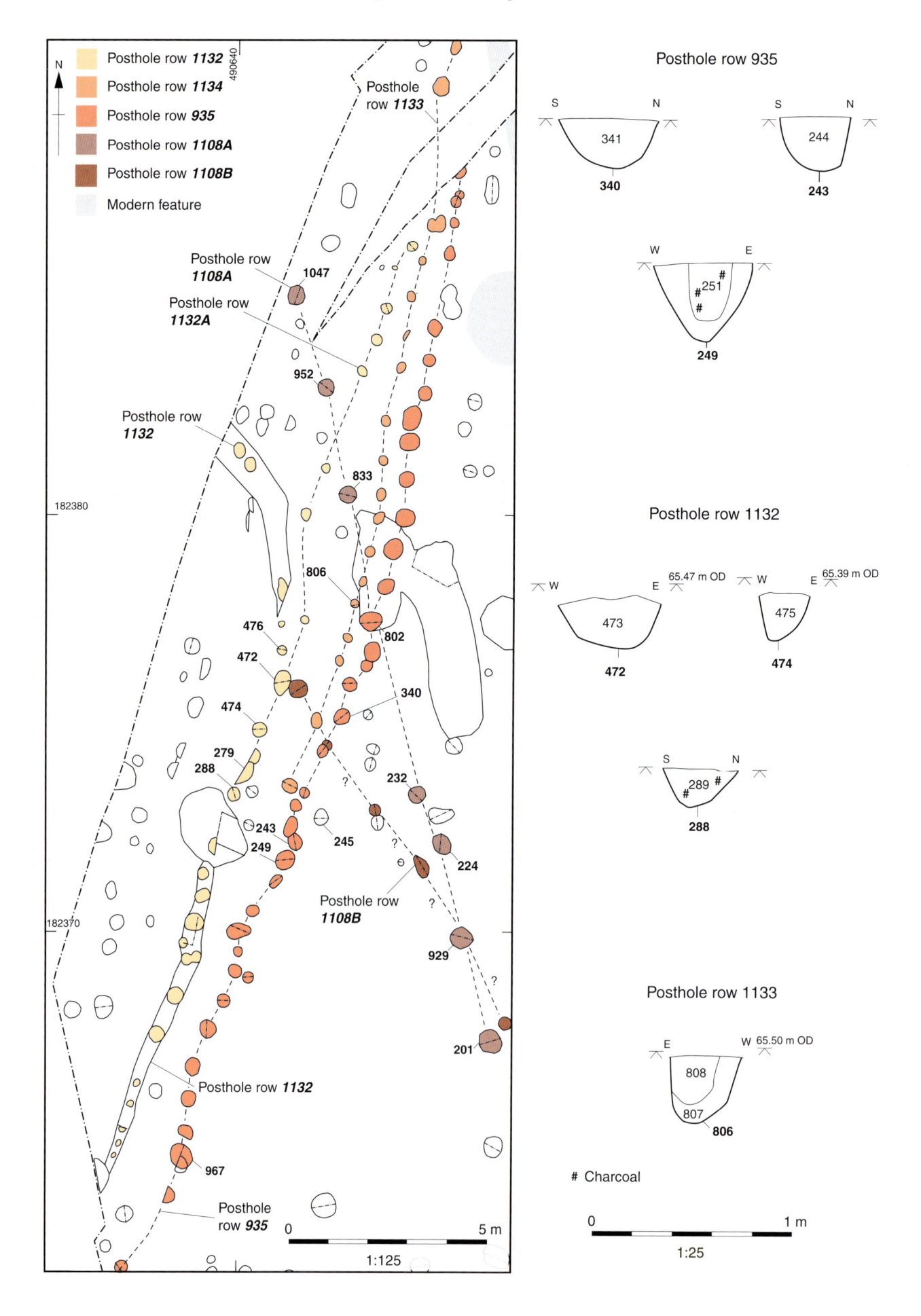

From Bronze Age enclosure to Anglo-Saxon settlement

of Mesolithic or early Neolithic struck flint. Single sherds of flint-tempered late Bronze Age (4 g) and sand and flint-tempered late Bronze Age-early Iron Age pottery (7 g) were found in the postholes of this row. A middle Bronze Age radiocarbon date (OxA-14358: 3120±30 BP; 1450-1310 cal BC) was also obtained from charred *Triticum* in one of the other postholes (279), but this is probably residual

WA Test-pit 12 was dug across the line of this posthole row and into the top of the tree-throw hole beneath, although no postholes of the row were recognised or recorded. Fifty-six sherds of late Bronze Age plain ware pottery were recovered from layer 1202 in this test-pit, which probably corresponds to the occupation soil recorded as overlying the posthole row in the 2000 excavation, although some sherds may have come from the row itself. This may indicate that this row went out of use some time before the end of the late Bronze Age.

Row 1132 was not contemporary with the widely-spaced row of postholes (1108A) tentatively identified running north-north-west from row 1108, which may indicate that 1132 is later than 1108, as the radiocarbon date also suggests. Their chronological relationship to the V-profiled ditch (574) is also uncertain.

Two of the rows (1133 and 935) were clearly not contemporary with possible Iron Age roundhouse 1134 (see Fig. 4.1). On the basis of the radiocarbon dates it is likely that 935 predates the structures in posthole circle 1117 (see below), but one or more rows could have been contemporary with either the posthole circle or any of the five possible four-post structures.

The interpretation of posthole rows 935, 1132 and 1133

Except for the more-widely spaced short row (1132A) continuing north from 1132, the postholes were of similar size to those of rows 1107 and 1108, and row 1132 were set within a probable palisade slot, albeit very shallow. It is therefore possible that at some stage in the site history these structures were the main, or only, defence for the site. The separate posthole rows do not however seem to have belonged to a more complex structure, since the postholes in one row do not appear to match those in the others, nor do the three rows seem to run parallel to each for the whole width of the excavation. They may alternatively have been internal fences within the enclosure defined by palisade 1106, the V-profiled ditch (574) or both. The change in alignment of posthole row 1132, turning north-west across the interior, and perhaps deliberately skirting around the edge of possible roundhouse 1134, may indicate that this is the more likely interpretation, but since so little of the interior lay within the excavations, this remains speculative.

Table 4.4: Summary of finds in posthole rows 935 and 1132

Posthole	Layer	Pottery (weight g)	Flake	Chips and waste flakes	Blade, bladelet and blade-like flake	Burnt unworked flint	Charred plant remains	Animal bone
935								
243	244						Wheat +	
							Cereal indet. +	
							Hazelnut shell +	
249	251					1	Cereal indet. +	Sheep/goat 1/2
288	289					1		
336	337		1	1				
340	341				1			
802	803		2	1				
802	804			1				
944	945				1			
967	968	1						
954	966		1					
1132								
472	473		2					
474	475		1					
279	283						Wheat + (residual)	

Fig. 4.6 (facing page) Detailed plan of posthole rows 935, 1108A and B, 1132, 1132A and 1133 and selected sections

The V-profiled ditch (574) and its rampart

The V-profiled ditch (574) lay from 3.7 m to 5.4 m to the east of palisade trench 1106, and ran roughly parallel to it and to posthole rows 1107 and 1108, curving slightly to the west near the southern end of the excavation. The ditch terminated near to the northern edge of the excavation, where there was an entrance into the hillfort (see below).

Three main sections were excavated across this ditch: sections 123, 227 and 125 (Figs 4.7 and 4.8; Plate 4.3). In these the ditch itself measured 5.3 m – 6.3 m wide and 1.8 m – 2.2 m deep, although at the south-east corner of the enclosure observations during the watching brief suggested a depth of 2.6 m or more. The ditch had a V-shaped profile whose sides generally sloped at 40-45° (section 125 is slightly oblique). In the two sections at right-angles to the line of the ditch the angle of the western (inner) side was slightly steeper (45°) than the eastern (outer) side (40°). The ditch was open long enough for some erosion at the top to occur (cf observations at experimental earthworks, Bell *et al.* 1996), creating a gentler profile. The sides of the ditch would probably originally have been straight, in which case the ditch would have been around 4.8 m wide.

In the southern part of the site, this ditch was cut through the lower, orange-brown subsoil layers (group 1105; Fig. 4.9, section 229). Soils (collectively called 1120) were found to the west of the ditch, representing either possible upcast forming a rampart associated with this ditch, or the topsoil buried below this upcast. Neither layers 1105 nor 1120 produced any finds. The interpretation of these deposits, and their chronological relationships with other features, is not straightforward, and they are discussed further below.

The V-profiled ditch 574 and its fills

The fills of the V-profiled ditch were divided into two by the standstill layer (1102). The deposits above this layer were part of the early-middle Iron Age rampart associated with the U-profiled ditch (460), and are discussed in Chapter 5; those below relate to the earlier filling of the ditch in the late Bronze Age.

In all three sections cut across the ditch, small primary deposits of gravel were found in the very bottom of the ditch (layers 521, 496 and un-numbered), and probably derive from erosion and collapse of the outer edges of the ditch (cf. Bell *et al.* 1996). In section 125, the primary fill was overlain by a thick layer of brown silty sand (495) that covered almost the whole width of the ditch, but in the other two sections the sequence of fills was more complex, although in both the fills appear to have derived largely from the eastern side at first, followed by fills mainly coming from the west. In section 123, the primary fill was overlain by deposits of orange and red brown sandy silts (520

Plate 4.3 The V-profiled ditch (574): section 125

Chapter 4

Fig. 4.7 The V-profiled ditch (574): plan

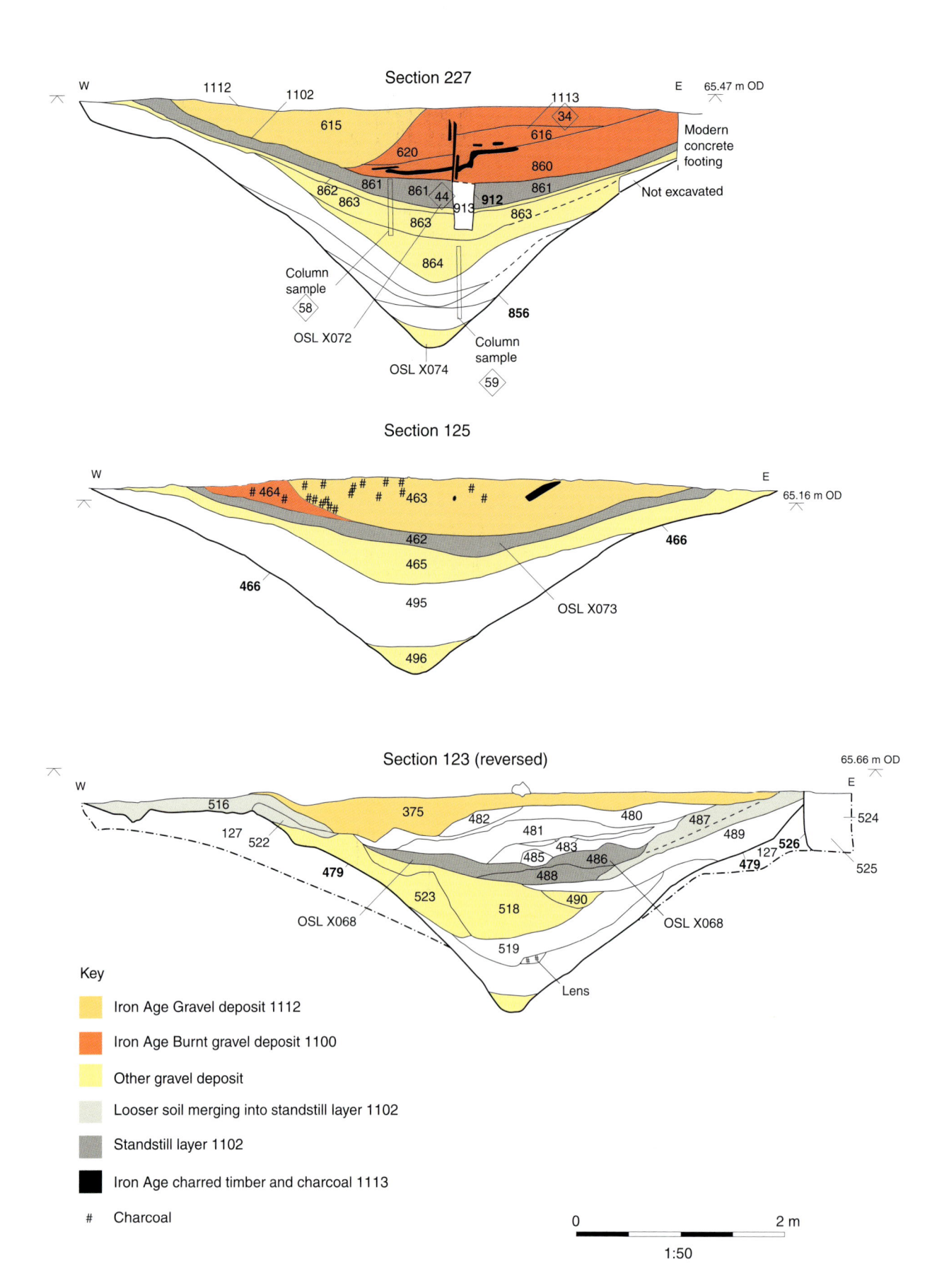

From Bronze Age enclosure to Anglo-Saxon settlement

Fig. 4.8 The V-profiled ditch (574): sections 227, 125 and 123

Chapter 4

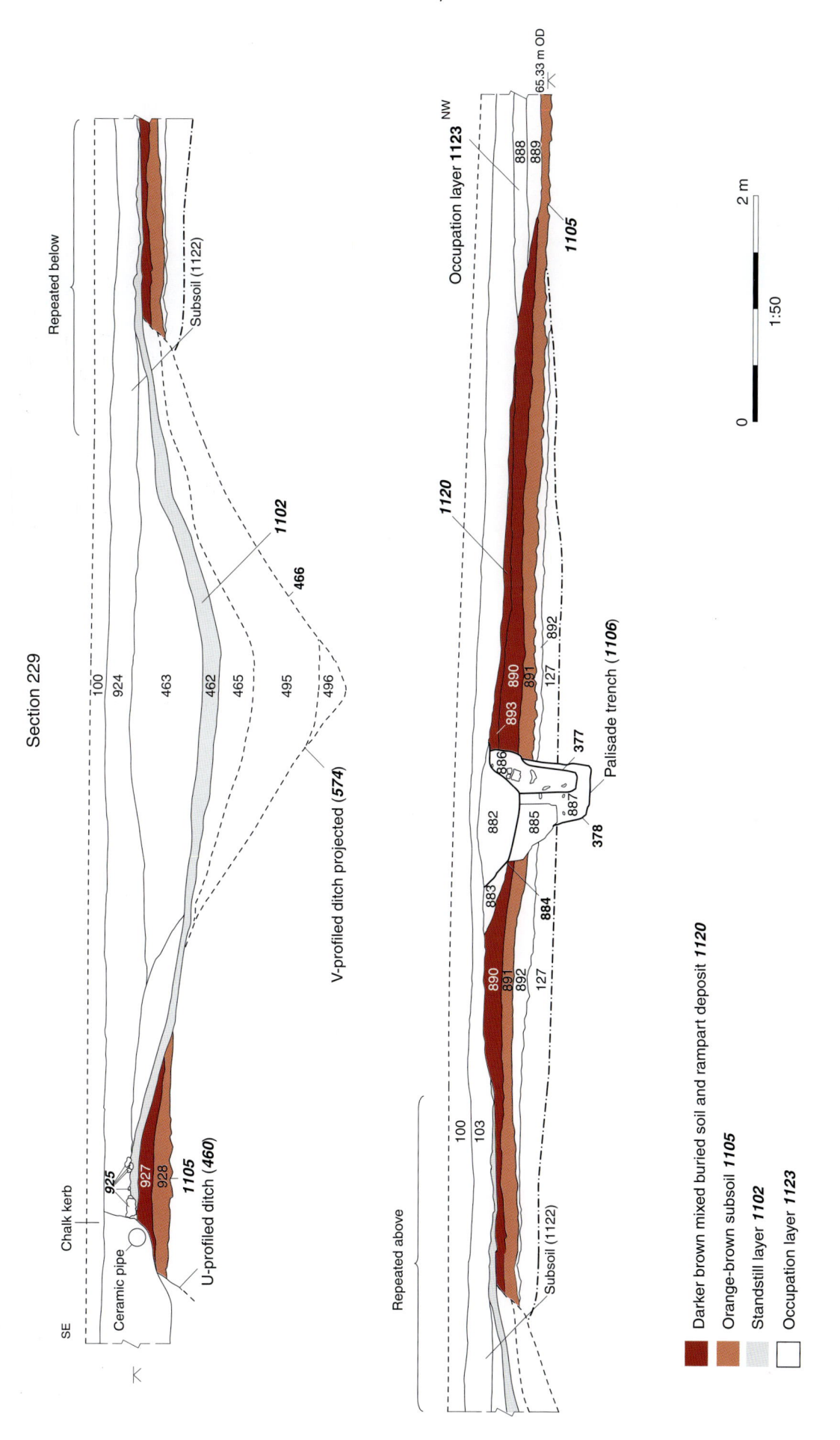

Fig. 4.9 The V-profiled ditch (574): section 229

Plate 4.4 The V-profiled ditch (574): section 123

and 519) which appear to have come into the ditch largely from the east, and only on top of these were there thicker deposits, gravelly in parts, which were deposited from the west (522, 523 and 518; 518 and 522 containing the most marked proportion of gravel) (Plate 4.4). In section 227 fills were deposited from either side of the ditch, though as in section 125 these fills were thicker, and extended further up the cut, on the west side. Only the upper layers (862, 863 and 864, below the standstill layer) however contained notable proportions of gravel.

It seems likely that most of the lower fills of the ditch were the result of natural silting processes, the larger proportion of fill on the west side perhaps being due to the slightly steeper angle of the ditch on this side, which resulted in greater erosion. The origin of the gravelly fills above this is less certain; they could still have eroded from the exposed upper ditch side, but the shallower ditch profile may indicate that erosion (or deliberate slighting) of the rampart was occurring. Erosion or slumping of the upcast rampart is likely to have occurred only once the ditch sides had eroded back and undermined it. Although the excavation of the ditch was limited, it does not appear to have been maintained by cleaning out or recutting.

In the top of the V-profiled ditch a bleached, brown-grey silt layer (1102) with strongly developed iron pan above and below it, was found all along the length of the ditch within the excavation. It represents a phase of very slow silting towards the top of the V-profiled ditch when the deposits around and in the ditch were stable. The layer, variably sandy or clayey, and its formation is discussed in detail later in this chapter.

Finds from the V-profiled ditch (574)

The V-profiled ditch contained few finds (Table 4.5). The small assemblage of pottery, mostly in flint-tempered fabrics, belongs to the late Bronze Age plain ware tradition (Barrett 1980), and on comparative grounds is dated to *c* 1150-800 BC. This includes much of a fineware biconical bowl from the layer immediately below the standstill layer (see Fig. 7.3. No.9), which could perhaps be as late as the 8th century BC. The later, flint and sand-tempered pottery in the standstill layer at the top of this ditch contains the highest proportion of decorated pottery in the sequence (see Table 7.8), and can be assigned to the end of the late Bronze Age and the beginning of the early Iron Age. The 73 sherds in this layer, mostly abraded, probably indicate the accumulation of material over a considerable period of time. There is otherwise little evidence for activity on the site in this period. The other finds comprise a few amorphous fragments of fired clay and struck flints, mostly flakes (Table 4.5).

Four Optically Stimulated Luminescence dates (hereafter OSL) were obtained from the V-profiled ditch (574) (see Chapter 9). An OSL date (X074) was obtained from the primary fill (see section 227). The OSL date has a range (1250-290 BC) which is very wide even at only 1 standard deviation. Three OSL

Table 4.5: Summary of finds in the V-profiled ditch (574), the standstill layer (1102) and the rampart associated with the U-profiled ditch (460)

Feature	Cut	Context	Pot (weight g)	Flake	Chips and waste flakes	Blade, bladelet and blade-like flake	Cores	Retouched pieces	Axe	Other worked flint	Burnt unworked flint	Fired clay (no. frags/weight (g))	Animal bone	Charred plant remains	Charcoal (excluding timber lacing)
Rampart associated with the U-profiled ditch (460)															
1100		644	3	3							2			Weed indet. +	Oak 31 Hawthorn/apple 1
1100		645	60	10	1	1				1					Oak
1100		569		1											
1100		724	43												
1100		616													
1112		615	45							2					
1112		463	56									Amorphous 1/11			
1112		994													
Standstill layer															
1102		861	298	8	5	1					1		Cattle 1/5 Horse 1/18 Unid. 1/1		
1102		462	62	3	1		1								
1102		648	213	1											
1102		1074													
V-profiled ditch															
574	580	581		47	6	5	1	3		1					
574	865	863	52												
574	865	864		1											
574	865	880	128		1	1	2	2							
574	878	838	133												
574	878	839										Amorphous 5/17			
574	993	1075	28												

55

dates (X068, X072 and X073) were obtained from the standstill layer (1102) at the top of the ditch. All the dates are very similar, and although one (X073) has a similarly wide range (1210-290 BC), the other two suggest a narrower date range, between 1080 and 370 BC. These dates indicate that the ditch belongs to the later Bronze Age or early Iron Age.

As the deposit was quite thick, and formed over a long period, we cannot be sure that the samples do not reflect different parts of the accumulation, so cannot simply reduce the range using the latest start and earliest end date. However, constraining the dates using Bayesian statistics, (see Chapter 9), the date from the primary ditch fill is narrowed considerably by the model to 1050-700 BC (95.4%), and those from the standstill layer at the ditch top to 870-540 BC (at 95.4% confidence). This date range is again consistent with the late Bronze Age-early Iron Age pottery associated with this layer.

The range for the V-profiled ditch is compatible with the date suggested for the plain ware from the V-profiled ditch (574) of c 1150-800 BC. It thus seems likely that the V-profiled ditch (574) was constructed in the later part of the late Bronze Age. The OSL dates suggest that the fills between (and including) these layers, were deposited over a period of less than 250 years, and probably less than 120 years.

Rampart (1120) associated with the V-profiled ditch

The darker brown deposits (group 1120) that lay above the orange-brown silts (1105) west of the ditch are interpreted as belonging to the rampart associated with the V-profiled ditch (574). At the south end of the site the darker brown deposit, here numbered 992 (see Fig. 4.3, section 273) was recorded as stopping just short of the standstill layer (1102) in the top of the V-profiled ditch, but just to the north (Fig. 4.9, section 229) the standstill layer overlay the equivalent soil 890. This demonstrates that the group 1120 deposits are either contemporary with the V-profiled ditch, or predate it. The edge of the ditch appeared to cut this soil, but this may be the result either of erosion of the ditch edge back into the rampart, or simply the later ditch fills overlying the original upcast.

Layer 992 contained a much higher proportion of gravel (80%) than the underlying layers. This gravel is most easily explained as a dumped deposit, part of the upcast from the V-profiled ditch (574). In section 229 there were two layers of the darker brown deposits, the lower of which (891) contained no more gravel (5%) than the surrounding layers, but the layer above (890/893) again contained a higher proportion of gravel (30%) than usual. This could perhaps be seen as the succession of dumped topsoil followed by underlying gravel dug out from the adjacent ditch. The proportion of gravel in the corresponding layer (927) on the eastern side of the V-profiled ditch was notably less (10%).

As described above, at the south end of the site an area of layer 992 was exposed west of the V-profiled ditch, and sealed the postholes of rows 1107 and 1108 and the palisade trench 1106, but not those within palisade trench 1106 (section 273). It is possible that some of the posts of the palisade survived above ground when layer 992 was deposited, but the absence of other postholes visible in the stripped area strongly suggests that most of the posts had been removed or cut off at ground level before the rampart was thrown up. West of the palisade trench 1106 no change in soil was observed in plan, but in section 273 (Fig. 4.3) the layer to the west of palisade trench was recorded as consisting only of the lower, orange brown silts (1105). Layer 1023 was, however, described as being more orange towards the base, and it seems likely that the distinction between the lower orangey layers (1105) and the darker brown upper layer (1120) was not clearly made on the section drawing.

On this interpretation the orange-brown silts (1105) below 1120 must represent the remains of the soil preserved below the rampart. The orange-brown silts do not have the character of a buried soil, although if these soils had indeed been ploughed (see Chapter 3) it is possible that the length of time between their last ploughing and their burial by the rampart had not allowed the formation of a developed soil profile. It is also possible that the top of the soil profile was removed as turf, perhaps for use in revetting the rampart (eg Avery *et al.* 1967). If the successive soils 891 and 890 are taken to represent redeposited topsoil and gravel from the excavation of the ditch, it is not clear why the redeposited topsoil should be darker than the underlying soils unless the topsoil had been removed from beneath the rampart.

It is alternatively possible, in view of their darker colour, that all or part of soils 1120 represent the buried topsoil below the rampart (see also Canti, Chapter 8). However, this seems unlikely, not only because of the high proportion of gravel in them, but also because 1120 overlay the posthole rows 1107 and 1108 and palisade trench 1106. A considerable length of time would have had to elapse between the removal or rotting of the posts in these structures for all traces of them to have disappeared from the soil into which they had been cut before the V-profiled ditch was dug (cf Collins 1948-9, 54, describing a turf line at Blewburton Hill, Oxfordshire, formed over a palisade trench before the box rampart was constructed), yet the line of the posthole rows, the palisade trench and the ditch match one another very closely, suggesting that they directly succeeded one another.

It remains possible that a thin buried soil did exist at the base of 1120, and was subsequently mixed by earthworm activity with the rampart deposits above; observations at experimental earthworks suggest that even soils and turf buried below a bank will become mixed by earthworm activity (Bell *et al.* 1996, 76). This might also explain the lack of a clear distinction between 1105 and 1120 in section 273, layer 1023. Modification once buried by the rampart had however clearly not obscured the differences between the various layers making up 1105 and 1120, nor details such as the postholes in palisade trench 1106, so the effects of this mixing on the stratigraphic relationships are believed to have been limited.

One further possibility that should be mentioned – if only to dismiss it – is that the gravel mixed into the darker brown soils 1120 derived not from the V-profiled ditch but from the later U-profiled ditch. However, where layer 992 was exposed adjacent to the rampart in the top of the V-profiled ditch, it was partly overlain by the standstill layer (1102) underlying the upcast rampart material from the U-profiled ditch (see Chapter 5 below), and beyond this the two deposits were clearly distinguishable from one another, not continuations of the same material.

To the east of the V-profiled ditch the soils overlying the gravel, an orangey layer overlain by a browner soil, were similar to 1105 and 1120 to the west; layer 928, which lay directly upon the natural gravel (127), corresponded with layer 891 (and hence formed part of group 1105), while layer 927 was similar to layer 890 on the west (and hence formed part of group 1120). The stratigraphic relationships between the darker brown deposits (1120), the V-profiled ditch (574) and the standstill layer (1102: 462 in section 273; see Fig. 4.3) are consistent with the darker brown deposits being a buried topsoil or upcast material, although the low level of gravel suggests that little upcast spoil may have been thrown out from the ditch on this side. Ditch 574 again appears to have been cut through these layers, but such an effect could also have been produced by erosion of the ditch edge back into the edge of the upcast spoil. The standstill layer which formed in the top of the V-profiled ditch (574) also extended beyond the ditch to the east over the darker brown deposits (1120).

No artefacts were found in these layers. Their date is, however, fixed by their relationship with the V-profiled ditch (574). This suggests that the rampart was constructed, and the soils below buried, in the later part of the late Bronze Age, probably between *c* 980-800 BC.

The extent and character of the rampart 1120

The rampart material extended west of the V-profiled ditch (574) for 6.7 m, to the edge of the more gravelly upper dark layer (893) and for 7.5 m to the edge of the occupation layer in the interior (1123; see Fig. 4.9, section 229). A symmetrical V-profiled ditch, on average 4.8 m wide and 2.0 m deep, would have provided an area of spoil, in section, of 4.8 m². This figure should be increased to allow for the fact that the sediment would have been less compact once it was dug than it would have been *in situ*. Avery (1993) suggests a ratio of 1:1.5. If the whole width of layer 1120 had been covered by the upcast spoil from the V-profiled ditch, it would have formed a mound just over 2 m high, whose angle of slope would have probably been relatively stable (see Fig. 4.4C).

There was no convincing evidence for a revetment to retain such a rampart. Two postholes (512 and 514) were found at the west edge of the ditch in the central slot cut across it, spaced 2.25 m apart (Fig. 4.7). The southerly posthole 512 was not revealed until the uppermost ditch fill had been removed, and the plan indicates that this posthole also underlay the standstill layer, so it was probably Bronze Age in date. Posthole 514 cut the lower fills of the V-profiled ditch, but lay just beyond the surviving edge of the standstill layer, so its date relative to this is uncertain. One further posthole was found 4.5 m south of 512 close to the edge of the V-profiled ditch, and another posthole (403) was excavated on the west edge of the northern cut across the V-profiled ditch, but its relationship to the standstill layer was not recorded. Although it is possible that a line of postholes lay below the edge of the standstill layer along the edge of the ditch, no such postholes were found in the southern slot across the ditch, Additionally, postholes 512 and 514 lay at the edge where the ditch was widest, and it seems unlikely that more postholes would not have been visible had such a line existed.

The extent of the standstill layer, however, may indicate that the rampart did not come right to the edge of the ditch. In oblique section 229 (Fig. 4.9) the standstill layer (1102) extended 1.8 m beyond the edge of the ditch, ending at a slight rise in the buried soil (890), and this might reflect the original position of the front of the rampart. The fact that the standstill layer ran almost horizontally beyond the edge of the ditch argues against the former presence of a rampart that had subsequently eroded; either the rampart had never extended over this area, or it had been deliberately and thoroughly removed. Unless the rampart was removed at the front before the stabilisation layer began to form, this would imply a berm between 1.6 m and 2 m wide between the ditch and the rampart (depending upon the allowance for erosion of the original upper edge of the ditch). No postholes were found that could be interpreted as having revetted the front of such a rampart.

Assuming a berm of 1.8 m, the remaining protected width of soil, and thus the width of the rampart, would have been between 4.9 m and 5.7 m. To accommodate the spoil from the V-profiled ditch an unrevetted rampart 5.7 m wide would have been about 2.5 m tall, or even higher if the width was less. The spread of standstill layer east of the ditch in section 229 suggests that very little bank material was dumped on the outer edge of the ditch. The angle of slope of such a rampart would have been about 45° (Fig. 4.4D), so may not have remained stable without some revetting; there may have been low turf walls at front and rear that would have created a stable rampart,

It is possible that some of the spoil from the V-profiled ditch was not used for a rampart, and was taken elsewhere. Another possibility is that the front of the rampart was deliberately slighted to fill in the ditch, removing a little of layer 890 in the process, and perhaps also accounting for the deposition of layer 516 west of, and sloping down into, the ditch in section 123. This would have enabled the standstill layer that formed subsequently to spread west of the ditch.

The entrance

The V-profiled ditch (574) ended near the northern edge of the main excavation in an area that had not only suffered considerable modern disturbance but which was also the location of the later hillfort entrance. A number of features found immediately to the north are interpreted, largely on the basis of extensive evidence for burning, as belonging to an entrance structure associated with the early-middle Iron Age defences, which were themselves burnt (see Chapter 5). Scant traces of a small number of pits and postholes were found that were cut by these early-middle Iron Age features, but none contained any finds. It is, nonetheless, possible that they were related to a late Bronze Age entrance structure associated with the V-profiled ditch.

Two of these features (1024 and 799) may have been pits or large postholes but had been almost entirely cut away by later features (see Figs 4.7 and 5.7). One of them (1024) was cut by an early Iron Age pit (1016) and lay around 5.5 m to the east of the V-profiled ditch (574).

Pit (1016) contained 40 sherds of late Bronze Age pottery and a little sand-tempered pottery presumed to be Iron Age, and *Alnus/Corylus* charcoal from the feature gave a radiocarbon date with a range of 790-520 cal BC (OxA-14296; 2508±27 BP). It is therefore plausible that feature (1024) belongs in the late Bronze Age, indeed the residual pottery of this date in pit 1016 may have been derived from it. However, it is not clear what function this feature would have performed in relation to an entrance so far outside the line of the defences, lying as it did east even of posthole row 1104. The other pit or large posthole (799) was cut by early-middle Iron Age gully 647 and lay just beyond the northern end of the V-profiled ditch (574). Both features were filled with sandy deposits in which the only trace of burning was charcoal staining in the upper fill of 799. This staining may however have infiltrated from gully (647) above, which contained substantial quantities of charcoal. A posthole (738) which was filled with a sandy deposit which contained only a few flecks of charcoal was also found near to the early-middle Iron Age gully (647) at the end of the V-profiled ditch. This posthole was cut by another (655) which contained burnt gravel and charcoal.

Although much disturbed by modern trenches, the truncated end of the V-profiled ditch was found, and projecting this upwards suggests that the line of the standstill layer, which survived around part of the end of the ditch, gives a reasonable indication of the end of the ditch. No relationships survived between the ditch fills and the pits and postholes just described, but if these features did belong to the late Bronze Age hillfort, the entrance structure would have stood right against the ditch end.

Posthole row 1104

One or more rows of postholes (1104) ran between the V- and U-profiled ditches (Fig. 4.10; Plate 4.5). The distribution of the postholes in this area was much less regular than in the other posthole rows. In places, particularly towards the north end, it appeared possible that it consisted of two rows, but these could not be traced clearly over any great distance. At the north end there was also a broken length of slot (698) running immediately west of three of the postholes over a distance of 3.2 m. This slot, which had a flat base, only survived at most 0.04 m deep, and the breaks were probably due to truncation. Its fill was similar to that of the adjacent postholes, but also contained a little charcoal. The slot, which was aligned just west of south-north, was in line with the V-profiled ditch adjacent, but not with the U-profiled ditch, and was believed to cut the edge of posthole 696 partway along.

Near the south-western corner of the excavation, two of the postholes (1110 and 898 – see Fig. 4.11) were cut into the darker brown soils (group 1120, here recorded as 920) and were covered by deposits forming the standstill layer (1102). Elsewhere, the postholes of this row were cut into the natural gravel (127) and were covered by the cultivation soil that covered much of the site. A number of postholes near the southern end of the excavation were overlain by the fills of the western edge of the U-profiled ditch. However, since this edge of the ditch probably eroded after the ditch was cut, the stratigraphic relationships in this area only show that the postholes predate the erosion of the ditch.

As the postholes stratigraphically predate the standstill layer (1102) in the upper part of the V-profiled ditch (574), the radiocarbon date from the latter gives a *terminus ante quem* of c 870-540 BC for the postholes (Table 2.1). Since they also cut dark brown deposits (1120) believed to be equivalent to those sealing posthole row (1108) on the other side of the V-profiled ditch, a date in the late Bronze Age is apparently indicated. This relationship probably also indicates that row 1104 was contemporary with the V-profiled ditch, although due to the low proportion of gravels in the dark brown soils here it is unclear whether it was the buried topsoil or the upcast soil from the ditch that these postholes cut.

Fig. 4.10 (facing page) Detailed plan of posthole row 1104 highlighting those containing charcoal, and selected sections

Chapter 4

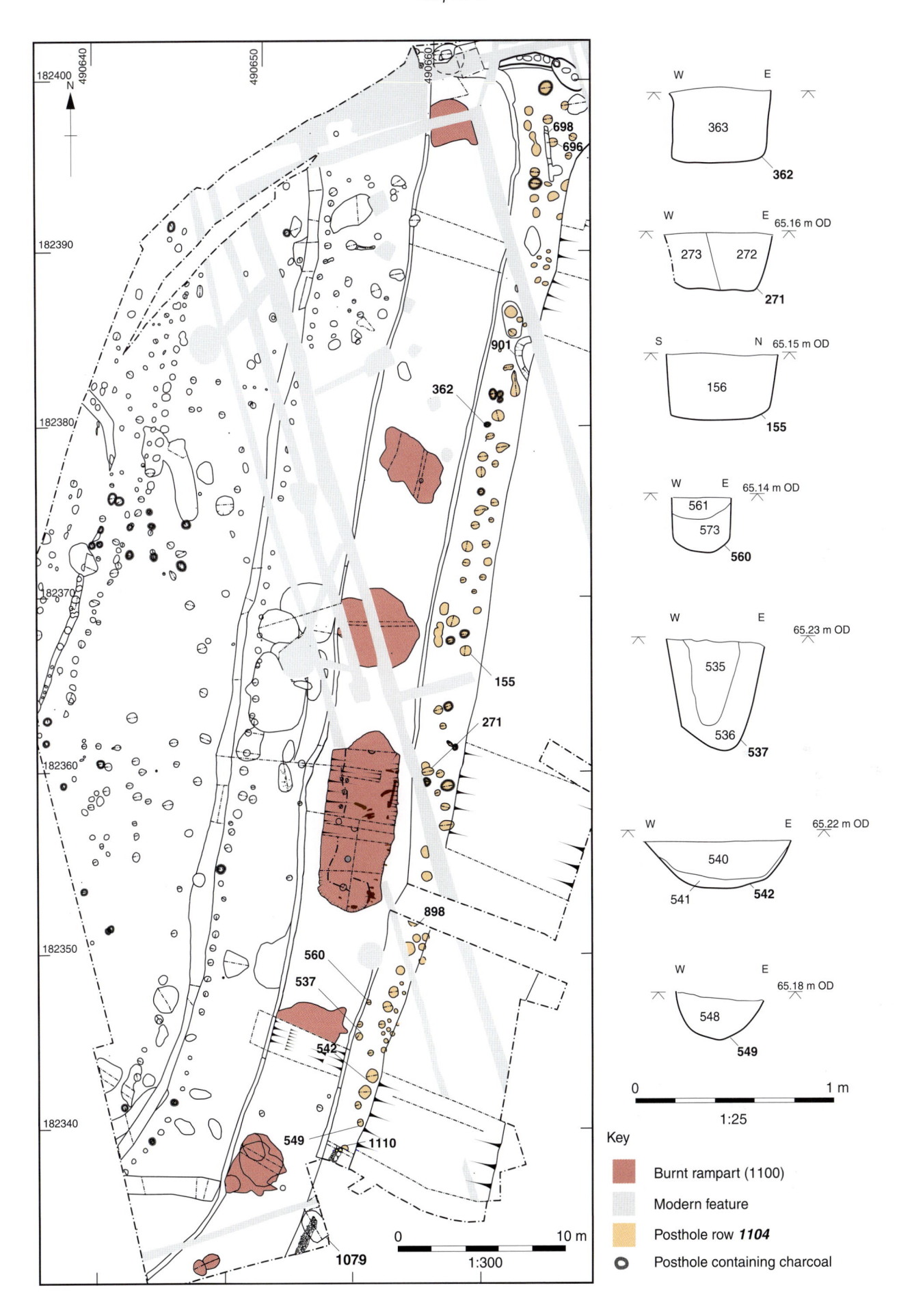

59

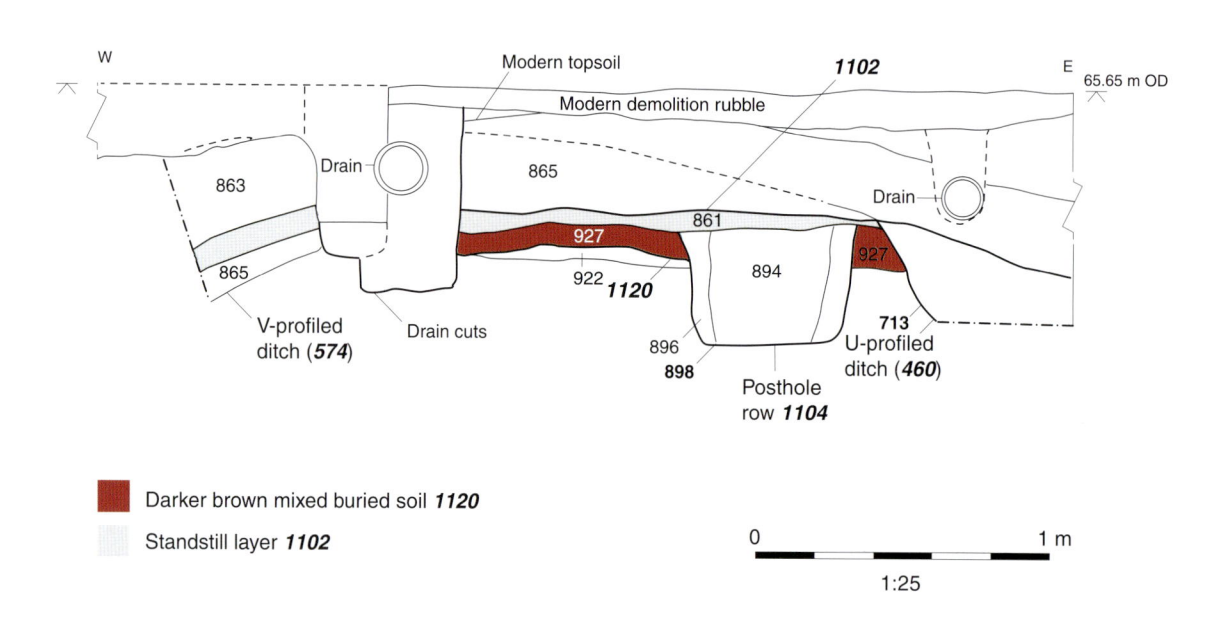

Fig. 4.11   Section 230

Plate 4.5   Posthole row 1104 between the Bronze Age and Iron Age ditches, showing postholes on the very lip of the U-profiled ditch

The postholes of 1104 were, on average, larger than those in the other posthole rows: 0.48 m wide and 0.29 m deep (Table 4.1). There was, however, considerable variation, this row containing some of the largest and some of the smallest postholes in any of the post rows (maximum width 0.83 m; minimum width 0.16 m), and differences in size did not help in defining coherent groups within the postholes, except that at the southern end a row of small postholes lay east of a line of larger postholes. Here (and to a smaller extent at the very north end of the row) the partial truncation of some of the postholes by the U-profiled ditch may have obscured the overall distribution of postholes. Otherwise postholes of different sizes were distributed without any obvious pattern.

Most of the postholes in the row were filled with grey brown sandy fills, and apart from the presence of charcoal (see below) no clear distinctions could be made on the basis of the slight differences in the fills. Post-pipes were recognised in only four, widely scattered postholes (898, 537, 271 and 675).

Due to their wide variety it is possible that the postholes in this 'group' comprise elements from more than one phase. There are a few intercutting postholes (271 and one unexcavated group of three), showing show that they cannot all have been contemporary, though these may represent replacements within a single phase of use. The position of the row might suggest that some parts of it might have been related to the early-middle Iron Age rampart associated with the U-profiled ditch (460). However, although a few contained flecks of charcoal, the fills of the postholes varied very little. To test the possibility that some belonged with the succeeding Iron Age rampart the correspondence of postholes containing charcoal with the burnt areas of the rampart associated with the U-profiled ditch

Table 4.6: Summary of finds in posthole row 1104

Posthole	Context	Pottery (weight g)	Flake	Chips and waste flakes	Blade, bladelet and blade-like flake	Microlith	Charred plant remains and charcoal	Animal bone
1104								
151	152		2	1	1			
153	154		3	1				
155	156		5					
157	158		2					
159	160		1					
161	162				1			
258	259		1					
263	264		3					
267	268		2		1			
269	270		2	1				
271	273		3		3			
309	277		1					
311	312		1	1				
315	316		1					
326	327			2				
350	351		2					
362	363		2			1		
371	372		2					
534	532			1				
534	533			1				
537	535	2					Cereal - 1 Hazelnut shell - 13 Clover - 1	
542	540		3				Cereal - 1 Hazelnut shell - 1	Cattle 1/5
549	548		1					
560	561						Cereal - 1 Weed indet. - 1	
671	672		3					
673	674		1					

(460) was plotted (Fig. 4.10), but the quantities of charcoal were very small, and the association is unconvincing.

Further evidence for more than one phase of activity in this area is curving gully 901, a feature surviving only 2.4 m long on the edge of the U-profiled ditch, overlain by its upper fills (Fig. 4.10). This shallow gully did not contain any finds, but had a rounded even profile 0.35 m wide and up to 0.19 m deep; it is unlikely to have been dug after the U-profiled ditch, and so was presumably Bronze Age or earlier. On the basis of the curvature, which was not even, any enclosure formed by it would have been small; it most resembles the gully found in WA Trench 6 (Fig. 2.2).

Dating evidence and other finds associated with posthole row 1104

Aside from flint flakes, very few finds were associated with posthole row 1104 (Table 4.6). The struck flint included a few chips, residual blades and a microlith. A single small sherd of pottery (2 g) in a flint-tempered fabric consistent with a late Bronze Age date came from posthole 537; the only other finds were a single fragment of cattle bone and charred plant remains. A sample of *Maloideae* charcoal from posthole 548 gave an early-middle Saxon date: cal AD 690-890 (OxA-14293: 1224±24 BP). It is possible that this posthole may have belonged to a much later phase than those overlain by the standstill layer, although there is no corroborative artefactual evidence for Saxon postholes. Alternatively, the charcoal may be intrusive. A further radiocarbon date, obtained from a charred hazelnut shell in posthole 537, gave an early Mesolithic date (8560-8290 cal BC; SUERC-4969: 9220±40 BP), and the shell is clearly residual.

The Wessex Archaeology evaluation also revealed postholes between two parallel ditches in Trench 3 (see Fig. 1.4). Although neither the ditches nor the postholes were dated, the width and relative positions of the ditches makes it very likely that these represent continuations of the V-profiled and the U-profiled ditch north of the entrance found at the north edge of the excavations. The seven identified postholes between the ditches had similar fills to those in posthole row 1104, and did not form clear lines; instead, like 1104, they were scattered across the full width of the area between the ditches. The general similarity to posthole row 1104 is therefore strong, and they may well belong to the same phase or phases of defence.

One of the seven postholes was cut by the upper edge of ditch 303, equivalent to late Bronze Age ditch 574. Neither the thick gravel upcast nor the standstill layer was evident from the soil descriptions, indicating that the ditch probably had a different pattern of infilling, but the presence of both ditches so close together strongly suggests that the rampart from the U-profiled ditch would have overlain the V-profiled ditch, so that the relationship between the V-profiled ditch and posthole row 1104 must have been established before the ditch was buried. There are two possibilities: either the posthole row had gone out of use by the time the V-profiled ditch was dug, or the row may have been contemporary with the ditch, but was dismantled while the ditch was still

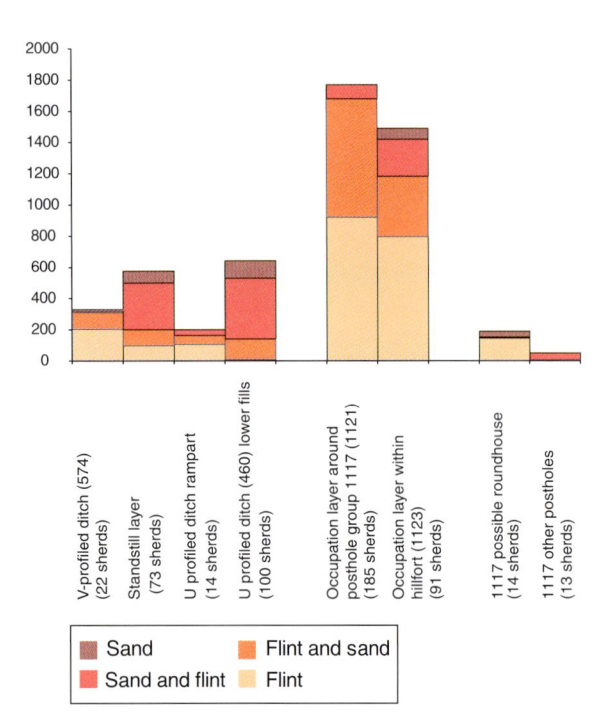

Fig. 4.12 Summary of quantities of pottery (weight, g) by fabric in major features

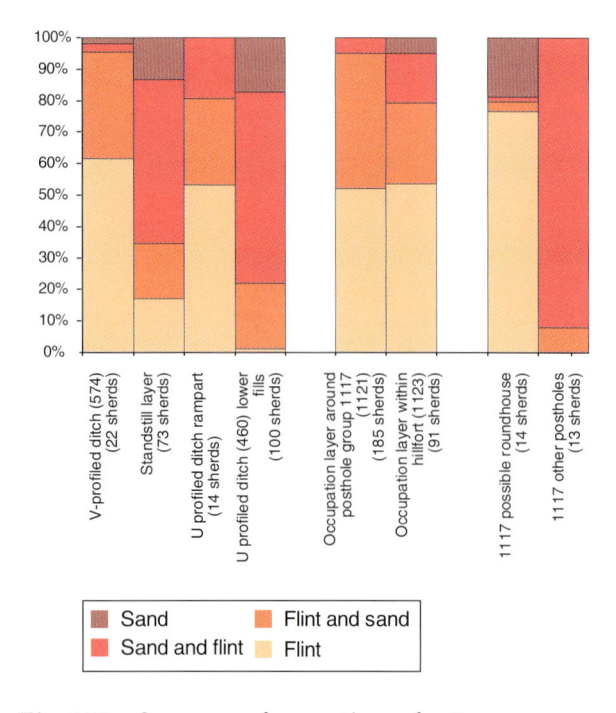

Fig. 4.13 Summary of proportions of pottery (quantified by weight) by fabric groups in major features

open, and the ditch subsequently eroded back to cut the posthole fill. In either case, one phase of posthole row 1104 would appear to have gone out of use before the ditch had reached the standstill phase.

Activity within the hillfort

Only a small area of the hillfort interior was excavated, and with the exception of the tree-throw holes and hollows discussed above (see Chapter 3), all of the features within the hillfort were postholes. The pottery, charcoal and other finds from the postholes cannot be shown to be integral to their function, and it is therefore often impossible to determine whether the finds were residual, intrusive or contemporary with the features. On the basis of the quantities of finds and radiocarbon dates, it seems that activity was most intensive in the late Bronze Age (Figs 4.12-13), but there was evidently activity in this area from the Mesolithic to the middle Iron Age.

This section describes features and finds that may date from the late Bronze Age and the late Bronze Age-early Iron Age, the most significant of which consist of two clusters of postholes (1117 and 1134), some of which might have been related to roundhouses or four-post structures.

Posthole group and possible roundhouse 1117, four-post structures FP1-3 and the occupation layer (1121 and 1123)

Near the south-western edge of the excavation was a scatter of postholes (1117) among which a semicircle of postholes that might have formed part of a roundhouse can be postulated (Fig. 4.14). Although it is not entirely clear which postholes should be assigned to the structure, it seems that around nine postholes might have belonged to it, spaced at intervals of 0.66-1.80 m (mean = 1.2 m). The postholes in this group were, on average, 0.35 m wide and 0.21 m deep, similar in size to those forming the posthole rows (Table 4.1). They did not differ much in size from the other postholes in this area (on average 0.40 m wide and 0.21 m deep), although there was more variation in the size of the other postholes.

This possible posthole circle had a diameter of only 5 m, and it could not be traced near the western edge of the excavation, where preservation was best, so whether this was really a roundhouse is unclear. Incomplete circles or oval structures were however recovered at Rams Hill (Bradley and Ellison 1975, figs 2.20-2.25), and semicircular post-built structures are also known in the Iron Age of the Thames Valley (Lambrick with Robinson 2009).

Within this same area several four-post structures can also be postulated, and are marked by dashed outlines as FP1, FP2 and FP3 (Fig. 4.14). FP1 lies within the area enclosed by the arc of postholes 1117, and is a rectangle 1.9 m east-west by 1.4 m north-south, comprising postholes 145, 147, 179, and 187. These four postholes ranged in depth from 0.16 m to 0.25 m, the western pair being larger but shallower than their eastern counterparts. FP2 is a square of side 2.1 m, and comprises postholes 206, 193, 181 and 1136 (unexcavated). The three excavated postholes were all of similar size; two were 0.26 m deep, and 193 was 0.33 m deep.

The third possible four-post structure, FP3, comprises postholes 149, 196, 179/181 and 206, and is slightly trapezoidal, measuring 2.8 m by 3.2 m – 3.6 m across. The two south-western postholes were both smaller and deeper (0.26 m) than the north-eastern pair (0.21m -0.23 m deep).

Dating evidence and other finds from posthole group 1117

The date of these possible structures, and of the other postholes in this area, is uncertain. They need not all have belonged to the same phase. Radiocarbon dates of 930-790 cal. BC and 910-800 cal. BC (SUERC 4968: 2700±40 BP and OxA-14359: 2687±27 BP) were obtained on charred spelt from posthole 206 for FP2/FP3, but this posthole was not part of the posthole circle.

The pottery from the postholes belonging to the possible posthole circle includes flint-, flint and sand-, sand and flint- and sand-tempered sherds; the other postholes in this area contained flint and sand- and sand and flint-tempered sherds, as well as clearly residual early Bronze Age sherds (see Table 7.12) The two sherds in sand-tempered fabrics from posthole 208 raise the possibility that the roundhouse dates to the middle Iron Age, rather than to the late Bronze Age indicated by the radiocarbon dates. However, sand-tempered pottery is known in the late Bronze Age, albeit forming a very small element in the assemblages in which it occurs.

The other finds (see Table 4.7) included a few fragments of animal bone, some charred cereal grains, a little chaff and some weed seeds, as well as a small quantity of probably at least partially residual flint, most of which consisted of flakes.

Finds associated with occupation layer within the hillfort and around posthole group 1117, including the decorated late Bronze Age bracelet

Identified in the 2000 watching brief excavation behind the preserved soil under the rampart of the V-profiled ditch was a band of subsoil (983=1121), darker than found elsewhere, and containing greater quantities of artefacts and charcoal (Table 4.8). The finds in this area included 1768 g of pot with sherds from all of the main late Bronze Age fabric groups but not the sand-tempered (and possibly middle Iron Age) wares, suggesting that activity was most intense in this area in the late Bronze Age. The density of finds in this area was greater than that in the occupation layer elsewhere (1123) which contained 1403 g of pot from a much wider area, and included not only sherds in all of the main late Bronze Age fabrics but also in Iron Age fabrics (Table

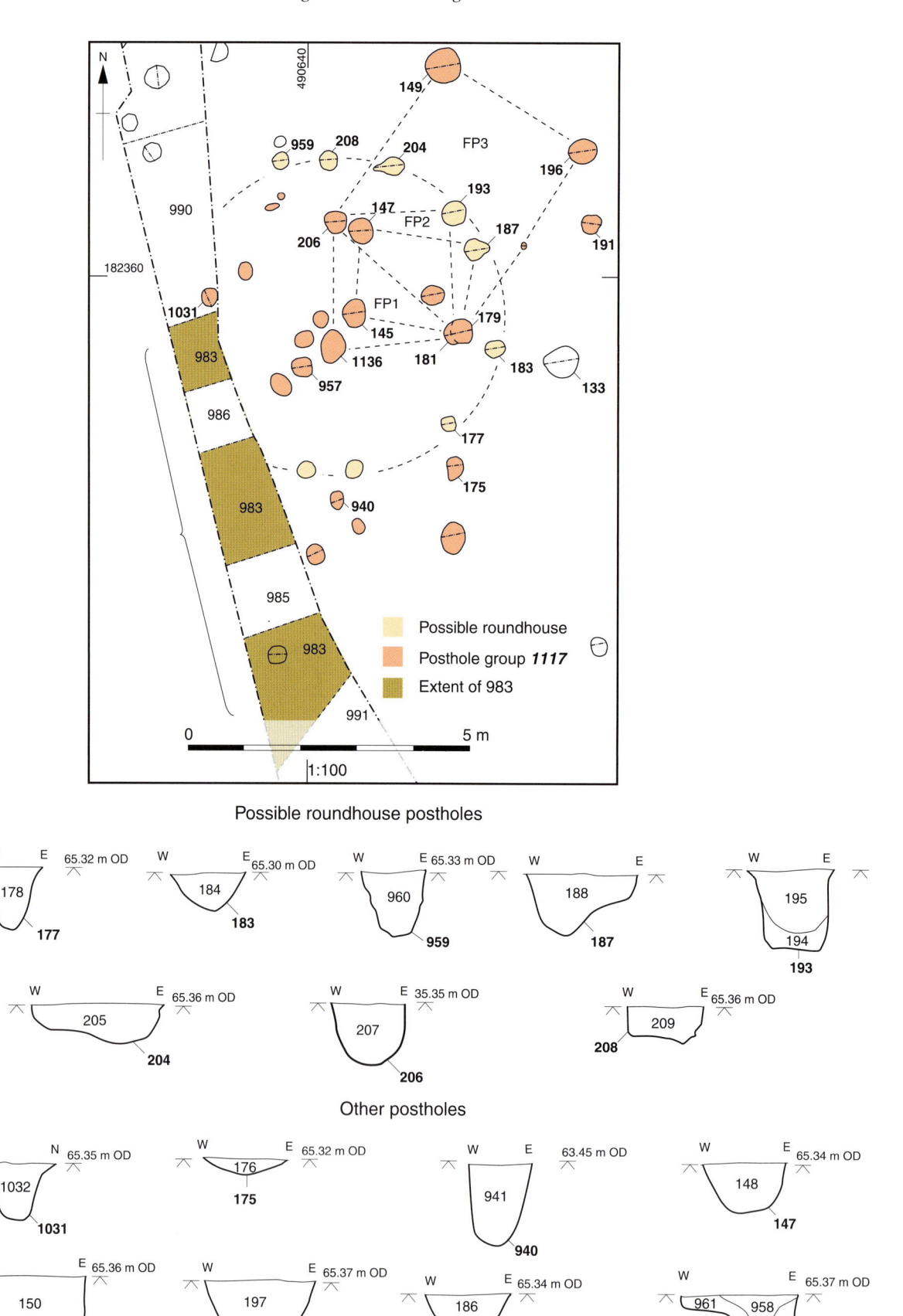

Fig. 4.14 Posthole group 1117, possible roundhouse and four-post structures FP 1-3: plan and sections

Table 4.7: Summary of finds in posthole group and roundhouse 1117

Pit	Layer	Pottery	Flake	Chips and waste flakes	Blade, bladelet and blade-like flake	Othe worked flint	Burnt unworked flint	Charred plant remains	Animal bone	Other finds
Roundhouse										
177	178		1							
206	207		2					Wheat grain 32 Barley grain 1 Cereal grain 136 Wheat glume 46 Weeds 16	Unid. 1/7	
208	209	5/25							Sheep/goat 2/2	Heat-fractured pebble
940	941	7/35		1					Unid. 3/9	
959	960	1/3	1						Unid. 1/2	
187	188		1							
193	195		5	1						
204	205	1/2	1		1					
Other postholes										
147	148	1/1	1				1	Wheat grain + Barley grain + Cereal indet. + Knotgrass +	Unid. 1/1	
149	150	10/45	2					Barley + Cereal indet. +		Hammmerstone 1
173	174		2		2					
181	182								Large mammal 1/3	
196	197		1	2				Hazel nut shell +		
185	186	1/8	2							
957	958	1/4	2							

4.8). It should be noted, however, that relatively intense activity in the late Bronze Age compared to other periods would increase the chances of material of that date being redeposited in later features. While the presence of late Bronze Age pottery in features may, therefore, provide a *terminus post quem*, it provides less certain evidence against the possibility that some of the features were later in date.

The occupation layer (1121) around posthole group 1117 also contained a few fragments of cattle bone, a few pieces of amorphous fired clay and fragments of worked stone including a rubber and a possible whetstone.

The most striking find, however, was part of a decorated late Bronze Age bronze bracelet (SF1173 – see Plate 7.2). The precise context of the bracelet is uncertain: it might have come either from occupation layer (1121) or the modern subsoil above (1122). On the basis of its composition (see Chapter 7, report by P Northover), it has been suggested that this bracelet belongs to the early part of the Ewart Park phase or perhaps to the Wilburton phase. The former suggestion corresponds most closely to the radiocarbon dates obtained from posthole (206) in posthole group 1117. The pottery, however, covers all of the late Bronze Age and would be equally consistent with a Wilburton date. The bracelet, then, could well have been deposited at the same time as most of the other material in this area.

Elsewhere within the hillfort the occupation layer (1123) also contained worked flint, fragments of fired clay from a hearth or oven, a piece of fired clay from a cylindrical loomweight, and a few fragments of cattle bone (Table 4.8).

Relationship of the occupation deposit to the posthole circle 1117

The layer of darker occupation soil did not survive within the main excavation area. It ran beyond the postholes on the southern edge of 1117 up to the edge of the preserved soil that probably indicated the limits of the former Bronze Age rampart, ending partway across the circle (see Fig. 4.14). No postholes were visible cutting through this deposit. Although only part of this layer was excavated, 1 m squares were excavated where the continuation of the posthole row was projected,

Table 4.8: Summary of finds in the occupation layers (1121 and 1123) within the hillfort

Pit	Layer	Pottery (weight g)	Flake	Chips and waste flakes	Blade, bladelet and blade-like flake	Cores	Retouched pieces	Other worked flint	Fired clay (no. frags/weight (g))	Worked stone	Animal bone	Other finds
Occupation layer near posthole group 1117												
1121/1122	964/962											Decorated bronze bracelet
1121	962	125	1									
1121	983	672							Amorphous 7/14	Worked frag/whetstone ? sandstone		
1121	985	417							Amorphous 9/15	Hammerstone? sarsen	Cattle 2/24	
1121	986	554								Rubber, pennant sandstone		
Occupation layer within the hillfort												
1123	104	294	114	21	25	6	3	6	Hearth/oven 1/88			
1123	990	310							Hearth/oven 3/158		Cattle 3/15	
1123	991	692							Cylindrical loomweight 1/37			
1123	217	14										
1123	219	4										
1123	888	89										

but no postholes were found on this line below the occupation layer, nor within the general occupation layer to the north (990).

Since the darker occupation deposit was not confined within the line of the posthole row, it may not have been associated. While the occupation deposit was rich in charcoal, the postholes in this area did not contain much charcoal, although most were filled with dark black-brown sandy silts. There were no marked differences between the fills of the postholes associated with the possible roundhouse and others in this area. The darker colour of the subsoil and the presence of more finds than elsewhere is perhaps better explained as the product of a midden having lain there than as resulting from domestic occupation associated directly with the possible structure. The two sand-tempered, and possibly middle Iron Age, sherds from posthole 208 in the posthole circle itself, although small, may provide the best *terminus post quem* for this structure.

Posthole group and possible roundhouse 1134, and possible four-post structures FP4-7

Further north, a second, looser group of postholes (1134) was found, within which the plan of a second possible roundhouse, with a possible entrance porch facing north, could be made out (Figs 4.1, and 4.15). It is again not entirely clear which postholes should

Table 4.9: Dimensions of four-post structures and their postholes

Structure No.	Length	Width	Posthole	Diameter (m)	Depth (m)
FP1	1.9 m	1.4 m			
			147	0.37 x 0.39	0.20
			187	0.45 x 0.36	0.25
			181	0.23 x 0.28	0.26
			145	0.36 x 0.44	0.16
FP2	2.1 m	2.1 m			
			206	0.31 x 0.33	0.26
			193	0.35 x 0.40	0.33
			179	0.28 x 0.37	0.24
			1136	0.40 x 0.52	
FP3	3.2 - 3.6 m	2.8 m			
			149	0.53	0.21
			196	0.50 x 0.48	0.24
			179	0.28 x 0.37	0.24
			206	0.31 x 0.33	0.26
FP4	1.6 - 1.8 m	1.5 - 1.7 m			
			787	0.24	0.16
			792	0.25	0.20
			789	0.38	0.28
			784	0.34	0.36
FP5	1.5 - 2.0 m	1.2 or 1.7 m			
			236	0.24	0.30
			234	0.28	0.16
			344	0.24	0.14
			226	0.31	0.18
			228	0.22	0.16
			230	0.28	0.26
FP6	1.6 - 1.7 m	1.3 - 1.5 m			
			336	0.34	0.18
			236	0.24	0.30
			230	0.28	0.26
			245	0.3	0.23
FP7	1.7 - 1.8 m	1.6 - 1.7 m			
			279	0.36	0.20
			336	0.34	0.18
			245	0.3	0.23
			241	0.23 x 0.15	0.27
FP5-6	3.0 - 3.2 m	1.7 m			
FP6-7	3.0 - 3.2 m	1.7 m			
FP5-7	4.8 - 5.0 m	1.7 m			

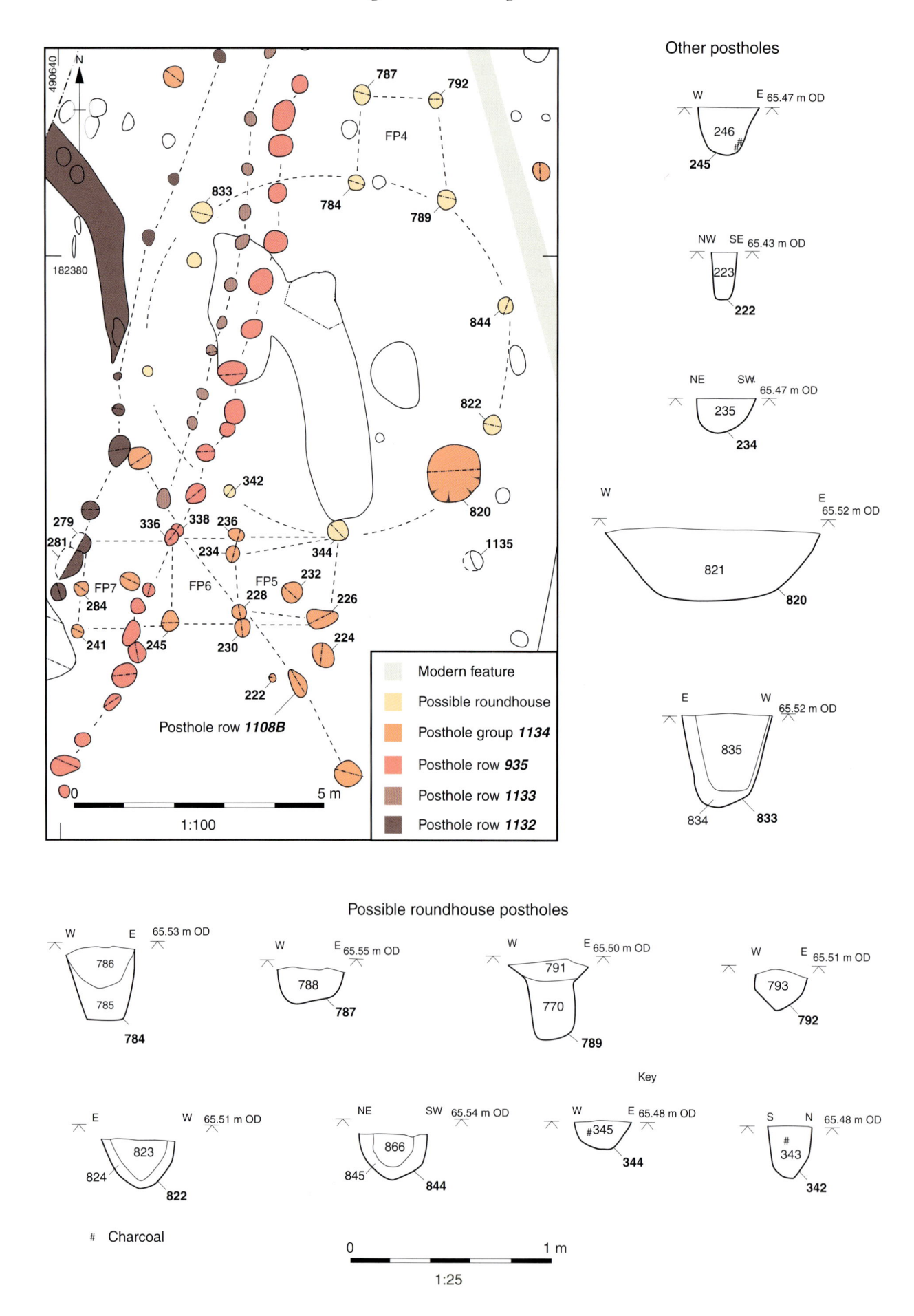

From Bronze Age enclosure to Anglo-Saxon settlement

be assigned to the structure, but around eight or nine postholes could be assigned to the posthole, set at rather larger intervals of 1.79 m – 3.64 m (mean = 2.7 m) than were the postholes associated with the other possible roundhouse (1117).

The postholes associated with both of the possible roundhouses were similar in size, those from group 1134 measuring 0.35 m wide and 0.27 m deep on average (Table 4.1). Again, however, they did not differ much from the other postholes in this area (on average 0.38 m wide and 0.23 m deep), although there was more variation in the size of the other postholes. The posthole circle was not symmetrical, and the possible porch on the north was skewed to the line of the building, so the coherence of this structure is not entirely convincing. If genuine, it would have had a diameter of only *c* 6 m.

With so many postholes in this area, it is all too easy to find possible structures, but some other possibilities deserve mention. Postholes 844, 822 and 1135 may well have belonged to posthole row 1108 (as suggested above), while the roundhouse porch may instead have been a four-post structure (labelled FP4 on Fig. 4.15), with other possible four-post or larger structures (labelled FP5, FP6 and FP7) to the south (see Table 4.9 for dimensions). Both FP4 and FP5 are of very similar size, but both are trapezoidal rather than square. In addition, in FP4 postholes 784 and 789 are both larger and deeper than 787 and 792 (see Fig. 4.15), and in FP5 postholes 344 and 226 are larger than the others, although if postholes 234 and 228 were those related to FP5, then all the postholes are of similar depth (0.14 m – 0.18 m). Postholes 230 and 236 could perhaps have resulted from a rebuild or shoring up of one side of FP5 using deeper postholes, or could belong to FP6, while FP7 is almost square. All of the postholes of FP6 share a charcoal-rich fill.

It is alternatively possible that structures FP5, FP 6 and possibly FP7 belong to a single, six- or eight-post structure (Fig. 4.15), to which posthole 284 may also have belonged (see Table 4.9 for dimensions). Postholes 279 and 336 both cut the adjacent postholes, and this putative structure would therefore probably have postdated the posthole rows with which it intersected.

The unexcavated postholes along the sides of FP4, one between 784 and 787, the other between 784 and 789, are matched in early Iron Age four-post structures on several sites, including Little Wittenham, Oxfordshire (Allen and Lamdin-Whymark 2005, fig. 29; Allen *et al.* 2006, fig. 8.7).

Finds associated with posthole group and possible roundhouse 1134

Apart from charcoal and burnt unworked flint, the postholes in group 1134 contained only a few flint

Table 4.10: Summary of finds from posthole group and possible roundhouse 1134

Pit	Layer	Flake	Chips and waste flakes	Blades	Burnt unworked flint	Charred plant remains	Animal bone	Other finds
Roundhouse								
784	786	1						
787	788	1	2					
789	790					Cereal indet. +		
Other postholes								
220	221				3			
222	223							Post-med wall plaster 1/2
228	229				1			
230	231	1			1			
232	233	1			3			
234	235						Large mammal 1/10 g	
234	235	1						
236	237	1			2			
245	246					Wheat +		
						Cereal indet. +		
						Dogwood +		
286	287	2		1	1			

Fig. 4.15 (facing page) Posthole group 1134, possible roundhouse and four-post structures FP4-7: plan and sections

flakes (Table 4.10) and a fragment of bone from a large mammal. However, a few charred cereal grains were present in posthole (789) belonging to the possible roundhouse, and charred Dogwood seeds and grain identified as wheat in posthole 245, the latter producing a radiocarbon date of OxA-14292, 2736±26: 970-810 cal BC. The posthole did not, however, lie upon the posthole circle of the putative roundhouse, although it was part of possible rectangular structures (FP6 and FP7), and was close to posthole row 935, with whose radiocarbon date the range from posthole 245 overlaps. A fragment of post-medieval plaster was found in one of the smallest postholes in this area (222), and this posthole may have been of recent date.

The date of the posthole circle remains very uncertain; on spatial grounds it was clearly not contemporary with posthole rows 935 and 1133, but could have been contemporary with either part of posthole row 1132, or with posthole row 1108A. The date of the possible four-post structures relative to the posthole rows is also uncertain, although charcoal was found within a group of postholes just south of the possible roundhouse that included three of the postholes belonging to FP5 (Fig. 4.10). This distribution of charcoal corresponds roughly to a minor concentration of burnt unworked flint (see Fig. 3.3), suggesting that the two were related. The postholes containing this concentration of charcoal and burnt unworked flint included examples from posthole row 1132 and 935 and postholes to the south-east, as well as from FP5, and so most probably derives from earlier activity, possibly at the back of the putative roundhouse, incorporated into the later structures.

A final concentration of postholes was identified near the northern edge of the excavation, between the V-profiled ditch (574) and the palisade trench (1106). No structures could be identified in their arrangement, and they yielded very few finds.

Activity outside the hillfort

Pit 3032 and residual late Bronze Age pottery in the outer ditch

Only a small sample of the area outside the V- and U-profiled ditches (574 and 460) was examined, and only in evaluation trenches. A correspondingly small number of features, most of them undated, were identified. In Trench 1 to the north-east of the main excavation, a probable late Bronze Age pit (3032) was identified (see Figs 1.4 and 5.8), subrectangular in plan with vertical sides and a flat base. It measured 1.15 m by 0.80 m wide, was 0.60 m deep and was filled with dark sandy silts, one of which (3036) was particularly rich in charcoal. This layer (3036) also contained late Bronze Age pottery (13 sherds, 50 g), a small assemblage of probably contemporary worked flint consisting of broad, thick flakes and a multiplatform flake core, and a sarsen stone rubber. A further 9 sherds of late Bronze Age pottery (50 g) and some worked flint was found in the upper fills (Table 4.11).

This pit is significant primarily because of its location. It lies outside the late Bronze Age defences, and some 2 m west of the edge of the outer ditch (3050) The small diameter of the pit makes it unlikely that the pit could have been dug through a rampart adjacent to the ditch, supporting the view that the outer ditch and its rampart are later than the late Bronze Age pit.

Small quantities of pottery similar to that from pit (3032) were also found in the outer ditch (3050; see below) nearby. Despite this evidence it seems likely that the outer ditch was related to the middle Iron Age activity on the site, and it is therefore described in the next chapter. Nevertheless, the pottery from the outer ditch and the small pit do provide evidence for late Bronze Age activity outside the late Bronze Age defences. The residual sherds of late Bronze Age pottery incorporated into the rampart of the U-profiled ditch (see Chapter 7

Table 4.11: Summary of finds in pit 3032

Pit	Layer	Pottery (no. of sherds/weight (g))	Flake	Cores	End and side scraper	Charred plant remains	Worked stone
3032	3034	Flint-tempered 7/22 Flint and sand-tempered 2/18	5		1		Stone rubber
3032	3035	Flint-tempered 13/50	2	1		Cereal + Hazel/Alder charcoal +	Cobble/hammerstone quartzite Rubber? sarsen

below) may also have derived from activity outside the V-profiled ditch, rather than from the interior. The nature of this activity is however uncertain.

The standstill layer (1102)

The standstill layer (1102) was a deposit of bleached, greyish clayey silt within the V-profiled ditch (574) that extended for the full length of the ditch within the excavation, and was visible along both edges as a thin line in plan (Fig. 2.1). It was up to 0.26 m deep, and towards the north end of the ditch iron-pan had developed both at the base of the layer and at the top. Within the ditch it was overlain by thick deposits of gravel interpreted as upcast from the adjacent U-profiled ditch. Where not truncated (at the south end of the site) the standstill layer also extended beyond the ditch to the west over the dark brown soil (1120) for c 1.8 m (Fig. 4.9, section 229), showing that there was no associated bank or rampart immediately adjacent to the ditch edge. To the east the standstill layer also overlay similar soil (927) and was overlain by a layer of chalk blocks (925) that probably formed the footing of a rampart associated with the U-profiled ditch (460; Fig. 4.9, section 229), before being cut by the U-profiled ditch, or at least by its eroded edge. The standstill layer was overlain by a thick deposit of gravel all along the length of the V-profiled ditch that is most likely to have been thrown up when digging the U-profiled ditch adjacent, and within this gravel layer were charred timbers interpreted as part of the timber framework of the rampart. This stratigraphic evidence confirms that the standstill layer predated the U-profiled ditch.

The standstill layer represents a phase in which the V-profiled ditch had become stable, and deposit accumulation was slow. The three OSL dates (X068, X072 and X073) obtained from the layer suggested that it formed in the late Bronze Age-early Iron Age (68.2%: 860-580 cal BC; 95.4%: 940-490 cal BC). The layer contained 73 sherds of pottery (see Table 7.8) of late Bronze Age or early Iron Age character, including the stratigraphically earliest sand-tempered sherds from the excavation. The pottery suggests that some activity continued in the area of the hillfort after the V-profiled ditch had largely silted up.

The other finds from the standstill layer (Table 4.5) consisted of a few fragments of animal bone, a single piece of burnt flint, and a small quantity of worked flint, most of which consisted of flakes.

The formation of the standstill layer

Why such a fine-grained clay deposit should have accumulated at all is difficult to explain, as the ditch fills below contained a high proportion of gravel, and should therefore have drained fairly freely. The fact that the standstill layer extended for a considerable distance either side of the ditch as an almost horizontal layer, yet was not thicker in the centre of the ditch, strongly suggests that the deposit formed in a much shallower hollow than appears in the sections, and that the underlying ditch fills were compacted considerably by the weight of the overlying Iron Age rampart. There would therefore have been little scope for water gathering in the ditch top to drain except through the underlying ditch fills. Iron pan was not observed in all the sections cut across this layer, but the formation of iron pan, or other mineralisation of the underlying gravel, would greatly have assisted the development of the deposit, by cementing the underlying gravel and thus preventing drainage. Once the deposit had begun to accumulate, it would have formed a virtually impermeable barrier to the drainage of any water that collected in the hollow in the ditch top, creating localised ponding and encouraging the deposition of more fine-grained clayey silt, and the development of further mineral accumulations such as the iron pan. The accumulation of this layer may have taken a considerable period of time, as both the pottery from it and the OSL dates from the lower and upper parts might suggest.

Chapter 5 – The early-middle Iron Age hillfort

INTRODUCTION

Following the accumulation of the standstill layer, a second, U-profiled ditch (460) was cut, and the spoil thrown out to help form a rampart alongside (Fig. 5.1). The U-profiled ditch ran parallel to the V-profiled ditch, and ended near the northern edge of the excavation, in line with the end of the V-profiled ditch. The evidence of the standstill layer suggests that the line of the V-profiled ditch may still have been evident as a distinct hollow up to 0.5 m deep at this time, and may well have held water when it rained.

No direct stratigraphic relationships existed between the V-profiled ditch (574) and the U-profiled ditch (460). However, in section 230 (see Fig. 4.11) the U-profiled ditch cut through the standstill layer (1102) that lay in the top of, and extended beyond, the V-profiled ditch (574). Furthermore, above the standstill layer the V-profiled ditch (574, see Fig. 4.8) was filled along its length with up to 1 m of redeposited gravel (1100, 1112 and 1113). This huge quantity of gravel most probably came from the excavation of the U-profiled ditch (460) immediately adjacent, and is interpreted as being used to form a rampart.

In addition, layers of burnt gravel similar to those found within the rampart formed some of the early fills down the west side of the U-profiled ditch (see below). It is thus clear that the U-profiled ditch (460) was later than the V-profiled ditch (574).

THE U-PROFILED DITCH (460)

Around 21 m of the 75 m length of the ditch that was exposed was excavated (just under 30%). The excavated sections at the north and south ends were dug by hand and extended by machine under archaeological supervision, but the 7 m length in the centre was dug entirely by hand, as was the ditch terminal.

The early-middle Iron Age ditch (460) was U-shaped in profile, with a flat base and steep, sometimes vertical sides (Figs 5.2-3; Plate 5.1). Near the top the sides splayed outwards. Observations of experimental earthworks (Bell *et al.* 1996) suggest that this is a product of a typical pattern of erosion in which the upper edges of the ditch collapse.

Plate 5.1 The U-profiled ditch (460) from the south

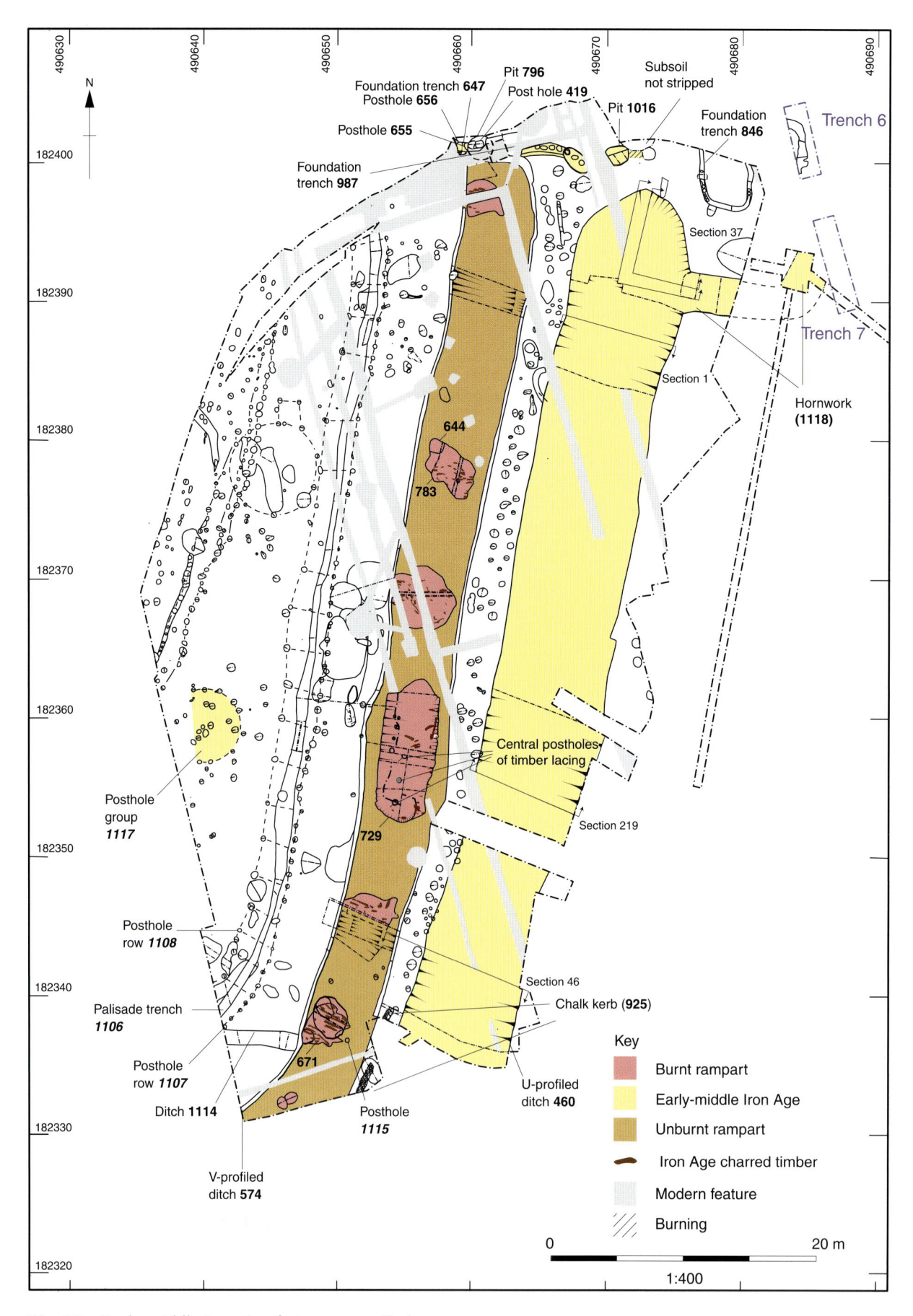

Fig. 5.1   Early-middle Iron Age features: overall plan

Therefore, it is likely that the sides of the ditch were originally straight (steeply sloping towards the north terminal, vertical further south). This implies that the current width of the ditch (6.5 m – 8.1 m) is greater than it would have been originally. Assuming that the sides were straight, the width of the ditch would have been around 4.4 m – 6.0 m. Its depth (ranging from 2.4 m to 2.8 m) is less likely to have been affected, although the (likely) depth of the original topsoil should be taken into account.

Erosion generally occurred around 1.5 m from the ditch bottom on the west (inner) side, and around 1.2 m on the east (outer) side. This may in part be due to the orientation of the ditch, with the sun at its hottest in the afternoon shining on the east side of the ditch, and the prevailing wind from the west meaning that the east side of the ditch was exposed to the worst weather. The survival of a near-vertical edge to such a height on the west was in part due to the burning and partial collapse of the rampart at an early stage in its filling, which covered and protected this side of the ditch from erosion.

The sections (Figs 5.2-3) show that the edges of the ditch bottom filled first, and that erosion from the sides gradually changed the ditch profile to a more rounded, and sometimes almost V-profiled shape. Very few finds, and no material suitable for radiocarbon dating, were found in the primary fills, so the cutting of the ditch is not directly dated. The character of the ditch fills, and their dating, will be considered after the rampart has been described.

THE RAMPART

The rampart associated with the U-profiled ditch was constructed directly upon the standstill layer (1102) within a hollow in the top of the late Bronze Age V-profiled ditch (574). All that survived of the rampart were the truncated deposits which had been protected within this hollow. Because of this truncation, the width of the surviving rampart deposits (5.3 m – 6.3 m) was probably rather less than the original width of the rampart.

In the previous chapter the standstill layer was described as a naturally formed deposit, but the possibility must also be considered that this could have been a layer of imported material laid down to form the base of the rampart. Due to the slope of the layer within the V-profiled ditch this possibility was not entertained on site, and no samples were taken to establish the origins of the deposit through micromorphology. The layer was a clayey silt, not a pure clay, and contained sand appropriate to the Taplow gravels on which the site sits. It is unclear where else such a deposit would have come from; the ling heather within the pollen from this layer rules out a deposit alongside the Thames, and on balance a natural origin for the deposit and the worn sherds found within it is more likely.

Despite the severe truncation, some details of the rampart construction still survived. Three main types of deposits were distinguished within this rampart: unburnt gravel deposits (1112); burnt gravel deposits (1100); and charred timber lacing

Plate 5.2 Charred timbers (783) and fire-reddened gravel from the rampart associated with the U-profiled ditch (460), with dark soil (644) in the background

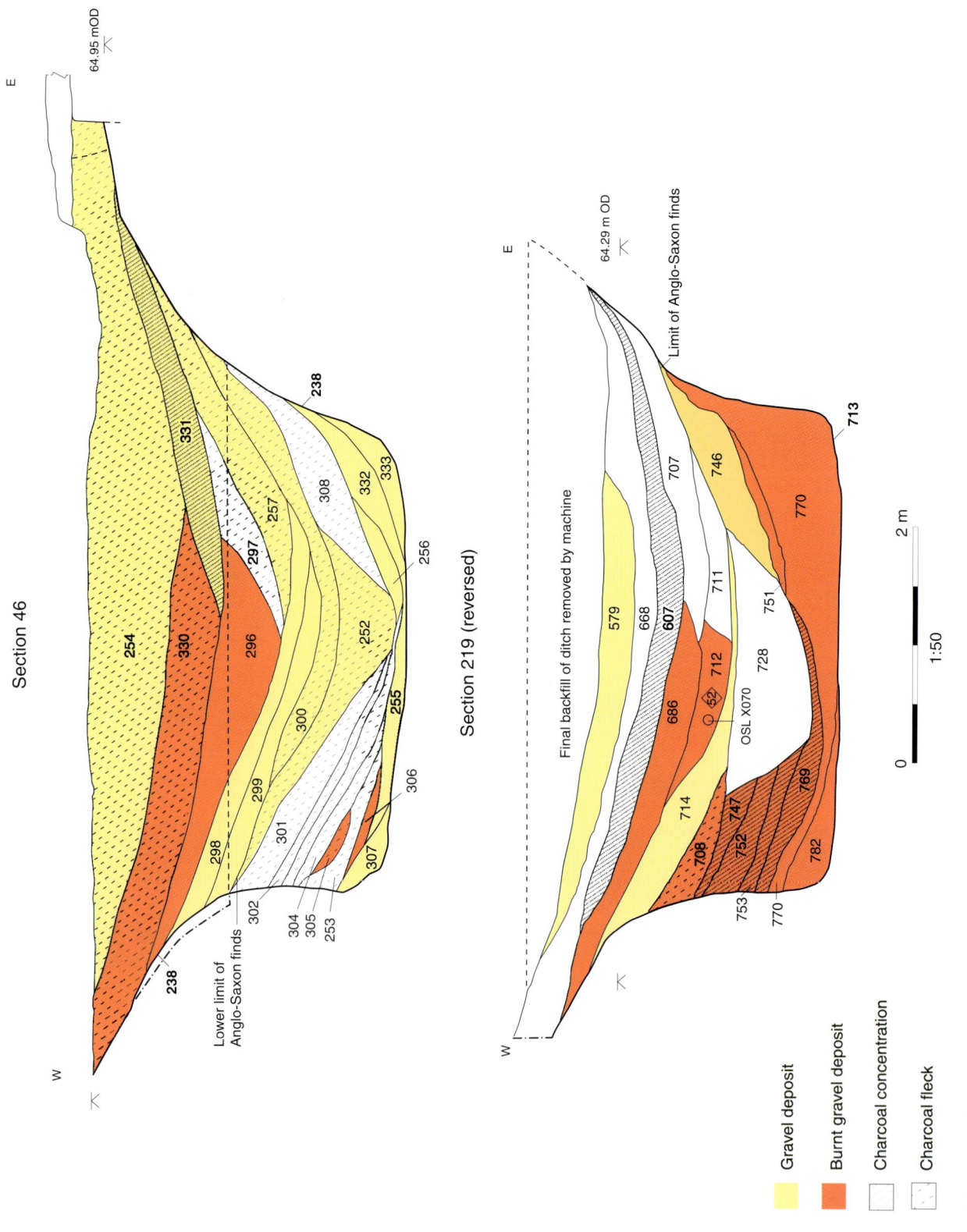

Fig. 5.2 The U-profiled ditch (460): sections 219 and 46

Chapter 5

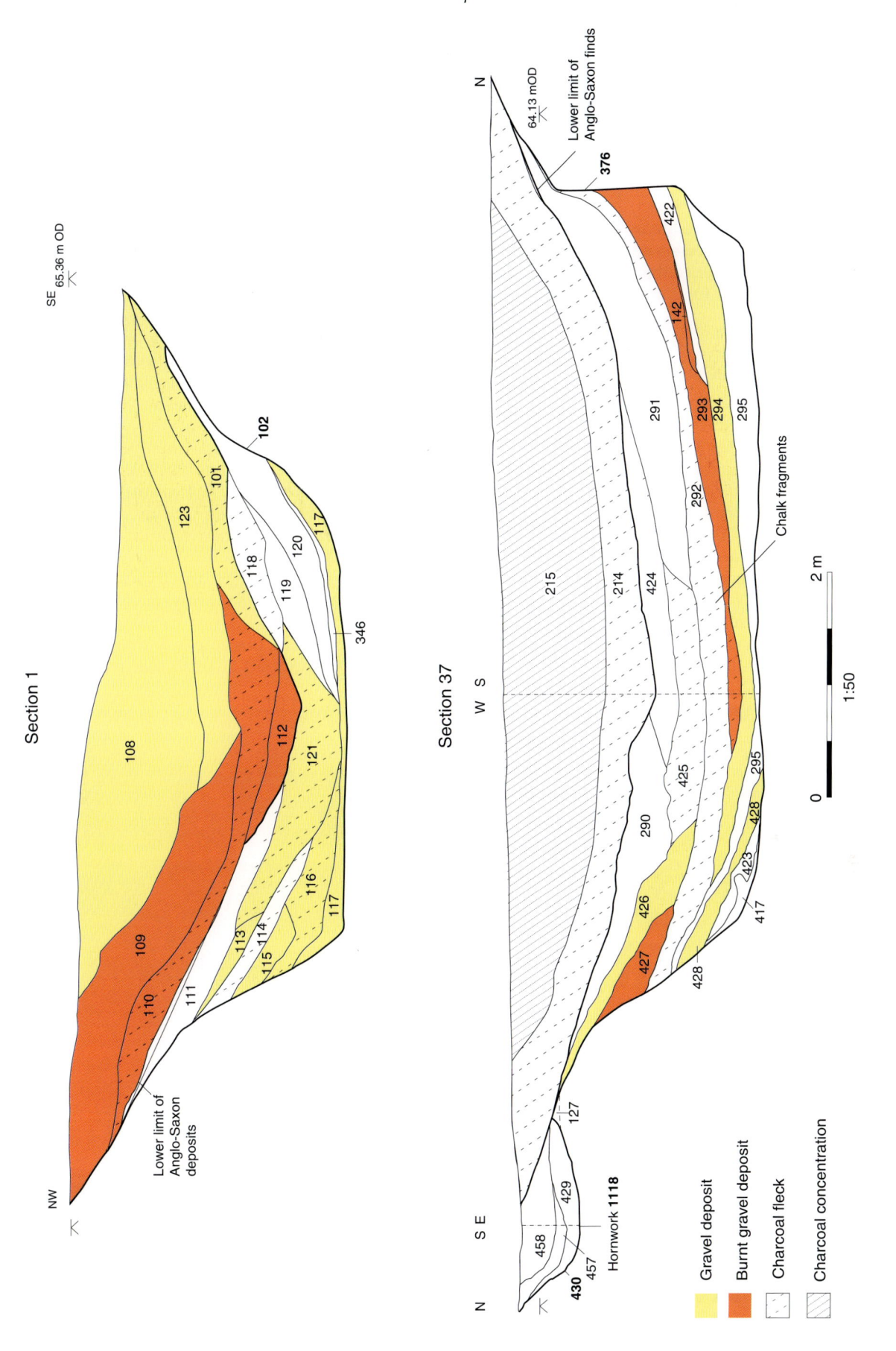

Fig. 5.3 The U-profiled ditch (460): sections 1 and 37

(1113). Occasional patches of dark soil were also found within the rampart, and one of these, layer (644) within burnt area 783 (see Fig. 5.5) was shown by particle size analysis to be very similar to the occupation layer within the late Bronze Age enclosure (see Canti Chapter 8). This suggests that some occupation material scraped up from the interior was incorporated into the rampart.

Intermittent but extensive areas of burning, and corresponding areas of preserved charred timber lacing, provide clear evidence that the rampart had been burnt, probably not long after its construction (Plate 5.2).

The chalk kerb (925) and posthole row 1104

At the southern end of the excavation, where the site was least truncated, a single course of chalk blocks (925), surviving for a length of 6.7 m from the southern baulk, was situated directly upon the standstill layer (1102), forming a wall or kerb 0.50 m wide and 0.08 m thick running NNE (Fig. 5.4; Plate 5.3). The blocks of chalk were varied in size, the largest being 0.26 m across. If these chalk blocks originally formed a kerb or façade for the rampart, their presence implies that the rampart originally extended over a metre further to the east than is suggested by the surviving deposits in the upper part of the V-profiled ditch.

Chalk was not reached in the ditch bottom in the excavation area, being covered by around 6 m of plateau gravel, but material for the chalk kerb could have been obtained from further down the hill slope, nearby.

If the kerb originally extended along the whole length of the rampart, then we might expect to find chalk in quite large quantities within the ditch. Only small quantities of chalk were found in the ditch, in sections 46 and 219 (see Fig. 5.2), near the southern end of the excavation, and at the northern end of the ditch in section 37 (see Fig. 5.3). No chalk was recorded in section 1. It therefore seems most likely that chalk was used only at the base of the rampart. Where it was found the chalk lay on the western, inner side of the ditch, in layers which lay near the middle of the sequence of fills (752, 304 and 291), but which were at the top of the layers which contained most charcoal and which seemed to be most directly related to the burnt rampart. This might indicate that collapse or erosion of the upper part of the rampart did not include chalk, which was only incorporated when erosion reached the lower part of the rampart.

Chalk was also found in the exposed top of a curving palisade slot (987) revealed during the watching brief at the north end of the site (Fig. 5.1; see also Plate 5.7). The post-pipes within this feature showed that the rampart at this point was retained

Plate 5.3   The chalk kerb (925): below it lies a posthole forming part of posthole row 1104

Fig. 5.4 (facing page)   The chalk kerb (925): plans and sections 236 and 279

Chapter 5

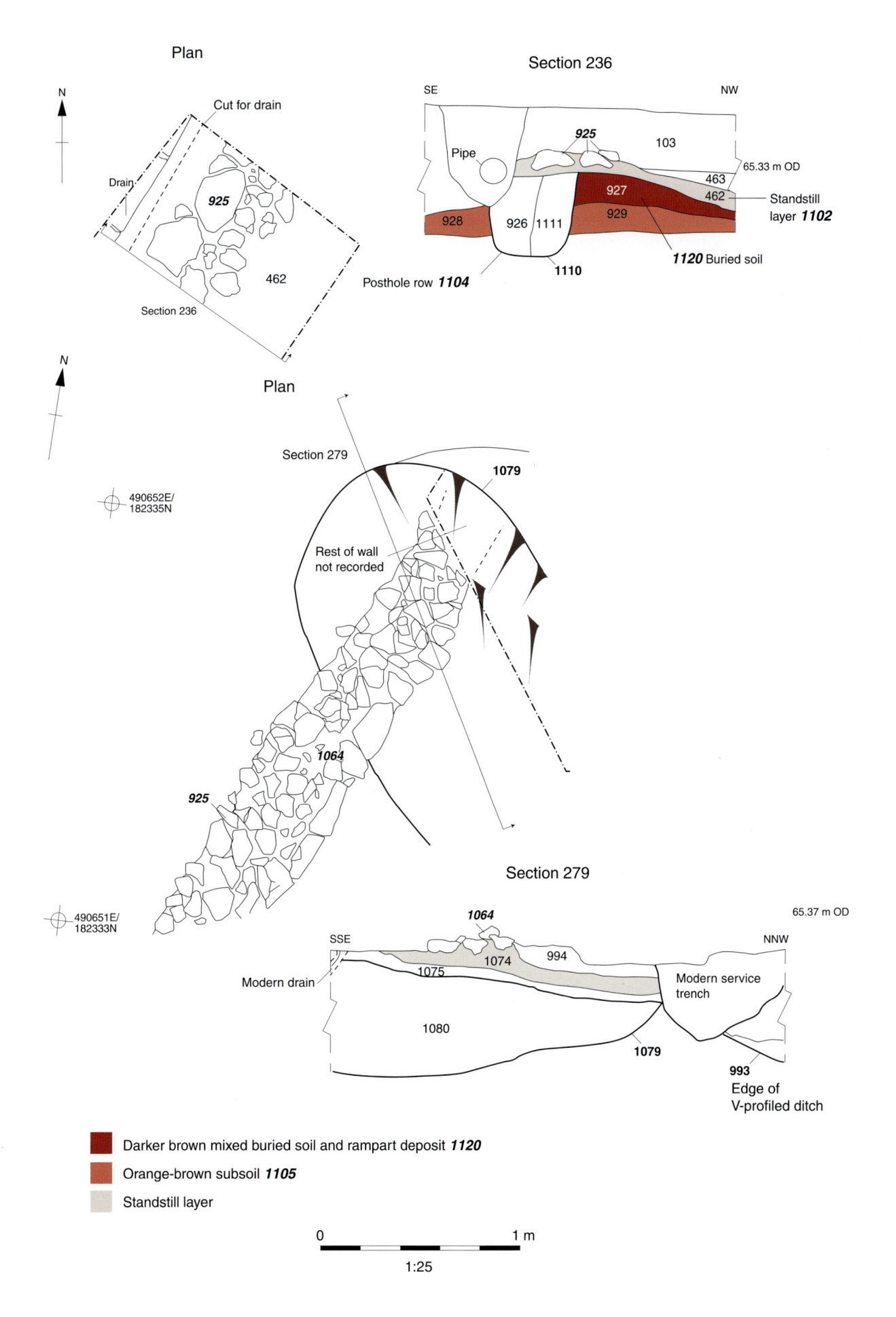

by a group of closely-spaced vertical timbers no more than 0.25 m apart (centre to centre). Fragments of chalk were found around and overlying several of the post-pipes; this may indicate that chalk was used around the posts as a decorative device, as it could have served little structural purpose in the narrow gaps between the vertical timbers.

The post-pipes within this feature showed that at the entrance the rampart was retained by a group of closely-spaced vertical timbers no more than 0.25 m apart (centre to centre). The post-pipes were filled with charcoal and burnt stone, indicating that they had been burnt like the burnt areas of the rampart.

A white, chalk-faced rampart would, no doubt have been visually striking, and would perhaps have recalled the appearance of hillforts built on the chalk downs. However, the evidence seems to suggest that chalk was used selectively, perhaps only at certain points along the rampart, and even then perhaps only to make a kerb at the foot of the rampart.

None of the chalk that was found, whether in the kerb at the south end of the site or in the palisade slot at the north end, appeared to have been burnt. While the kerb at the south end may fortuitously have escaped burning, this seems less convincing in the curving foundation trench, where the chalk apparently directly overlay charcoal and burnt stone, and raises another interpretation of the chalk kerb, that it was laid after the original timber-laced rampart had been burnt, as a secondary facing to the rampart, probably at the base of a turf revetment. This would explain the fragments of chalk apparently overlying the post-pipes in palisade 987, and would be consistent with the stratigraphic position of the chalk in the U-profiled ditch, suggesting that at this location the chalk could have derived from the construction of a chalk kerb, not from its demolition or erosion. The limited survival of chalk in the palisade slot, however, and the limited time available for its investigation, mean that its relationship to the postholes in the palisade cannot be taken as certain.

The timber rampart structure

In the areas where the rampart had been burnt, the remains of a charred timber structure were found (Figs 5.1 and 5.5; Plates 5.2 and 5.4), that may have constituted both a platform or corduroy along the base of the rampart, and a consolidating framework within the rampart. The timbers were preserved particularly well at the southern end of the excavation where the site was least truncated; to the north the wood was more fragmented.

The least comminuted pieces included a split roundwood timber and fragments from timbers over 2 m long, suggesting that the lacing had originally been constructed with substantial pieces of wood. Almost all the charcoal associated with this rampart has been identified as oak. The few fragments of *Pomoideae* charcoal also found within the rampart

Plate 5.4 Charred timbers (1113) and fire-reddened gravel (1000) from the rampart associated with the U-profiled ditch

Chapter 5

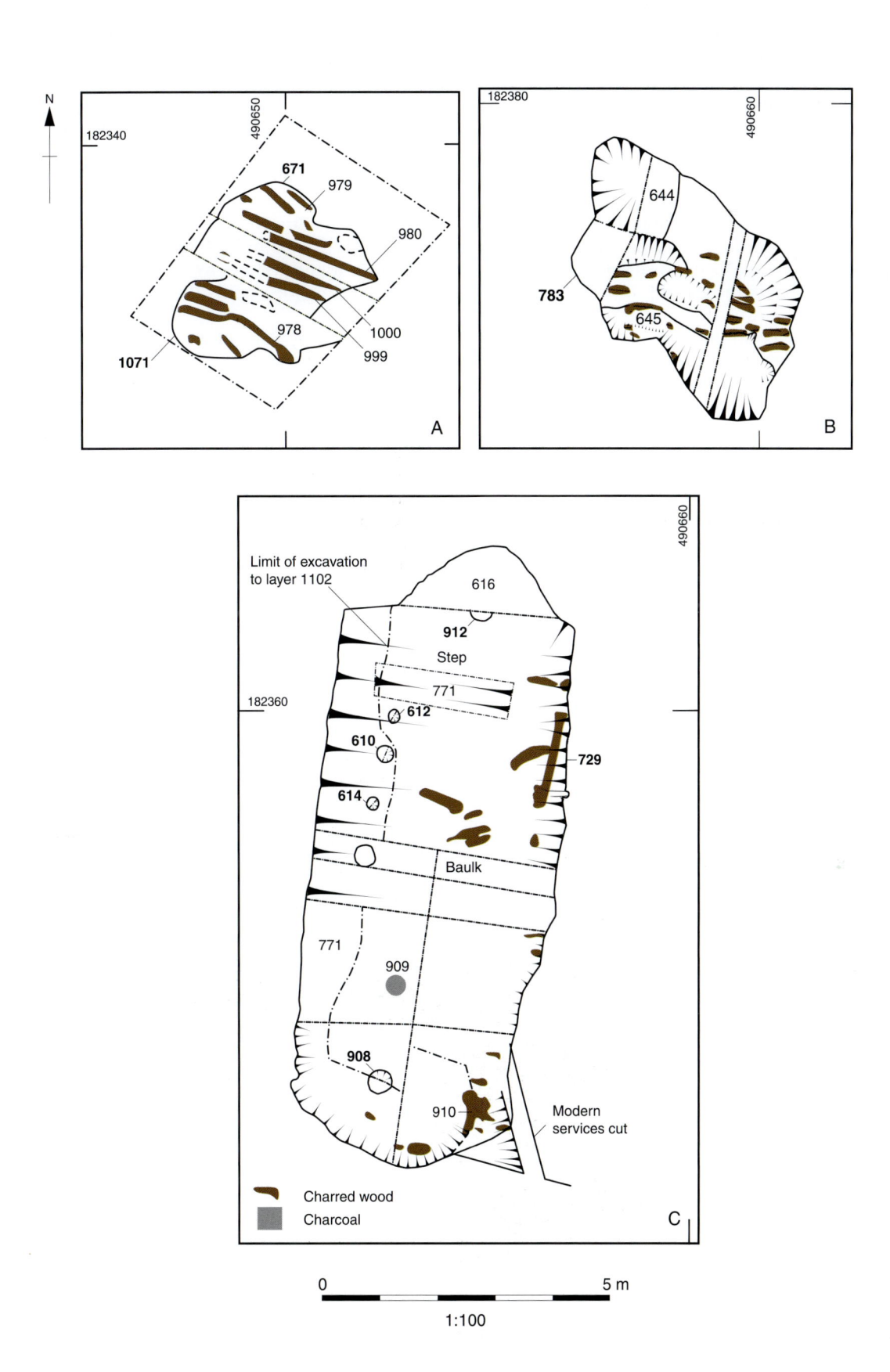

Fig. 5.5 Selected plans of charred timbers (1113) within areas of burnt rampart

may derive from stray, incidental inclusions, rather than deliberate use of woods of this genus.

Most of the charred timbers lay transversely across the rampart. Where they were best preserved, it was clear that these transverse timbers were quite closely spaced, some contiguous with one another, others up to 0.25 m apart. It was the consistent alignment of these timbers which provides the clearest indication that they have remained essentially *in situ*. One of the charred timbers may not have been straight (context 978, Fig. 5.5A), perhaps indicating that selection of material for the corduroy included only roughly-prepared roundwood, although it is possible that the charred timber in question was in fact two shorter straight lengths of wood.

A few pieces of wood lay parallel to the line of the rampart on the eastern edge of the burnt area (eg Plate 4.5). If the front of the rampart had been defined either by the line of chalk blocks (925) or by postholes within line 1104, then these longitudinal timbers would have lain up to 2 m from the front of the rampart. Although in one or two cases a transverse piece lay upon the longitudinal timbers, the charred wood was not well enough preserved to show whether or how these pieces were joined. This does however demonstrate that the lacing had some kind of internal structure.

Two postholes (912 and 908), nearly 8 m apart, were found below the largest burnt area in the middle of the site, cut up to 0.50 m deep into the standstill layer (1102) near the centre of the surviving rampart deposits (Figs 5.1 and 5.5C). A circle of black charcoal (909) showing in the standstill layer between them may represent another burnt post (Fig. 5.5C). The remains of charred vertical timbers were found in these postholes and in the sediments above (Fig. 4.8, section 227; Plate 5.5). At the south end of the excavation a further posthole (1115), 0.3 m in diameter and nearly 0.8 m deep, was identified below another patch of burnt gravel, cutting the standstill layer in the centre of the ditch.

A 2.5 m-long row of four postholes, three of which (610, 612 and 614) were excavated, was found in the top of the burnt gravel 616 to the west of 908 and 912 (Fig. 5.5C). The postholes were spaced 0.7 – 0.95 m apart, and varied in depth from only 0.12 m to 0.30 m deep. All had dark fills consisting predominantly of charcoal. The standstill layer (1102) was exposed below 612, and the postholes had not penetrated to this layer.

There was no evidence within the surviving rampart of any timbers that may have joined the posts in this posthole row, and no clear distinction between the deposits on either side of this row, so the timber elements were not intended to form solid compartments within the rampart, and more likely were used as anchors for timbers retaining the rampart at the front and back, although they may

Plate 5.5 Section 227 across the V-profiled ditch, showing the standstill layer cut by posthole 912, and the remains of the charred upright continuing through the burnt gravel rampart above

also have been joined to one another at intervals within the rampart contruction to provide lateral stability.

All of the horizontal charred timbers lay at, or very near, the base of the rampart deposits, either directly upon the standstill layer or, more usually, above the first layer of rampart deposits. No traces of any further timbers were found in the V-profiled ditch where the gravel rampart was not burnt, but without burning any such timbers would have decayed entirely, and the gravel was not sufficiently compacted to have preserved horizontal post-voids. The one narrow slot excavated see Fig. 5.1) could well have fallen between the postholes along the centre of the ditch. The presence of horizontal timbers in every burnt patch suggests that the timbers may originally have constituted a complete layer or corduroy along the base of the rampart. Even though it is claimed that transverse timbers are structurally more effective at preventing subsidence if they are positioned nearer the top of a rampart (Avery 1993, 41), several hillforts are known in which the ramparts were constructed on a raft of timber (eg Crickley Hill, Leckhampton and Rainsborough; ibid., 44). At Taplow the use of such a structure might have been motivated by a desire to stop the new rampart from subsiding into the remains of the V-profiled ditch. Evidently, however, this was not entirely successful since some of the timbers sloped down into the hollow left as the underlying ditch fills settled under the weight of the rampart (Fig. 4.8, section 227).

Some ramparts, for instance Bickerton (Avery 1993, 44), have more than one layer of timbers at intervals up the rampart. The depth of rampart deposits which survived above the timbers at Taplow was modest (a maximum of 0.55 m), and this may mean that any further layers of timber would have been above the surviving top of the rampart. The depth of burnt gravel that survived in the rampart deposits, and the quantities which were found in the U-profiled ditch, would have required substantial amounts of timber to heat such a large quantity, perhaps indicating that there were originally timbers further up the rampart, which may either have burnt more completely than those at the base of the rampart, or have been truncated (see also below).

Sediments

The sediments that surrounded the timbers and made up the bulk of the rampart were varied. Most consisted of sandy deposits mixed with varied proportions of gravel (from 5% to 80%). In sections 123 and 227 (see Fig. 4.8) the lower surviving deposits contained less gravel than the upper fills, and the almost clean gravel fills were deeper on the west side. This perhaps reflects the expected deposition sequence if these soils derive from the excavation of the U-profiled ditch, the first soils being mixed topsoil and subsoils deposited close to the ditch, the pure gravels overlying and lying behind them. However, section 125 (Fig. 4.8) has a more homogeneous fill, and deposits with high proportions of gravel occurred both above and below the charred timbers.

Variations in the proportion of gravel might also reflect natural variation in the deposits into which the U-profiled ditch was cut. Some of the initial ditch fill might have been derived from the remains of the late Bronze Age rampart (as the presence of residual flint-tempered pottery suggests – see Table 4.5), while the rest might have derived from the ditch sides. Either way, the differences in the sediments do not appear to indicate a deliberate and consistent strategy on the part of the builders.

The form of the rampart

The rampart may have been constructed on a foundation raft which was composed of closely spaced transverse timbers and by at least one line of longitudinally placed timbers which lay within the rampart towards, but probably not at, its front. The front of the original rampart may have been marked by a kerb of chalk blocks, or possibly, by some of the posts within the erratic row 1104, although the absence both of clear evidence for these posts being burnt, and corroborative dating evidence, suggests that this is unlikely.

On the basis of the small area investigated, a row of vertical posts may have run parallel to the U-profiled ditch along the centre of the surviving rampart, some 2 m behind posthole row 1104. Since no postholes were found which might have been related to structural elements retaining the back of the rampart, it seems likely that on its western side the timber lacing either ended within the rampart or was of the Hod Hill type, in which the rear vertical timbers were not set into the ground (cf. Ralston 2006, fig. 16). Alternatively, the rampart may have rested against the pre-existing rampart of the V-profiled ditch, doing away with the need for revetment at the back (Fig. 5.6A). Beyond these details the reconstruction becomes increasingly speculative.

If the front was retained by only a low chalk kerb, it is perhaps likely that the front sloped upwards from this kerb to the row of posts within the rampart. If they were sufficiently long, these posts might have projected from the top of the rampart, and have been used as the framework for a breastwork. If that were the case, it seems likely that the rampart deposits would have formed a walkway behind the breastwork. Since there was no indication of any structure retaining the back of the rampart, it is possible that the rampart simply sloped downwards from this walkway.

Alternatively, the front of the rampart could have consisted of a taller vertical revetment sitting either on the chalk kerb or on the standstill layer, perhaps consisting of turf or based on a horizontal sill-beam. If this was the case, then a walkway might have

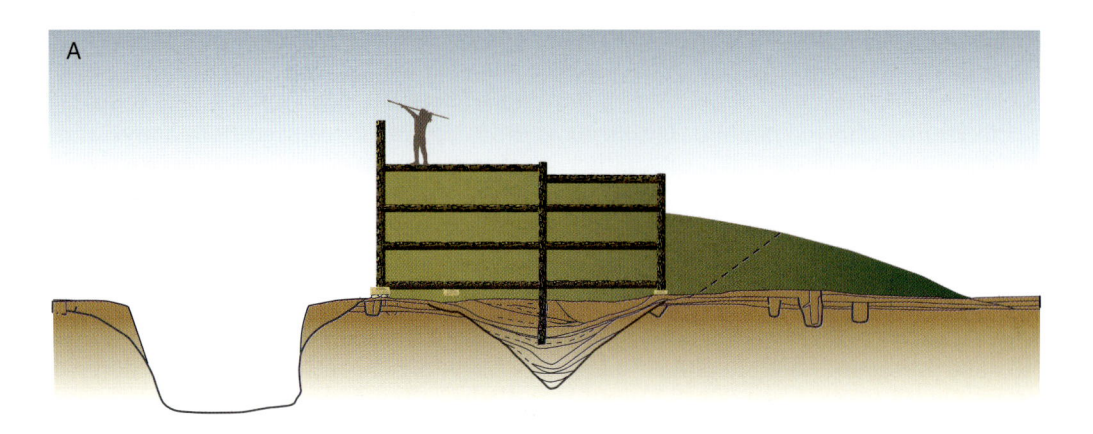

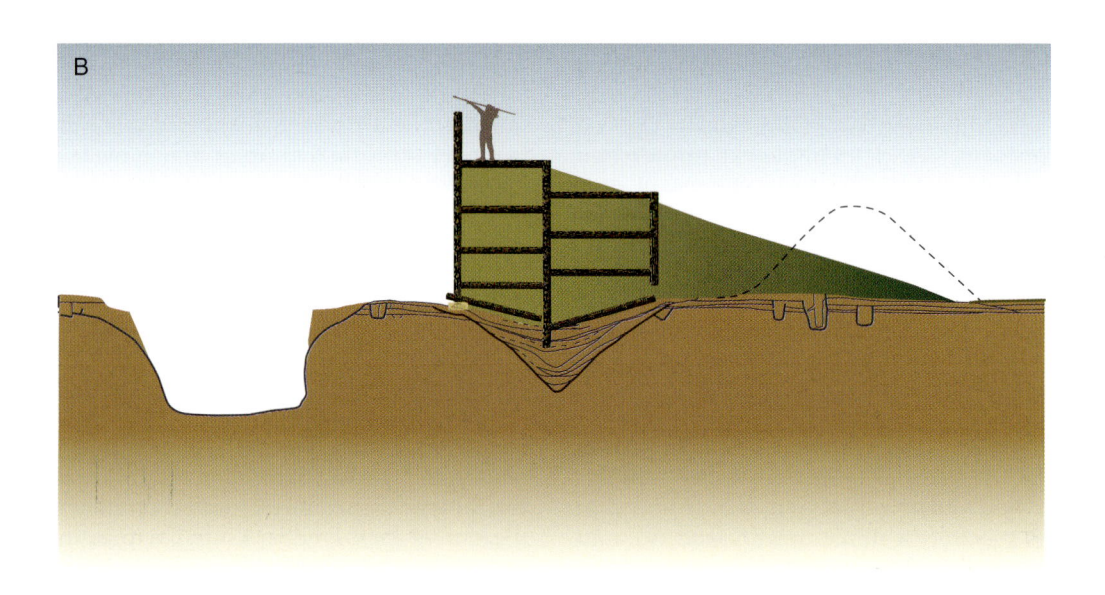

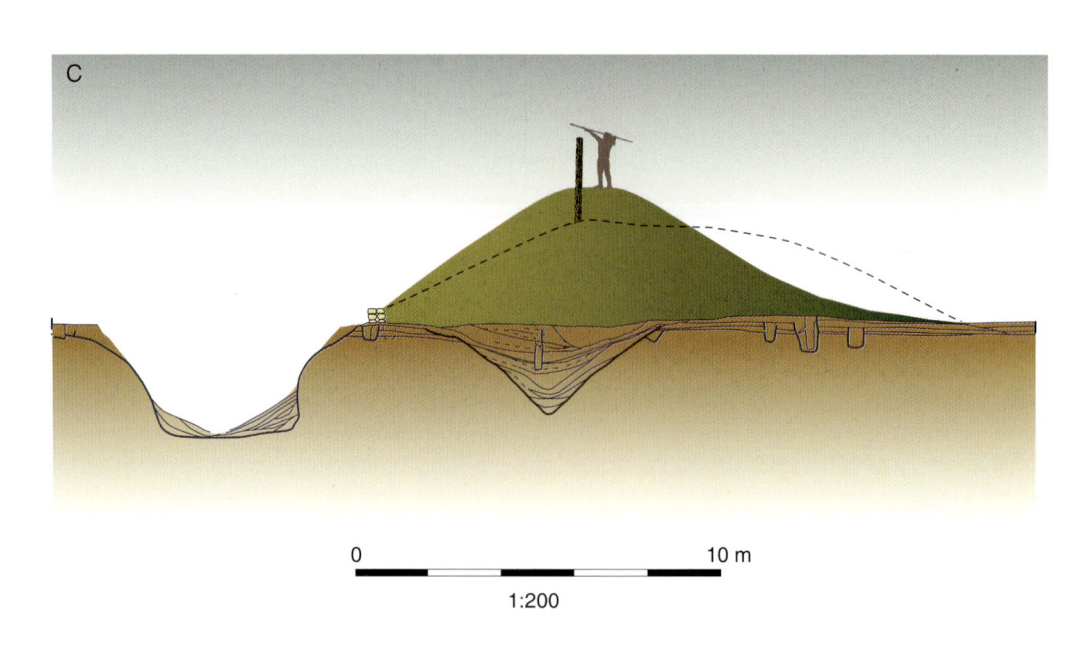

From Bronze Age enclosure to Anglo-Saxon settlement

0   10 m
1:200

84

been formed between the front of the rampart and the row of postholes within the rampart, and the rampart deposits might than have sloped down to the back of the rampart from the central row of posts (Fig. 5.6B).

A rough idea of the size of the rampart might be obtained from the quantity of spoil obtained from excavating the U-profiled ditch, although further material might have been obtained from the remnants of the rampart associated the V-profiled ditch, while an appreciable volume of timber was probably also included within the rampart. The sections across the U-profiled ditch suggest that it was originally on average 5 m wide and nearly 3 m deep, or in cross-section an area of c 15 m^2. The minimum width of the rampart is given by the distance from the chalk kerb (925) to the western edge of the surviving rampart deposits, a distance of roughly 7 m. Excluding any adjustment for compaction or the volume of timber within the rampart, the ditch would have provided enough material for a rampart 2.17 m tall of this width (with a rectangular cross-section), For an unrevetted dump rampart a height of around 4.3 m is possible with this volume of material. Increasing the bulk of the spoil to 150% as suggested by Avery (1993) for freshly-excavated and uncompacted material, a fully encased rectangular box-rampart might have been 4 m high, and an unrevetted dump rampart of triangular cross-section nearly 8 m high. The latter is implausible, as the spoil would not have been stable at such a steep angle of rest. Given that there is evidence for timber lacing, the rampart is more likely to have approximated to a rectangular shape.

Another possibility is that the rampart extended all the way back to the rampart of the V-profiled ditch, as there is no certain evidence that this was demolished. In this case the overall width of the rampart would have been considerably greater, and the height of the rampart somewhat less (Fig. 5.6C). What is clear, however, is that the ditch would have provided more than enough material for an imposing rampart.

DESTRUCTION OF THE HILLFORT DEFENCES

The burning of the rampart

The burning of the early-middle Iron Age rampart was revealed by seven areas of fire-reddened gravel within which the charred remains of the rampart's timber lacing were preserved. These areas were quite localised, implying either that the fires were more or less restricted to these areas, or that the fires only burnt in a way which left archaeologically detectable remains in these areas. This may have been a product either of setting fires only in certain areas or of the local conditions affecting the way in which the fire burnt. In addition, the features that were related to the entrance into the hillfort all also contained evidence of burning. Some of the conditions which appear to affect the way in which timber-laced ramparts may burn are discussed below.

Burnt gravel deposits lying above the standstill layer (1102) and thus forming part of the early-middle Iron Age rampart survived to depths of 0.7 m (Plate 5.6). Considerable quantities of burnt gravel were also found within the associated U-profiled ditch (460; see below), presumably having eroded from the rampart. The original depth of burnt deposits in the rampart was, therefore, probably much greater than the 0.7 m that survived.

Experiments involving bonfires built upon gravelly surfaces suggest that the heat does not penetrate to any great depth and that reddening will occur only to depths of up to 0.05 m (Canti and Linford 2001). The burnt rampart deposits are, therefore, clearly much too thick to have been burnt purely by a fire built above them. On these grounds, Canti (Chapter 8) suggests that the fire-reddened deposits have been redeposited (and hence did not constitute *in situ* rampart deposits). We disagree with Canti for two reasons. The first is that charred timbers within these deposits do appear to have remained *in situ* (ie essentially in the positions they were in after the rampart had burnt). They include lines of parallel large, intact carbonised horizontal timbers, as well as some vertical elements. The second reason is that to produce the quantities of fire-reddened gravel that remained in the rampart and the U-profiled ditch – assuming that reddening occurs only to a depth of 0.05 m – would require building a fire covering an extraordinarily large area, or repeatedly burning large quantities of gravel, either of which seems implausible. There was no indication in the ditch fills that the rampart had been partially demolished before it was burnt.

Rather than being the product of dumping, as Canti proposes, we suggest that the depths of fire-reddened gravel at Taplow could have been produced by the burning of the timber lacing within and below the rampart deposits. Experiments involving burning timber-laced ramparts which attempt to reproduce the processes which lead to the creation of vitrified forts suggest that vitrification is likely to have been the product of a fire burning within and, perhaps most crucially, below the ramparts. This was the conclusion reached by McHardy (1906) as a result of his experiments, and has been reiterated by Childe and Thorneycroft (1937) and Ralston (1986; 2006, chap. 7). Childe and Thorneycroft's experiments, in particular, are relevant to Taplow Court since they involved reconstructed ramparts which, although built of stone and turf, had timber lacing which may have been similar to that at Taplow. Although these experi-

Fig. 5.6 (facing page) Schematic reconstructions of the Iron Age defences associated with the U-profiled ditch

Plate 5.6 Fire reddened gravel (1100) in the rampart associated with the U-profiled ditch (460)

ments in vitrification do not provide precise analogies for the rampart at Taplow (because they involve stone-built ramparts), they have highlighted several factors which influence the way in which timber-laced ramparts burn, and have also emphasised very clearly the way in which variations in conditions can have marked effects on the way in which the fire burns.

In all of the vitrification experiments, the timber lacing was set alight by building a fire against the outside of the rampart. Of course, this is only effective if the timber lacing is exposed on the outer face of the rampart. There is no direct evidence for or against this at Taplow, although the large number of transverse timbers raises the possibility. Nor is there any evidence at Taplow for an external fire. However, Canti and Linford's observations suggest such surface fires are unlikely to leave extensive evidence of reddening, and such a fire might only have been marked by easily dispersed ash.

It is not, however, the external fire which is significant, but rather the ensuing burning within the rampart. Once the internal timbers are burning the rampart sediments may act like a clamp to retain the heat within the rampart. This seems to be one of the significant factors which allows temperatures of over 950° C (which are required for vitrification) to be reached. The temperatures at which a deposit will redden depend upon various factors, such as its composition (and in particular its iron oxide component) and the presence of an oxidising atmosphere (Canti and Linford 2001). Canti and Linford suggest that in general, while some deposits may redden at c 300° C, a minimum temperature of c 500° C is usually required. At Taplow, Canti's analysis (see Chapter 8) indicated that the gravels will redden at the lower end of the range, at c 300-350° C. Given that much higher temperatures have been achieved in the vitrification experiments, it would seem that temperatures sufficient for reddening could have been reached quite easily at Taplow. The oak from which the timber lacing was constructed was an ideal fuel for obtaining high temperatures, and the oak charcoal in the U-profiled ditch was partly vitrified, suggesting that temperatures in excess of 800° C may have been reached. Although the oak charcoal where vitrification was observed came from an Anglo-Saxon deposit within the ditch, there was considerable burnt gravel and charcoal from the rampart deposited in the ditch during this period, and none of the non-oak charcoal was similarly vitrified.

A second crucial factor affecting the burning is the supply of air into the rampart. Too great a supply of cold air may reduce the temperature within the rampart (Ralston 1986). It is possible that high temperatures within ramparts are produced only as a result of the conversion of the internal timber into charcoal, and this requires a reducing atmosphere (Childe and Thorneycroft 1937, 54). At the same time, if the rampart deposits are too dense, they may choke the fire (Ralston 1986).

The atmosphere of the fire raises significant issues in relation to the burnt rampart at Taplow. The first involves the contrast between reddened gravel – which implies an oxidising atmosphere – and carbonised timber – which implies a reducing atmosphere. The second involves the extent to which the sand and gravel sediments that made up most of the rampart would have effectively dampened the fire. In the absence of more experiments, no definitive answers can be given to the questions raised by these issues, but some possibly significant points can be noted. It is, for example, possible for oxidising and reducing conditions to be produced at different stages and in different parts of a fire (as ceramic production shows). A contradiction is not, therefore, necessarily implied by the presence of evidence for both oxidation and reduction. The sediments from which the rampart was composed may have been significant in this respect. That they did allow in sufficient air to produce oxidising conditions is implied by the quantities of reddened gravel, and it is perhaps worth noting that the sediments may not have been well compacted after having been dug from the ditch, especially if the fire was set soon after construction. Furthermore, the presence of timber lacing may have allowed further air to enter the rampart.

In the vitrification experiments discussed above, it was sometimes the case that the collapse of the stone from which the rampart was made as the timbers burnt stifled the fire below (Ralston 1986). The same effect may have occurred at Taplow where the collapse of the upper part of the rampart as its timbers burnt away (in oxidising conditions) may have reduced the flow of air and hence produced the reducing conditions which lead to the carbonisation of the lower timbers. It is also possible that less air could reach the lower timbers anyway since they lay within the hollow left by the V-profiled ditch (574). If this was the case, conditions conducive to the reddening of considerable quantities of gravel might have been produced, the carbonised lower timbers producing high temperatures while the sediments above were still exposed to sufficient air for oxidisation to occur. It is perhaps also worth noting that, being excavated from the ditch, the rampart deposits would probably have contained very little organic material (which may have a reducing effect; Canti and Linford 2001).

In sum, the rampart must have been burnt *in situ*. The high temperatures required to redden the gravels in the rampart were probably produced by the burning of the timber lacing at the base of the rampart. The transformation of this timber in a reducing atmosphere into charcoal may have been crucial in reaching high temperatures. The rampart deposits probably acted like a clamp, retaining heat within the rampart. However, the reddening of the gravel would have required an oxidising atmosphere and some air must, therefore, have been able to penetrate the upper parts of the rampart. One possibility is that, as the horizontal timbers burnt from the outer face of the rampart, air was drawn in along the resulting void, keeping the timbers smouldering as in a charcoal clamp due to the surrounding rampart soils, but providing air to the overlying already heated rampart gravels.

The circumstances in which the rampart was burnt are difficult to infer. There is no indication that any of the features lying within the hillfort were burnt, and it is, therefore, unlikely that the rampart burnt as a result of a wider fire. Nor is there any indication – other than the burning itself – that the hillfort was attacked. No slingstones or other weapons were found. The vitrification experiments discussed above suggest that setting fire to a rampart in this way is no easy matter. It might, therefore, be argued that the fire is unlikely to have been set during an attack, but more probably derives from an attempt to slight the defences once the hillfort had already been captured. The localisation of the burnt areas within the rampart might be taken to indicate that this was intended more as a symbolic – rather than entirely effective – destruction. However, it is possible that the burning of the timber lacing was an unintended consequence of a fire intended to destroy external features such as the breastwork and façade of the rampart (if that was constructed of timber). The localisation of the burning might, therefore, be nothing more than a product of the local conditions.

A further possibility, depending upon the length of time it took for the primary fills of the U-profiled ditch to accumulate, is that the rampart was burnt deliberately by the inhabitants of the hillfort. If the timber rampart had become unstable due to subsidence into the V-profiled ditch, firing the rampart might have been a deliberate attempt to destroy the revetted rampart in favour of a *glacis* style dump rampart. Although a considerable quantity of burnt and unburnt gravel fell into the U-profiled ditch as a result, the ditch remained open to a depth averaging 2 m thereafter. This would have made most sense as a preliminary to the construction of the outer ditch (3050), which would thereafter have formed the principal line of defence, leaving the U-profiled ditch and its rampart surviving as still appreciable defensive features even after the rampart had been burnt (see Chapter 6).

The lower fills of the U-profiled ditch (460)

The fills within the U-profiled ditch (460) were examined with the aim of identifying deposits that might have been related to the destruction of the rampart (see Figs 5.2-3). Evidence of fire was, however, less evident than might have been expected. There was, for example, no clear horizon marked by a concentration of charcoal. The paucity of charcoal is not, however, as surprising as it might seem. Given the way in which the rampart appears to have burnt, charcoal might have been produced primarily at the base of the rampart where it has remained *in situ*, the higher timbers being more thoroughly burnt to ash.

Table 5.1a. Summary of finds in the U-profiled ditch (460): section 219, cut 713. The double line marks the boundary between prehistoric and Anglo-Saxon deposits; the dashed lines mark the deposits containing the clearest evidence for fire, related to the burning of the associated rampart

Context	Prehistoric pot	Early-Middle Saxon pot	Flint	Burnt unworked flint	Horse	Cattle	Domestic fowl	Large mammal	Medium mammal	Pig	Sheep/goat	Dog	Red deer	Roe deer	Unid. bone	Rotary quern lava	CPR	Charcoal	Other finds
579	4	7/166	6			1/99	1/2	5/62	6/12	1/16	2/2				37/25	7/12	Wheat grain - 25; Rye grain - 14; Barley grain - 20; Oats grain - 27; Cereal grain - 82; Wheat glume - 2; Wheat rachis node - 16; Rye rachis node - 10; Rye or barkey rachis node - 4; Weeds - 284	Oak - 32; Hazel - 1 fragment; Beech - 61 weight 16/167; Hawthorn/apple - 1; Blackthorn - 1; Willow - 2	Cu alloy spiral headed pin; Fe knife - whittle tang; Fired clay - annular loom weight
668																			
607	3	39/485	2			2/24	16/714	3/4	28/316	26/98	11/93	6/58	5/83	1/40	7/94	97/163		Oak; Beech	Fe knife; Fired clay - amorphous 4/6; oven/hearth 1/15; Pos smithing hearth bottom - 442 g
686				6		1/90													
707		3	3			1/189		4/156		2/53					2/27				
712	3	1/1	2			3/43													
711			3	3	2/105												Rye +; Cereal indet. +		
714	8														1/1				
708	17														4/8				
728						2/264		1/25	2/4										
746								1/14										Oak	
747																			
751																			
752	7		1																
753									1/3										
769																		Oak	
770																			
782																			

Less outstanding indications of burning were, however, found within the ditch.

Of the four sections cut across the U-profiled ditch, three (sections 37, 46, and 219) lay near to burnt areas of the rampart. Not surprisingly, these three sections contained considerably more evidence of burning than the fourth (section 1), supporting the contention that the effect of the fires was localised. The evidence for burning in these three sections consisted of charcoal and fire-reddened (oxidised), gravelly deposits. Such evidence was mostly found in layers deposited from the western, inner side of the ditch, and hence probably derives from erosion of the rampart.

In the three sections cut near to burnt areas, the largest quantities of charcoal occurred in burnt gravelly deposits near the base of the ditch. In two of these sections one or two layers of primary fill which did not contain evidence for burning lay below the layers containing charcoal. These unburnt layers comprised orangey-brown sand and gravel, probably eroded from the upper edges of the ditch. In section 219 (see Fig. 5.2), only a single layer (782) had accumulated below the layers containing charcoal, but this layer contained burnt gravel. Observations at experimental earthworks (Evans and Limbrey 1974; Bell *et al.* 1996, chap. 12) suggest that these primary deposits are likely to have formed quite quickly, perhaps within a year or two of the excavation of the ditch. Assuming that the ditch was not later recut or cleaned out (of which there was no indication), the fills therefore suggest that the rampart was burnt quite soon after it was constructed.

The charcoal and reddened gravel in the layers above this primary fill may then have accumulated over a longer period. The sections do not provide clear indications of an increased rate of deposition among the first layers containing evidence for burning, as one might expect following the destruction of the rampart. It is, however, possible that the berm and the continued presence of the chalk kerb (see below) slowed the erosion of rampart deposits into the ditch. Burnt gravels occur from above the primary fill, and continue up to the top of the ditch.

From about halfway up the ditch, the deposits contain Anglo-Saxon finds (the date of which is supported by radiocarbon dates (see below, Chap. 6), and the deposition of burnt rampart deposits into the ditch thus appears to have continued over a considerable period. The quantity of charcoal generally decreased up the profile, and what there was in the upper levels may have derived from Anglo-

Table 5.1b. Summary of finds in the U-profiled ditch (460): section 1, cut 102

Context	Prehistoric pot	Early-Middle Saxon pot	OXAC 11th C pot	Flint	Burnt unworked flint	Horse	Cattle	Domestic fowl	Large mammal	Medium mammal	Pig	Unid. bone	Rotary quern lava	Other finds
108				6		1/242	1/51		3/41		1/14	10/7	38/191	Fe knife
123				1			2/133		7/28			14/10	5/78	
109														Modern copper pipe - pushed vertically into deposits from top of ditch to form an earth
110			1/3	4	1	9/298	1/11	2/46	2/15	2/55	25/46	51/479		
122				7			1/108		1/63		1/36		7/317	
112														
101		1/6		14					1/15					
118				3										
111														
121	34			5										Post-med wall plaster 1/3 g fired clay - hearth/oven 3/44
113														
119														
114														
120				4			1/19							
115														
346														
116				2										
117														

Saxon activity rather than the rampart itself, since it did not all consist of oak charcoal (Tables 5.1a-d).

At the entrance, decayed chalk pieces which may have formed part of the kerb were found in layer 292, which lay near the top of the layers containing most charcoal (Fig. 5.3, section 37). Smaller quantities of chalk were also found in layers 752 and 304, near the top of the layers containing most charcoal in sections 219 and 46 respectively (Fig. 5.2). If this chalk had formed part of the kerb of the rampart, its presence in the ditches in these levels might indicate the final collapse of the front of the rampart into the ditch.

Finds from the lower fills of the U-profiled ditch (460) and its rampart

A total of 100 prehistoric sherds were found in the ditch, though only 59 came from the prehistoric fills. The pottery from the ditch consisted predominantly of sherds in sand and flint-tempered fabrics but included also significant proportions in sand-tempered fabrics, the latter generally more common in the middle Iron Age. The sequence in section 46 (Fig. 5.2) is as follows: one early Iron Age sherd came from layer 255 at the very bottom of the ditch, together with six late Bronze Age sherds, and fourteen residual late Bronze Age sherds came from the charcoal-rich fills interspersed with burnt rampart gravels. These were overlain by an indeterminate Iron Age sherd from layer 256, and middle Iron Age sherds in layer 252 above that. At the terminal of the ditch the burnt rampart gravels contained middle Iron Age sherds as well as residual late Bronze Age sherds, and a group of middle Iron Age sherds came from a charcoal-flecked fill (292) above that. No material suitable for radiocarbon dating was recovered from the primary fills of the ditch, and it was decided not to date charcoal associated with the burnt gravel spills in the ditch, as these were derived from the rampart. Charcoal from charred timbers within the rampart were dated, and gave dates of 710-390 cal BC (OxA-14267: 2390±27 BP) and 750-400 cal BC (OxA-14295: 2428±BP). When modelled (see Chapter 9) the range is reduced to 510-390 cal BC, suggesting that the ditch and rampart were constructed in the 5th century BC, at the end of the early Iron Age or in the early part of the middle Iron Age. This is consistent

Table 5.1c. Summary of finds in the U-profiled ditch (460): section 46, cut 238

Context	Prehistoric pot	Flint	Burnt unworked flint	Cattle	Large mammal	Medium mammal	Pig	Sheep/goat	Dog	Roe deer	Unid. bone	Rotary quern lava	Charcoal
254	4											9/66	
331													
331													
296													
297													
257		1		9/788	12/121	10/41	3/16	1/5	1/41	3/73	26/40		
298													
299													
300													
252	63												Oak
308													
301													
256	20	1											
302													
303													
304													
305													
253	72			2/13									
306													
255	115				1/14								Oak
332													
333													
307													

with the middle Iron Age sherds in the lower secondary fills of the U-profiled ditch (460). A third sample submitted for dating gave a modern result, and this was presumably intrusive charcoal from the construction of the Plessey buildings.

Compared to the quantities of Anglo-Saxon finds in the upper fills of the U-profiled ditch (which are discussed in Chapter 6), relatively few finds were recovered from the lower levels (Table 5.1a-d). The contrast in the quantities of finds probably reflects the fact that the ditch was used to deposit rubbish in the Anglo-Saxon period, whereas during the Iron Age, what little settlement activity is suggested by the evidence would have been concentrated behind the rampart.

While the material within the ditch may, nonetheless, have been related in large part to activity during the use of, and after the abandonment of the fort, the material contained within the rampart must derive from activity predating or contemporary with its construction. The pottery in the rampart deposits (1100 and 1112) comprised 14 sherds in a mixture of flint-tempered fabrics and sand and flint-tempered fabrics. The sherds were relatively large and well-preserved but were probably residual; lenses of dark soil (eg cxt 644) – similar to the late Bronze Age occupation layer within the defences – were found within the rampart gravels (see Canti, Chapter 8), suggesting that some soil from the interior was incorporated into the rampart during construction. The quantity of pottery in the four sections cut across the U-profiled ditch varied, but no pattern was apparent in the spatial distribution.

Aside from the pottery, both the ditch and the rampart contained small numbers of pieces of worked flint. Again, the presence of greater numbers in the rampart deposits than in the ditch probably reflects the inclusion of residual material in the rampart. Within the ditch most of the flint lay near northern end (sections 1 and 37).

In contrast, most of the other finds in the ditch were found in the southern sections (nos 219 and 46). They included small numbers of animal bones, among which cattle was the only species identified. Only a single fragment of animal bone, from a large mammal, was found in the northern sections. The only remaining finds were a few fragments of fired clay from section 1 of the ditch and the rampart. Overall, the small quantities of finds in the ditch seem to represent nothing more than stray fragments, incidentally incorporated into the deposits.

Table 5.1d. Summary of finds in the U-profiled ditch (460): section 37, cut 376

Context	Prehistoric pot	Early-Middle Saxon pot	Roman pot	Flint	Burnt unworked flint	Cattle	Large mammal	Medium mammal	Pig	Sheep/goat	Roe deer	Unid. bone	Rotary quern lava	Charcoal	Human bone
215	83	5/42	1/12	5		12/322	4/20	1/17				1/25	10/22	Oak	
214	38	7/46	1/42	10	3	6/358	7/178		2/34	1/11		22/62	83/494		2 fragments human left humerus
290				6											
424															
425															
426															
427															
291	92			10											
292	44														
416				1											
293	18			2											
421															
422															
294				2											
295	20			1											
428															
423															
417				4											

THE ENTRANCE

A group of features all showing signs of burning was found at the northern end of the excavations (Fig. 5.7), probably representing the remains of one or more structures associated with the entrance through the U-profiled ditch (460). The group consists of a pit (1016) and an area of burning to its east, which may have been associated with a row of postholes set within a foundation trench (987 – possibly continuing as 647) further west (Plate 5.7). These features probably all belonged to one side of a timber-lined passageway. However, since only one side of this structure was revealed, and even that was heavily disturbed by recent activity, the form of the structure remains uncertain. The ditch of a hornwork (1118) was also found, extending east from the end of the U-profiled ditch (460).

Pit 1016

Just over 2 m to the north of the end of the U-profiled ditch an oval pit (1016) was identified, measuring 1.60 m by 1.00 m wide and 0.66 m deep (Fig. 5.7, section 267). Pit 1016 lay within a larger feature (1024 – see Chapter 4), most of which had, however, been cut away either by pit 1016 or by recent foundation trenches. The fills of 1024 contained no charcoal or other evidence of burning. This feature may either have been a very large posthole within which 1016 was the post-pipe, or may have been feature relating to an earlier version of the gateway.

It is suggested that pit 1016 may originally have held a gatepost, marking the eastern end of the entrance structure, although a band of further burning (not investigated) extended between areas of modern disturbance 2 m further east. The pit was filled with two layers of dark brown silty clay containing large quantities of charcoal and burnt flint. Most of the charcoal seems to have been of oak and may derive from a post that had burnt *in situ*. The charcoal also included some *Alnus/Corylus*, which is less likely to have been directly related to the entrance structure, and may have been residual. A radiocarbon date on a fragment of this *Alnus/Corylus* charcoal gave a date which is slightly earlier than that suggested for the U-profiled ditch (790-520 cal BC (95.4%), 770-540 (68.2%); OxA-14296).

Pit 1016 also contained a substantial quantity of pottery (Table 5.2). Most of this was in flint-tempered (11 sherds, 92 g) and flint and sand-tempered fabrics (25 sherds, 251 g), but there was also 10 sherds (28 g) of sand-tempered pottery in its lowest fill. This pottery, as well as the large quantities of charcoal and burnt stone, suggest that the pit was contemporary with the U-profiled ditch, and was burnt at the same time as the rampart associated with that ditch. The pit also contained two flint chips and a few fragments of animal bone.

Plate 5.7 View of curving palisade trench 987 at the entrance, showing the burnt post-pipes and chalk in the top, looking west.

Chapter 5

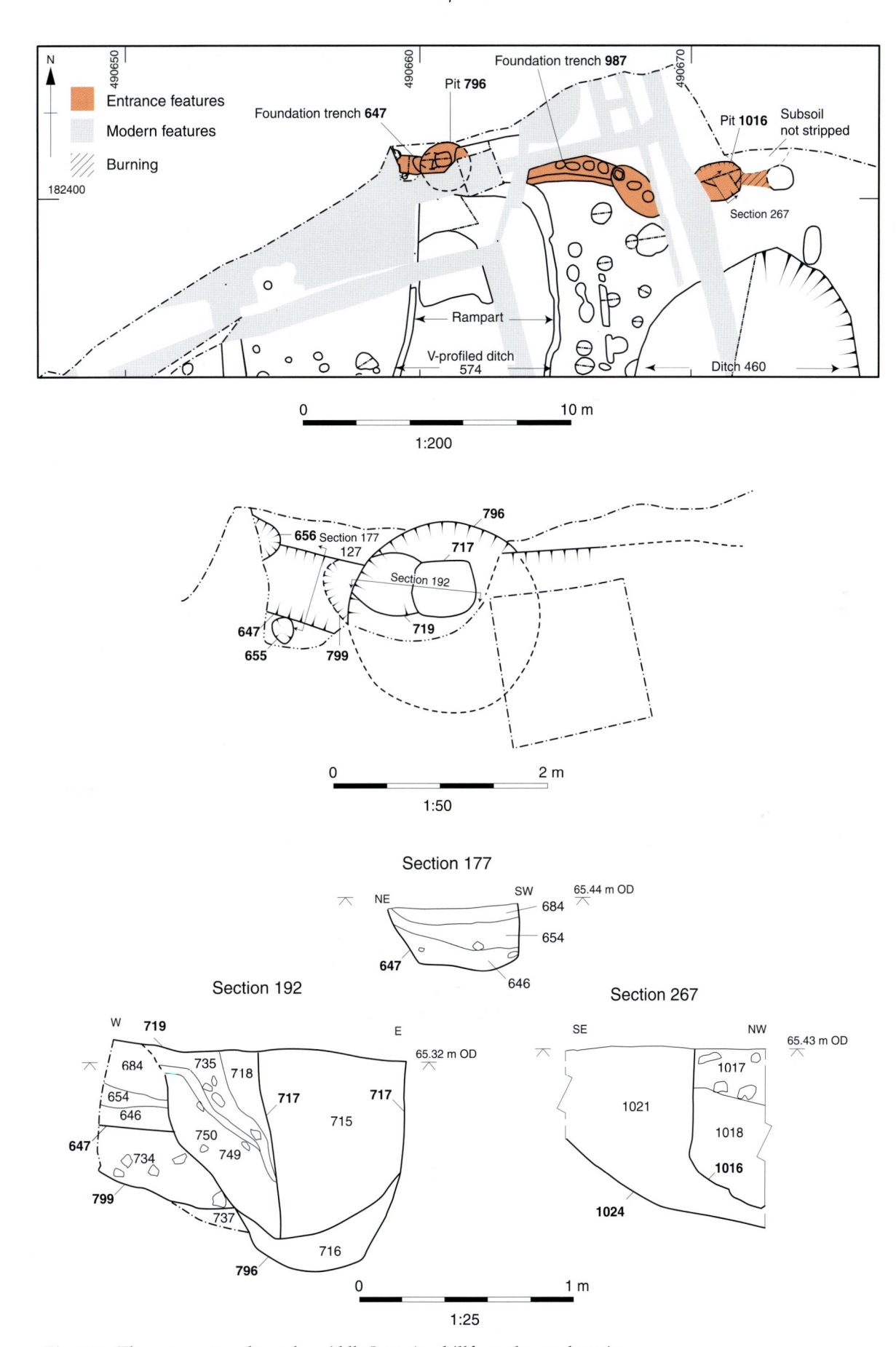

Fig. 5.7 The entrance to the early-middle Iron Age hillfort: plan and sections

Table 5.2. Summary of finds from features associated with the entrance to the early-middle Iron Age hillfort

Feature	Context	Pottery (no. of sherds/weight (g))	Flake	Chips and waste flakes	Burnt unworked flint	Charcoal	Other finds
Hornwork 1118	124		5				
Pit 1016	1018	Flint 10/46		2	30	Oak +	Cattle 2/14
		Flint and sand 5/34					Large mammal 1/20
		Sand and flint 15/142					Sheep goat 1/1
		Sand 10/28					Unid. 1/3
Pit 1016	1017	Flint 1/46					
		Flint and sand 3/39					
		Sand and flint 2/36					
Gully 647	654						Burnt mudstone pebble
Posthole 719	717	Flint and sand 1/10					Oak charcoal
		Sand and flint 3/228					

Posthole row and foundation trench 987

To the west of pit 1016 lay a curved alignment of seven close-set postholes set within a palisade trench (987), which ran for just under 5 m, roughly east-west, from the end of the V-profiled ditch (574) to near pit 1016. A possibly distinct gully seemed to run part of the way along the southern side of the palisade trench. None of these features was excavated, but the post-pipe fills of the palisade trench (generally indicating timbers 0.3 – 0.4 m across) contained charcoal, and a packing of burnt stone. Chalk fragments lay in the top of the trench, mainly around the post-pipes but in one case apparently overlying the post-pipe as well (see Plate 5.7).

Although the date of these features in relation to the ditches and palisades cannot be established on the basis of stratigraphy or artefacts, the evidence for burning suggests that they were contemporary with the U-profiled ditch, and that like pit 1016, the posts were burnt at the same time as the rampart associated with that ditch.

Gully 647 and associated features

To the west of trench 987 a sequence of further features, unfortunately badly disturbed, was found. The earliest feature (799; see detailed plan in Fig. 5.7) may have been a pit, most of which had been removed by later activity. It was filled with brownish sandy deposits. The upper of these was stained by charcoal, although this may have infiltrated from the fill of gully (647) above.

A length of around 1 m of this gully survived. It was 0.46 m wide, 0.25 m deep and was U-shaped in profile. It contained three layers of black or reddish brown sandy fills, all of which contained substantial proportions of burnt gravel and charcoal. It is the evidence for burning in these fills which suggests that this gully formed part of the early-middle Iron Age hillfort entrance. Very similar deposits were found in two nearby postholes (655 and 656: both 0.23 m wide and 0.24-0.28 m deep), one of which (656) was, however, cut by the gully. The other (655) cut an earlier, larger posthole (738) measuring 0.60 m wide by 0.60 m deep.

The gully (647) was in turn cut by a probably circular pit (796: 1.27 m wide and 0.98 m deep). The bottom of this pit was filled with greyish sandy clay fills; the top by brownish and yellowish sandy deposits, containing varying proportions of gravel – none of which appeared to have been burnt – and no charcoal.

Subsequently a large posthole (719), 1.12 m wide and 0.85 m deep, was cut into this pit. A large, square post-pipe (717), nearly 0.60 m wide, was preserved on the eastern side of this posthole. It was filled with a dark grey silty sand which contained a little oak charcoal. Some of the packing deposits on the western side of this posthole contained burnt gravel and flecks of charcoal. Between these deposits, however, occurred others which lacked evidence for burning, and it seems likely that the burned material was redeposited, perhaps deriving from gully 647 where it had been disturbed by the cutting of pit 796.

Besides the possible correlation of gully 647 with the burning of the early-middle Iron Age rampart, the chronology of all of these features is uncertain. The only finds were four large sherds in flint and sand-tempered fabrics found in the post-pipe (715) within posthole 719, which, on the basis of their stratigraphic relationship with gully 647, are probably residual (Table 5.2).

Apart from the chalk kerb, pit 796 and posthole 719 are the only features that could be interpreted as belonging to a restoration of the hillfort after the rampart had been burnt. The lack of dating evidence however means that it is impossible to know whether this activity occurred shortly after the rampart was burnt, or (possibly) in the Anglo-Saxon period nearly a millennium later.

The hornwork (1118)

The entrance was also provided with a probable hornwork (1118). All that remained of this was a ditch, 2.8 m wide and 0.78 m deep, with steep sides and a flat base, which was found at the edge of the main excavation and in an evaluation trench to the east (Fig. 5.1). From near the end of the U-profiled ditch (460), the ditch ran eastwards for 8 m where it curved to the north. It must have ended just a short distance further north since no traces of it were found in WA Trenches 6 or 7 to the north.

The hornwork ditch appeared to have been cut by the U-profiled ditch, and its fills were certainly overlain by the Anglo-Saxon and later fills in this ditch (Fig. 5.3, section 37). However, it is possible that this apparent stratigraphic relationship was created by erosion of the outer edge of the U-profiled ditch. The shallow depth of the hornwork may indicate that it was not added to the U-profiled ditch until silting of the ditch was well underway (ie after the burning of the rampart sometime in the middle to late Iron Age).

The hornwork ditch was filled with generally silty sand deposits of varied colours, none of which suggested burning and which contained very little charcoal. The only finds recovered from the ditch were five flint flakes.

The hornwork seems to have been a relatively slight structure. That no trace of an associated rampart survives in the more truncated northern part of the site is unsurprising, but given the size of the ditch (and assuming that this was proportional to the size of the rampart), a rampart, if one existed, is unlikely to have been very large. The rampart would presumably have lain on the inner side of the ditch, occupying the space between the hornwork ditch and the end of the U-profiled ditch, extending up to pit 1016 where the wooden entrance structure may have begun. It is reasonable to assume that a similar hornwork would have existed on the other side of the entrance. Although it appears that the hornwork was not a very substantial structure, it would, nonetheless, have had the effect of elongating the entrance, and of narrowing the approach to the gate itself, which presumably lay between the larger ramparts associated with the U-profiled ditch (460).

The entrance structure

Plainly the evidence is insufficient to provide a clear picture of the original form of the entrance. What there was, however, suggests that a timber-lined passageway extended outwards (eastwards) from the end of the rampart for around 5 m, ending close to the end of the U-profiled ditch. This passageway may have been continued by a relatively low bank (compared to the main rampart), that ran behind the hornwork ditch. This ditch probably curved round to the north at its end, narrowing the outermost entrance. The timber-lined passageway and hornwork would have extended the entrance for a distance of around 20 m from the rampart where, presumably, the main gate stood. Unfortunately the area at the end of the rampart was very badly disturbed, and it is, therefore, not surprising that no gate postholes were found at the end of the rampart. The large pit (1016) at the end of the U-profiled ditch might have held a further gatepost related to an outer gate, but it is also possible that the large post it could have held simply formed the end of the timber-lined passageway.

Presumably a walkway over the entrance would also have been positioned between the ramparts. However, it is also possible that such a walkway extended outwards, beyond the rampart where it could have been supported by the posts forming the timber-lined passageway. This might provide another explanation for the position of the large pit (1016) near the end of the U-profiled ditch.

THE OUTER DITCH (3050)

The remains of an outer ditch (3050) were found to the north-east of the main excavation area in Trench 1 of the Phase 2 excavations in 2005 (Fig. 1.4; Plate 5.8), as well as in WA Trench 5 nearby (which unfortunately ran along the length of the ditch), and to the east in the watching brief. This ditch was not bottomed in either the evaluation trench or the watching brief. The most complete section (which was stepped) was obtained in Trench 1, but even there the eastern edge of the ditch lay just beyond the edge of the excavation (Fig. 5.8).

The ditch had a broad, V-shaped profile; the lower slope on the west (inner) side was around 37°; that on the east (outer) side c 32°. The slope became shallower towards the top, probably as a result of erosion, suggesting that the original ditch would probably have been slightly narrower than it measured in section. When excavated it was over 12 m wide and was 3.35 m deep. Its original width, assuming the sides of the ditch were straight, would have been closer to 10 m. The gravelly lowest fill (3051) probably derived from natural erosion of the sides of the ditch. It contained a single sand and flint-tempered sherd. Above this lay deposits of orange-brown sandy silts that contained a further sand and flint-tempered sherd, and worked flint. Like the U-profiled ditch, the fills above these deposits contained Anglo-Saxon finds (Table 5.3). No evidence of burning was found in this ditch.

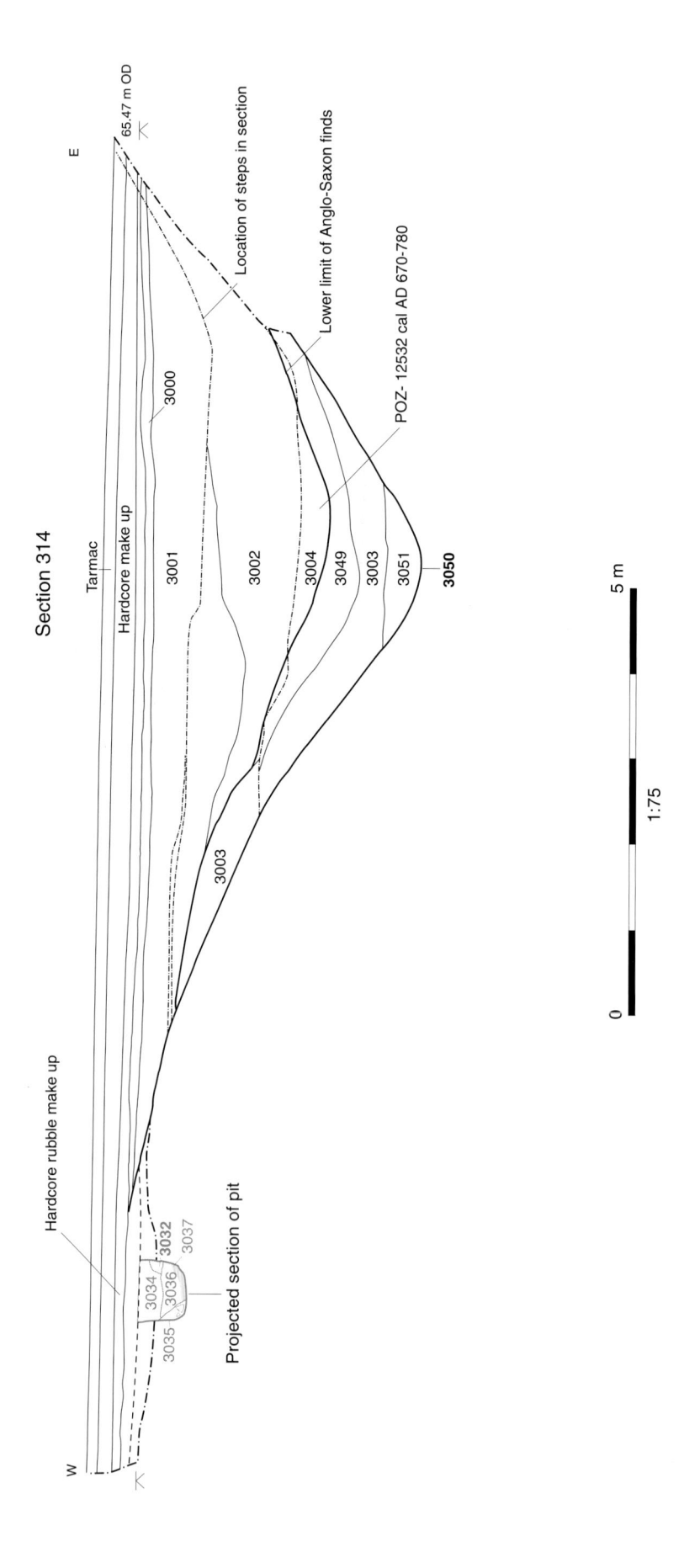

Fig. 5.8   *The outer ditch (3050): section 314*

Plate 5.8 The outer ditch (3050) in 2005 evaluation Trench 1

Table 5.3: Summary of finds in the outer ditch (3050). The double line marks the boundary between prehistoric and Anglo-Saxon deposits

Context	Prehistoric pot	Roman 1st-2nd C AD	Early-Middle Saxon pot	OXAC 11th C pot	Flint	Pig	Sheep/goat	CPR	Charcoal	Other finds
3001					3					
3002			1/14	1/18	12					
3004		1/6	5/115			1	1	Wheat grain +++ Rye grain + Barley grain ++++ Oat grain +++ Cereal grain indet. ++++ Rye rachis + Hazel nut shell ++ Weeds ++	Beech ++++ Oak +++	Import late Roman sherd 1/38 Rotary quern fragment, Millstone Grit
3049	1/7				13					
3003					5					
3051	1/19				9					

Fig. 5.9 Schematic reconstruction of the Iron Age multivallate defences

The area to the west of the ditch had been truncated by the construction of a car park. This would have removed any traces of a rampart that might have survived. With the exception of the uppermost fill (3001), the upper fills of the outer ditch (3004 and 3002), which contained Anglo-Saxon finds, appeared to have been deposited from the eastern, outer side. The fill (3003) above the primary fill (3051) and below the Anglo-Saxon levels, however, was deeper on the west and extended further up the western side of the ditch. While this material might therefore have originated in a bank on that side, the uneven silting may simply result from greater erosion from the steeper slope on the western side of the ditch. The uppermost fill (3001) contained a high proportion of gravel, and probably represents the final slighting of any surviving rampart to level the ditch.

Although it seems likely that this ditch belonged to the early-middle Iron Age phase of activity, its date is uncertain. As a consequence, it is impossible to determine how the outer ditch related to the U-profiled ditch (460). On the slender grounds of the absence of evidence for burning, it has been suggested that the outer ditch may not have been strictly contemporary with the U-profiled ditch (460), and might have been constructed to replace the U-profiled ditch when its rampart was destroyed. However, whether intended as a replacement, or as a deliberate decision to make the defences multivallate, the effect was to create a multivallate fort (Fig. 5.9), as the presence of Anglo-Saxon finds at depth in both ditches 460 and 3050 shows that both ditches remained open as substantial features until, and beyond, the end of the Iron Age.

Evidence for activity within the early-middle Iron Age hillfort

Very little clear evidence was found within the excavated area of the hillfort for early-middle Iron Age activity potentially contemporary with the U-profiled or outer ditches (460 and 3050). Two sherds of middle Iron Age pottery from posthole 208 in posthole circle 1117, and seven sherds in posthole 940 just outside on the south, provide some evidence that this structure may date from this period (see Chapter 4 *Posthole group and possible roundhouse 1117*). Otherwise, no internal features

Table 5.4: Summary of sand-tempered pottery within the hillfort

Group	Cut/feature	Context	No. of sherds	Weight (g)
Tree-throw hole 1003	1003	1004	1	8
Palisade trench 1106	569	571	1	3
Posthole row 1107	506	507	1	1
Roundhouse 1117	940	941	7	35
Occupation layer				
1123	104	217	1	14
1123	104	104	2	24
1123	104	104	1	9
1123	888	888	1	10
1123	991	991	2	15
Total			17	119

can be dated to this period nor does any of the radiocarbon-dated material derive from the early-middle Iron Age. The best evidence of early-middle Iron Age activity is pottery, and especially that in sand-tempered fabrics. Such fabrics also occur in the standstill layer (1102) and thus appear to have been in use from the late Bronze Age-early Iron Age. Their distribution may, therefore, reflect activity over a very long period from the end of the late Bronze Age, and not just activity in the early-middle Iron Age. Even so, very little of this pottery was found; single sherds associated with tree-throw hole 1003, palisade trench 1106 and posthole row 1107 (Table 5.4). A further 48 sherds (292 g) were found in the modern subsoil, and seven sherds (72 g) in the occupation layer (1123) within the hillfort.

Within the excavated area there was thus only limited activity inside the early-middle Iron Age hillfort. The area of the interior of the hillfort exposed in the excavation was, however, only a maximum of 720 sq. m, and if the defence works are taken into account, could have been as little as 350 sq. m. This is likely to represent a very small proportion of the whole hillfort interior, so the apparent level of activity may not be representative of the actual level overall (see also Chapter 11 *Extent of the hillfort*).

Chapter 6 – Late Iron Age and Roman activity and Anglo-Saxon occupation

EVIDENCE FOR LATE IRON AGE AND ROMAN ACTIVITY

Three sherds of Roman pottery, found in the upper fills of the U-profiled and outer ditches (460 and 3050), provide the only evidence for activity in the period between the middle Iron Age hillfort and the earliest Anglo-Saxon activity. These few sherds were mixed with Anglo-Saxon finds, and it is possible that they were collected by the Anglo-Saxon occupants. One of the sherds from the U-profiled ditch (460, layer 215) was a base that may have been deliberately trimmed and smoothed into a disc (see Biddulph, Chapter 7).

While this evidence suggests that the area had been abandoned, a much larger quantity of poorly preserved and hence possibly redeposited Roman pottery (404 sherds, 2104 g) was found in the TCAST trenches down the slope to the south of the main excavations. These sherds suggest activity predominantly in the 1st and 2nd centuries AD, but continuing also in the 3rd and 4th centuries, and clearly indicate the presence of a Roman settlement somewhere nearby. Roman pottery was also found on the cricket ground to the east of Taplow Court. While the pottery alone cannot provide much insight into the nature of this activity, it does suggest that settlement continued in the area for a much longer period that is evident in the main area of the excavation.

THE ANGLO-SAXON EVIDENCE

Anglo-Saxon activity (Fig. 6.1) includes a poorly preserved inhumation (105) dating from the late 6th-7th century AD (Plate 6.1) and finds dating from c 650-980 AD, recovered from the upper fills of the U-profiled and outer ditches (460 and 3050). These finds include a sherd that possibly formed part of a late Roman vessel imported from the eastern Mediterranean. It is also possible that foundation trench 846 belonged to an Anglo-Saxon building (see Fig. 6.1 and Plate 6.2) .

The evidence suggests that there may have been a hiatus of as much as 200 years between the use of the hillfort in the Roman period and the resumption of activity in the Anglo-Saxon period. Although the finds provide only a shadowy image of Anglo-Saxon activity within the former hillfort, their proximity to the Taplow Mound lends them a special interest.

Inhumation 105 and other human remains

The partial remains of the skeleton (107) of an adult male (Fig. 6.2; Plate 6.1) were found in a subrectangular grave cut (105) just to the north of the end of the U-profiled ditch (460). The grave had a flat base and near-vertical sides. Its northern end had been removed by a machine cut, and all of the grave was severely truncated. The surviving part was 1.50 m long and 0.50 m wide, and survived to a depth of only 0.06 m. Not surprisingly, the bones were fragmented and poorly preserved, but sufficient of the left arm, the vertebrae, the hips and the right and left legs survived to show that the inhumation had been extended and supine. The head, which had been cut away by the machine, would have lain to the north. A radiocarbon determination (SUERC-4963: 1390±40 BP) on the left femur gave a result of cal AD 590-680. A highly corroded iron whittle tang knife in several pieces (SF12), which lay beside the left hip, is consistent with this date, and was the only associated artefact.

Further human remains, consisting of two fragments from an adult left humerus, were found in one of the Anglo-Saxon upper fills of the U-profiled ditch (460, context 214, cut 376, see Fig. 5.3, section 37). These two fragments were associated with large quantities of Anglo-Saxon finds and do not seem to have been deposited with any care. A copper alloy double spiral-headed pin (SF1171; Plate 7.3) was found in another context within the same ditch (context 579, cut 713, see Fig. 5.2, section 219). Such pins are often associated with Anglo-Saxon burials. It is therefore possible that both the pin and the femur reflect the disturbance of another Anglo-Saxon burial or burials, though given the contexts of the finds, such disturbance would have to have occurred in the Anglo-Saxon period. Stray human bone is occasionally found in Anglo-Saxon settlements in non-funerary contexts such as *Grubenhäuser* (Tipper 2004, 152-3). Alternatively the pin could derive from a domestic context, and the bones may be residual, and not Anglo-Saxon.

The condition of the hillfort in the Anglo-Saxon period

Quite large assemblages of Anglo-Saxon finds were recovered from the upper fills of the U-profiled and outer ditches (460 and 3050). While these finds suggest that the ditches became almost completely

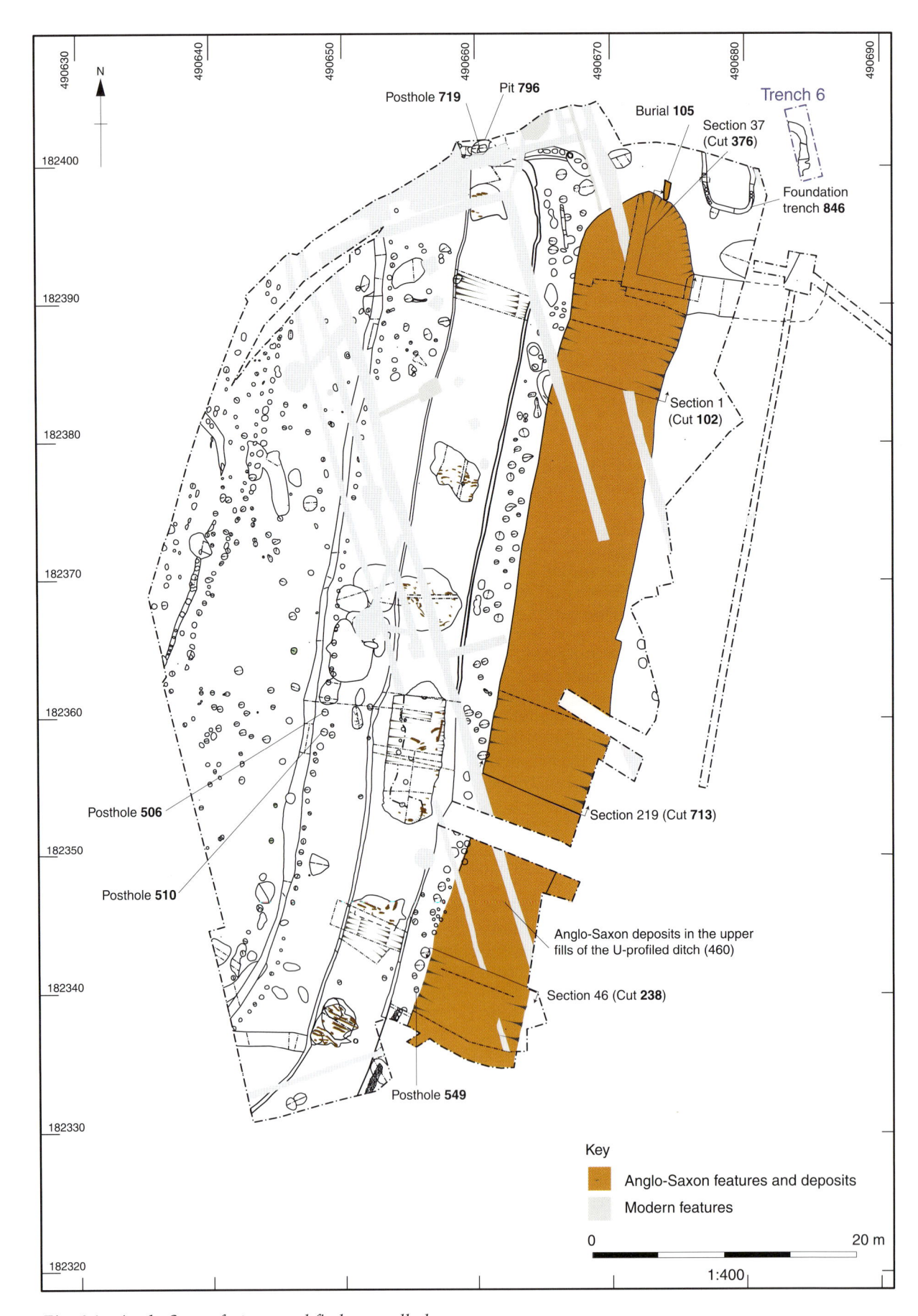

Fig. 6.1 Anglo-Saxon features and finds: overall plan

Chapter 6

Plate 6.1 Anglo-Saxon inhumation 107, in grave 105

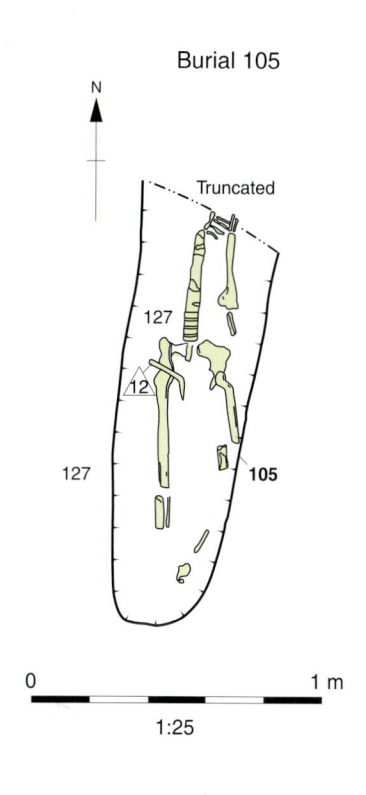

Fig. 6.2 Inhumation 105: plan

filled over the course of the Anglo-Saxon occupation, they also show that they must have survived as appreciable features well into the Anglo-Saxon period, probably over 2 m deep in the case of the outer ditch and at least 1.65 m in the case of the U-profiled ditch. The extent to which the ramparts survived is less clear. However, since the upper fills of the U-profiled ditch (which contained Anglo-Saxon finds) contained large quantities of fire-reddened gravel probably derived from the rampart, it seems likely that at the beginning of the Anglo-Saxon occupation at least the inner rampart still existed as an appreciable feature. Overall, it seems likely that the hillfort ditches, and perhaps also the ramparts, would still have formed notable earthworks.

Radiocarbon dates indicating activity in the Anglo-Saxon period were obtained from both the U-profiled ditch (460) and the outer ditch 3500. A radiocarbon date of cal AD 550-650 (OxA-14432: 1451±30 BP) was obtained on horse bone from layer 711, and another of cal AD 770-970 (SUERC-4971: 1165±35 BP) on a charred *secale cereale* grain from layer 579. They are earlier than the 11th-century date suggested for the small sherd of Cotswolds-type ware near the top of the ditch, which provides a *terminus post quem* for the final filling of the ditch. A wheat grain from deposit 3004 in the outer ditch (3050) gave a radiocarbon date of cal AD 670-870 (Poz-12532: 1255±30 BP).

In addition, *Maloideae* and *Alnus/Corylus* charcoal was dated in two postholes in posthole row 1107 (510 and 506: OxA-14297, 1258±24: cal AD 670-810 and SUERC-5150, 1305±35: cal AD 650-780) within the interior, and from another in posthole row 1104 (549: OxA-14293, 1224±24: cal AD 690-890). However, stratigraphy shows that the postholes in row 1107 and some of those in row 1104, cannot have been Anglo-Saxon. While it is possible that some of the postholes in row 1104 might be Anglo-Saxon in date, it seems more likely that these posthole rows belonged to earlier periods. The only other potential indications of renovations to the hillfort defences were pit 796 and posthole 719, both of which cut features that related to the burning of the entrance of the early-middle Iron Age hillfort (Plate 6.2). There is however no other evidence for the date of these

Plate 6.2 Burning in posthole 717/719 at the entrance to the Iron Age hillfort

features, which could have been Iron Age. Overall, given the quantities of Anglo-Saxon debris in the hillfort ditches, the quantity of evidence which might indicate an attempt to renovate the defences is very slight, although it is possible that fences were planted in the tops of the surviving ramparts, which would have left no archaeological trace except at the entrance.

Aside from the inhumation, only the debris of domestic Anglo-Saxon occupation was found. There were no traces of sunken-featured or timber buildings (foundation trench 846 being the only possible exception). It nonetheless seems likely that the location of Anglo-Saxon activity would have been influenced by the location of the surviving Iron Age defences. It is possible, for example, that a focus of Anglo-Saxon activity lay between the U-profiled and outer ditches (460 and 3050), even though only two undated postholes and a tree-throw hole with environmental evidence consistent with the Anglo-Saxon period were found in the limited excavations in this area. Otherwise, it is difficult to account for the occurrence of debris in both ditches, unless the debris had been carried some way from the main focus of the settlement.

Anglo-Saxon finds in the top of the U-profiled and outer ditches (460 and 3050), including the possibly east Mediterranean sherd

Alongside small quantities of residual flint, the ditches contained quite large quantities of animal bone, pottery and fragments of lava probably derived from rotary querns. The fills of the U-profiled ditch (460) included pottery from about half-way up (contexts 711 in section 219; and 299 in section 46 (see Fig. 5.2), and contexts 214 in section 37; 112 and 101 in section 1 (see Fig. 5.3). Near the top of layer 110 (section 1), a single small sherd (3 g) of Cotswolds-type ware (Oxford fabric OXAC; Mellor 1994) was found, probably dating to the 11th century. The pottery assemblage included a few, possibly deliberately collected Roman sherds, one of which may have been trimmed into a disc, as well as a sherd in layer 3004 in the outer ditch 3050 that possibly came from a late Roman vessel imported from the eastern Mediterranean (see Tomber below, Chap. 7, and Plate 7.1). Other finds include a single fired clay annular loomweight and fragments of three iron knives. Further fragments of fired clay, some from a hearth or oven, and a large fragment of slag that may have been part of a smithing hearth bottom, were found in the U-profiled ditch (460).

The animal bone included cattle, horse, pig, sheep/goat, dog, domestic fowl and red and roe deer, and seems to have been more evenly distributed in the ditches than the pottery, although there was little bone in the outer ditch (3050).

Assemblages of charred plant remains consisting largely of wheat, rye, barley and oat grain but including also some chaff of the same species and weed seeds were found in both ditches. They came from the uppermost fill (579) of the U-profiled ditch (Table 5.1a) and the lowest Anglo-Saxon fill (3004) of the outer ditch (3050) (Table 5.1d). Charcoal from a variety of species was found in the same contexts.

While in general the composition of the assemblage is typical of Anglo-Saxon settlements, the relatively large quantities of deer bone may be an indication of high status. Together with the imported, late Roman sherd and the double spiral-headed copper pin which was found in layer 579 in section 219 across the U-profiled ditch (460; Fig. 5.2), the indications of high status activity are strong.

Insofar as the limited extent of excavation allows us to see, the pottery seems to have been distributed unevenly along the ditches (see Tables 5.1a-d), and, although no joining sherds were found in different parts of the ditches, the mean sherd weights (1.0 g to 12.4 g, except one context with a mean sherd weight of 23.7 g) are comparable to those associated with sunken-featured buildings (Tipper 2004, table 5.2), many of which contain redeposited material. The size and preservation of the Anglo-Saxon assemblages at Taplow is variable, and it is possible that some of this material had been redeposited. Some assemblages such as that from context 579 combined rich charred plant remains with large potsherds; others contained well-preserved animal bones with pottery and other finds (eg cxt 607); these are unlikely to be the result of redeposition. A small sherd of Cotswold-type ware (3 g) which was most common in the 11th century (although it does occur as early as the late 9th century) was found near to the base of the Anglo-Saxon deposits (layer 110) in section 1 across the U-profiled ditch (context 460; Fig. 5.2), but here the only significant finds from above this were fragments of lava quern, which could have been redeposited. In the outer ditch, a larger sherd of the same type (18 g) was found in a deep deposit (3002) that may have accumulated over some time above the main deposit containing Anglo-Saxon finds (layer 3004). Given the disturbance the site has suffered – including a copper pipe pushed vertically into the fills of the U-profiled ditch (down to layer 109) to form an electrical earth – it is possible that the small sherd in layer 110 was intrusive.

Other Anglo-Saxon finds: tree-throw hole 3030 and the TCAST trenches

Evidence for Anglo-Saxon activity from other parts of the site was very limited. A tree-throw hole (3030), measuring 0.80 m wide and 0.35 m deep, located in Trench 3 of the Phase 2 excavations (see Fig. 1.4) contained an assemblage of charred cereals and other plants, the varieties of which are suggestive of an Anglo-Saxon date. However, aside from charcoal, the tree-throw hole contained no other finds, and it must be possible that the charred plant remains were redeposited.

Anglo-Saxon pottery, generally similar to that found in the U-profiled and outer ditches (460 and 3050) was also found in the TCAST trenches. Notable within the assemblage was a decorated sherd that is likely to be among the earliest Anglo-Saxon pottery on the site, dating from the 5th to the 6th centuries (Fig. 7.8.3).

Foundation trench 846

A shallow foundation trench (846), measuring 0.31 m – 0.38 m wide and surviving to between 0.19 m and 0.33 m deep, was found in the north-eastern corner of the main excavation (Fig. 6.3; Plate 6.3). It formed a U-shape in plan, around 3.5 m wide and extending about the same distance from the edge of the excavation. Within this trench close-set circular postpipes, marked by dark brown sandy marks set within orange brown sandy silt packing, were found once the top was trowelled down. Part of a further, rather irregular, curving gully, varying from 0.45 m to 0.65 m wide and from 0.20 m – 0.25 m deep was found in Wessex Archaeology Trench 6, about 3 m to the east of foundation trench 846. Excavation in this feature did not reveal any post-pipes, so although similar in dimensions to 846, it may not have been associated.

Neither feature is dated, foundation trench 846 containing only a few pieces of flint and some charred plant remains (Table 6.1). Although a few of the post-pipes contained occasional flecks of charcoal, others did not, so the structure with which

Table 6.1. Summary of finds in foundation trench 846

Pit	Layer	Flake	Burnt unworked flint	Charred plant remains
846	872			Barley + Cereal indet. + Hazel nut shell + Grass +
846	850	4	1	

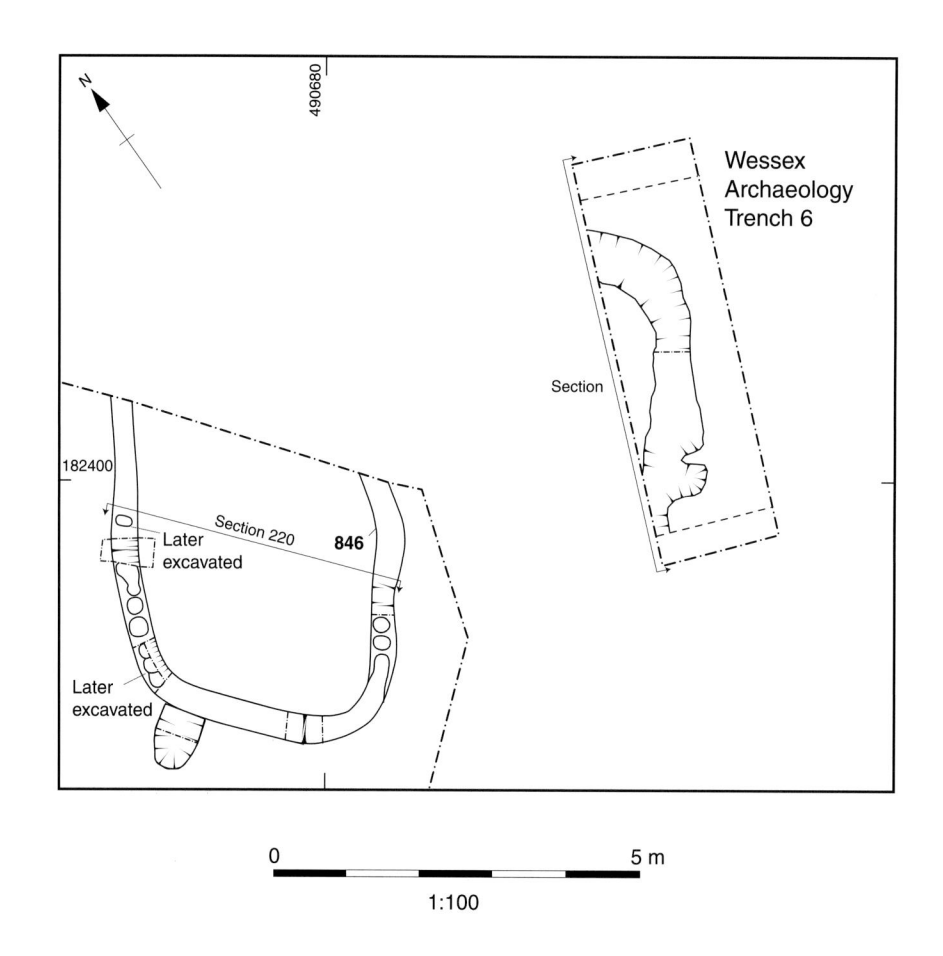

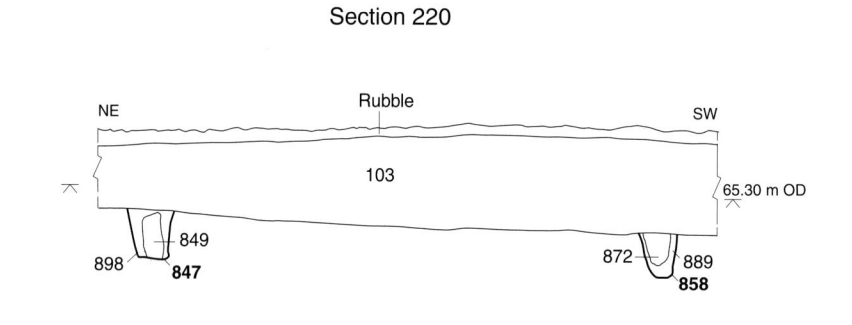

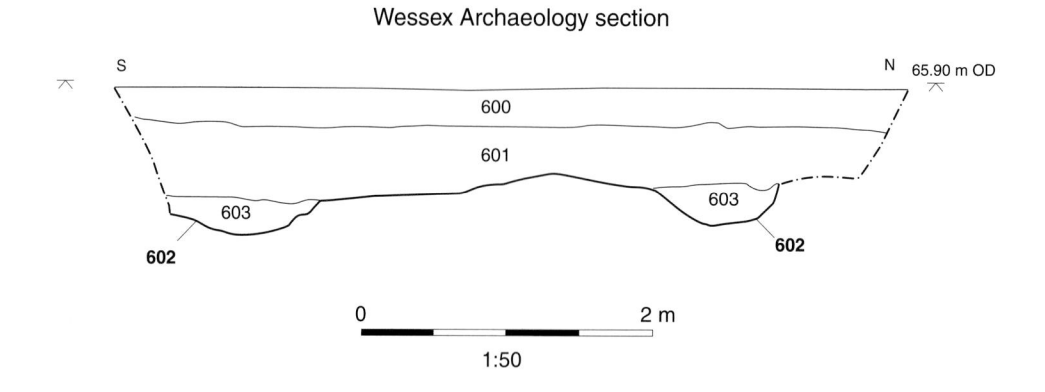

Fig. 6.3 Detailed plan and sections of post-in-trench structure 846 and Wessex Archaeology Trench 6

the foundation trench was associated does not seem to have burnt down.

Its function is as uncertain as its date. The post-in-trench construction was similar to that found in the late Bronze Age posthole rows. It might have been the end of a double palisade, but no corresponding features were found to the south or in evaluation trenches to the north. Another possibility, that it might have been a structure associated with the entrance to the early-middle Iron Age hillfort – perhaps a guardhouse tucked behind the hornwork (see below) – can perhaps be excluded on the grounds that the rest of the entrance to the hillfort seems to have been burnt. A third possibility is that it formed the foundation of an Anglo-Saxon or later structure. Post-in-trench construction is a characteristic of the middle and late Anglo-Saxon periods, and an Anglo-Saxon burial and occupation evidence were recovered from the adjacent ditch (460). However, the structure is both irregular (trapezoidal rather than rectangular) and narrow (c 4 m) for an Anglo-Saxon building. Given its position across part of the entrance to the hillfort, an Anglo-Saxon or even a medieval date, when the ditches had finally been filled in, is perhaps most likely, but ultimately this structure cannot be related with any confidence to any of the phases of activity at Taplow Court.

Plate 6.3   Foundation trench 846

Chapter 7 – Artefacts

FLINT

by Kate Cramp and Hugo Lamdin-Whymark

A total of 2610 struck flints and 252 pieces (5.9 kg) of burnt unworked flint were recovered during the main excavation at Taplow Court (Table 7.1). The flintwork ranges in date from the Mesolithic to the late Bronze Age and comes from a range of features, including pits, tree-throw holes, postholes and ditches. An illustrated selection of flint is shown in Figure 7.1 with an accompanying catalogue (Table 7.2).

Mesolithic activity is represented by a scatter of residual finds, including one *tranchet* axe (Fig. 7.1.1), two microliths (one illustrated, Fig. 7.1.2) and three microburins (not illustrated). The small collections of flintwork from tree-throw holes 814 and 914, located on the western edge of the excavated area, might also belong to this period, but cannot be clearly distinguished from the larger assemblages of flintwork from tree-throw holes 497 and 816, which are technologically earlier Neolithic in appearance and, given their fresh condition, probably came from *in situ* deposits.

To the south-east of these features, a group of intercutting hollows (Group 1119) produced a substantial assemblage of 867 struck flints. With the exception of the assemblage from pit 578, these flints are probably contemporary with the sherds of Collared Urn recovered from the same deposits. Tree-throw hole 899, *c* 25 m to the north-east of the intercutting hollows, produced a technologically similar assemblage that may also be of early Bronze Age date.

Methodology

The artefacts were catalogued according to broad debitage, tool or core type. The terminology for retouched forms follows standard morphological descriptions, for example Bamford (1985, 73-7), Healy (1988, 48-9) and Saville (1981, 7-11). Chips were defined as pieces whose broadest surface was less than 10 mm^2, including small flakes or fragments of flakes (Newcomer and Karlin 1987, 33). In order to avoid any sampling bias, a distinction was made between chips that were excavated by hand and those that were recovered by sieving.

Burnt unworked flint was selectively retained and includes bulk samples of reddened material from the burnt rampart gravels (1100) that were collected by M G Canti for comparison with experimentally burnt sediment (see Canti, Chapter 8). The remaining burnt unworked flint from the rampart gravels was discarded once quantified by piece and by weight.

Following a brief assessment of all of the flint, the assemblages from tree-throw holes 814, 914, 497 and 816 and pit 578 were analysed in more detail. Attributes recorded included butt type (after Tixier *et al.* 1980, fig. 47), extent of dorsal cortex, termination type (Cotterell and Kamminga 1987) and hammer mode (Onhuma and Bergman 1982). The classification of flake type used Harding (1990) with slight modification. The presence or absence of platform edge abrasion and dorsal blade scars was also recorded. Metrical analysis was carried out on all complete pieces within a sample, and involved recording the length, breadth and thickness to the nearest millimetre, using standard methods (Saville 1980).

The assemblages from tree-throw holes 497 and 816 and pit 578 were also subjected to refitting analysis. The refitting exercise involved laying out the flintwork from each feature and grouping the material according to visual similarities in colour and composition. Attempts to find knapping refits and conjoins were made both within and, in some cases, between assemblages.

Condition

The assemblage was in highly variable condition. Flintwork recovered from negative archaeological features, such as pits and tree-throw holes, was generally very fresh and unabraded. Material from layers, particularly topsoil and subsoil deposits, usually displayed considerable post-depositional damage suggesting that these deposits had been extensively reworked. While the majority of flints were uncorticated, an incipient white or bluish-white cortication was present on a small number of pieces.

Raw materials

Raw material supplies were abundantly provided by the deposits on which the site is situated. The local nodules are of variable size, ranging in colour from light greys to dark browns. Thermal flaws and cherty inclusions are common and may have affected the flaking quality of the nodules. In general, the flint type associated with the Mesolithic and Neolithic flintwork is of a consistently higher quality than that found in the later assemblages. In particular, preference was shown for nodules with a thin, beige-coloured cortex in the earlier periods; far less

Table 7.1 Summary of flint by type

	Wessex evaluation	Watching brief	Excavation (phase 1)	Excavation (phase 2)	Total
Flake	90	311	1288	37	1726
Blade	16	50	129	3	198
Bladelet	3	5	25		33
Bladelike flake	8	15	55	5	83
Rejuvenation flake tablet		2	8		10
Core face/edge rejuvenation flake		2	8		10
Other rejuvenation flake	2		4	2	8
Levallois flake	1				1
Microburin			3		3
Chip	7	4	32	1	44
Sieved chips 4-2mm	25				25
Sieved chips 10-4mm	5				5
Irregular waste	3	55	163	3	224
Single platform flake core		10	25	2	37
Multi-platform flake core	6	8	25	2	41
Single platform blade core	1	5	8		14
Opposed platform blade core	1		1		2
Other blade core			1		1
Core on a flake	3	2	11	1	17
Unclassifiable core		5	6		11
Partially worked nodule	1	14	30	3	48
Retouched flake		1	15	1	17
End scraper		1	11		12
Side scraper	1		1		2
End-and-side scraper		1	6	1	8
Other scraper			2		2
Notch	1		3		4
Denticulate		2	2		4
Microlith			2		2
Awl			1		1
Spurred piece			1	1	2
Truncated blade		1			1
Axe			2		2
Hammerstone		2	8		10
Other heavy implement		1	1		2
Total	174	497	1877	62	2610
No. of burnt unworked flints	2	6	243	1	252
Weight (g) of burnt unworked flints	613	216	5053	39	5921

Table 7.2 Catalogue of flint illustrated in Figure 7.1

Fig.	Area	Small find number	Category	Feature	Cut	Deposit
1.1	Excavation	1172	Tranchet axe	Upper subsoil (Group 1122)	-	103
1.2	Excavation		Microlith	Fill of palisade trench (Group 1106)	597	626
1.3	Watching brief	5048	Truncated blade	Early Neolithic (?) tree-throw hole	813	814
1.4	Watching brief	5100	Single platform blade core	Early Neolithic tree-throw hole	816	817
1.5	Excavation	478	End-and-side scraper	Early Bronze Age pit (Group 1119)	642	552
1.6	Excavation	904	Awl	Early Bronze Age pit (Group 1119)	700	555
1.7	Excavation	68	Axe	Early Bronze Age pit (Group 1119)	578	550
1.8	Excavation	372	Rejuvenation flake tablet	Early Bronze Age pit (Group 1119)	578	550

selection seems to have occurred in the Bronze Age.

The use of Bullhead flint is represented by two flakes from earlier Neolithic tree-throw hole 816 and one flake and one partially-worked nodule from early Bronze Age hollow 642. Two additional pieces, including a second partially-worked nodule, came from unstratified or modern deposits. Bullhead flint is characterised by a dark green cortex overlying an orange or buff-coloured band. It occurs in the Bullhead Bed in the south-east of the country (Rayner 1981, 357; Shepherd 1972, 114), which outcrops some 1.5 km from the site, but has also been identified in the Kennet gravels (Healy *et al.* 1992) and around Eton and Maidenhead (T Durden pers. comm.). Nodules of Bullhead flint, therefore, need not have travelled particularly far to reach the site, and in view of this it is perhaps unsurprising that nodules were being introduced to the site in an unprepared state.

The assemblage

There follows a broadly chronological discussion of the flint assemblage, with detailed reference to the Mesolithic assemblage, the Neolithic tree-throw holes and the group of early Bronze Age pits.

Mesolithic

The Mesolithic assemblage takes the form of a residual spread across the site. Diagnostic pieces include a complete *tranchet* axe from the subsoil (Fig. 7.1.1) and a second possible flaked axe fragment from layer 964. Two microliths were recovered, one of which corresponds to Jacobi's class 1a (Fig. 7.1.2) while the other (not illustrated) compares most closely with class 4 (Jacobi 1978, 16, fig. 6). Three microburins, the by-products of microlith manufacture using the microburin technique (Inizan *et al.* 1992, 69, fig. 24), can also be dated to the Mesolithic period. Two of these are distal microburins; the third is a proximal example.

Although less chronologically distinctive, some of the blades in the assemblage are also likely to be of Mesolithic date. These pieces are usually narrow in form, with dorsal blade scars and abraded platform edges; several exceed 90 mm in length.

Some of the blade cores, including the opposed platform example from the palisade trench 1106 (cut 564, deposit 562), probably belong to same industry.

Dating the Mesolithic assemblage is problematic, given that most of the flints occur as redeposited finds in mixed contexts. Both microliths are broad-blade forms which, when dominant in a collection, usually indicate a date in the early Mesolithic (Jacobi 1978); it may be significant that a charred hazelnut shell from posthole row 1104 was radio-carbon dated to the 9th millennium BC (8560-8290 cal BC (SUERC-4969: 9220±40 BP). A late Mesolithic date for some or all of the assemblage, however, cannot confidently be ruled out.

A small number of blades and associated debitage from tree-throw holes 814 and 914 were originally thought to be Mesolithic assemblages. This, however, has not been confirmed by the results of the technological and metrical analysis, which reveal an industry indistinguishable from that represented by the early Neolithic flintwork. In the absence of any independent evidence linking them to Mesolithic activity in the area, these small assemblages are discussed alongside the other early Neolithic tree-throw hole collections (see below).

Neolithic

Alongside the flint from three-throw holes 814 and 914, assemblages of Neolithic flintwork were recovered from tree-throw holes 497 and 816 (Table 7.3). It is probable that other residual Neolithic flints were recovered from elsewhere on site, although no diagnostic types have been recorded.

Tree-throw hole 497

The single fill of tree-throw hole 497 contained 74 fresh, uncorticated flints (Table 7.3). The assemblage is dominated by flakes (41 pieces), although blades, bladelets and bladelike flakes are also present in small quantities and provide 20% of the debitage (excluding chips). This figure falls within the expected range for an early Neolithic industry (Ford 1987a), although the results of the metrical analysis seem to show that the flints are slightly less blade-like than those from tree-throw hole 816 (Figs 7.2 A and C). This may be of chronological significance,

---

Comments

Flaked axe. Butt end lightly burnt and consequently broken. Tranchet-style removal across blade end. Probably Mesolithic.
Class 1a (Jacobi 1978, 16, fig. 6).
Small, plunging blade with oblique retouch truncating distal end.
Simple platform with abraded edge. 54 g
Thick, angular, secondary flake. Probably hard-hammer struck. Abrupt retouch (c 80degs) to distal end and minimal, semi-abrupt retouch to right-hand side. A couple of large flake removals taken inversely.
Awl manufactured on flake, abruptly retouched across bulb and along distal left-hand side to form convergent point.
Flaked axe. Slightly twisted profile.
Thick tablet. Large sand-gloss spot on ventral surface.

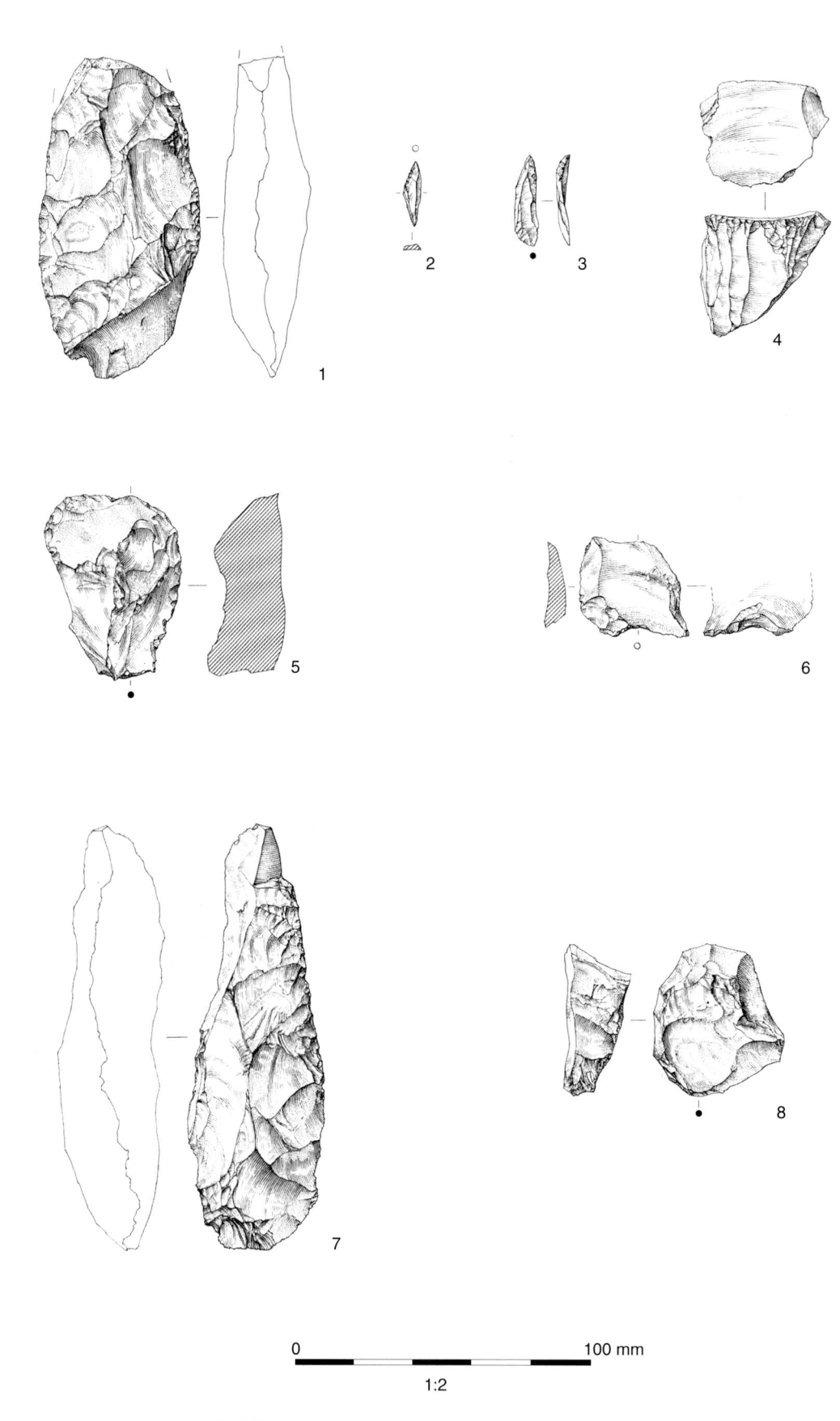

From Bronze Age enclosure to Anglo-Saxon settlement

Fig. 7.1 *Selected worked flint*

perhaps indicating a later date for the material from this tree-throw hole.

The assemblage contains seven cores, including one example made on a flake. These range in weight from 22 g to 61 g and were utilised for the production of both flakes and blades. Most exhibit platform edge abrasion. A single partially worked nodule was also recovered, along with several chips and pieces of irregular waste that reflect the deposition of some knapping waste.

The refitting analysis identified a knapping refit between a flake and a core. No further refits were found, despite the presence of visually similar material with a distinctive beige cortex. This suggests that, while the assemblage clearly contains a significant knapping component, much of the debitage has been removed.

The assemblage contains seven retouched pieces, including two end scrapers (one of which was deliberately broken), one spurred flake and two retouched blades. Both retouched blades are in a slightly damaged condition and are probably residual Mesolithic artefacts. One of the blades is 72 mm long and has been minimally retouched along one edge. Some rounded use-wear was noted in association with a distal spur. Use-wear was also occasionally noted on unretouched flints within the assemblage.

Tree-throw hole 813

Tree-throw hole 813 contained 13 struck flints in fresh, uncorticated condition (Table 7.3). The collection includes four blades, two of which are exceptionally long and narrow (Fig. 7.2.B). Most pieces have been removed using a soft-hammer percussor following an episode of platform edge abrasion; the blades generally have linear or punctiform platforms and exhibit dorsal blade scars. A small core (26 g) was recovered from the same deposit, along with an obliquely truncated blade (Fig. 7.1.3). Technologically, the flintwork would be consistent with a Mesolithic or early Neolithic industry. Closer dating is not possible in the absence of diagnostic types.

Tree-throw hole 816

Tree-throw hole 816 contained an assemblage of 95 struck flints and a single piece (76 g) of burnt unworked flint (Table 7.3). The flints are in fresh condition and display a light, incipient cortication. Technologically and morphologically, the flintwork is consistent with an early Neolithic industry.

The assemblage is dominated by flakes (45 pieces), although blades, bladelets and bladelike flakes are numerous, representing 37.3% of all debitage (excluding chips); this is visible in the

Table 7.3 Flint by type from tree-throw holes 497, 813, 816 and 914.

	497 / 467	813 / 814	817	816 / 819	Total:	914 / 915	Total
Flake	41	6	37	8	45	1	93
Blade	5	4	16	3	19	1	29
Bladelet	2		4		4		6
Bladelike flake	4		7	1	8		12
Rejuvenation flake tablet			1		1		1
Core face/edge rejuvenation flake		1	1		1		2
Chip	4		4		4		8
Irregular waste	3		5		5		8
Single platform flake core	2	1	1		1	1	5
Multi-platform flake core	2						2
Single platform blade core	2		2		2		4
Core on a flake	1		1		1		2
Unclassifiable core			1		1		1
Partially worked nodule	1		1		1		2
Retouched flake	4		1		1		5
End scraper	2		1		1		3
Spurred piece	1						1
Truncated blade		1					1
Total	74	13	83	12	95	3	185
No. of burnt struck flints	4 (5.7%*)		19 (24.1%)	1 (8.3%)	20 (22%)		24 (13.6%)
No. of broken struck flints	20 (28.6%)	2 (15.4%)	34 (43%)	5 (41.7%)	39 (42.9%)		61 (34.5%)
No. of retouched tools	6 (8.6%)	1 (7.7%)	2 (2.5%)		2 (2.2%)		9 (5.1%)
No. of burnt unworked flints			1		1		1
Weight (g) of burnt unworked flints			76		76		76

* Percentage of total assemblage, excluding chips

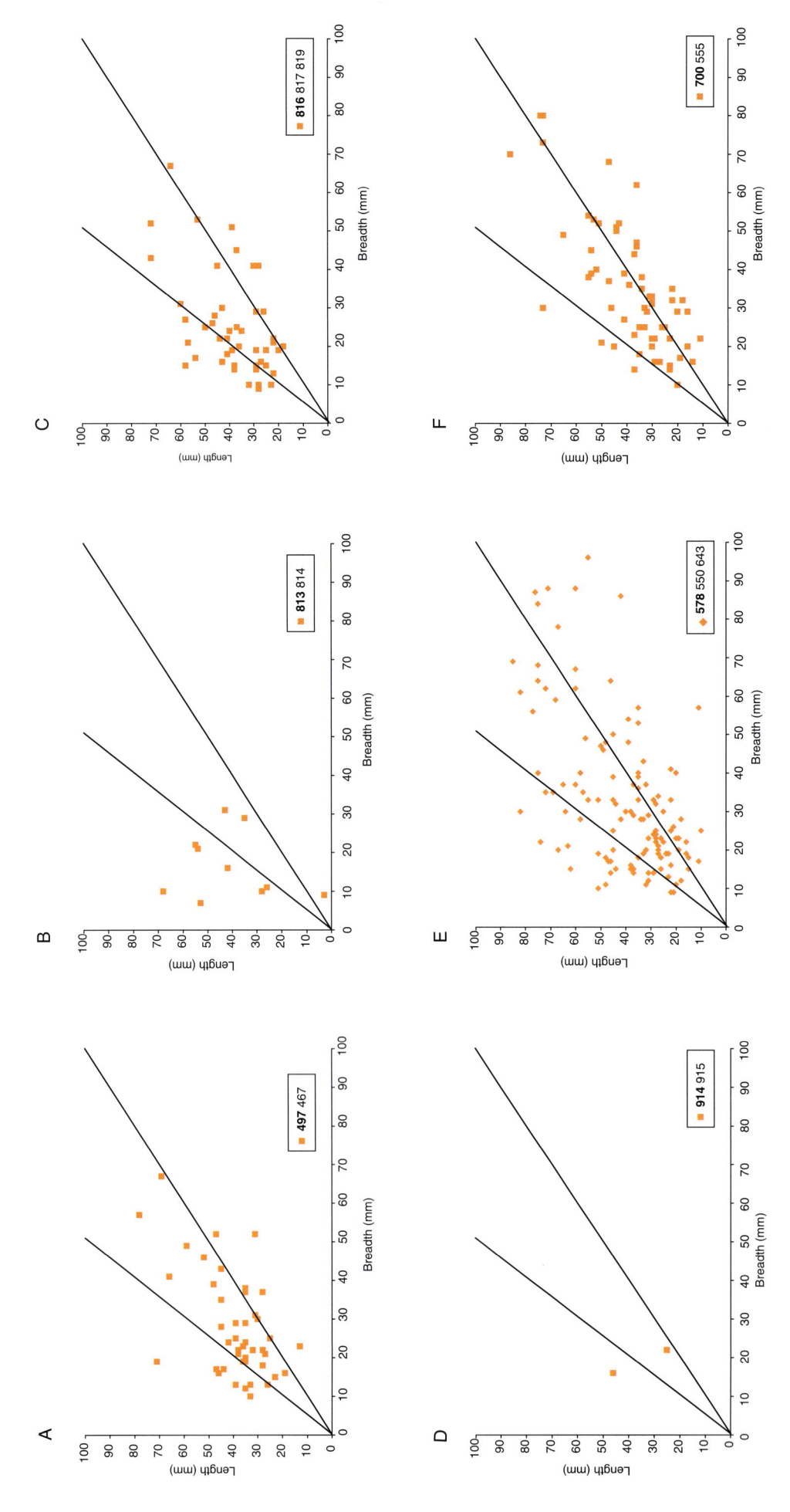

Fig. 7.2 Length and breadth of complete flints from (A) tree-throw hole 497 (B) tree-throw hole 813 (C) tree-throw hole 816 (D) tree-throw hole 914 (E) pit 578 and (F) pit 700.

results of the metrical analysis (Fig. 7.2 C). The hammermode seems to have been mixed, although soft-hammer percussion appears to have been preferred for blade production. Both flakes and blades show careful preparation and removal, and several display the dorsal scars of previous blade removals.

A refit between the two snapped fragments of a single flake was found across deposits 817 and 819, while a conjoin between two fragments of a blade was found within deposit 819. The presence of refitting material *between* deposits might suggest that a relatively short period elapsed between the deposition of the lower and upper fills, although it is possible that the flint was redeposited when the tree fell.

The assemblage contains some knapping waste, including five cores, one partially worked nodule, five pieces of irregular waste and four chips. The cores were mostly aimed at the production of blades and bladelets (eg Fig. 7.1.4), although several of the associated blades do not have dorsal blade scars, suggesting that both types of removal were produced from a single core. The presence of a rejuvenation tablet in the assemblage reflects a controlled knapping strategy involving periodic adjustment of the flaking angle.

Two retouched pieces were recovered, including one end scraper made on a cortical flake with semi-abrupt retouch along one edge. Several unretouched pieces had also been utilised and, significantly, a high proportion of the assemblage had been burnt (20 pieces or 22%).

Tree-throw hole 914

Tree-throw hole 914 contained three struck flints in fresh condition (Table 7.3 and Fig. 7.2 D). Along with one flake and one blade, the assemblage includes a small flake/bladelet core with platform edge abrasion. The flintwork is technologically similar to that from tree-throw hole 814, although the very limited number of flints allows only broad dating to the Mesolithic or Neolithic.

Early Bronze Age

The early Bronze Age assemblage was mostly contained within a series of intercutting hollows (1119) in the central part of the excavated area. The flintwork was accompanied by several sherds of Collared Urn and, on independent technological grounds, was probably contemporary with the ceramic assemblage.

A total of 868 struck flints and one fragment (1 g) of burnt unworked flint were recovered from the group of five hollows (Table 7.4). The hollows contained between 29 and 314 flints. The assemblage is dominated by broad, short, thick flakes. Many are of exceptionally large proportions, with several reaching 80 mm in length. Any platform preparation tends to consist of rough chipping of the platform edge rather than the fine abrasion that characterises the earlier Neolithic industries from the site. Platforms tend to be plain or cortical, rather than linear or punctiform, and often display prominent bulbs with crushing at the point of impact associated with the use of direct, hard-hammer percussion (Onhuma and Bergman 1982). Two flint hammerstones were recovered from the group.

The presence of numerous irregular flake cores, partially worked nodules and pieces of irregular waste suggests an unspecialised flake industry. From the low incidence of platform edge abrasion and rejuvenation flakes, it seems that platforms were rarely prepared or adjusted between episodes of flaking, while the number of multiplatform flake cores in the collection (16 pieces) suggests that an alternative platform was sought each time the original platform became unworkable. The retouched component is heavily scraper-based (nine pieces, for example Fig. 7.1.5), but also includes seven retouched flakes, one notched flake and one awl (Fig. 7.1.6). A flaked axe was recovered from hollow 578 (Fig. 7.1.7).

A small quantity of blade material is present in each pit, providing between 4.5% and 12% of the debitage component in each case. The majority of these are probably either accidental removals or residual Mesolithic flints. The assemblage from hollow 578, however, contained an unusually high percentage of blades (17.9%) and on account of this, requires further discussion.

Hollow 578

The assemblage from hollow 578 contains a series of fresh, finely struck blades, some exceeding 90 mm, which account for nearly 18% of the debitage component. The majority display platform edge abrasion and dorsal blade scars and, where it can be determined from bulb morphology, most have been soft-hammer struck. In contrast to the thick, plain platforms that typify the other assemblages in the group, linear and punctiform platforms are common within this collection. The careful knapping strategy is also reflected by the presence of three rejuvenation flakes, including one tablet (Fig. 7.1.8).

When compared to the assemblages from the other hollows, the flintwork from hollow 578 is technologically anomalous and may represent the redeposited contents of an earlier feature, perhaps cut by the excavation of the hollows. The results of the technological and metrical analysis certainly seem to indicate an earlier origin for the majority of the flintwork. The debitage is distinctly more blade-like than a sample from hollow 700 and is much more closely aligned with the assemblages from Neolithic tree-throw holes 497 and 816 (Figs 7.2.A, C, E and F). While it is possible that the blades are specialised early Bronze Age pieces – blanks for backed knives, for example – their striking resemblance to those from the Neolithic tree-throw holes suggests that they might be contemporary with the Neolithic assemblages.

Table 7.4 Flint by type from the early Bronze Age intercutting pits (group 1119) and tree-throw hole 899

		578	578 total		642		642 total			700	700 total	702	703	Total
	550	643	551	552	553	557		555	701	722		554	706	
Flake	110	34	144	18	51	145	9	223	114		50	167	45	22	601
Blade	11	12	23	2	4	4	1	11	4	3	2	6	2	1	43
Bladelet	1		1	1		3		4					1		6
Bladelike flake	7	1	8	2	7	6		15	2			2	3	2	30
Rejuvenation flake tablet	1		1												1
Core face/edge rejuvenation flake	2		2			1		1	1			1	1		5
Chip	5		5		3	3		6	2		4	6	1		18
Irregular waste	3	2	5		4	23	1	28	26		27	53	5	3	94
Single platform flake core	1		1	1		2	1	4	2		1	3	1		9
Multi-platform flake core				1		8	1	10	4			4	2		16
Single platform blade core	2	1	3										1		4
Core on a flake	1		1		1			1	1			1			3
Unclassifiable core	1		1			1		1	1			1			3
Partially worked nodule	1		1	1		1		2	4		3	7	2	1	13
Retouched flake	1	1	2		3			3	2			2			7
End scraper				1		1		2	1			1			3
Side scraper									1			1			1
End-and-side scraper	1		1		1			1	2			2			4
Other scraper													1		1
Notch	1		1												1
Awl												1			1
Axe	1		1												1
Hammerstone						1		1	1			1			2
Other heavy implement						1		1							1
Total	150	51	201	26	75	200	13	314	169	3	87	259	65	29	868
No. of burnt struck flints	7 (4.8%*)	2 (3.9%)	9 (4.6%)	1 (3.8%)	6 (8.3%)	9 (4.6%)	1 (7.7%)	60 (19.5%)	3 (1.8%)		1 (1.2%)	4 (1.6%)		1 (3.4%)	74 (8.7%)
No. of broken struck flints	47 (32.4%)	17 (33.3%)	64 (32.7%)	7 (26.9%)	21 (29.2%)	44 (22.3%)	6 (46.2%)	78 (25.3%)	27 (16.2%)		6 (7.2%)	32 (12.6%)		2 (6.9%)	176 (20.7%)
No. of retouched tools:	4 (2.8%)	1 (2%)	5 (2.6%)		5 (6.9%)	3 (1.5%)		8 (2.6%)	8 (4.8%)			8 (3.2%)	1 (1.6%)		22 (2.6%)
No. of burnt unworked flints:							1		1			1	1		1
Weight (g) of burnt unworked flints:															1
% of debitage provided by blades:			17.9%					11.4%					4.5%	11.5%	12.0%

* Percentage of total assemblage, excluding chips

Table 7.5 Flint by type from the main stratigraphic groups

	Evaluation	460	574	935	1099	1100	1102	1103	1104	1105	1106	1107	1108	1112	1117	1118	1119	1121	1122	1123	Total
Flake	90	76	57	10	41	14	12	2	42	22	77	13	18		18	5	601	1	316	114	1529
Blade	16	16	7	3	3	1	1		4	1	11	2	1				43		30	19	158
Bladelet	3	1	2						2	1	1	1					6		8	1	27
Bladelike flake	8	3			2				1	1	3				1		29		10	6	63
Rejuvenation flake tablet		2									3						1		2	1	9
Core face/edge rejuvenation flake						1								1			5				7
Other rejuvenation flake	2												1	1					1	1	6
Levallois flake	1																				1
Microburin											2								1		3
Chip	7	1			2				3		1						18		1		33
Sieved Chips 4-2mm	25																				25
Sieved Chips 10-4mm	5																				5
Irregular waste	3	3	7	3	3	1	6		4	3	11	3	1		2		94		44	21	209
Single platform flake core		1	1	1	1		1			1	4		1		2		9		5	1	29
Multi-platform flake core	6		2						1		2	1					16		7	2	36
Single platform blade core	1				1												4		2	1	9
Opposed platform blade core	1										1										2
Other blade core													1								1
Core on a flake	3				3												3		3	2	14
Unclassifiable core		1								1	1						3		3		9
Partially worked nodule	1	5	1							2	1						13		16	2	41
Retouched flake		1			1												7		2		11
End scraper			1		1								1				3		2	1	9
Side scraper	1																1				2
End and side scraper			1														4		1	1	7
Other scraper											1						1				2
Notch	1										1						1			1	4
Denticulate			3								1										4
Microlith									1												2
Awl																	1				1
Axe																	1		1		2
Hammerstone		1										1			1		2		3	2	10
Other heavy implement																	1		1		2
Total	174	111	82	17	58	17	20	2	58	32	122	21	24	2	24	5	867	1	459	176	2272

The proportion of the flint which dates from the early Bronze Age (if any) is unknown as this component cannot be confidently isolated on technological grounds. The percentage of blades (17.9%) is towards the lower end of the range predicted for earlier Neolithic assemblages (Ford 1987a), and may provide slim evidence in favour of the inclusion of some later material. A knapping refit between a single platform blade core and a blade, however, suggests that the assemblage maintains its integrity and has not been significantly disturbed.

Later Bronze Age

A large number of struck flints were recovered from Bronze Age and later contexts, including the occupation layer within the hillfort (1123) and the modern subsoil (1122; Table 7.5). These assemblages contain large numbers of unretouched flakes, many of which are thick and irregular. The flintwork recovered from these layers is generally in poor condition and is probably largely residual, although its composition and technological appearance suggests that much of it dates to the Bronze Age. While it is difficult to identify secure groups, a few possible examples were isolated. These include 24 struck flints from the postholes of one of the possible roundhouses (1117). These flints are in fresh condition and may derive from *in situ* deposits within contemporary Bronze Age features.

Discussion

The Mesolithic assemblage consists of a residual spread across the site which, with obvious limitations, has been defined by the distribution of diagnostic tools. These include one *tranchet* axe (Fig. 7.1.1), two microliths (Fig. 7.1.2) and three microburins. No spatial patterning was noted in the distribution of these finds. Some of the blades and blade cores may also be Mesolithic in origin, but these pieces could not be reliably separated from material of early Neolithic date. Refining the chronology any further is difficult given the residual context of the flintwork. It may be significant that the 9th millennium BC radiocarbon date from the hazelnut agrees with the early Mesolithic date cautiously suggested for the two broad-blade microliths.

The Neolithic assemblage includes four coherent collections from tree-throw holes. Substantial quantities of fresh flintwork were recovered from tree-throw holes 497 and 816. Two of the tree-throw holes (813 and 914) contained very small quantities of flint, and are assumed to be Neolithic simply on account of their proximity to similar assemblages of demonstrably Neolithic date; a Mesolithic origin for these two collections is not therefore dismissed. Broadly contemporary activity can be demonstrated at the Taplow Mill Site 2, some 500 m to the southwest, which produced a small collection of residual Mesolithic microliths, along with an assemblage of over 300 flints from an early Neolithic tree-throw hole (Durden and Lamdin-Whymark forthcoming).

The Neolithic assemblage from Taplow Court appears fairly mixed in composition, combining knapping waste with numerous retouched, utilised and burnt pieces, and may reflect the deposition of middened material into a convenient hollow (eg Evans *et al.* 1999). The refitting analysis identified occasional knapping refits and conjoins within the assemblage, but no long sequences were found. Furthermore, the presence of a conjoining flake between deposits suggests that the deposition of the flintwork might not have been a single event. The relatively high frequency of burnt pieces (Table 7.3), particularly compared to the early Bronze Age assemblage (compare Table 7.4), might indicate that some of the material was originally contained within a hearth.

The early Bronze Age assemblage recovered from the scoops is particularly significant given its association with Collared Urn pottery. The assemblage represents an opportunistic approach to flaking quite distinct from careful blade-based technology of the Neolithic industry. From its composition and technological characteristics, the flintwork has close parallels with that from the northern scatter at Maidenhead Thicket, some 5.5 km to the northeast of Taplow Court (Boismier 1995). This broadly contemporary scatter was interpreted as the remains of a residential site, while two scatters to the south were considered to have been generated in the course of specialised quarrying or extraction activity. While the Taplow Court pit group contains substantial evidence of knapping activity in the form of cores and chips, these are combined with numerous retouched and utilised pieces that suggest a more generalised working area, perhaps located close to a settlement, comparable to that related to the northern scatter at Maidenhead Thicket (ibid., 63).

At the nearby Taplow Mill Site 2 (see Fig. 1.3), a series of natural hollows and tree-throw holes produced a substantial late Neolithic/early Bronze Age assemblage (Durden and Lamdin-Whymark forthcoming); a spread of broadly contemporary flintwork was recovered from the layer that sealed these features. The assemblage there is marked by a near-absence of retouched tools, pottery, fired clay and burnt stone, but contains several concentrations of large unworked flint nodules, perhaps stockpiled for later use. The composition of the assemblage does not suggest activity appropriate to a nearby settlement as seen at Taplow Court, but may represent a specialised location within the same territory.

The remaining flint assemblage from Taplow Court is less spatially distinct but can be grouped by shared technological characteristics. These flints, many of which have been redeposited in reworked layers, probably relate to activity associated with the construction and use of the hillfort in the late Bronze Age.

PREHISTORIC POTTERY

by Emily Edwards

A total of 1056 sherds (10.4 kg), ranging in date from the early Bronze Age to the middle Iron Age, was recovered from the Conference Hall excavation and subsequent 2005 evaluation at Taplow Court (Table 7.6). The pottery includes a sequence of stratified groups dating from the late Bronze Age through to the middle Iron Age, although the early Iron Age is poorly represented. The early Bronze Age material is from a group of five hollows (1119), although residual sherds were also recovered from other contexts.

A further 2613 prehistoric sherds were recovered from the five trenches excavated by TCAST (see Tables 7.13-14). The pottery from Trenches 1-3 was examined by Kate Brown and that from Trenches 4-5 was scanned by the author for vessel forms and fabrics for the purposes of comparison with the pottery from the main excavation.

The assemblages from successive stratigraphic events reveal a change over time from flint-tempered to sand-tempered fabrics, via flint and sand-tempered fabrics. It should be stressed that the assemblages are not large, and that quite a high proportion of the pottery is likely to be residual because such a long sequence of prehistoric features was cut in the same place.

Table 7.6 Quantities of pottery from the main excavation by phase. Codes: EBA: early Bronze Age; MBA: middle Bronze Age; LBA: late Bronze Age; LBAEIA: late Bronze Age to early Iron Age; EIA: early Iron Age; MIA: middle Iron Age; IA: Iron Age; IND: indeterminate; EPREH: early prehistoric; LPREH: late prehistoric; PREH: prehistoric

Date	Sherd Count	Weight (g)
EBA	52	240
MBA	3	47
LBA	912	8556
LBAEIA	23	665
EIA	1	19
MIA	46	366
IA	11	304
IND	8	11
Total	1056	10208

Methodology

Preliminary recording was carried out using the OA prehistoric pottery recording system, which is based on Prehistoric Ceramics Research Group guidelines (1997). This characterises pottery by fabric, form, surface treatment, decoration and colour. Each fabric has been examined microscopically using a binocular microscope (x 20) and differentiated according to the size and type of major inclusions. Small crumbs were not assigned to a fabric type. The sherd count does not include fresh breaks. Vessels were counted according to rims, decorated sherds and other groups of sherds that could reasonably be said to represent a single vessel. A representative sample of the pottery has been illustrated from both the main excavation and the TCAST trenches (Figs 7.3-7, and a detailed catalogue is included at the end of the report (Tables 7.15-16).

Condition

The condition of the material varies. A large proportion of the assemblage (87%) consists of body sherds, while 6% are rims and 2% bases. Only 17 partial profiles were reconstructable, and no whole vessels or complete profiles were found. For over half of the contexts the mean sherd weight was 5 g or less.

The condition of the pottery restricts the extent to which particular assemblages can be dated. Of the 81 contexts containing pottery, only 14 produced assemblages of 20 or more sherds, and some of these contexts were subdivisions of the same layers, so that only eight context groups produced pottery groups of any size. One assemblage of more than 20 sherds came from early Bronze Age hollow 642 in group 1119, two from the subsoil over the hillfort interior (1122), seven from the prehistoric occupation layer in the interior (groups 1123 and 1121, plus a group recovered from WA Trench 12), two from the standstill layer in the V-profiled ditch (1102), one from layer 1118 in a pit associated with the entrance to the Iron Age hillfort (1016), one from a pit (3032) adjacent to the outer defensive ditch, and a residual group in one of the Anglo-Saxon upper fills (215) of the U-profiled ditch (460).

Pottery was recovered from only 28 discrete features other than the hillfort ditches; these included the early Bronze Age hollows (1119), postholes associated with one of the possible roundhouses (1117), the posthole rows (1107, 1108 and 1104) and palisade trench (1106), as well as a few pits and tree-throw holes. For most of these the total pottery assemblage for the whole feature group was less than 20 sherds.

Summary of provenance and dating

There were thus few good groups from discrete features. Most of the material came from ditches or the occupation layer and an unknown proportion may have been residual. The material from the V-profiled ditch (574) (see Figs. 7.3.4-9) has 10th- to 9th-century BC parallels at Runnymede (O'Connell 1986) while the pottery from the occupation layer 1121 and 1123 (a deposit of mixed dates; see Fig. 7.5.17-29) includes vessels which also have 10th- to 9th-century BC parallels at Lot's Hole (A. Barclay pers. comm.). The V-profiled ditch (574) was overlain by the standstill layer (1102) which contained pottery dating to the end of the late

Bronze Age and the beginning of the early Iron Age, while the overlying rampart gravels (1100 and 1112) contained redeposited late Bronze Age forms (Fig. 7.3.14-16). Pottery from the lower fills of the U-profiled ditch (460) was also of mixed date ranging from late Bronze Age through to Iron Age (Fig. 7.5.32-3). This fits the chronology indicated by radiocarbon dates, which suggest that the ditch was dug between 510 and 390 BC, although these dates also imply that some, at least, of the pottery described here as middle Iron Age should more accurately be termed early-middle Iron Age. Pottery recovered from postholes associated with the possible roundhouse (1117) was equally mixed, and either some must have been residual, or the posthole group includes examples of different dates. The pottery recovered from the posthole rows (1107, 1108 and 1104) and the palisade trench (1106) was also of varied dates, ranging from the early Bronze Age to the early-middle Iron Age. The discrete features included pit 1016, radiocarbon dated to 790-520 BC, which contained late Bronze Age pottery (see Fig. 7.3.4), but also included five Iron Age sherds.

Fabrics

A total of 10 fabrics were recorded (Table 7.7). The early Bronze Age sherds are tempered with very little other than rare fine grades of grog (the Biconical Urn fragment is unusual in being hard-fired and sand and grog-tempered). Most of the late Bronze Age pottery is flint-tempered or flint and sand-tempered. Sandy, gritless fabrics are also present, making identification of intrusive later material at Taplow difficult. The early-middle Iron Age vessels were predominantly burnished, fine sand- and sand and flint-tempered fabrics, although a coarser fabric containing high percentages of large ironstone pellets was also present.

A change in fabrics over time, from flint- to sand-tempered, was revealed quite clearly by stratified ceramic assemblages, although these assemblages were small (see Figs 4.12-13). The fills of the earlier, V-profiled ditch (574) contained 23 sherds (context 880 is the only exception), of which 59% were of flint-tempered fabrics. This total includes residual middle Bronze Age sherds. In the standstill layer (1102) in the top of this ditch, which produced 73 sherds, only 17% were in flint-tempered fabrics, and

Table 7.7 Fabric descriptions with % of total sherd count

Fabric group	Fabric code	% of total sherd count	Common name	Description
Sand	Ai	11.29	Fine Sand	Well sorted 20-25% quartzite sand, less than 3 mm in size. Occasional 1-3% ferruginous pellets and organic material.
	Aii	0.76	Coarse Sand	Poorly sorted 20-25% quartzite sand, from 3-5 mm
Sand and flint	Bi	16.22	Fine Sand and Flint	Well sorted 30% quartzite sand, less than 3 mm in size. Moderately sorted 10-15% crushed flint, 3-4 mm. Occasionally 1-2% ferruginous pellets and 7% organic material.
	Bii	0.09	Coarse Sand and Flint	Poorly sorted 30% quartzite sand, up to 5 mm. Poorly sorted crushed flint, 15-20%, up to 5 mm. Occasionally 1-2% ferruginous pellets.
Flint and sand	Ci	30.83	Fine Flint and Sand	Well to moderately sorted, 10-20% flint sized 2-4 mm. Moderately well sorted, 7-10% sand, sized 2-3 mm. Occasionally 1-2% ferruginous pellets.
	Cii	1.71	Coarse Flint and Sand	Poorly sorted, 20-25% flint sized 4-7 mm. Moderately well sorted, 7-10% sand, sized 2-3 mm. Occasionally 1-2% ferruginous pellets.
Flint	D	27	Fine Flint	Well to moderately sorted flint, 10-15%, sized up to 4 mm.
	E	8	Coarse Flint	Poorly sorted 20% flint, sized up to 8 mm.
Grog	H	2.94	Fine Grog	Moderately well sorted angular grog, 2-3% up to 4 mm. Occasionally 1-2% flint and 10% fine sand.
Others	G	0.09	Organic	5-7% voids, organic impressions within section.
	I	0.57	Coarse Quartzite	20% crushed quartzite, up to 7 mm.
	J	0.38	No inclusions	No visible inclusions.
	K	0.47	Indeterminate	Too small for fabric to be determined.

Table 7.8 Summary of the number of sherds and decorated sherds, and weight and proportions of ceramic fabrics in the ditches and ramparts (excluding Saxon pottery). Contexts are shown in stratigraphic order with the earliest at the bottom. The four sections cut through the U=profiled ditch (460) are shown separately with the fills within each section in stratigraphic order.

						Weight (g)									Percentage (by weight)					
Feature	Context	Total no. sherds	Total weight (g)	No decorated sherds	Coarse Flint	All Flint	Flint & sand	Sand & flint	All flint & sand	Sand	Grog	Others	Coarse Flint	All Flint	Flint & sand	Sand & flint	All flint & sand	Sand	Grog	Others
U-profiled ditch																				
460	121	1	34					34	34							100	100			
460	252	1	63				35		35	28					56		56	44		
460	256	3	20					20	20							100	100			
460	253	14	72					72	72							100	100			
460	255	7	115	1				115	115							100	100			
460	215	21	83				35		35	48					42		42	58		
460	214	7	38				13	12	25	13					34	32	66	34		
460	291	14	92				27	65	92						29	71	100			
460	292	9	44					27	27	17						61	61	39		
460	293	6	18				11	2	13	5					61	11	72	28		
460	295	6	20				6	14	20						30	70	100			
460	579	2	4	3			4		4						100		100			
460	607	1	3				3		3						100		100			
460	712	1	3					3	3							100	100			
460	714	1	8					8	8							100	100			
460	708	5	17					17	17							100	100			
460	752	1	7		7	7							100	100						
Total		100		4	7	7	134	389	523	111			1	1	21	61	82	17		
U-profiled ditch rampart																				
1100	616	1	43				43		43						100		100			
1100	644	3	3				3		3						100		100			
1100	645	2	60		21	21		39	39				35	35		65	65			
1112	463	1	45		45	45							100	100						
1112	994	7	56		41	41	9		9			6	73	73	16		16			11
Total		14		0	107	107	55	39	94			6	52	52	27	19	45			3
Standstill layer																				
1102	462	6	62				20	42	62						32	68	100			
1102	861	30	298	3	63	63		227	227	8			21	21		76	76	3		
1102	1074	37	213	6	35	35	81	29	110	68			16	16	38	14	52	32		
Total		73		9	98	98	101	298	399	76			17	17	18	52	70	13		
V-profiled ditch																				
574	863	7	52	7	41	52							79	100						
574	880	9	128	8	11	11	111		111	6			9	9	87		87	5		
574	1075	3	28	2	15	15					13		54	54					46	
574	838	3	133	3	50	124		9	9				38	93		7	7			
Total		22		20	117	202	111	9	120	6	13		34	59	33	3	35	2	4	

the majority (70%) were in fabrics tempered with both flint and sand. This layer was also the earliest to contain sherds tempered only with sand, albeit in small quantities.

Above this, the deposits (1100 and 1112) representing the rampart of the U-profiled ditch (460) contained 14 sherds, a mixture of flint and sand-tempered fabrics and flint-tempered fabrics, the latter probably residual. The rampart associated with the U-profiled ditch was constructed of sediments deriving from the cutting of the ditch and perhaps also from the hillfort interior (see Canti, Chapter 8, deposit 664), and therefore may reflect mainly the debris from earlier activity carried on outside and possibly inside the first V-profiled ditch, not necessarily from activity contemporary with the construction of the rampart. The number of sherds was small compared to those of the earlier assemblages, though the individual sherds were relatively large and well-preserved.

Flint-tempered fabrics were almost absent from the fills of the U-profiled ditch (460), the sections of which (102, 238, 376 and 713; Figs 5.2-3) are shown separately in Table 7.8. There were 59 sherds from Iron Age deposits, of which a high proportion were in fabrics tempered with both flint and sand. Most noticeable, however, was the increase in the quantities of sand-tempered fabrics (17% overall). The limited quantities of pottery from the TCAST trenches identified as early Iron Age are also predominantly in sand-tempered fabrics.

This gradual chronological shift in temper was noted by Longley as long ago as 1991 (Longley in Needham 1991, 163). Flint temper is consistent with early late Bronze Age material (Longley and Needham 1980, 40-65), while later assemblages such as that from Petters Sports Field (O'Connell 1986) employ sandier fabrics, again present in large quantities at Taplow Court. The gritted bases noted within this assemblage (see Fig. 7.4.7) can also be paralleled at Lot's Hole, Petters Sports Field and Runnymede.

It should be stressed, however, that at Taplow the proportion of residual pottery in some contexts is likely to have been high, eg. the rampart deposits (1100 and 1112) associated with the U-profiled ditch (460). The extent of the change is, therefore, likely to be slightly obscured or understated by the Taplow Court assemblages. The sequence is comparable to that suggested by Timby for the pottery from excavations along the adjacent Maidenhead to Windsor and Eton Flood Alleviation channel (in Allen *et al.* in prep. b). Although residuality makes precise interpretation difficult, the relative proportions of flint and sand temper appear (in this part of the Thames Valley) to correspond to chronological distinctions within the late Bronze Age and early Iron Age. The middle Iron Age fabrics are also typical of the period within the middle Thames Valley, and the grog fabrics are consistent with early Bronze Age traditions.

As well as the broad development from flint-tempered to sand-tempered fabrics, Table 7.8 also indicates that there may also have been a development from flint and sand-tempered fabrics (in which flint is more common than sand) to sand and flint-tempered fabrics (in which sand is more common than flint). Most of the limited proportion of pottery in these fabrics in the V-profiled ditch (574) was in flint and sand-tempered fabrics, whereas in the overlying standstill layer (1102) and in the U-profiled ditch most of the pottery in these fabrics was in sand and flint-tempered fabrics. However the small size of the assemblages makes this suggestion highly tentative.

Sources of raw materials

Taplow sits on Black Park Terrace Gravels, over the phosphatic Upper Chalk and the fossil free Reading Beds. The gravels are 4 m thick on the hilltop and contain poorly sorted, unconsolidated flint gravels interleaved with moderately sorted loose sand. As the Gravels are almost purely sandy in places (and contain little actual gravel), the clay is most likely to have derived from river bank deposits of clay from the Reading Formation.

Forms

Evidence for vessel form (Table 7.9) could be obtained from only a very small percentage of the assemblage (2.6% of the sherd count and 37% of the vessel count) due to the condition of the material. However, it was possible to establish the presence of biconical bowls and tripartite jars in the late Bronze Age phases, the latter of which were recovered from the hillfort interior in the modern subsoil (1122), the occupation layer (1123 and 1121), the rampart gravels (1100) associated with the U-profiled ditch (460), the standstill layer (1102) and a pit (1016) associated with the entrance to the early-middle Iron Age hillfort.

The only middle Iron Age forms (Fig. 7.5 nos 30 and 33), which were recovered from a posthole (208) associated with the possible roundhouse (1117) and from context 252 in the U-profiled ditch (460; cut 238, section 46) respectively, were ovoid and globular jars (Ai and Av).

The late Bronze Age rim forms are typical of most assemblages of this period, simple upright forms being the more dominant and expanded forms being almost absent. The straight-walled or ovoid jar forms are however characteristic of assemblages of the earlier part of the late Bronze Age, becoming rare or absent in later assemblages (Longley in Needham 1991; Morris 2004). Other decorative traits, such as finger-tipping on the exterior of the rim or the shoulder, are more characteristic of the later part of the period, ie after 950 BC (ibid.). The excavations at Taplow produced examples belonging to both periods. The middle Iron Age rims were simple rounded or everted rounded rims.

Table 7.9 Late Prehistoric Vessel Forms at Taplow

Form Code	Form Type	Sherd Count/Weight (g)	Vessel Count
Ai Total	Ovoid Jar	5/80	5
Aii Total	Tripartite Jar with short upright neck	10/185	8
Aiii Total	Slack Shouldered Jar	7/218	7
Aiv Total	Long necked tripartite jar	3/47	3
Aix Total	Tripartite Jar with flared rim	1/8	1
Av Total	Globular Jar	1/28	1
Biv Total	Flared rimmed round bodied bowl	1/8	1
Bv Total	Biconical bowl	1/57	1
Bvi Total	Bipartite Bowl	2/30	1
Total		31/661	28

Decoration and surface treatment

A total of 53 sherds were decorated, of which three sherds were twisted cord decorated Collared Urn sherds, while the remainder were late Bronze Age-early Iron Age (Table 7.10). Few of these were assigned a form. Decoration among the jars (Fig. 7.3. nos 4, 10 and 11) was confined to the body and rim, and included finger rustication on the body and base, finger impressions on the rim, various means of cabling on the rim (including slashed, incised and fingertip impressions). The finer biconical bowls were decorated with horizontal lines (Fig. 7.3.9). Surface treatment was not commonly noted. Burnishing was noted on five vessels (including Fig. 7.3 nos 9, 12, 14, and Fig. 7.5.17, the last internally), two of which were bowls. The surface of 15 vessels was smoothed. None of the Iron Age sherds was decorated although No. 30 was trimmed and No. 31 was smoothed (Fig. 7.5). The stratified groups of pottery suggest that here, as more broadly (Barrett 1980), decoration became more common in the late Bronze Age-early Iron Age. However, decoration remained rare at Taplow in all of the later prehistoric phases.

Table 7.10 Types of decoration noted within the Taplow assemblage

	Nosh	Weight (g)
Beaded rim & horizontal band around shoulder	1	57
Cabled rim.	15	1884
Faded twisted cord	3	4
Finger wiping on the body	15	337
Impressed finger nail on the body	2	9
Impressed fingertips on rim and neck.	13	202
Fingertip rustication around the base	2	362
Line under rim	1	4
Groove creating impression of beading	1	2
Total	54	2875

Pottery by groups

The early Bronze Age hollows (1119)

A total of 53 early Bronze Age sherds were identified, including 44 (186 g) of Collared Urn. These derived from relatively thin walled vessels manufactured from sand and grog-tempered fabrics. They included collar sherds and faded twisted cord decoration (eg. Fig. 7.3.3). A single vessel rim diameter was measurable (260 mm), on which the undecorated collar had been formed by means of an applied and pinched strip of clay which formed a peaked collar base. Although size and form were not discernible due to the size of the sherds, these few details suggested a late date for this Collared Urn group (Burgess 1986). A fragment of Collared Urn rim recovered from pit 133 (Fig. 7.3.1) was of a similar fabric and firing to those from the hollows.

Early Bronze Age occupation deposits are still relatively rare in the Thames Valley and in southern Britain generally (Tomalin 1995, 102; Healy 1995, 180; Longworth 1984). Small quantities of Collared Urn have been found in possible domestic contexts at a number of sites within the Eton Rowing Course project. At Yarnton, in the Upper Thames, a round-house radiocarbon-dated to the early Bronze Age was associated with a Biconical Urn (Edwards and Barclay in G Hey in prep.).

In addition to the Collared Urn from the hollows, feature 578 contained a shoulder fragment of Biconical Urn. This was a smoothed, fine vessel which was manufactured from a fabric containing sand and grog temper and was decorated with a smoothed cordon (Fig. 7.3.2). The underside of the cordon was also decorated with rounded impressions, probably made with a flat-ended object rather than a fingertip. The presence of early to middle Neolithic flint in pit 578 (contexts 550 and 643) was noted but there is little doubt about the date of this sherd. Another rim with a cordon just below it (Fig. 7.3.3) may also come from a Biconical Urn. The rim of this vessel was very irregular, the cordon crudely executed and the overall finish very poor.

The V-profiled ditch (574)

A total of 22 sherds (241 g) were recovered from four contexts within the V-profiled ditch, each containing 9 sherds or less. A minimum of five vessels was represented by one early Bronze Age rim, one middle Bronze Age cordon (Fig. 7.3.8) and half of a profile from a biconical bowl (Fig. 7.3.9). Also noted was one closed, flat topped rim from a plain ware ovoid jar (Fig. 7.3.6), a form which dates to the earlier part of the late Bronze Age (1150-950 BC, see below).

The most indicative piece from this group was the finely flint-tempered biconical bowl (Fig. 7.3.9, context 880) with beaded rim and horizontal incised line. This has been assigned to Potterne type 3.2 and Runnymede type 8/4, although it should be made clear that no identical parallels have been found. Runnymede Type 8 is characterised by a proper flange and has a curved upper profile, whereas Type 4 has a longer, straighter upper profile and an internal moulding at the shoulder, which is not present on the Taplow example. Although this vessel type is distinctive and much discussed in terms of chronology, there are few clearly non-residual examples associated with good groups from discrete or well-stratified features. It is consistent with vessels from contexts C/D-J within the late Bronze Age channel from Area 6 at Runnymede (Needham 1991, 167 and 187, fig. 84, no. 104). The radiocarbon dates for these phases put these vessels at 925-875 cal BC or 825-750 cal BC (ibid., 351, fig. 133). It is also paralleled closely by a bowl from pit 405 at Petters (O'Connell 1986, 64 and 71, fig. 56, no. 259), where it is associated with a tripartite jar with a decorated shoulder. O'Connell states that there is evidence for the appearance of biconical bowls with incised decoration in the middle Thames Valley by the 8th century and in the Thames Estuary (Mucking) at an earlier date. The similar vessel from Weybridge (Closebrooks 1977, 31 and fig. 19, no. 146) does not come from a stratified feature and is much more curvilinear in profile than the Taplow vessel. More examples were recovered from the midden within Area 1 at Runnymede (Longley and Needham 1980, 13 and 59, fig. 37, nos 425-6) but the author suggests that the material from this midden could be expected to span the entire occupation of the site. A whole example was found within pit 3475, Area 3100 at Reading Business Park 1 (Hall 1992, 76, fig.48, no. 146) and was associated with carinated, concave necked jars and a fingernail decorated shoulder. Hall states that this pit was stratified above a pit containing Plain Ware, which may put the vessel's earliest date in the 8th century BC. Beyond the Thames Valley at Potterne in Wiltshire, Morris dates these vessels to the 9th to the 6th century BC (Gingell and Morris 2000, 156 and fig. 47, no.11).

Otherwise, the group from the V-profiled ditch consisted of sherds which varied from reasonably large late Bronze Age sherds (70 x 70 mm) to small and abraded early and middle Bronze Age sherds (20 x 28 mm), the early Bronze Age being represented by a grog tempered, simple rounded and incurved rim and the middle Bronze Age by a heavily flint-tempered applied cordon (Fig. 7.3.8). The two largest sherds weighed 57 g and 74 g, although 13 sherds weighed under 10 g.

The majority of the later Bronze Age sherds had rough surfaces and were manufactured using coarse flint- or fine flint and sand-tempered fabrics. This included one sherd from a flat-rimmed ovoid jar (Fig. 7.3.6). One base sherd was gritted on the underside (Fig. 7.4), which is a feature typical of pottery from both Runnymede and Petters Sports Field. Decoration was minimal and occurred only on the biconical bowl (Fig. 7.3.9).

The occupation layer (1121 and 1123)

A total of 407 (5121 g) sherds were recovered from contexts within the occupation layer, of which six contained over 20 sherds (not including the Wessex Archaeology evaluation material). These sherds varied from reasonably large late Bronze Age sherds (80 x 50 mm) weighing over 40 g to small and abraded sherds weighing under 10 g. This was by far the richest deposit in terms of numbers and variety of vessels (Fig. 7.5.17-28); a total of 39 vessels were identified, of which two were burnished, eight were smoothed, one was wiped and the remainder were roughened. One rimsherd appears to belong to the biconical bowl from the V-profiled ditch. A total of 15 partial vessel-profiles were noted. Vessel forms included short and long necked carinated jars (Fig. 7.5 nos 18, 19, 23 and 24), ovoid jars and slack-shouldered jars (Fig. 7.5.25-7). Rim forms included both upright and everted rounded, flattened, squared, pointed, slightly beaded and T-shaped rims. One cabled rim and one pinched base were noted. The majority of sherds were manufactured using fine flint and fine sand (see Table 7.11). It is possible that, although much of this material appears to be contemporary with the V-profiled ditch, there is some mixing of material of differing dates within this area.

The standstill layer (1102)

A total of 73 sherds (573 g) were recovered from contexts within the standstill layer, two of which contained over 30 sherds. A minimum of six vessels was represented by small fragments of rims and one sharply carinated shoulder (Fig. 7.3.10-13). Each of these rims was decorated with spaced deep diagonal grooves or contiguous diagonal scallops (Needham 1996, 115; O'Connell 1986, 57). The featured sherds from this group were much more worn and broken (on average 75 x 40 mm) than those from the V-profiled ditch below and no sherd weighed more than 36 g. Although the majority of the sherds were roughened, a small number of sherds were smoothed and burnished, and coarse flint fabrics were entirely absent from this group. The dominant fabric was one containing fine sand, 10% flint upwards of 1 mm across and 1% up to 3 mm across. No bases were gritted. Apart from the simple cabled rims (see above) and the carinated shoulder, single fragments of a long necked tripartite jar (Fig. 7.3.10), a short necked carinated jar (Fig. 7.3.11) and a bipartite burnished bowl (Fig. 7.3.12) were noted. These cabled rims appear within both Runnymede and Petters Sports Field assemblages but without decorated shoulders closer dating becomes difficult. The finer flint and sand fabrics point, however, to a late Bronze Age/early Iron Age date.

The rampart gravels (1100 and 1112)

A total of 14 sherds (207g) were recovered from contexts within the rampart gravels, none of which contained more than seven sherds. A minimum of four vessels were represented by three jar forms and a rim (Fig. 7.3.14-16), all of which weighed 39 g or above. No decorated sherds were present, although one vessel was smoothed and burnished. Condition varied, as nine very small sherds weighing from 1-5 g were also present alongside the larger sherds. These small sherds were not merely recently broken fragments from the larger sherds, as they were all of different fabrics or from

Table 7.11 Summary of pottery in posthole-rows, trench 1106 and subsoil layers

Group	Feature	Context	Total weight (g)	Coarse flint	All flint	Flint & sand	Sand & flint	All flint and sand	Sand	Grog	Organic	Others
Modern subsoil												
1122	103	103	388	158	243	99	46	145				
1122	964	964	3447	967	1471	1437	247	1684	292			
1122	971	971	25			25		25				
Occupation layer												
1123	104	104	294	68	68	104	89	193	33			
1123	104	217	14						14			
1123	104	219	4							4		
1123	888	888	89			64	15	79	10			
1123	990	990	310	14	120	188	2	190				
1123	991	991	692	108	519	28	130	158	15			
Occupation layer near posthole group 1117												
1121	962	962	125	99	99	26		26				
1121	983	983	672	68	332	321	19	340				
1121	985	985	417	144	308	66	43	109				
1121	986	986	554	79	183	346	25	371				
Palisade trench												
1106	569	571	4						3			1
1106	597	598	4						4			
Posthole row												
1104	537	535	2	2	2							
Posthole row												
1108	1052	1053	36		36							
Posthole row												
1107	500	499	23				23	23				
1107	506	507	1						1			
Subsoil												
1105	1023	1023	54			54		54				

different contexts. Forms included a burnished bipartite jar (Fig. 7.3.14) with concave neck (O'Connell 1986, 68, type 10), one tripartite jar (Fig. 7.3.15) of a Runnymede type 12 form (O'Connell 1986, 63 and fig. 46, no. 56) which dates to the later phase of the late Bronze Age (950-750 BC), one straight-walled jar (Fig. 7.3.16) and one simple squared rim (not illustrated). The straight-walled, ovoid jar is of a type which was not common at Runnymede, Petters Sports Field or Eldon's Seat but which was recovered from the early land surface at Weybridge (Closebrooks 1977, 37-40, figs 16, nos 57 and 17), is very common at Green Park (Reading Business Park; Morris 2004, 66) and which also occurs at Aldermaston (Bradley *et al.* 1980, 234, 242). These parallels date this form to the earlier phase of the late Bronze Age (1150-950 BC).

The posthole rows (935, 1104, 1107 and 1108) and the palisade trench (1106)

A total of 19 late Bronze Age sherds, one middle Iron Age shoulder sherd, one early Bronze Age body sherd and one middle Bronze Age body sherd were recovered from eleven contexts within the posthole rows, almost all of which contained single sherds. A minimum of two late Bronze Age vessels were represented by two small, simple rims; the rim of one was decorated with impressed fingertips and the other was burnished. The sherds were dated according to fabric, sherd thickness and surface treatment. The condition of the sherds was almost universally poor, the majority weighing less than 8 g and only four body sherds weighing over 23 g. These larger sherds included a thick-walled middle Bronze Age sherd and the middle Iron Age shoulder.

The U-profiled ditch (460)

A total of 100 sherds (641 g) were recovered from 17 contexts within the U-profiled ditch, one of which contained over 20 sherds and two more of which contained between 10 and 20. Sherds of differing dates were recovered from five of these contexts: contexts 214, 215, 252 and 293 contained both late Bronze Age and middle Iron Age pottery while context 255 contained early Iron Age and late Bronze Age – early Iron Age sherds. In total, 28 sherds (164 g) were middle Iron Age, one was early Iron Age and eight (110 g) were late Bronze Age – early Iron Age. The remaining 56 (299 g) were late Bronze Age. Condition ranged from very small to medium. Although 16 sherds weighed over 10 g, the group was very fragmented with no sherds weighing over 34 g. The dominant fabrics both contained fine flint and fine sand.

A minimum of six vessels was represented by rims and a carinated shoulder, two of which were middle Iron Age (Fig. 7.5.32). The late Bronze Age rims included a simple form, a smoothed, pointed rim from a tripartite vessel, an everted pointed form and a flat form decorated with finger impressions. One further early Iron Age slack shoulder sherd was decorated with a finger pit (Fig. 7.5.33).

The possible roundhouse (1117) and surrounding postholes

A total of 27 sherds (157 g) were recovered from eight contexts (mostly postholes) associated with posthole group 1117, none of which contained over 10 sherds (five contexts contained single sherds). Only two sherds weighed over 10 g and the group was very broken, abraded and of mixed date. Posthole 185 contained a single early Bronze Age sherd while posthole 208 contained two middle Iron Age sherds (Fig. 7.5.31) and one late Bronze Age sherd. Fine flint and sand fabrics were dominant (see Table 7.12).

A total of six vessels were represented by rim and shoulder fragments, two of which came from ovoid jars. All surfaces were roughened and no decoration was noted. The early Bronze Age rim was flat and internally expanded, while the late Bronze Age forms were simple squared, beaded or everted with an internal bevel (Fig. 7.5.30). The beaded rim may be a fragment of a beaded, biconical bowl similar to that found in the V-profiled ditch. The middle Iron Age sherd from posthole 208 is a fragment of an organic-tempered globular jar.

Other discrete features

A further 115 sherds (716 g), including three early Bronze Age sherds, 100 late Bronze Age sherds, one late Bronze Age-early Iron Age sherd, four Iron Age sherds and one middle Iron Age sherd were found in other features. The group was of mixed condition, with very broken material alongside larger fragments weighing up to 76 g. The majority of these were plain body sherds, with the exception of three finger-decorated late Bronze Age sherds and one earliest Iron Age sherd decorated with a curvilinear design. The late Bronze Age and earliest Iron Age fabrics contained flint and sand, while the early Bronze Age sherds were all untempered.

Pottery recovered by TCAST

A total of 2613 sherds were recovered from the TCAST Trenches, 2175 (12,268 g) of which were scanned for the purpose of comparison with the OA assemblage (see Tables 7.13 and 7.14), and a selection of which has been illustrated (Figs. 7.6-7).

A total of 40 early Bronze Age sherds were noted by Kate Brown (Trenches 1-3) and the author (Trenches 4-5). Those from the latter included a sherd decorated with a single comb-impressed line (Fig. 7.6.35). The late Bronze Age and late Bronze-early Iron Age sherds included a higher quantity of recognisable forms. Although to a large extent there was a high degree of similarity in fabric and form between this and the assemblage from the main

Table 7.12 Summary of pottery associated with features within the hillfort

Group	Feature	Total number/weight (g)	Flint	Flint & sand	Sand & flint	Sand	Grog	Organic	Others
Posthole-row 935									
935	967	1/18		1/18					
Posthole-row 1132									
1132	288				1/7				
1132	954	1/4							
Roundhouse 1117									
1117	959	1/3	1/3						
1117	208	5/25	2/11	1/4	1/3			1/7	
1117	940	7/35				7/35			
1117	204	1/2		1/2					
Other postholes 1117									
1117	149	10/45			10/45				
1117	147	1/1			1/1				
1117	185	1/8					1/8		
1117	957	1/4		1/4					

excavation, there were some significant differences in that a higher proportion of straight sided, thin walled jars (Fig. 7.6.52) and ovoid jars (Fig. 7.6.35 and 38) were represented among the earlier late Bronze Age sherds (1150-950 BC). A slack-shouldered jar with triangular stamps on the shoulder (Fig. 7.6.43) is paralleled with a late Bronze Age vessel from a pit at Yarnton (Edwards and Barclay in prep.). A peculiar, thin-walled rim sherd was deeply indented in such as way as to resemble a comb (Fig. 7.6.52).

The early Iron Age was more strongly represented than was the case in the Conference Hall excavation. Incised decoration was noted on a pedestal base (Fig. 7.7.60) and rim, and a sand-tempered Aii style jar with a T-shaped rim (Fig. 7.7.61) was decorated with horizontal wiping or tooling curving down at the ends where the strokes met. These vessels are particularly important as they represent elements that were absent from the assemblage from the main excavation: the fine decorated wares of the earliest Iron Age and the carinated jars of the early Iron Age.

Although little is known of the disturbed contexts from which this assemblage was recovered, a wider variety of material was recovered from these trenches than from within the hillfort.

Table 7.13 Quantification by sherd count of pottery from TCAST Trenches 1 to 3

	Trench One	Trench Two	Trench Three	Total
EBA	19	4	14	37
LBA	42	23	18	83
EIA	136	66	60	262
MIA	14	34	8	56
Total	211	127	100	438

Table 7.14 Summary quantification of assemblages from TCAST Trenches 4 and 5

Date	Minimum Vessel Count	Sherd Count	Weight (g)
EBA	3	3	28
LBA or EBA	3	5	38
LBA	183	1427	9649
LBA to EIA	90	543	1691
EIA	41	123	604
EIA or MIA	5	37	101
MIA	3	3	43
EPREH	2	2	8
LPREH	3	21	66
IA	1	4	21
IND	1	2	3
PREH	3	5	16
Total	338	2175	12268

Discussion

The presence of both Collared Urn and Biconical Urn at Taplow is of considerable interest. As very few examples of non-funerary Collared Urns are known, this pottery style has been viewed in the past as having been created purely for funerary use (see Tomalin 1995, 102; Healy 1995, 180). Although Longworth (1984) lists four other Collared Urn sites in Buckinghamshire, they are all cremation burials deposited in or near burial monuments. There is no such evidence at Taplow Court, although the nature of the activity to which the 40 sherds from the TCAST trenches related is unclear. Longworth was able to cite few non-funerary assemblages (Longworth 1984) and Tomalin (1995) mentions only one more recent find at West Row Fen in Suffolk (Martin and Murphy 1988). Longworth cited only one non-funerary site situated in the Thames Valley: an isolated pit at Sutton Courtenay in Oxfordshire.

It is, however, possible that early Bronze Age settlements were commonly associated with such pottery. It is rare for early Bronze Age fabrics (with the exception of Beaker fabrics) to survive in a condition sufficient for positive identification to be possible (Healy 1995, 180), and the scarcity of Collared Urns in non-funerary contexts may be due simply to poor preservation. The apparently exclusive nature of Collared Urns and either Food Vessels or Biconical Urns has also been noted (Healy 1995, 181). The identification of a possible Biconical Urn fragment (Fig. 7.3.2) is, therefore, also of some interest. The form of the illustrated fragment matches closely that of a complete Biconical Urn

Table 7.15 Catalogue of illustrated prehistoric pottery from the main excavation

Figure Number	Feature	Interpretation	Intervention	Context	Date	Count	Weight (g)	Fabric group	Vessel type	Rim diameter	%rim present
7.3.1	133	EBA pit	133	135	EBA	1	15	J			
7.3.2	1119	EBA hollows	578	550	EBA	1	10	H	BU		
7.3.3	1119	EBA hollows	642	553	EBA	1	7	A	CU		
7.3.4	1016	E-MIA pit	1016	1017	LBA	3	39	C	Aii	120	6
7.3.5	574	LBA V-profiled ditch	878	838	LBA	3	9	B			
7.3.6	574	LBA V-profiled ditch	878	838	LBA	1	50	D	Ai	330	10
7.4.1	574	LBA V-profiled ditch	878	838	LBA	1	74	E			
7.3.8	574	LBA V-profiled ditch	865	863	MBA	2	11	E			
7.3.9	574	LBA V-profiled ditch	865	880	LBA	1	57	C	Bv	200	8
7.3.10	1102	LBA-EIA standstill layer	861	861	LBA	1	13	B	Aiv		
7.3.11	1102	LBA-EIA standstill layer	861	861	LBA	1	14	B	Aii		
7.3.12	1102	LBA-EIA standstill layer	861	861	LBA	2	30	B	Bvi	120	8
7.3.13	1102	LBA-EIA standstill layer	861	861	LBA	1	8	B			
7.3.14	1100	E-MIA Rampart	616	616	LBA	1	43	C	Bvi		
7.3.15	1112	E-MIA Rampart	463	463	LBA/EIA	1	45	D	Aii	320	6
7.3.16	1112	E-MIA Rampart	994	994	LBA	1	41	D	Ai		
7.5.17	1122	modern subsoil	964	964	LBA	1	8	D		160	10
7.5.18	1122	modern subsoil	964	964	LBA	2	19	C	Aii	140	9
7.5.19	1122	modern subsoil	964	964	LBA	1	6	B	Aii	130	40
7.5.20	1122	modern subsoil	964	964	LBA	1	11	D	Aiii	110	7
7.5.21	1122	modern subsoil	964	964	LBA	1	4	D	Aiv	160	8
7.5.22	1122	modern subsoil	964	964	LBA	1	13	E			
7.5.23	1122	modern subsoil	964	964	LBA	4	147	A	Aiv		
7.5.24	1122	modern subsoil	964	964	LBA	1	51	D	Aiii	250	10
7.5.25	1121	LBA-MIA occupation layer	962	962	LBA	1	58	D	Aiii	230	6
7.5.26	1121	LBA-MIA occupation layer	983	983	LBA	1	14	C	Aiii	120	9
7.5.27	1123	LBA-MIA occupation layer	104	104	LBA	1	56	C	Ai	130	40
7.3.28	1123	LBA-MIA occupation layer	991	991	LBA	1	33	B		340	5
7.5.29	1117	Posthole group and roundhouse	149	150	LBA	1	21	D	Ai	120	9
7.5.30	1117	Posthole group and roundhouse	208	209	MIA	1	7	G	Av		
7.5.31	460	E-MIA U-profiled ditch	238	252	LBA	1	28	A			
7.5.32	460	E-MIA U-profiled ditch	238	255	EIA	1	19	B			
7.5.33	460	E-MIA U-profiled ditch	713	708	MIA	3	9	B	Av	150	7
7.5.34		NOT USED									

Chapter 7

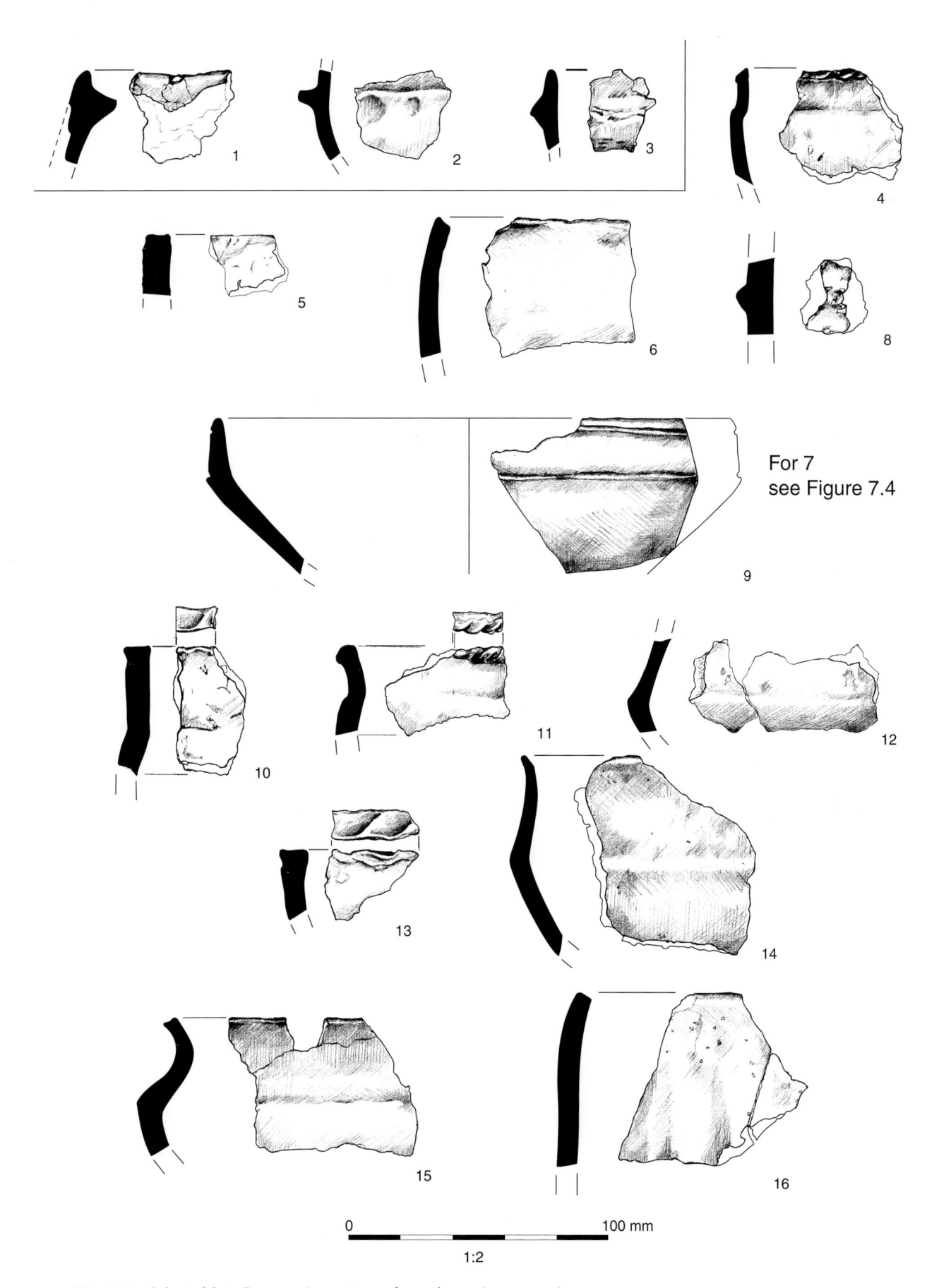

For 7
see Figure 7.4

0   100 mm
1:2

Fig. 7.3   Selected late Bronze Age pottery from the main excavations

Table 7.16 Catalogue of illustrated prehistoric pottery from the TCAST trenches

Figure number	Context	Fabric	Sherd count	Weight (g)	Vessel type	Date	Surface treatment	Decoration
7.6.35	316	AS1	1	7		EBA		Single line of comb
7.6.36	301	F2	3	50	Ai	LBA		
7.6.37	306	AF2	1	12	Aii	LBA		
7.6.38	306	F2	1	6		LBA		Impressed fingernail on rim top
7.6.39	312	F1	1	14	Ai	LBA	Burnished	
7.6.40	401	F2	1	21	Bvi	LBA		
7.6.41	401	F2	1	13		LBA		Partial deep fingernail impressions on the rim
7.6.42	401	F2	1	13	B	LBA		
7.6.43	402a	FA1	1	54	Aiii	LBA		Impressed triangular stamp on shoulder and finger marks on internal curve of shoulder.
7.6.44	402a	AF1	1	13	Aii	LBA	Trimmed	
7.6.45	402a	AF1	1	3		LBA		Small circular impressions on outside of rim
7.6.46	402a	AF1	1	10	Ai	LBA		
7.6.47	402A	A1	1	12	Aix	LBA		Incised lines on outside of rim
7.6.48	402a	A1	1	11		LBA		Impressed fingernail on outside of rim
7.4.49	402a	AF1	1	14	Ai	LBA		
7.6.50								NOT USED
7.6.51	402a	AF1	1	4		LBA		Finger tip and nail on shoulder
7.6.52	402a	F1	1	1		LBA		Very deep fingernail incisions
7.6.53	404	F3	1	32	Av	LBA		
7.6.54	404	F2	1	27		LBA		Straight-walled jar with impressed fingertips on the rim
7.7.55	404	F2	1	12	Avii	LBA	Smoothed	
7.7.56	404	F2	1	11	Aii	LBA	Smoothed	
7.7.57	404	FA2	1	11		LBA		Bevelled rim
7.7.58	404	F2	1	11		LBA		
7.7.59	402a	FA1	2	26	Aiii	LBA		
7.7.60	404	F1	1	11		EIA	Burnished	Burnished and incised pedestal base
7.7.61	402a	FA1	1	99	Aii	EIA		Flat, expanded rim, horizontal interleaved wiping

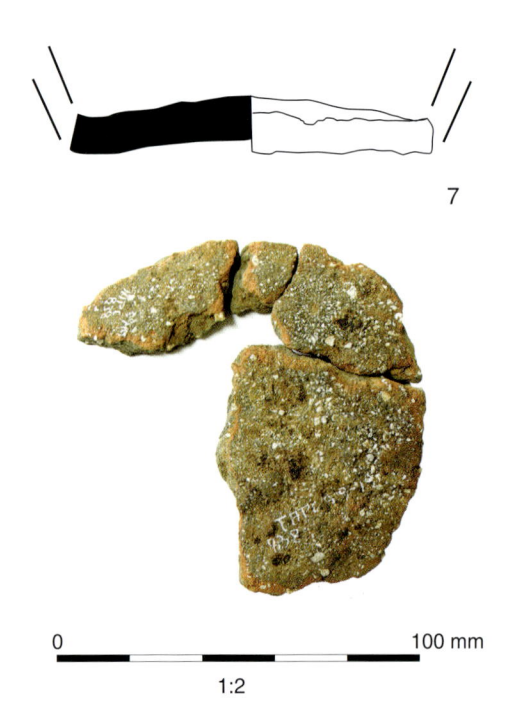

recovered at Barrow Hills, Radley, Oxfordshire (Barclay and Halpin 1999, fig. 5.9). The tapered rim above a cordon (Fig. 7.3.3), which closely matches a vessel from Long Wittenham, Oxfordshire, may also belong to this tradition (Case *et al.* 1964/5, fig. 29, no.2).

The association of later Bronze Age plain ware with the Taplow hilltop enclosure relates it to a number of post-Deverel-Rimbury sites from South-East England. There were significantly less featured sherds present than at many other contemporary sites, and the small size of the assemblage and lack of good groups from discrete features has restricted the information on activity areas, condition, taphonomy, status and ceramic exchange and interaction which can be gleaned from the Taplow assemblage.

Comparable later Bronze Age and early Iron Age pottery has been recovered from a number of adjacent sites including the Taplow to Dorney pipeline (McSloy in Hancocks forthcoming), the

Fig. 7.4 (left) Late Bronze Age gritted base from the V-profiled ditch

Chapter 7

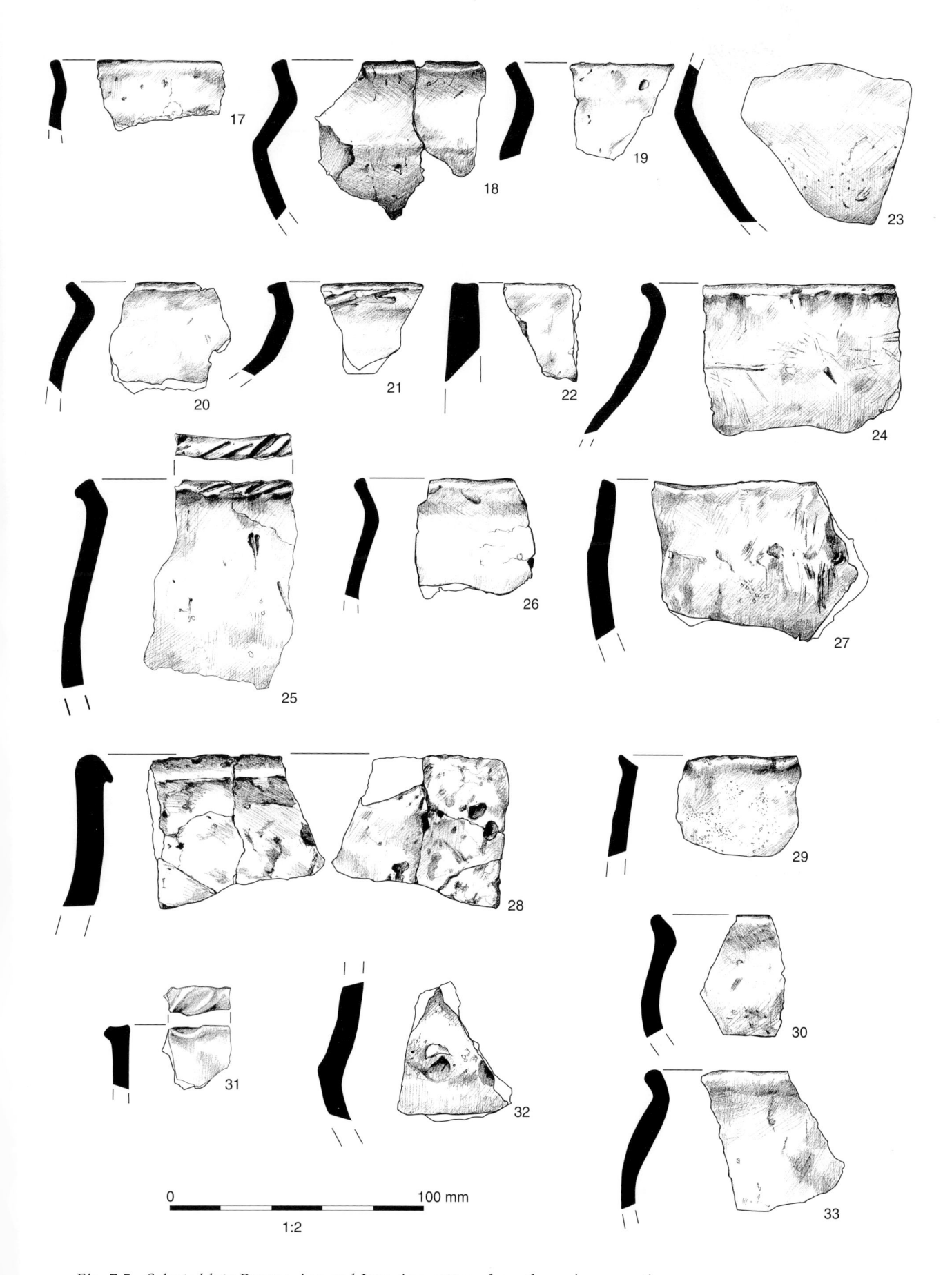

Fig. 7.5 Selected late Bronze Age and Iron Age pottery from the main excavations

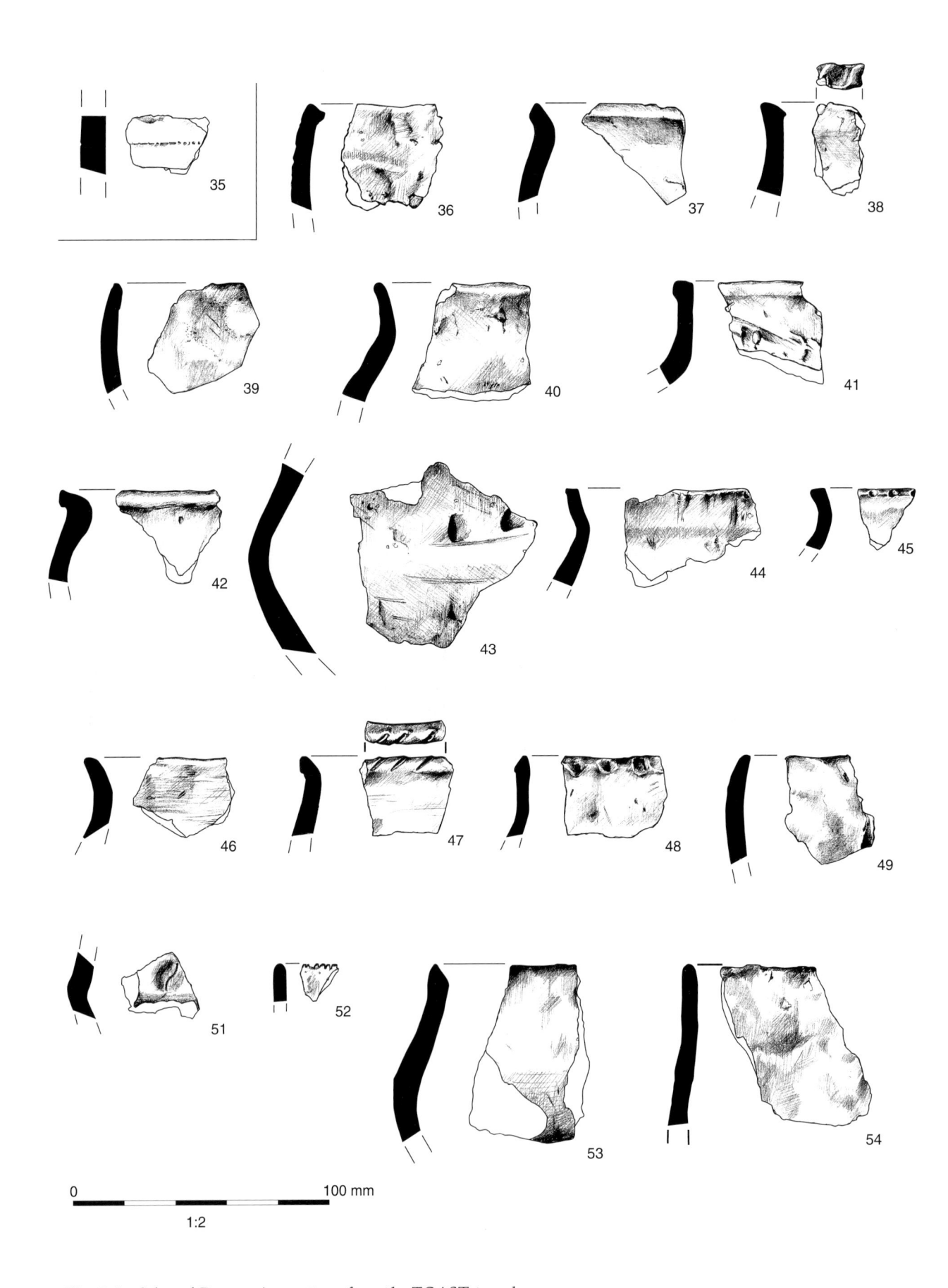

Fig. 7.6 Selected Bronze Age pottery from the TCAST trenches

Chapter 7

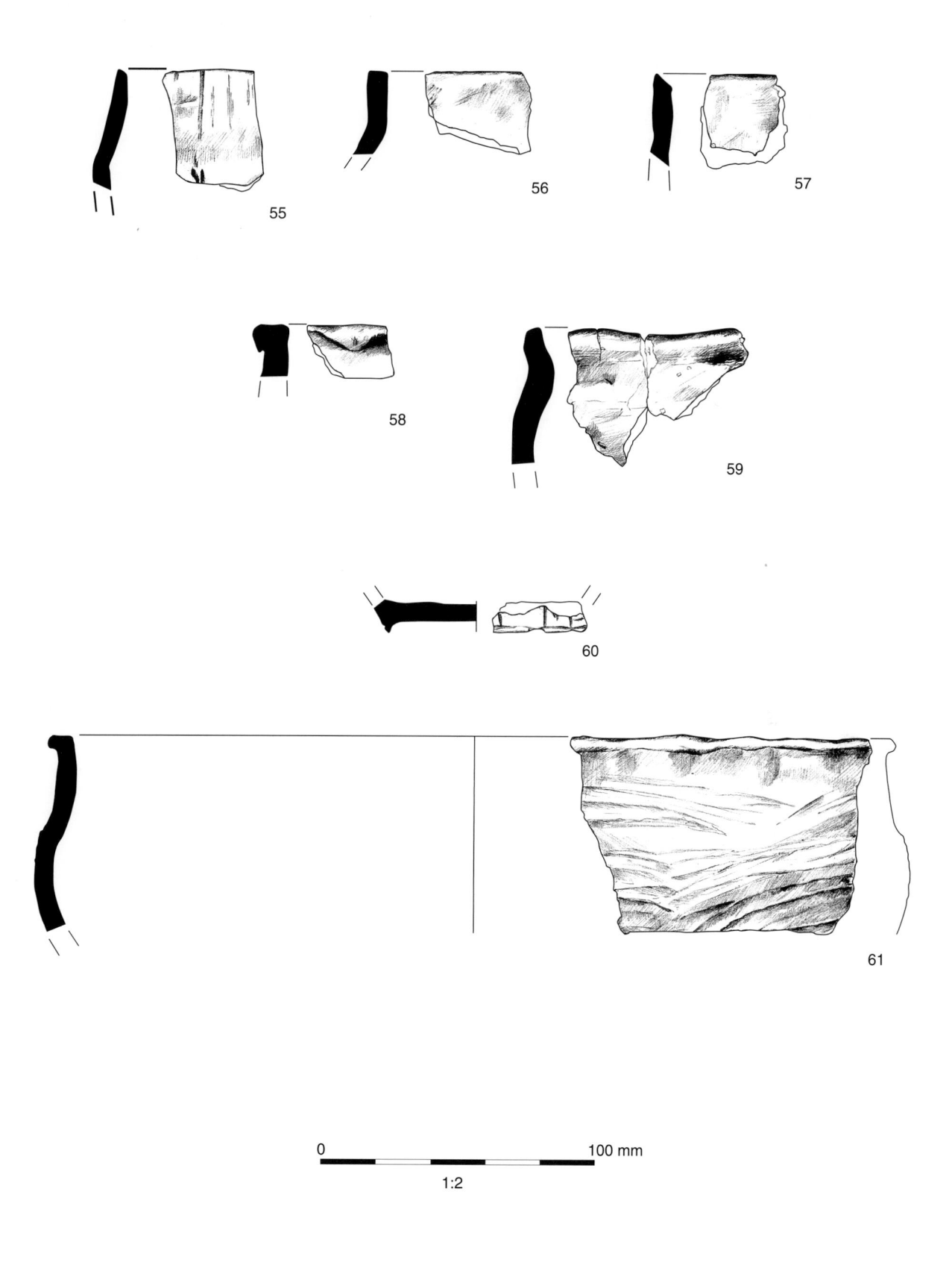

Fig. 7.7 *Selected late Bronze Age and early Iron Age pottery from the TCAST trenches*

Eton Rowing Course, the Maidenhead, Windsor and Eton Flood Alleviation Scheme (Allen *et al.* in prep. b) and Cippenham (Ford 2003). Other relevant published assemblages come from Runnymede (Longley and Needham 1980) and Petters Sports Field (O'Connell 1986), Ivinghoe Beacon (Cotton and Frere 1968), Reading Green Park (Brossler *et al.* 2004), Reading Business Park (Moore and Jennings 1992), Aldermaston and Knight's Farm (Bradley *et al.* 1980).

LATE IRON AGE AND ROMAN POTTERY

by Edward Biddulph

Although just three Roman sherds were recovered from the main excavation (from the U-profiled and outer ditches, 460 and 3050), a much larger quantity (404 sherds, 2104 g) was recovered from four of the five TCAST trenches (Table 7.17). The pottery was sorted macroscopically and, where necessary, at x20 magnification by context into fabric groups. Groups were assigned fabric codes from OA's standard recording system for late Iron Age and Roman ceramics (Booth nd) and weighed. All pottery was additionally quantified by sherd count, while forms were quantified by estimated vessel equivalents (EVE) and minimum number of vessels (MV) based on rim count. Typology followed the scheme set out in Booth (nd). Sherds were typically small and abraded, making precise identification and dating of form and fabric difficult. (The possibly eastern Mediterranean late Roman sherd found in the outer ditch (3050) is discussed in a separate report below.)

Wares (Table 7.18)

S20. South Gaulish samian ware
F51. Oxfordshire red/brown colour-coated ware
W20. General sandy white wares
W21. Verulamium-region white ware
W30. General fine white wares
Q20. General oxidised white-slipped wares
E13. 'Belgic-type' ware, organic- and grog-tempered
E30. 'Belgic-type' ware, medium to coarse sand-tempered
E40. 'Belgic-type' ware, shell-tempered
E60. 'Belgic-type' ware, flint-tempered
E80. 'Belgic-type' ware, grog-tempered
O10. General fine sand oxidised wares
O20. General coarse sand oxidised wares
O80. Oxidised coarse tempered wares
R10. General fine sand grey wares
R20. General coarse sand grey wares
R30. General fine/medium sand grey wares
R90. Coarse 'storage jar' fabrics, usually grog-tempered

Table 7.17 Quantification of LIA and Roman pottery from the TCAST excavations by trench

	Trench			
	2	3	4	5
Sherds	21	117	57	209
Weight (g)	133	735	212	1024
MV	1	9	3	21
EVE	0.05	0.53	0.17	1.61

Table 7.18 Quantification of LIA and Roman pottery from the TCAST excavations by ware

Wares	Sherds	% Sherds	Weight (g)	% weight	MV	% MV	EVE	% EVE
S30	1	<1%	2	<1%				
F51	2	<1%	6	<1%				
W20	1	<1%	1	<1%	1	3%	0.05	2%
W21	3	1%	9	<1%				
W30	1	<1%	2	<1%				
Q20	3	1%	22	1%				
E13	1	<1%	6	<1%				
E30	23	6%	107	5%	1	3%	0.05	2%
E40	2	<1%	6	<1%				
E60	36	9%	239	11%	1	3%	0.05	2%
E80	61	15%	392	19%	7	21%	0.57	24%
O10	11	3%	26	1%				
O20	24	6%	115	5%	1	3%	0.1	4%
O80	7	2%	76	4%				
R10	75	19%	276	13%	7	21%	0.53	22%
R20	8	2%	92	4%	2	6%	0.12	5%
R30	139	34%	643	31%	13	38%	0.82	35%
R90	2	<1%	75	4%	1	3%	0.07	3%
B10	2	<1%	6	<1%				
B20	2	<1%	3	<1%				
Total			2104		34		2.36	

B10. Hand made black-burnished ware 1
B20. Wheel made black-burnished ware 2

So-called 'Belgic' E wares typically date to the 1st century AD (Booth 1995, 108). Grog-tempered wares (E80) dominated the category. Some pieces contained other inclusions besides grog, but the size of the sherds made further division impractical. Flint-tempered wares (E60) also made a significant contribution. These represent something of a regional tradition; they were important, for example, at Park Farm, Binfield, some 12 km to the south-west (ibid.), and at Datchet to the south (Biddulph unpubl.). Sandy wares (E30) contributed a lesser amount to the assemblage, although the category may be under-represented if small, undiagnostic sherds were assigned to the R30 category instead. While the flint and sandy wares possibly arrived from a suspected 1st-century kiln site at nearby Knowl Hill (Over 1973, 66), other as yet undiscovered production sites may have existed closer to Taplow. Shell-tempered and organic-tempered fabrics (E40 and E13 respectively) made a token appearance. Medium-coarse sandy reduced wares (R30) accounted for a large part of the post-conquest pottery. Sources were presumably local in most cases. Potters from further afield may have been responsible for a few pieces; a storage jar represented by a single sherd currently assigned to R30 may have arrived from Alice Holt. Fine grey wares (R10) were also important. The white slip and barbotine dot decoration surviving on some pieces recalled Highgate Wood C ware (Tomber and Dore 1998, 136), but the fabric was not identical and source remains uncertain. Other reduced wares only made minor contributions. Oxidised wares (O), like the reduced wares, were probably locally made. Coarse fabric O80 invariably contained grog and was used mainly for storage jars. Both hand and wheel made black-burnished wares reached the site probably after c AD 130, though the small sherds prevented identification of source. White wares (W) arrived in part from the Verulamium region (W21) between AD 50 and 160 (Davies et al. 1994, 41). A sherd of central Gaulish samian ware (S30) dated to the 2nd century represents the sole continental import. Two sherds of Oxfordshire colour-coated ware (F51) were the latest known pieces, dating after AD 240.

Vessels

The TCAST assemblage was quantified by EVE and vessel class (Table 7.19). Rim sherds were relatively few and poorly preserved; on average just 7% of the total rim circumference of each vessel represented by a rim survived. Jars (C) dominated the assemblage as expected. Neckless bead-rimmed jars (CH) and storage jars (CN) were typical of 'Belgic' wares, while necked, medium-mouthed jars (CD) were available in 'Romanised' reduced wares. Beakers (E) were additionally encountered in white wares. Rims were largely undiagnostic. However, a 1st-century butt-beaker (EA) was tentatively identified in fabric E80, while at least two poppy-headed beakers (EF) were seen in fine grey ware. Body sherds with barbotine dot decoration hint at further vessels. Type EF was current in the late 1st and 2nd century AD. Bowls comprised straight or curving sided types (HB and HC respectively) and occurred in 'Belgic' and reduced wares. The latter type included out-turned or bead rims characteristic of 2nd-century vessels. A decorated Drag. 37 samian bowl arrived from central Gaul. Lids were unusually well-represented at 20% by EVE. Typically they form only a minor part of any assemblage. At Binfield, for example, they accounted for 0.5% of all forms by EVE (Booth 1995, table Mf.9). Why ceramic lids should be so strongly represented at Taplow is unclear, but hints, perhaps, at the presence of a nearby pottery production site, with lids forming a major part of the repertoire.

Table 7.19 Quantification of the TCAST pottery by EVE arranged by vessel class.

Ware	C Jar	C/E Jar/beaker	D Jar/bowl	E Beaker	H Bowl	L Lid	Total	% total
W20				0.05			0.05	2%
E30					0.05		0.05	2%
E60	0.05						0.05	2%
E80	0.25			0.21		0.11	0.57	24%
O20						0.1	0.1	4%
R10	0.1			0.13	0.1	0.2	0.53	22%
R20	0.12						0.12	5%
R30	0.5	0.05	0.05	0.08	0.08	0.06	0.82	35%
R90	0.07						0.07	3%
Total	1.09	0.05	0.05	0.47	0.23	0.47	2.36	
% total	46%	2%	2%	20%	10%	20%		

Condition and chronology

The assemblage was poorly preserved. Sherds were small – as the mean sherd weight of 5 g indicates – and abraded. Each context yielded 17 sherds on average. Six out of 24 contexts yielded more than 30 sherds, but were themselves chronologically mixed. The figures are consistent with a redeposited assemblage, much disturbed through later activity. However, the material nevertheless points to the presence of a late Iron Age and Roman settlement in the vicinity of the site. The paucity of diagnostic elements within the assemblage provides only the broadest outline of the date of such a settlement. The 'Belgic' wares suggest occupation during the early 1st century AD. This continued beyond the Roman conquest; the samian, poppy-headed beakers and Verulamium-region ware place activity in the 2nd century, though perhaps not continuing too far beyond AD 160. There was some limited activity in the late 3rd or 4th century AD. Ceramic supply was predominantly local, although Verulamium and samian wares reveal wider trading links.

Roman pottery from the hillfort

Two sherds were recovered from Saxon fills of the U-profiled ditch 460. Context 214 produced a base sherd, probably from a jar, in a sandy grey ware (R30). The base is half-complete, with a neat break across the centre, although there is no strong indication that the breakage is deliberate. Source is unknown, but it probably came from local kilns. Context 215 yielded a base sherd, probably from a beaker, in a fine grey ware (R10). The base, complete and with smooth edges, was disc-shaped, and may have been deliberately trimmed and shaped into a counter. However, the junction of the base and wall, particularly of beakers, tends to be relatively weak, and a disc-shaped sherd can result even from casual breakage. Even so, it is possible that the pottery had been deliberately selected and curated prior to deposition.

ANGLO-SAXON POTTERY

by Paul Blinkhorn

The bulk of the Anglo-Saxon pottery from both the main excavation (Table 7.20) and the TCAST trenches (Table 7.21) comprised early/middle Saxon hand-built wares with the same basic range of fabrics. The scant chronological evidence suggests that activity at both sites started during the pagan early Saxon period (c AD 450 – 850). A single small sherd of decorated pottery provides the evidence for the earliest Saxon activity in the TCAST trenches. The main excavation did not produce any decorated pottery, but did yield radiocarbon dates spanning the period AD 550-970. The feature which produced the latest of the radiocarbon dates (AD 770-970) contained only hand-built pottery, so it seems likely that there was also activity at the site in the middle Saxon period. Two small sherds of late Saxon pottery, which could conceivably date to the later part of the radiocarbon date range, were found in the U-profiled and outer ditches (460 and 3050), and so it is possible that there was continual activity at the site from the early to late Saxon periods.

Methodology

The pottery was initially bulk-sorted and recorded on a computer using DBase IV software. The material from each context was recorded by number and weight of sherds per fabric type, with featureless body sherds of the same fabric counted, weighed and recorded as one database entry. Feature sherds such as rims, bases and lugs were individually recorded, with individual codes used for the various types. Decorated sherds were similarly treated. In the case of the rimsherds, the form, diameter and the percentage remaining of the original complete circumference was all recorded. This figure was summed for each fabric type to obtain the estimated vessel equivalent (EVE).

The terminology used is that defined by the Medieval Pottery Research Group (MPRG 1998) and to their minimum standards (MPRG 2001). All the statistical analyses were carried out using a Dbase package written by the author, which interrogated the original or subsidiary databases, with some of the final calculations made with an electronic calculator. All statistical analyses were carried out to the minimum standards suggested by Orton (1998-9, 135-7).

Fabrics

The same range of early/middle Saxon (AD 450-850) hand-built pottery was noted in both the main excavation and the TCAST trenches. The hand-built Anglo-Saxon pottery occurred in the following fabrics:

F1: Sandy. Dense subangular clear, grey and pink quartz c 0.5 mm

F2: Chaff. Dense chaff voids up to 10 mm, very sparse subangular quartz and calcitic material <0.5 mm

F3: Sparse quartz. Fine sandy matrix, sparse to moderate subrounded quartz up to 1 mm, rare red iron ore up to 2 mm, rare calcitic material up to 1 mm and sparse to moderate chaff up to 3 mm

These fabrics are very typical of the range of types noted at a number of sites in the region.

Anglo-Saxon pottery from the main excavation

The pottery assemblage comprised 70 sherds with a total weight of 913 g. The estimated vessel equivalent, by summation of surviving rimsherd circumference was 0.22. The assemblage comprised

Table 7.20 Occurrence of Anglo-Saxon pottery in the main excavation by number and weight (in g) of sherds per context by fabric type. E/MS = early-middle Saxon

Context	F1 No	F1 Wt	F2 No	F2 Wt	F3 No	F3 Wt	OXAC No	OXAC Wt	Date
101			1	6					E/MS
103	2	17							E/MS
110							1	3	11th C?
214	3	17	4	29					E/MS
215			5	42					E/MS
579	7	166							E/MS
607	35	397	3	81	1	7			E/MS
712			1	1					E/MS
3002	1	14					1	18	11th C?
3004	4	50	1	65					E/MS
Total	52	661	15	224	1	7	2	21	

early/middle Saxon hand-built material, and a single sherd (3 g) of Saxo-Norman material. The pottery occurrence by number and weight of sherds per context by fabric type is shown in Table 7.20. Each date should be regarded as a *terminus post quem*.

Fabrics

The hand-built Anglo-Saxon pottery occurred in the following fabrics:

F1: 52 sherds, 661 g, EVE = 0.27

F2: 15 sherds, 224 g, EVE = 0

F3: 1 sherd, 7 g, EVE = 0

In addition, two sherds (21 g) of late Saxon – early medieval Cotswolds-type ware (Oxford fabric OXAC; Mellor 1994) were noted. The Cotswolds-type sherds are very abraded, and many of the inclusions leached out, suggesting that they are likely to be redeposited. Such pottery is common in the region in the early-mid 11th century, but a few examples have been found in secure contexts dating to the later 9th century in Cricklade, and in Oxford a single vessel is known which is dated to the early 10th century (Mellor 1994, 51). In the west and north of Oxfordshire, the earliest securely dated finds suggest it was not arriving in any significant quantity until the late 11th century. These are among the most easterly finds of the ware in the Thames Valley, and so caution must be applied to the dating of the sherd. For this reason, it seems most likely that they date from the 11th century here, although they could conceivably be a century or two earlier.

Chronology

All the Saxon hand-built material was undecorated, making it impossible to date other than to within the broad early/middle Saxon periods, AD 450-850. The Anglo-Saxons appear to have generally stopped decorating hand-built pottery around the turn of the 6th-7th centuries, and vessels with fabrics similar to the ones from this site are known from both early and middle Saxon sites along the length of the Thames Valley. For example, at Radley Barrow Hills near Abingdon (Blinkhorn 2007, 231) a range of decorated early Saxon pottery in quartz- and chaff-tempered fabrics was noted, whereas at the sites excavated before the construction of the Maidenhead, Windsor and Eton Flood Alleviation scheme, less than 5 km to the south-east of this site, similar wares were found in association with middle Saxon Ipswich Ware and continental imported wares (Blinkhorn 2002, table 4.1). Such wares are also common at middle Saxon sites in the City of London (Blackmore 1988; 1989), and chaff-tempered wares were found in association with Ipswich Ware at Lechlade, Glos. (Blinkhorn, forthcoming).

A radiocarbon date of cal AD 550-650 (OxA-14432) from the lowest of the Anglo-Saxon fills in the U-profiled ditch, although not associated with any pottery, suggests that Anglo-Saxon activity began in the area of the main excavation late in the 6th century AD or early in the 7th. The later radiocarbon date of cal AD 770-970 (SUERC-491) from the same ditch indicates that there was also middle-late Saxon activity here. The context which produced the later date (layer 579) produced only hand-built pottery, so it seems likely that this context at least is of middle Saxon date, or is possibly even late Saxon, as hand-built pottery has been found in quantity in late Saxon deposits in the region, at places such as Dorchester (Mellor 1994, 36). It is possible that the hand-built 'early Saxon' tradition in Oxfordshire continued into the late Saxon period, and that some of the pottery from Taplow is, in fact, of early late Saxon date.

As noted above, Cotswolds ware, although generally a late Saxon or Saxo-Norman ware, is known from late 9th-century deposits to the west of Taplow, and so the sherds from this site could conceivably date to within the span of the later radiocarbon date.

Vessel forms

Only three rimsherds were present, all of simple everted form, a common type for pottery of the period. Two are illustrated (Fig. 7.8. nos 1 and 2). None of the bodysherds showed any evidence of form or decoration other than a single flat basesherd, and it seems likely that all the Anglo-Saxon hand-built pots were in simple globular forms. These can also be paralleled at the sites noted above.

Anglo-Saxon pottery from the TCAST trenches

The pottery assemblage comprised 32 sherds with a total weight of 293 g. The estimated vessel equivalent (EVE), by summation of surviving rimsherd circumference was 0. The same range of fabric types was noted, as follows:

The pottery occurrence by number and weight of sherds per context by fabric type is shown in Table 7.21. Each date should be regarded as a *terminus post quem*.

F1: 8 sherds, 42 g, EVE = 0
F2: 6 sherds, 66 g, EVE = 0
F3: 18 sherds, 185 g, EVE = 0

Chronology

The bulk of the Anglo-Saxon material was undecorated, so the comments concerning chronology already made in relation to the pottery from the main excavation also apply here. However, a single small sherd in fabric 1 from context 404 had a fragment of incised line decoration (Fig. 7.8.3). This would suggest that the sherd in question is of early Saxon date, but unfortunately, such decoration was extremely common throughout the pagan early Saxon period, and so the sherd can only be broadly dated to that period (the 5th-6th century).

Discussion

The two groups of pottery have the same range of fabric types. However, the proportions in the two areas are quite different. The group from the main excavation favours fabrics F1 and F2, whereas F3 is the major ware from the TCAST trenches. The main excavation produced radiocarbon dates spanning the period from AD 550 to 970. The pottery from the TCAST trenches appears to belong to a similar period, although the single decorated sherd may have been slightly earlier (5th or 6th century) than anything found in the main excavation. Although there must have been considerable overlap in the chronology of the pottery from the two areas, it is possible that the apparently quite different proportions of the fabrics at the two sites is evidence of a change in pottery use over time.

The probability that the pottery from the two areas was composed of significantly different fabrics can be tested statistically using the chi-squared test (Drennan 1997). The data in this test is shown in Table 7.22. Computing this data gives a chi-squared value of 44.09 with 2 degrees of freedom, where $p > 0.0001$. This suggests that the difference is significant. Testing the strength of the result using Cramer's V (ibid.) returns a value of 0.66. This suggests that there are grounds to believe that the difference in the fabric proportions is significant, but this cannot be stated with absolute confidence, probably due to possible distortions from the relatively small assemblage size. While it is therefore possible that the

Table 7.21 Occurrence of Anglo-Saxon pottery in the TCAST trenches by number and weight (in g) of sherds per context by fabric type

	F1		F2		F3		
Context	No	Wt	No	Wt	No	Wt	Date
23					1	27	M11thC?
30					1	11	E/MS
201	5	25			1	3	E/MS
202	1	6					E/MS
301			1	13	1	7	E/MS
302			1	36	4	65	E/MS
304					1	5	E/MS
306	1	9			1	13	E/MS
310					2	16	E/MS
401			1	2	2	10	E/MS
402			2	11			E/MS
404	1	2	1	4	4	28	ES
Total	8	42	6	66	18	185	

Table 7.22 Early/middle Saxon pottery occurrence in both the main and TCAST excavations by number of sherds per fabric type

	F1	F2	F3	Total
Main excavation	52	15	1	62
TCAST trenches	8	6	18	32
Total	60	21	19	94

differences in the proportions of fabrics reflect differences in the chronological emphasis of activity in the two areas, overall the chronological range of the pottery appears to be similar. Certainly, the context from the main excavation that produced the radiocarbon date (layer 579) produced only sherds in F1, suggesting that this fabric may be of middle Saxon date. However, the decorated sherd from the TCAST trenches is in the same fabric, so it would appear that this particular fabric type had a long life. Furthermore, the decorated sherd was the only sherd in that fabric from Trench 4, F3 forming the bulk of the admittedly somewhat small assemblage.

Catalogue of illustrated Anglo-Saxon pottery

Fig. 7.8.1: Context 607, F1. Rimsherd. Brownish-grey sandy fabric. E/M Saxon.

Fig. 7.8.2: Context 607, F1. Rimsherd. Dark grey sandy fabric. E/M Saxon.

Fig. 7.8.3: TCAST (TC99) Context 404, F1. Decorated sherd. Light grey fabric with darker surfaces. Outer surface is smoothed and lightly burnished, with a fragment of a single incised cordon.

The possibly eastern Mediterranean late Roman sherd

by Roberta Tomber

The form and general appearance of a single sherd (Plate 7.1) found in the lowest of the Anglo-Saxon upper fills (3004) in the outer ditch (3050) initially suggested that it might have been of eastern Mediterranean origin, possibly allied to late Roman Amphora 1 Class 44 (Peacock and Williams 1986). A thin section was made from the sherd in order to assess this attribution. In thin section the sherd has a silty clay matrix with abundant colourless mica and occasional iron-rich inclusions. A larger fraction of inclusions is moderately common, comprising medium- to coarse-sand grade quartz, polycrystalline quartz and, rarely, chert. Iron-rich clay pellets can also be seen. The closer examination of the fabric does not support the initial identification. While there is nothing particularly distinctive about the fabric, it could nevertheless easily have originated in the eastern Mediterranean and the sherd could have derived from a flagon or other vessel type from that region. A grain of wheat from the same layer gave a radiocarbon date of cal AD 670-870 (Poz-12532: 1255±30 BP).

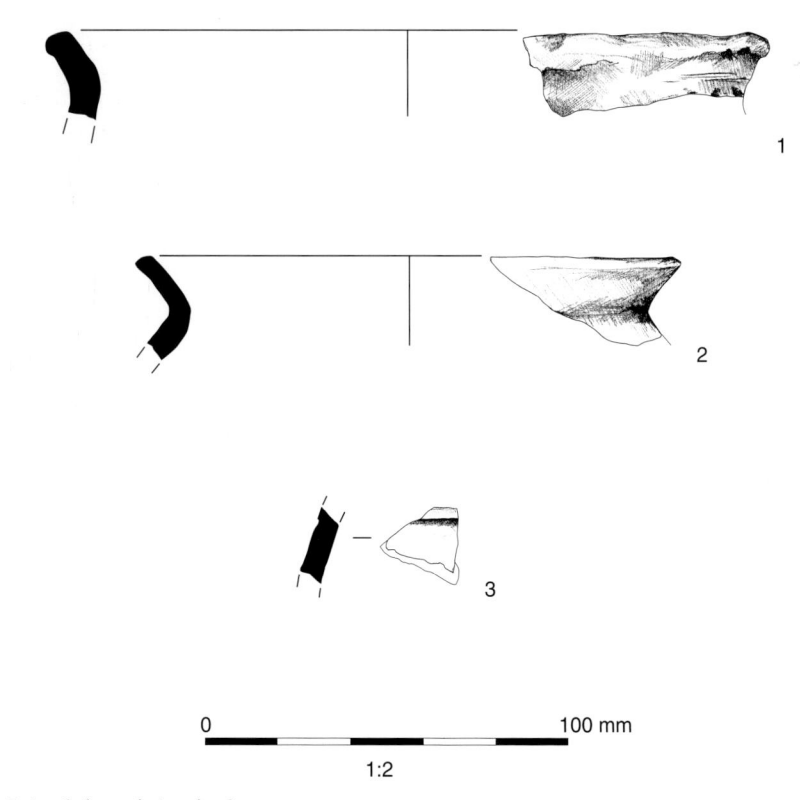

Fig. 7.8 Selected Anglo-Saxon pottery

Plate 7.1 The sherd possibly from an imported, eastern Mediterranean vessel

METALWORK

The bronze bracelet

A fragment of a bronze bracelet (SF1173) was found either in the occupation layer (1121) or the modern subsoil above (1122) within the hillfort. Unfortunately, after the analysis reported below had been completed, the bracelet went missing, possibly stolen. It is not, therefore, possible to provide a full description of this find. The only records of it that survive are the analysis reported below and an x-ray (Plate 7.2). The x-ray shows that just under half of the circumference of the bracelet survived. It appears to have formed a rather flattened circle, with a maximum diameter of over 62 mm, and, seen from above, had a diameter of 5 mm. The outer edge of the bracelet is marked by much stronger image on the x-ray than the interior, suggesting that the outer edge was thicker than the inner. The excavator recalls that the bracelet was decorated on the side with two or three indented parallel lines running perpendicular to the circumference of the bracelet.

Analysis of the bronze bracelet
by Peter Northover

The decorated bronze bracelet described above (SF 1173) was submitted for compositional analysis. A single sample, labelled Ox 301 was removed using a handheld modelmaker's electric drill with a 0.9 mm diameter bit. The sample was hot-mounted in a carbon-filled thermosetting resin, ground and polished to a 1 µm diamond finish. Analysis was by electron probe microanalysis with wavelength dispersive spectrometry; operating conditions were an accelerating voltage of 25 kV, a beam current of 30 nA, and an X-ray take-off angle of 40 E. Thirteen elements were sought, as listed in Table 7.23; pure element and mineral standards were used with a counting time of 10 s per element. Detection limits were typically 100-200 ppm with the exception of 400 ppm for gold.

Five areas, each 30x50 µm, were analysed on the sample; the individual compositions and their means, normalised to 100%, are shown in Table 7.23. All concentrations are in weight %.

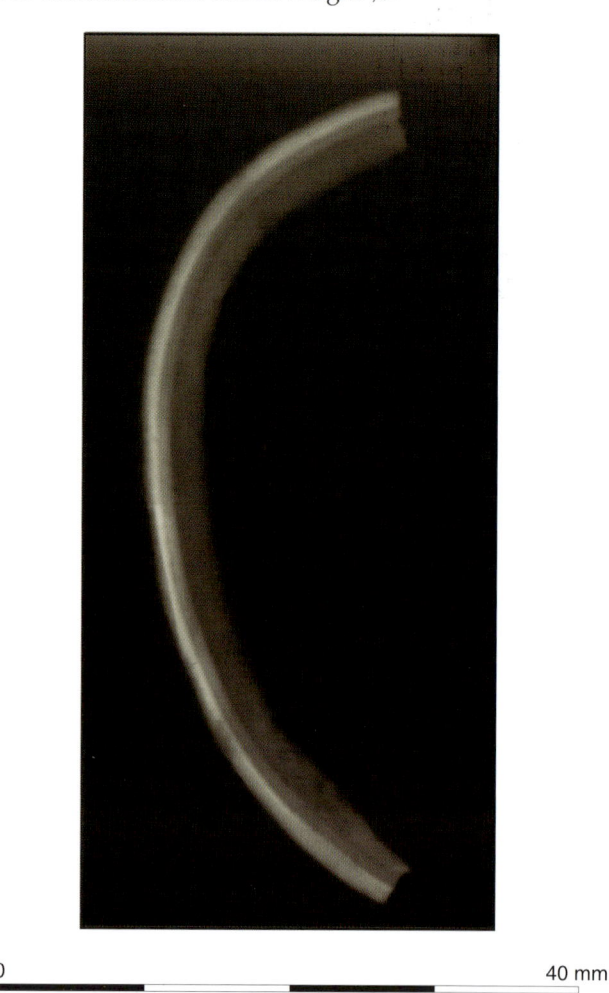

Plate 7.2 X-ray of Bronze Age bracelet fragment

Table 7.23 Analysis of the bracelet

Sample	Fe	Co	Ni	Cu	Zn	As	Sb	Sn	Ag	Bi	Pb	Au	S
OX 301/1	0.83	0.02	0.28	91.56	0.04	0.20	0.47	5.90	0.49	0.01	0.17	0.00	0.03
OX 301/2	0.45	0.01	0.21	90.40	0.00	0.26	0.64	7.50	0.17	0.05	0.24	0.03	0.05
OX 301/3	0.07	0.04	0.23	92.09	0.02	0.26	0.64	6.26	0.26	0.00	0.12	0.00	0.01
OX301/4	0.00	0.02	0.26	90.66	0.00	0.25	0.61	7.09	0.23	0.01	0.83	0.00	0.03
OX301/5	0.00	0.00	0.25	89.42	0.00	0.24	0.87	7.39	0.24	0.00	1.47	0.13	0.00
OX301/Mean	0.27	0.02	0.25	90.83	0.01	0.24	0.64	6.83	0.28	0.01	0.57	0.03	0.03

The metal

The bracelet was cast in a low to medium tin bronze with 6.82% tin; lead was present in the sample at 0.57%, but this may reflect a residual alloy level of 1-2% elsewhere in the sample. The principal impurities were 0.27% iron, 0.25% nickel, 0.24% arsenic, 0.64% antimony, and 0.28% silver; there were also small traces of cobalt, zinc, bismuth and sulphur.

The dating of the bracelet to the late Bronze Age on typological grounds is supported by the composition since an impurity pattern with Ni, As, Sb, Ag and Sb > As is, in Britain, only found in that period. It is particularly characteristic of the Wilburton period, and typically Wilburton forms. However they continue into the Ewart Park period, although with decreasing frequency. Within the Ewart Park period they are more common and more persistent in eastern England and Scotland. It should be added that it is believed that late Bronze Age metal of Irish origin also has Sb > Ag but that metal does not have the level of nickel seen here.

It is difficult to assign this composition specifically to the Ewart Park or Wilburton period without taking note of its typology. However, the antimony content is at the lower end of the Wilburton range and a date early in the Ewart Park period is to be preferred. Even here the current evolution of our understanding of late Bronze Age chronology may blur this picture further. Work in progress by the present writer and colleagues is suggesting that the evolution of the Ewart Park sword, and perhaps other associated types, was taking place in parallel with that of the Wilburton sword rather than subsequent to it. This may ultimately affect the dating of some hoards such as Marston St Lawrence and Blackmoor to which we would otherwise look for parallels for this composition. The tin content could be consistent with either period as there was a marked drop in the tin content of the bronze imported into southern Britain on which local industries were dependent. Wilburton metalwork tends to be marked by a high lead content, especially for non-utilitarian pieces. In the Ewart Park period there is a much greater range of lead contents and it appears that some groups did not add lead but used some scrap already containing lead. Lead contents took longer to reach British levels across the Channel and it is possible that this bracelet was either made directly from a piece of imported bronze without other mixing, or could be of continental origin itself.

Conclusions

The composition of this bracelet is best associated with a dating in the first part of the Ewart Park period, from the latter part of the 11th century BC to the end of the 10th. The metal originated on the continent and, metallurgically, there is no reason why the bracelet could not have been made there.

Other metalwork
by Leigh Allen

A total of 18 metal objects were recovered from the excavations at Taplow Court. The assemblage comprises 11 copper alloy objects, five iron objects and two lead objects. In general the copper alloy objects are in good condition, although this is probably because the majority of the objects are post-medieval or modern in date. The only notable copper alloy object is a spiral headed pin of Saxon date. The ironwork is in very poor condition. The objects are fragmentary and the x-rays indicate that very little of the original metal still survives. The ironwork includes the remains of 4 knives that are possibly Saxon in date and a fork of post-medieval date. The lead objects include a musket ball and are post-medieval in date. The metalwork assemblage has been x-rayed and visually examined. Table 7.24 lists the objects.

Copper alloy objects

The most notable copper alloy object is a spiral headed pin (SF 1171; Plate 7.3) from the upper, Anglo-Saxon fills of the U-profiled ditch (460; context 579, cut 713). The pin has two spirals at the head that curl inwards. The shaft is straight and there is no collar. Similar examples have been found at Hamwic and Kingsworthy, and numerous examples have been recovered from Anglo-Saxon cemeteries. These delicate pins are often found in pairs, and from the position on the body they are believed to have been used on clothing or to secure shrouds. Originally

Table 7.24 Summary of metal objects other than the bronze bracelet. CA = copper alloy; Fe = iron; Pb = lead

Context info	Context	SF	Object	Material	Date
Modern subsoil 1122	103	2	Coin	CA	1709
Modern subsoil 1122	103	4	Coin	CA	1875
Modern subsoil 1122	103	1	Coin	CA	c19th/20th
Modern subsoil 1122	103	3	Coin	CA	1862
Modern subsoil 1122	103	-	Coin	CA	1890
Modern subsoil 1122	103	6	Button	CA	Post med
Modern subsoil 1122	103	11	Sheet fragment	CA	-
Modern subsoil 1122	103	7	Mount	CA	Post med
Modern subsoil 1122	103	10	Strip	CA	-
Modern subsoil 1122	103	9	Buckle	CA/Fe	Post med
Modern subsoil 1122	103	5	Strip	Pb	-
Modern subsoil 1122	103	8	Musket ball	Pb	Post med
Modern subsoil 1122	964	-	Fork	Fe	Post med
Saxon grave 105	107	12	Knife	Fe	Saxon
U-profiled ditch, Saxon upper fills, cut 102	123	-	Knife	Fe	Saxon
U-profiled ditch, Saxon upper fills, cut 713	579	1171	Pin	CA	Saxon
U-profiled ditch, Saxon upper fills, 713	579	-	Knife ?	Fe	Saxon
U-profiled ditch, Saxon upper fills, 713	607	501	Knife	Fe	Saxon

Plate 7.3 The Anglo-Saxon spiral-headed pin

believed to be 6th century in date, they are now thought to be slightly later. The Southampton examples suggests that they were current well into the 8th century and may have continued in use into the 9th and 10th centuries (Hinton and Parsons 1996, 28-30, fig. 11). Such spiral headed pins were decorative personal ornaments, generally assumed to be an item of female attire. They are commonly found in Anglo-Saxon cemeteries.

The remaining copper alloy objects are all post-medieval/modern in date and were recovered from subsoil within the hillfort.

Iron objects

The ironwork comprises four knives of Saxon date and a fork of post-medieval date. SF 12 from context 107, fill of grave 105, is a highly corroded whittle tang knife in a number of fragments. It has a flat back which angles down at the tip. The blade edge is very damaged. The burial probably associated with this knife has been radiocarbon dated to cal AD 590-680 (SUERC-4963: 1390±40 BP). The knife was the only artefact associated with this inhumation.

Two of the knives recovered from the Anglo-Saxon fills of the U-profiled ditch (460) are small in comparison to SF 12. They also have with straight backs that angle down at the tip. The example from context 123 has a straight blade edge but SF 501 from context 607 has a slightly worn blade edge giving the knife the characteristic S-shaped blade of late Saxon knives. The final knife fragment is a short section of a whittle tang from context 579, another fill of ditch 460. These knives are domestic items and suggest settlement in the vicinity of the ditch.

Lead objects

The lead objects include a musket ball (SF 8) of post-medieval date and a fragment of lead, both recovered from the modern subsoil (1122) within the hillfort.

FIRED CLAY
by Emily Edwards

Introduction

A total of 78 fragments (775 g) of fired clay, including parts of annular, cylindrical and pyramidal loomweights, were recovered from the excavation area. The fired clay was recovered from the early Bronze Age hollows (1119), the V- and U-profiled ditches (574 and 460), the palisade trench (1106), the rampart gravels associated with the U-profiled ditch (1100) and the occupation layer (1123 and 1121).

Methodology

Table 7.25 gives a summary quantification of the fired clay by number of fragments and weight. The fired clay was examined for evidence of wattle or other impressions, possible objects and structural pieces. A record was made of the various fabrics, which were examined under x20 magnification. Condition was recorded using a numerical system ranging from 0 (unidentifiable) through to 6 (identifiable).

The degree to which a fragment was fired was also measured on a grade of 1-4:

1 = Oxidised all the way through

2 = Unoxidised all the way through

3 = Oxidised exterior and unoxidised interior

4 = Irregularly fired throughout

Condition

The assemblage consists of broken and abraded fragments which vary in size. All of the material is less than 10% complete and 78% of the assemblage comprises amorphous fragments weighing under 10 g. The identifiable fragments and parts of objects varied in weight from 11 g to 88 g. The generally small size of the fragments may simply reflect the fact that much of the fired clay was residual.

Fabrics

There was little variation in the fabrics used to manufacture the fired clay fragments. All contain coarse sand (A), although some were more silty (B). None of the fabrics appears to have involved any form of clay paste preparation. Many of the inclusions, such as quartzite pebbles and ferruginous ironstone pellets, are naturally occurring materials rather than deliberately added temper.

Table 7.25 Summary of fired clay. Type Codes: A - amorphous; LW - loomweight; TLW - Triangular loomweight; PLW - Pyramidal Loomweight; ALW - Annular loomweight,; CLW - cylindrical loomweight; O - Object; HO - Hearth or oven.

Group	Feature	Cut	Context	Count	Weight (g)	Fabric	Type	Firing	Completeness
1119	EBA hollows	578	643	4	7	A	A	1	6
		642	551	2	3	A	A	1	0
		642	553	1	2	A	A	1	0
		642	553	1	3	A	A	1	0
		642	553	1	8	A	A	1	0
		642	553	1	9	A	A	1	0
		642	553	1	25	AB	HO	3	6
		642	553	2	2	A	A	1	0
		642	553	2	6	A	A	1	0
		642	553	2	22	A	A	1	0
		642	553	5	5	A	A	1	0
1106	Palisade trench	569	911	1	11	A	A	1	0
574	V-profiled ditch	878	839	5	17	A	A	3	6
1121	Occupation layer	983	983	7	14	A	A	1	0
		985	985	9	15	A	A	1	0
1122	Modern subsoil	964	964	1	7	A	HO	3	6
		964	964	1	26	A	CLW	1	0
		964	964	1	29	AB	HO	3	6
1123	Occupation layer	104	104	1	88	AB	HO	3	6
		990	990	3	158	A	HO	3	6
		991	991	1	37	A	CLW	1	5
1100	Rampart gravels (burnt)	644	644	2	49	AB	PLW	3	5
460	U-profiled ditch	102	121	3	44	A	HO	1	6
		713	579	16	167	A	ALW	3	5
		713	607	1	15	A	O	1	6
		713	607	4	6	A	A	1	6

Range and variety of material

The assemblage includes annular, cylindrical and pyramidal loomweights. Fragmented objects include a piece that is possibly the end of a pierced slab (Longley and Needham 1980, 31-2).

Provenance

A total of 22 fragments (92 g) of fired clay were recovered from the early Bronze Age hollows (1119) where they were associated with Collared Urn sherds. These fragments are all amorphous with the exception of one that could be the corner of an object, with a smoothed interior surface.

From the rampart gravels (1100), two refitting (49 g) fragments of a pyramidal loomweight were recovered.

A total of 24 fragments (232 g) of fired clay were recovered from the U-profiled ditch (460), including an Anglo-Saxon loomweight from the upper fills, while five fragments, all amorphous, were recovered (7 g) from the earlier V-profiled ditch (574), and a single amorphous fragment (11 g) was recovered from the palisade trench (1106).

A total of 21 fragments (312 g) were recovered from the occupation layer (1123), most of which were amorphous. A cylindrical loomweight (Plate 7.4) and part of an unclassified object (context 104) were, however, identified. Three fragments of fired clay (62 g) were recovered from the modern subsoil (1122) within the hillfort. These included the end of a cylindrical loomweight. The fabric of this piece is suggestive of sandstone rather than fired clay.

Fired clay by category (excluding amorphous fragments)

Loomweights

A total of 20 (279 g) fragments of a minimum of four loomweights were recovered from four contexts; two of these were identified as cylindrical loomweights, one as a pyramidal 'loomweight' and one as an Anglo-Saxon annular loomweight.

Cylindrical weights (see Plate 7.4) such as those recovered from the occupation layer (1123) within the hillfort, are rare in the Upper Thames Valley and are generally considered to be middle Bronze Age.

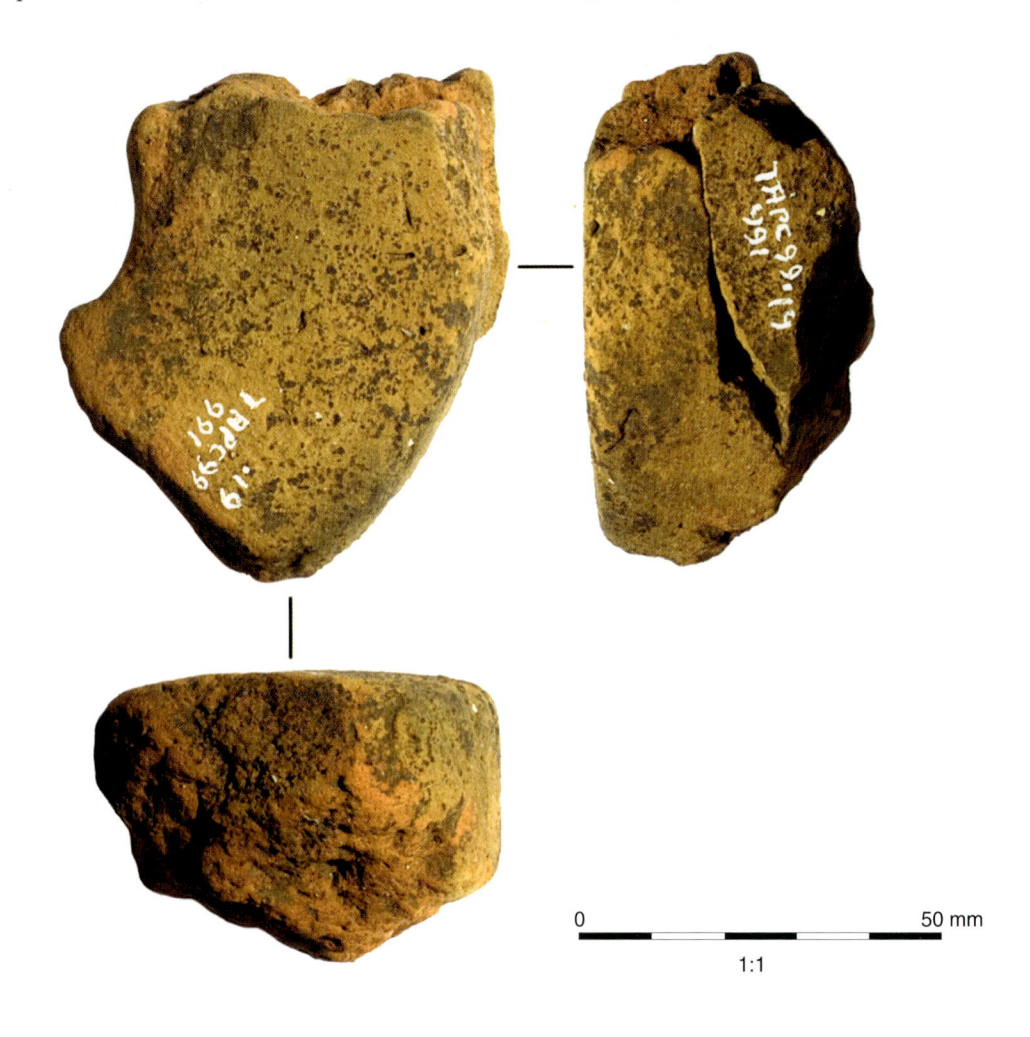

Plate 7.4 Fragments of fired clay from a cylindrical loomweight

Possible exceptions to this general date range, however, include weights recovered at Pingewood from a context associated with middle and late Bronze Age pottery (Johnston and Bowden 1985). One unpublished weight from Oxford was comb decorated and could be of early Bronze Age date (Alistair Barclay pers. comm.). These exceptions are important, as the Taplow Court example was recovered from deposits which were not sealed (991, part of the occupation layer 1123 and 964, part of the modern subsoil 1122) but which contained almost exclusively late Bronze Age and later pottery (although the lower subsoil of the occupation layer, context 219, contained one early Bronze Age sherd). De Roche (pers. comm.) has suggested, on the basis of experiments, that these weights would have hung horizontally (rather than vertically) underneath the loom.

Pyramidal 'loomweights' with a single piercing through the narrow top end were first made in the late Bronze Age, and continued to be produced in the Iron Age. The occurrence of such a weight from the burnt rampart gravels (1100) appears to be consistent with the residual late Bronze Age pottery recovered from these deposits. This type is paralleled in the late Bronze Age at Runnymede Bridge (Longley and Needham 1980, fig. 17), Reading Business Park (Moore and Jennings 1992, fig. 52) and Aldermaston, Berkshire (Bradley et al. 1980, fig. 19). Although usually described as loomweights, the absence of wear on the perforations of such objects suggests that they were not, in fact, used in this way. They may instead have been used as oven or hearth furniture (Poole 1991 and pers. comm.).

The annular loomweight fragment, from one of the upper fills (579) of the U-profiled ditch (460), was associated with Saxon, late Bronze Age and post medieval pottery. The occurrence of Saxon pottery is consistent with the form, which is diagnostically Saxon (Hamerow 1993, 66).

Oven or hearth clay

A large rectangular, angular fragment from context 990 in the occupation layer (1123) may be oven clay, as may an object from the hollow containing Collared Urn 1119 (context 553) and those from contexts 104 in the occupation layer (1123) and 964 in the modern subsoil (1122).

Hearth or oven material may include large thick blocks of fired clay and perforated rectangular or plaque shaped slabs. Interpretations of pierced slabs include cooking or ventilation (Champion 1980, 237-8). Such slabs have been recovered from Runnymede Bridge, Surrey (Longley and Needham 1980, figs 17 and 58), Mucking (Bond 1988, fig. 27), Potterne (Lawson 2000, fig. 65) and Petters Sports Field, Surrey (O'Connell 1986). The fragment from context 121 in the U-profiled ditch (460) is shaped similarly to those depicted in Longley and Needham (1980, figs 17 and 58) although the crucial perforation is not evident.

Oven material, in contrast, has not been recovered from any of the major Bronze Age sites in the middle Thames Valley. It can be difficult to recognise and is poorly understood. Oven and hearth features are ephemeral, and surviving fragments may consist of fired earth from clay-floored hearths or thick and curved pieces from the base or sides. Functions can be presumed to include cooking and feasting although such deposits can also be considered to indicate a potting (open firing) or cremation (pyre debris) site. Given the absence of any other evidence for pottery production or cremation at Taplow these latter functions seem unlikely in this case.

Other objects

A squared fragment from the U-profiled ditch (460, context 607) appeared to be the end of a slab or tile.

Discussion

Fired clay is a good indicator of domestic and industrial activities, which include cooking, textile production and pottery manufacture. The spindle-whorls and loomweights recovered provide an insight into the textile producing techniques of the community. Loomweights are used on vertical, warp-weighted looms, usually attached (via loops) to the warp threads. It is very rare for prehistoric British textiles to survive but those that have been recovered have contributed to an understanding of the types of cloth which such looms could produce (Wild 2003, 7-12; Barber 2003). By the Iron Age it is apparently the case that warp-weighted looms were used to produce more complicated weaves. Overall this small assemblage is representative of everyday domestic activities carried out at various times during the Bronze Age and the Saxon period.

WORKED STONE
by Ruth Shaffrey

Introduction

From a total of 30 contexts at Taplow Court producing utilised stone, there are 11 items of interest, all of which have been examined with the aid of a x10 magnification hand lens. They include six hammerstones, one rubber, one processor and three saddle querns plus a number of lava fragments. The site also produced unworked pebbles utilised as pot boilers. Stone was retrieved from early Bronze Age, late Bronze to middle Iron Age and Saxon contexts, with the bulk being from the late Bronze to middle Iron Age occupation layer within the hillfort.

Description

The worked stone comprises both rotary and saddle quern fragments. Three further fragments of stone have remains of worked surfaces but are too small for the function to be determined. The rotary quern fragments (approximately 200) are all of lava and were recovered from the upper (Saxon) fills of the U-profiled and outer ditches (460 and 3050). Most are small and weathered fragments, but at least two retain worked surfaces indicative of their use as rotary querns. Combined they weigh 1659 g. The recovery of lava quern fragments from Saxon contexts along the middle Thames Valley is commonplace. Excavations at Lake End Road West, Dorney, nearby produced some 13 kg of fragments (Roe 2002, 37).

Three saddle querns (one complete and two fragments) are probably late Bronze or Iron Age in date. The complete saddle quern (SF 174 from the modern subsoil, 1122) is a formed example with a shaped and pecked under-surface and worn grinding surface. This is especially worn at the edges where it shows some signs of polish. Tool marks running across the width of the stone are unusual and it seems very likely that the quern was used for something other than grinding grain, such as, for example, processing fruits, tubers or legumes (Wright 1991, 35), crushing nuts, or powdering minerals (Barker 1985, 12). One face on a small unworked cobble (context 138, fill of a posthole in posthole row 1108) has been worn concave through use. It could have been used for sharpening small implements like a similar item from nearby Staines (Robertson-Mackay 1987, 118) or for grinding or mixing small quantities of material, perhaps spices or dye. This processor is similar to a number of unworked quartzite pebbles, which were used as hammerstones (six in total) and which were mostly recovered from the occupation layer or the modern subsoil (1121 and 1122: contexts 964, 985 and 986). Some show limited abrasion on one or more faces while others reveal more substantial damage through percussion. At least one has also been utilised as a pot-boiler.

The majority of the stone would have been collected locally from the Thames Gravels especially the assorted cobbles and the boulder utilised for a saddle quern which is of pale brown, iron rich, slightly micaceous sandstone. Although it has been worked into a formed saddle quern, it retains part of the original iron rich skin of the boulder on the base. The only imported stone from the site consists of two probable quern fragments of Lodsworth Greensand from West Sussex. These finds add to a growing number in the middle Thames valley region including the nearby sites of Marsh Lane East and Lot's Hole on the Maidenhead to Windsor and Eton flood alleviation scheme (Roe in prep.), Runnymede Bridge (Freestone 1991, 138) and Laleham's Farm (Roe pers. comm.). These suggest that Lodsworth Greensand was reaching the area with some regularity during the late Bronze to early Iron Age and that its distribution was more widespread at this early date than provisionally determined by Peacock (1986).

Catalogue

Complete saddle quern, formed. Pale brown iron rich slightly micaceous sandstone. Lower surface largely shaped with pecking, though unevenly. Part of original surface remains. Grinding surface is concave and tooled into fine grooves across the stone. Wear is greatest around the edges of the stone where the surface is extremely smooth and has some signs of polish. Measures 276 mm x 180 mm x 88 mm thick. Modern subsoil 1122, ctx 971. SF 1174.

Hammerstone. Quartzite pebble with abrasion on surviving end and large flake removed from other end. Measures >118 mm long x 106 x 47 mm. Buried subsoil 1105, ctx 1023.

Thin probable saddle quern. Lodsworth Greensand. Flat stone worn on both faces. One possible original curved edge. Stone is very thin and tapers away from this edge. Measures 110 x 135 x 11-20 mm thick. Modern subsoil 1122, ctx 103.

Possible hammerstone. Quartzite pebble. Waterworn pebble with some slight abrasion at one end. Measures 75 x 31 x 45 mm. Early Bronze Age hollows 1119, hollow 133, ctx 135.

Processor. Medium grained, well-sorted quartz sandstone. Rounded waterworn pebble with one worn concave surface. Probably used for grinding or mixing small quantities of some substance. Measures 101 x 75 x 45 mm. Late Bronze Age posthole row 1108, posthole 136, ctx 138.

Possible hammerstone. Quartzite pebble. Burnt and cracked potboiler. Measures 63 x >36 x 45 mm. Early Bronze Age hollows 1119, hollow 642, ctx 553. SF 899.

Hammerstone. Fine grained quartz sandstone, possibly sarsen. Abraded on several faces. Measures 68 x 64 x 50 mm. Late Bronze Age-middle Iron Age occupation layer 1121 or modern subsoil 1122, ctx 964.

Probable saddle quern or rubber fragment. Lodsworth. Chunk with one flat and worn surface. One curved edge. Measures >104 x 78 x 47 mm. Late Bronze Age-middle Iron Age occupation layer 1121 or modern subsoil 1122, ctx 964.

Large hammerstone. Flint. Cobble with many flakes removed on several sides. Probably used as a hammerstone. Measures 87 x 87 x 71 mm. Late Bronze Age-middle Iron Age occupation layer 1121 or modern subsoil 1122, ctx 964.

Possible hammerstone. Sarsen. Hand-sized pebble with some abrasion on one end. Measures 71 x 68 x 38 mm. Late Bronze Age-middle Iron Age occupation layer 1121, ctx 985.

Rubber. Possible pennant sandstone. One worked curved face and one edge remain, the other edges are all broken. Burnt. Measures > 42 mm x 49 mm x 19 mm thick. Late Bronze Age-middle Iron Age occupation layer 1121, ctx 986.

Chapter 8 – Environmental evidence

HUMAN SKELETAL REMAINS
by Peter Hacking

Introduction

The human skeletal remains comprise an extended Anglo-Saxon burial (see Fig. 6.2, skeleton 107, grave 105), which lay near the northern end of the U-profiled ditch (460) in what would have been the entrance into the early-middle Iron Age hillfort, and two isolated fragments of a left humerus from one of the upper, Anglo-Saxon fills of the U-profiled ditch (context 214, see Fig. 5.3, section 37).

Methodology

The sexing of the adult individuals was based on pelvic morphology and metric data (Workshop 1980). It was not possible to age the skeleton more specifically than as an 'adult' due to damage to the pubic symphysis and the auricular surface. Due to the incompleteness of the bones of the arms and legs it was not possible to calculate the stature of the individual.

Results

Grave 105, skeleton 107 (see Fig. 6.2; Plate 6.1)

All the bone from skeleton 107 is fragmented and in poor condition. The bones present are the left humerus and ulna, left and right hemipelvis and femora, right tibia and fibula, left talus and calcaneum and numerous very small spinal fragments.

The bones are from an adult. Both sciatic notches are narrow, indicating a male skeleton. A third trochanter is present on the left femur, but there is no evidence of any pathology.

The U-profiled ditch (460), cut 376, layer 214

Two broken pieces of the left humerus of an adult, 123 mm of mid-shaft and a 65 x 45 mm distal fragment, were found in one of the upper, Anglo-Saxon fills of the U-profiled ditch.

ANIMAL BONE
by Emma-Jayne Evans

A total of 940 fragments of animal bone and teeth were recovered from the main excavation. Many of the fragments of hand-collected bone had broken during excavation and were refitted, reducing the number of bones and teeth to 464 fragments. A further 57 fragments were recovered from the sieved material, bringing the overall fragment count to 521.

Methodology

Identification of the bone was undertaken using the OA reference collection and published guides. All the animal remains were counted and weighed, and, where possible, identified to species, element, side and zone (Serjeantson 1996). Fusion data, butchery marks, gnawing, burning and pathological changes were also noted when present. Ribs and vertebrae were only recorded to species when they were substantially complete and could be accurately identified. Undiagnostic bones were recorded as small (small mammal size), medium (sheep size) or large (cattle size). The separation of sheep and goat bones was undertaken using the criteria of Boessneck (1969) and Prummel and Frisch (1986), in addition to the use of the reference material at OA. Where distinctions could not be made, the bone was recorded as sheep/goat (s/g).

The condition of the bone was graded using the criteria stipulated by Lyman (1996), grade 0 being the best preserved bone and grade 5 indicating that the bone had suffered such structural and attritional damage as to make it unrecognisable.

The quantification of species was carried out using the total fragment count. In addition the minimum number of individuals (MNI) was calculated using the zoning method (Serjeantson 1996). Tooth eruption and wear stages were measured using a combination of Halstead (1985), Grant (1982) and Levine (1982), and fusion data were analysed according to Silver (1969). Measurements of adult, that is, fully fused bones were taken according to the methods of von den Driesch (1976). Withers heights were calculated using Fock (1966) and Kieserwalter (Boessneck and von den Driesch 1974, 334).

Results

The bone from this site has survived in reasonably good condition with the majority of the bone according to Lyman's grading scoring 3, and some grades 1 and 2 (Table 8.1). However, almost all the bone has some degree of fresh damage, and there are many small fragments of broken bones. The condition of the bone has allowed for the identification of gnawing marks, butchery marks and pathological changes on a number of bones, particularly on the bones from the Anglo-Saxon period.

Table 8.1 Condition of the hand collected and sieved animal bone

Phase	Features	1	2	3	4	5
Anglo-Saxon	U-profiled ditch (460) upper fills	4%	52%	39%	4%	1%
Early-middle Iron Age	U-profiled ditch (460) lower fills and pit 1016	14%	33%	29%	24%	
Late Bronze Age to middle Iron Age	occupation layer (1121 and 1123), posthole row 1104, posthole groups 1117 and 1134			6%	38%	56%
Late Bronze Age - early Iron Age	standstill layer (1102)				67%	33%
Late Bronze Age	posthole row 935				100%	
All phases		4%	18%	54%	24%	

A total of 146 fragments were identified to species, 28% of the total fragment count. From the site as a whole all the main domestic species are represented, with roe deer and red deer representing wild species (Table 8.2). No fish or small mammal bones were recovered.

Very few fragments of bone have been recovered from either the Bronze Age or Iron Age phases, and the bone that has been recovered is in poorer condition than that from the Anglo-Saxon phase. There is thus little information about the use of animals during later prehistory, particularly as almost all the identified bones were teeth. Aside from a horn core in posthole 542 in row 1104 and a fragment of large mammal longbone from posthole 234 in posthole circle 1134, the only exceptions are from the early-middle Iron Age deposits in the U-profiled ditch (460), in which fragments of mandible and tibia were found.

The 13 cattle bones from the late Bronze Age and Iron Age contexts comprise 8 molars, and fragments of a horncore, a mandible and a tibia. The tibia has been chopped through the shaft suggesting marrow extraction, and the mandible has been aged to 18–30 months. The 3rd molar of the mandible only has two cusps instead of the usual three, which is a commonly seen non-metric trait among cattle third molars.

The horse bones from this phase comprise a molar from the standstill layer (1102) which has been aged to 8-11 years. Horses appear in the archaeological record in the middle Bronze Age, and become common on sites of the later Bronze Age and Iron Age, so their presence here is unremarkable. Sheep/goat was represented only by four molars.

The Anglo-Saxon bone survived in marginally better condition, and forms the majority of the assemblage. This period also provides the greatest variety of species, with pig, dog, domestic fowl and red and roe deer present as well as the domestic species that were present in earlier phases. The number of bones is large enough to allow consideration of a wider range of questions relating to animal husbandry.

Due to the slightly better condition of the Anglo-Saxon bone, there is more variety in the skeletal elements present, of which teeth are the minority rather than the majority. The cattle bones suggest a minimum of five individuals, one of which had a withers height of 1.22 m, which appears to be average for this period (Clutton-Brock, 1976). Three mandibles from the Anglo-Saxon phase have been aged as 8-18 months, 18-30 months and adult, and two as old adult. Fusion data of the Anglo-Saxon cattle suggests that at least one animal died before reaching 7-10 months, one before reaching $1-1^{1}/_{2}$

Table 8.2 Total number of animal bones identified to species and phase

Phase	Features	cattle	s/g	pig	horse	dog	domestic fowl	red deer	roe deer	unid.	Total
Anglo-Saxon	U-profiled ditch (460) upper fills	62	10	23	5	7	4	12	2	350	475
Early-middle Iron Age	U-profiled ditch (460) lower fills and pit 1016	6	1							15	22
Late Bronze Age to middle Iron Age	occupation layer (1121 and 1123), posthole row 1104, posthole groups 1117 and 1134	6	2							7	15
Late Bronze Age - early Iron Age	standstill layer (1102)	1			1					1	3
Late Bronze Age	posthole row 935			1							1
Undated and modern contexts		3								2	5
Total		78	14	23	6	7	4	12	2	375	521

years, one at approximately 2 – 2^1/$_2$ years, and one animal at approximately 3^1/$_2$-4 years. Both cut and chop marks were noted on the Anglo-Saxon bones, indicating that they had been processed for meat and marrow. Articulations were only seen between a radius and ulna, and no burning, pathologies or gnawing marks were noted.

The sheep/goat bones, although few in number, give a minimum number of four for the Anglo-Saxon phase. A single mandible gave an age at death of one individual as 3-10 months, and an unfused pelvis suggests that at least one individual died before reaching 6-10 months. Dismemberment marks were recorded on a humerus, and the unfused pelvis had been burnt.

The pig bones from the Anglo-Saxon phase give a minimum number of four. Four mandibles could be aged, suggesting that one died as an immature animal, and three as adults. One of the adult mandibles had an abscess on the medial aspect, at the base of the 3rd molar. Two unfused scapulae give ages at death of before 1 year, two unfused tibiae gives a further age at death of before 2 years, and an unfused ulna suggests another individual died before reaching 3-3^1/$_2$ years. Only one bone had evidence of cut marks: an atlas that has been chopped, probably when removing the head. A 4th metatarsal has carnivore gnawing. There was no evidence of burning or articulations between any of the bones.

The horse remains give a minimum number of one. A single mandible has been aged as 6-9 years, and a complete radius gave a withers height of 1.32 m (c 13 hands). There are a minimum number of three dogs from the Anglo-Saxon phase. All appear to come from adult individuals. There was no evidence of butchery marks, gnawing, burning or pathologies on any of the bones, and, although none were seen to articulate, five of the six from the Anglo-Saxon phase came from fill 607, and may belong to the same animal. Four bones of domestic fowl, representing a minimum of one individual, were also found. Two of the bones articulate, and it is likely that these two, along with one other also from ditch fill 607, originate from one individual.

While red deer is only represented by a mandible and radius the roe deer bones represent a minimum of four individuals. The deer bones from ditch fill 607 comprise a molar, a fragment of antler and five mandibles, and those from ditch fill 257 comprise a skull fragment and two further mandibles. The two roe deer bones from ditch fill 686 were left and right adult mandibles, and are possibly from the same animal. All the mandibles appear to be from adult individuals, except one which was from a young animal, probably less than 1 year old. One of the adult mandibles has cut marks on the lateral aspect, possibly as a result of dismemberment or skinning.

Discussion

The few bones from the Bronze Age and Iron Age were recovered from a number of features, including ditches, pits, occupation layers and the postholes of possible roundhouses, whereas almost all of the Anglo-Saxon bone was recovered from the U-profiled ditch (460). There appear to be distinct groups of material deposited within this ditch, such as the collection of roe deer remains from fill 607, which may indicate the deposition of material from one episode of roe deer butchery.

The bones from the Bronze Age and Iron Age are too few to provide much information beyond the presence of certain species. The bones from the Anglo-Saxon phase, although still a small sample, provide rather more information. The numbers of cattle bones in comparison to those of sheep and pig suggest that these animals were the main source of food for the local inhabitants. Literary sources would suggest that during the Anglo-Saxon period domestic pigs were kept in very great numbers, although as boned salt pork was the most common way in which pork was prepared and eaten, it is likely that pig bones are under-represented in the archaeological record (Clutton-Brock 1976). Literary sources also suggest that hunting was an invaluable supplement to the diet at the time, and this is supported by the presence of both red and roe deer at Taplow. The relatively high proportion of roe deer and red deer bones in this small assemblage might indicate that the site was of quite high status, as deer, and red deer in particular, appear to be connected with high status sites during this period (Clutton-Brock 1976).

Horse remains are commonly found in small numbers on Anglo-Saxon sites. The withers height of the horse at Taplow is close to the average for this period, in which horses usually averaged 14 hands (Clutton-Brock 1976). The only bird species found at this site was domestic fowl, which is a familiar domestic bird on Anglo-Saxon sites, and was commonly eaten during this period.

It is likely that the animal bones from Anglo-Saxon deposits at Taplow Court represent domestic waste. The assemblage is relatively typical for the Anglo-Saxon period, but the presence of a relatively high proportion of deer bones suggests a high status site. Within the U-profiled ditch (460) there appear to be distinct sites of both butchery and disposal, evidenced particularly by the roe deer and dog bones. However, as this is a small assemblage, it is difficult to determine if this is typical of the site or not.

CHARRED PLANT REMAINS
(excluding charcoal)

by Mark Robinson

Introduction

Bulk samples for charred plant remains were taken from features representing all of the major phases of activity in the main excavation. Fifty-six samples of up to 40 litres were floated for charred plant remains. Assessment established that 18 of them contained carbonised remains other than charcoal. Seven of these samples were regarded as having the potential for detailed analysis. The remaining 11 samples ranged from late Bronze Age to Anglo-Saxon in date and contained small quantities of mostly unidentifiable cereal grain.

Methodology

Each sample was floated in water onto a 0.3 mm mesh using a flotation machine. The dried flots were sorted under a binocular microscope and the remains recovered identified by comparison with reference material at magnifications of up to x50. The results are given in Table 8.3 in roughly chronological order, nomenclature following Clapham *et al.* (1987).

Mesolithic

Although no features of this date were found, a charred hazelnut shell from a posthole (row 1104) was radiocarbon-dated to the 9th millennium BC, showing the exploitation of woodland resources at this time.

Earlier Neolithic tree-throw hole 497

Sample 22 from context 498 in earlier Neolithic tree-throw hole 497 contained nut shell fragments of *Corylus avellana* (hazel) but cereal remains were absent. At least temporary occupation of the site exploiting woodland resources is suggested.

Early Bronze Age hollows (1119)

Sample 35 from context 553 in early Bronze Age hollow 642 contained a little cereal grain including hulled wheat, possible *Triticum dicoccum* (emmer wheat) and hulled *Hordeum vulgare* (six-row hulled barley). In contrast to the earlier Neolithic activity represented in tree-throw hole 497, the settlement associated with the early Bronze Age hollows (1119) was clearly using the products of arable agriculture.

Middle Bronze Age

A middle Bronze Age radiocarbon date was obtained on a charred grain of *Triticum sp.* from a posthole in the interior (posthole row 1132). This demonstrates the continuation of arable agriculture locally in the middle Bronze Age. It was not possible to distinguish whether this was *Triticum dicoccum* (emmer wheat) or *Triticum spelta* (spelt wheat); spelt replaced emmer as the principal crop during the middle-late Bronze Age, and is known from middle Bronze Age enclosures locally at the Eton Rowing Course (Robinson in Allen *et al.* in prep. b).

Posthole row 1104

Three postholes from a row (1104) running parallel to and just outstide the V-profiled ditch (574) were found to contain small quantities of hazelnut shell fragments and unidentifiable cereal grain. As described above, some of the hazelnut shell was dated to the early Mesolithic; the charred cereal grains may be contemporary with the postholes, some of which at least date to the late Bronze Age, but as an Anglo-Saxon radiocarbon date was obtained on charcoal from another of the postholes, the grain may also be intrusive, and relate to the later Anglo-Saxon use of the site (see below).

Late Bronze Age posthole group 1117

A substantial assemblage of charcoal and crop processing remains was found in a posthole (206, sample 49, context 207) which may have formed part of a roundhouse or four-post structure within posthole group 1117 (see Fig. 4.14). Two radiocarbon dates, both spanning the very late 10th to the end of the 9th centuries BC, were obtained on charred cereal grains. Cereal grain predominated but chaff and weed seeds were also present. Almost all the identifiable grain was *Triticum sp.* (wheat). The chaff confirmed the presence of both *Triticum dicoccum* (emmer wheat) and *T. spelta* (spelt wheat), which were represented by their glumes. There was a single grain of *Hordeum sp.* (barley) and wild food remains such as nutshell fragments were absent. The weed seeds were mostly from arable weeds including *Vicia* or *Lathyrus sp.* (vetch or tare), *Fallopia convolvulus* (black bindweed) and *Bromus* cf. *secalinus* (brome grass). One of the weeds, *Galium aparine* (goosegrass), tends to be associated with autumn-sown crops. The assemblage was perhaps derived from the dehusking and cleaning of hulled wheat. It is possible that the emmer and spelt had been grown as a mixed crop rather than the remains being from the processing of separate crops. A stone of *Crataegus* cf. *monogyna* (hawthorn) was more likely to have been from a fruit on twigs used as fuel than from food waste.

Anglo-Saxon fills of the U-profiled ditch (460)

The Iron Age sediments in the U-profiled ditch (460) did not contain identifiable charred plant remains other than charcoal. However, early and middle Saxon debris, including crop-processing remains, accumulated in its upper fills. Sample 51 from Context 579, one of the uppermost surviving fills, contained a rich mixed assemblage of cereal grain, chaff, nut shell fragments and weed seeds. A radiocarbon date of 770-970 cal AD (SUERC-4971) was obtained from one of the cereal grains. Cereal grain comprised around a third of the remains in the sample including free-threshing *Triticum sp.* (rivet or bread wheat), hulled *Hordeum vulgare* (six-row hulled barley), *Secale cereale* (rye) and *Avena sp.* (oats). The identity of the oats as *Avena sativa* (cultivated oats) could not be confirmed since floret bases were absent but the size range of the grains was appropriate for cultivated oats. Chaff only comprised 6% of the assemblages. Rachis fragments of free-threshing *Triticum* and *S. cereale* predominated but it was not possible to identify any of the wheat rachis fragments to species level. It is therefore uncertain whether the wheat was *T. turgidum* (rivet wheat) or *T. aestivum* (bread-type wheat). Interestingly, there were a couple of glumes of hulled wheat, one of which could be identified as *T. dicoccum* (emmer wheat). Remains of other cultivated plants were absent but nutshell fragments of *Corylus avellana* (hazel) comprised 6% of the assemblage.

Weed seeds comprised over half the assemblage. Almost all were from plants appropriate to arable cultivation. Indeed, one species, *Agrostemma githago* (corn cockle), is very closely linked to the cultivation of cereals and flax. The most numerous weed seeds were of *Rumex* sp. (dock), *Vicia* or *Lathyrus* sp. (vetch or tare), *Bromus* cf. *secalinus* (brome grass) and *Chenopodium album* (fat hen). The gravel terrace on which the site is situated has a very light well-drained soil. A significant presence of seeds of two wet ground plants, *Eleocharis S. palustris* sp. (spike rush) and *Carex* sp. (sedge) suggested that some of the crops had been grown on damper ground, perhaps closer to the river. Another of the weeds, *Anthemis cotula* (stinking mayweed), tends to be associated with heavy calcareous soils while the presence of *Galium aparine* (goosegrass) raises the possibility that some of the crops were autumn-sown.

The abundance of weed seeds suggested that the main sources of the charred assemblage were the cleaning of various cereal crops. This material had been mixed with shell fragments from the opening of hazelnuts. The results show that a range of cereals was being cultivated and that the source of some of the crops was beyond the immediate vicinity of the site. Woodland resources were also being exploited.

Anglo-Saxon fills of the outer defensive ditch (3050)

Sample 303 from context 3004 in the outer hillfort ditch was only assessed, but provides useful additional information about the Anglo-Saxon occupation. The sample contained a high concentration of mixed cereal grains including short free-threshing grains of *Triticum* sp. (rivet or bread wheat), hulled *Hordeum* sp. (hulled barley) and *Avena* sp. (oats) along with a small quantity of *Secale cereale* (rye). A charred *Triticum Sp.* grain was radiocarbon dated to 1255 ±30 BP (Poz-12532), which calibrates at 95% confidence to cal AD 670-870. Arable weed seeds, particularly *Chenopodium album* (fat hen), were present although there was little cereal chaff. In addition to the remains related to cereal processing, there were also nut shell fragments of *Corylus avellana* (hazel). This sample also contained much charcoal of *Fagus sylvatica* (beech) and *Quercus* sp. (oak).

Discussion

The earlier Neolithic charred remains from tree-throw hole 497 were of typical Neolithic character, being mainly hazelnut shell fragments, and the early Mesolithic hazelnut shell fragments were similarly characteristic of the period. The early Bronze Age remains from the group of hollows (1119) comprised what were probably the most important cereals of this period. The continuation of arable agriculture in the middle Bronze Age is unremarkable for the area, though the limited evidence may represent cereals imported from elsewhere rather than grown close to the site. The remains from the posthole row (1104), in showing the possible continued importance of gathered wild food plant remains beyond the end of the Neolithic, were of a different character from those from the probably late Bronze Age roundhouse (1117). It is, however, possible that they were residual from earlier activity on the site. The higher concentration of crop remains from the late Bronze Age, in comparison with the earlier contexts, follows the usual trend. The late Bronze Age settlement was similar to some other late Bronze Age settlements in the middle Thames Valley such as Runnymede Bridge (Greig 1991) in that both emmer and spelt wheat were being used.

The rich Anglo-Saxon samples from the upper fills of the U-profiled ditch (460) and from the outer ditch (3050) make a useful contribution to our knowledge of the period, and provide a similar picture to other local sites of this period such as Lake End Road West at Dorney (Pelling, 2002). The results suggested a developed arable economy using all the major cereal crops known from the Anglo-Saxon period: free-threshing wheat, six-row hulled barley, rye and oats. Unfortunately, it was not possible to confirm the identity of the free-threshing wheat although it is likely to have been *Triticum aestivum* (bread wheat). Rye was a minor crop in Roman Britain but becomes common by the middle Anglo-Saxon period. In addition to these four cereals, there was a slight presence of chaff of emmer wheat. Given that there was Bronze Age settlement on the site it is possible that these remains were residual. However, there is some evidence of a middle Anglo-Saxon resurgence of the cultivation of emmer wheat in the middle Thames Valley (Pelling and Robinson 2000).

The high proportion of beech charcoal from the outer ditch sample is also of interest, and gives some evidence on the origin of the Chiltern beechwoods, which were possibly of post-Roman origin.

CHARCOAL

by Rowena Gale

This report presents the analysis of charcoal obtained from the early Bronze Age hollows (1119), the early-middle Iron Age rampart gravel (1100) associated with the U-profiled ditch (460), and the

Table 8.3 Summary of charred plant remains (excluding charcoal)

		Earlier Neolithic tree-throw hole	Early Bronze Age hollow	Bronze Age posthole row			Probably late Bronze Age roundhouse posthole	Early Saxon fill of U-profiled ditch
Context Group		497	1119	1104	1104	1104	1117	460
	Context	498	553	535	540	561	207	579
	Sample	22	35	25	26	29	49	51
	Volume (litres)	10	40	10	10	4	9	40
	No. of items/litre	2	0.1	1.5	0.2	0.75	25.666	12.85
CEREAL GRAIN								
Triticum cf. *dicoccum* Schübl. emmer wheat		-	1	-	-	-	5	-
T. spelta L.	spelt wheat	-	-	-	-	-	2	-
T. dicoccum Schübl. or *spelta* L.	emmer or spelt	-	2	-	-	-	11	-
Triticum sp. - short free-threshing	rivet or bread wheat	-	-	-	-	-	-	21
Triticum sp.	wheat	-	-	-	-	-	14	4
Secale cereale L.	rye	-	-	-	-	-	-	14
Hordeum vulgare L. hulled lateral	six-row hulled barley	-	2	-	-	-	-	1
Hordeum sp. - hulled median	hulled barley	-	-	-	-	-	-	2
Hordeum sp. - hulled	hulled barley	-	-	-	-	-	-	7
Hordeum sp.	barley	-	-	-	-	-	1	10
Avena sp.	oats	-	-	-	-	-	-	27
cereal indet.		-	-	1	1	1	136	82
Total cereal grain		0	5	1	1	1	169	168
CEREAL CHAFF								
Triticum dicoccum Schübl. - glume	emmer wheat	-	-	-	-	-	3	1
T. spelta L. - glume	spelt wheat	-	-	-	-	-	4	-
T. dicoccum Schübl. or *spelta* L. - glume	emmer or spelt	-	-	-	-	-	39	1
Triticum sp. - free threshing - rachis node	rivet or bread wheat	-	-	-	-	-	-	16
Secale cereale L. - rachis node	rye	-	-	-	-	-	-	10
Secale or *Hordeum* sp. - rachis node	rye or barley	-	-	-	-	-	-	4
Total chaff		0	0	0	0	0	46	32
NUTS								
Corylus avellana L. - nutshell frags	hazel	20	0	13	1	1	-	30
WEED SEEDS								
Ranunculus cf. *repens* L.	creeping buttercup	-	-	-	-	-	-	1
Brassica rapa L. ssp. *sylvestris* (L.)	wild turnip	-	-	-	-	-	-	3
Brassica or *Sinapis* sp.	wild mustard, turnip etc	-	-	-	-	-	-	6
Agrostemma githago L.	corn cockle	-	-	-	-	-	-	4
Silene sp.	campion	-	-	-	-	-	-	1
Stellaria media gp.	chickweed	-	-	-	-	-	-	1
Chenopodium album L.	fat hen	-	-	-	-	-	-	21
Atriplex sp.	orache	-	-	-	-	-	1	-
Malvaceae	mallow	-	-	-	-	-	-	1
Vicia or *Lathyrus* sp.	vetch or tare	-	-	-	-	-	1	52
cf. *Medicago lupulina* L.	black medick	-	-	-	-	-	-	2
cf. *Trifolium* sp.	clover	-	-	1	-	-	-	5
Crataegus cf. *monogyna* Jaq.	hawthorn	-	-	-	-	-	1	-
Fallopia convolvulus (L.) Löve	black bindweed	-	-	-	-	-	4	2
Rumex sp. (not *acetosella*)	dock	-	-	-	-	-	2	61
Urtica dioica L.	stinging nettle	-	-	-	-	-	-	1
cf. *Anagallis arvensis* L.	scarlet pimpernel	-	-	-	-	-	-	1
Odontites verna (Bell) Dum.	red bartsia	-	-	-	-	-	-	1

Table 8.3 (continued) Summary of charred plant remains (excluding charcoal)

		Earlier Neolithic tree-throw hole	Early Bronze Age hollow		Bronze Age posthole row		Probably late Bronze Age roundhouse posthole	Early Saxon fill of U-profiled ditch
Odontites verna (Bell) Dum.	red bartsia	-	-	-	-	-	-	1
Galium aparine L.	goosegrass	-	-	-	-	-	1	2
Galium sp.	bedstraw etc	-	-	-	-	-	-	2
Anthemis cotula L.	stinking mayweed	-	-	-	-	-	-	11
Lapsana communis L.	nipplewort	-	-	-	-	-	-	1
Eleocharis S. *Palustres* sp.	spike-rush	-	-	-	-	-	-	10
Carex sp.	sedge	-	-	-	-	-	-	7
Bromus cf. *secalinus* L.	brome grass	-	-	-	-	-	1	22
Gramineae indet.	grass	-	-	-	-	-	3	18
weed indet.		-	-	-	-	1	2	48
Total weed seeds		0	0	1		0	1	16	284

Anglo-Saxon upper fills of the U-profiled ditch (460). Identification was undertaken to indicate the use of woodland resources and to obtain environmental data.

Methodology

Bulk soil samples were processed by flotation and sieving (see Robinson above). The resulting flots and residues were scanned under low magnification and the charcoal separated from plant macrofossils. Segments of narrow roundwood were rare. Charcoal fragments measuring >2 mm in radial cross-section were considered for species identification.

The condition of the charcoal varied from firm and well-preserved to poor and friable. The samples were prepared using standard methods (Gale and Cutler 2000). The anatomical structures were examined using incident light on a Nikon Labophot-2 compound microscope at magnifications up to x400 and matched to prepared reference slides of modern wood. When possible, the maturity of the wood was assessed (ie heartwood/sapwood).

Results

Context details and the taxa identified are presented in Table 8.4. Classification follows that of *Flora Europaea* (Tutin, Heywood *et al.* 1964-80). Group names are given when anatomical differences between related genera are too slight to allow secure identification to genus level. These include members of the Pomoideae (*Crataegus, Malus, Pyrus* and *Sorbus*) and Salicaceae (*Salix* and *Populus*). When a genus is represented by a single species in the British flora, it is named as the most likely origin of the wood, given the provenance and period, but it should be noted that it is rarely possible to name individual species from wood features, and exotic species of trees and shrubs were introduced to Britain from an early period (Godwin 1956; Mitchell 1974). The anatomical structure of the charcoal was consistent with the following taxa or groups of taxa:

Aceraceae. *Acer campestre* L., field maple
Corylaceae. *Corylus avellana* L., hazel
Fagaceae. *Fagus sylvatica* L., beech; *Quercus* sp., oak
Oleaceae. *Fraxinus excelsior* L., ash
Rosaceae. Subfamilies:
    Pomoideae, which includes *Crataegus* sp., hawthorn; *Malus* sp., apple; *Pyrus* sp., pear; *Sorbus* spp., rowan, service tree and whitebeam. These taxa are anatomically similar; one or more taxa may be represented in the charcoal.
Prunoideae. *Prunus spinosa* L., blackthorn.
Salicaceae. *Salix* sp., willow, and *Populus* sp., poplar.
    In most respects these taxa are anatomically similar.

Discussion

Early Bronze Age hollows (1119)

Sample 35 was obtained from fill 553 of hollow 642, one of the group of early Bronze Age hollows (1119). The hollow was stratigraphically one of the latest of the group and is associated with a radiocarbon date of 1740-1530 cal BC (OxA-14268). Evidence of cereal grain was sparse and the function of the hollow is unclear. The charcoal was identified as mainly oak (*Quercus* sp.), blackthorn (*Prunus spinosa*) and the hawthorn/*Sorbus* group (Pomoideae), although field maple (*Acer campestre*) and ash (*Fraxinus excelsior*) were also recorded. Although conifer wood was recorded during the assessment examination (Challinor 2004) and identified by Mark Robinson as yew (*Taxus* sp.), further evidence of softwood was not forthcoming during the full analysis of the charcoal. Softwood is rarely found in archaeological contexts and, in this instance, the total quantity of coniferous wood present appears to have been isolated at the assessment stage. In view of the broad range of species named, it seems probable that the charcoal represents fuel debris from an unknown activity.

Early-middle Iron Age rampart gravels (1100)

Evidence from burnt structural material associated with the hillfort attests to the conflagration of the early-middle Iron Age defences. Sample 31 was recovered from the burnt rampart gravels (1100; context 644). As a whole, the gravels (1100 and 1112) extended along the length of the ramparts and included the charred remains of a corduroy of timbers (1113) lying across the ditch. The charcoal was very fragmented and consisted almost entirely of oak (*Quercus* sp.), including heartwood, sapwood and a small amount of roundwood. In addition, a fragment from the hawthorn/*Sorbus* group (Pomoideae) was indentified. If, as seems possible, the burnt corduroy timbers gave rise to a substantial proportion of this charcoal, the evidence from this sample is consistent with that from the rampart structure (1113), which included the burnt remains of oak timbers.

The timber structure (1113)
by Dana Challinor

The timber structure (1113) of the rampart associated with the early-middle Iron Age U-profiled ditch (460) appears to have been constructed entirely of *Quercus* sp. (oak). The charcoal samples from the gravel deposits belonging to the rampart (1100) are likely to represent the collapsed remains of the same structure. The charred wood timbers within the rampart (1113) were not well preserved. The charcoal crumbled when the samples were unwrapped and was quite infused with sediment. The condition of the timber limits the conclusions that can be drawn about the kind of timber used to construct the rampart, how it was worked, and how the rampart was constructed. A few details could, however, be made out. In some samples, there appeared to be some roundwood (on the basis of the curvature of the rings) but it was not possible to count growth rings or to identify a bark edge. This is also confirmed by the photographs and site plans of the timbers when first uncovered (eg. Plates 5.4 and 5.5). The poor preservation of the charred timbers meant that the conversion of the wood for the structure was only tentatively identified in one sample. Timber 1000 appeared to have been produced by splitting a piece of roundwood in two. Although the bark edge was not preserved and the ring sequence was incomplete, a count of the surviving rings indicated that the tree was a minimum of 30 years old when felled.

Anglo-Saxon deposits in the U-profiled ditch (460)

A large sample of charcoal was recovered from context 579, one of the upper fills of the U-profiled ditch (460) which is associated with a radiocarbon date of cal AD 770-970 (SUERC-4971). A high ratio of beech (*Fagus sylvatica*) was present in the sample but was too fragmented to assess origins from coppiced sources. Oak was also fairly common and, although difficult to verify, probably included roundwood. Other species included the hawthorn/*Sorbus* group (Pomoideae), blackthorn (*Prunus spinosa*), willow (*Salix* sp.)/poplar (*Populus* sp.) and hazel (*Corylus avellana*; Table 8.4). Although fragmented, the hazel derived from fast-grown roundwood, which may imply the use of coppice stems. Most of the oak charcoal was partially vitrified, a condition usually attributed to burning at temperatures exceeding 800° C (Prior and Alvin 1983). Non-oak species, however, exhibited no signs of vitrification. Finds of associated pottery and abundant charred cereal grains (Robinson 2004) would be consistent with the disposal of domestic waste. If the ditch fill included deposits of waste material from various sources/hearths, this could explain the differential in preservation/vitrification of the charcoal. It is, however, also possible that the vitrified oak was residual, and derived from erosion of the burnt early-middle Iron Age rampart.

Environmental evidence

The hillfort was located on raised ground on the northern river terrace of the Thames Valley. Underlying soils consist of sand and gravel. In the present day, the surrounding parkland includes wooded strips adjacent to the river. The limestone hills of the Chilterns rise some distance north of the site.

Trees and shrubs identified from pollen from the late Bronze Age V-profiled ditch (574) include lime (*Tilia* sp.), pine (*Pinus* sp.), yew (*Taxus* sp.), hazel (*Corylus avellana*), oak (*Quercus* sp.) and heather (*Calluna vulgaris*) and there was some evidence to suggest the presence of heathland in the late Bronze Age/early Iron Age, contemporary with the stand-still layer (1102; see Parker below).

Evidence from fuel debris (charcoal) from the early Bronze Age hollows (1119) suggests that the area supported woodlands of oak, field maple and ash. Shrubby species including blackthorn and the hawthorn/*Sorbus* group probably grew in marginal woodland or in more open sites. Hazel also grew in the area – hazelnut shells, possibly residual, were frequent in posthole row 1104 (see Robinson above). Although hazel typically grows as understorey, the trees only fruit in sunlit areas. The windborne pollen of pine is often carried over long distances but, clearly, both yew and pine grew in the vicinity of the site, thus providing a source for the yew charcoal. Although not present in the prehistoric charcoal, wetland species such as alder (*Alnus gluti-*

Table 8.4 *Summary of analysed charcoal (excluding the burnt rampart timbers 1113). Key: h = heartwood; r = roundwood (diameter <20mm); s = sapwood (diameter unknown). The number of fragments identified is indicated.*

Sample	Context	Feature	Acer	Corylus	Fagus	Fraxinus	Pomoideae	Prunus	Quercus	Salicaceae
Early Bronze Age										
35	553	hollows 1119	3	-	-	1	15	16	17h, 3s	-
Early-middle Iron Age										
31	644	rampart gravel 1100	-	-	-	-	1	-	6h, 24s, 1r	-
Anglo-Saxon										
51	579	U-profiled ditch 460	-	1r	61	-	1	1	8h, 24s	2

nosa) and willow (*Salix* sp.) probably formed patches of woodland on the damp floodplains.

The construction of a rampart incorporating an oak structure around the hillfort during the early-middle Iron Age suggests that oak woodland was still quite abundant at this time (alternatively, although less likely, stocks could have been imported via the river). The felling and conversion of such large quantities of timber probably had quite a serious impact on the character of local woodland. Evidence from sites in other parts of the Thames Valley suggests that while some vestige of woodland cover remained on the river terraces in the late Bronze Age/early Iron Age, much of the landscape had been cleared for arable farming (Robinson and Wilson 1987).

It is interesting to note the predominance of beech (*Fagus* sp.) in the Anglo-Saxon deposit in the U-profiled ditch (460). The distribution of beech in the Chilterns and its environs prior to the medieval period is uncertain. At the time of Domesday (1086) the Chilterns formed the second largest woodland in England (Rackham 1986, 78) and in the following centuries woodland industries focussed on coppicing and pollarding beech, mostly for fuel (Marren 1992, 59). Although beech charcoal from the U-profiled ditch (460) was too comminuted to evaluate whether it originated from managed woodland or not, a small fragment of hazel stem from the same context indicates fast growth comparable to that of coppice.

PHYTOLITHS AND POLLEN
by Adrian G Parker

Four sediment columns from the V-profiled and the U-profiled ditches (574 and 460) were submitted for pollen assessment. Following standard preparation procedures all samples yielded very poor to no pollen preservation. A few samples yielded low counts but the pollen was poorly preserved implying oxidation of the samples and pollen deterioration and destruction. During the pollen preparation stages subsamples were examined to see if pollen was being lost during each step taken. This showed that no pollen was present. However, it did reveal large quantities of phytoliths in some samples.

Phytoliths, also called plant opals or opaline silica, are solid deposits of SiO_2 ($SiO_2.H_2O$) that are produced in living plants and precipitated in and among their cells in organs such as stems, leaves, and inflorescences (Piperno 1988; Pearsall 2000; Ball *et al.* 1999; Runge 1999). In some instances taxa may produce characteristic morphotypes which may permit identification to genera, families or rarely species and thus provide information concerning past vegetation, agriculture and human-plant relationships (Ishida *et al.* 2003; Parker *et al.* forthcoming).

Phytolith analysis offers an alternative technique from which palaeobotanical information can be derived, especially where conditions are not particularly favourable for pollen analysis. In the UK the application of this technique is in its infancy (Powers-Jones 1994; Hodson 2002). However, more use has been made of the technique in the Americas and Middle East (Fredlund and Tieszan 1994; Ishida *et al.* 2003).

Methodology

A total of 8 samples were prepared for phytolith analysis (Table 8.5). To remove the coarse sand and gravel fractions, 5 g of sediment from each sample was sieved (2 mm mesh). The samples were treated with 25 ml 6% HCl in order to remove any carbonate fraction. None was observed. Organic matter was removed using 10% NaOH and by heating the samples for 20 minutes. The samples were repeatedly rinsed using distilled deionised water until the supernatant liquid was clear. The samples were next deflocculated using 25 ml of 2% Calgon shaken continuously for 30 minutes. The samples were then passed through a 212 μm sieve, and the residues rinsed with distilled water and centrifuged. This was followed by heavy liquid separation using zinc iodide (2.35 sg). Material less than 5 μm in size was removed using the vacuum filtration method of Theunissen (1994). Samples

Table 8.5 Summary of phytolith analysis

	Ditch 460 57:607	%	Ditch 460 57:707	%	Ditch 460 56:711	%	Ditch 460 56:728	%	Ditch 574 58:861	%	Ditch 574 58:863	%	Ditch 574 59:864	%	Ditch 574 59:865	%
Poaceae short cell																
Round	22	3.6	3	1.0	0	0.0	4	2.3	8	2.5	7	2.5	0	0.0	0	0.0
Oblong	75	12.3	25	8.3	4	23.5	25	14.3	50	15.4	42	14.9	25	37.3	0	0.0
Square/Rectangle	45	7.4	41	13.6	0	0.0	10	5.7	28	8.6	20	7.1	0	0.0	0	0.0
Round-Trapezoid	60	9.8	5	1.7	0	0.0	1	0.6	15	4.6	5	1.8	0	0.0	0	0.0
Bilobate	18	2.9	20	6.6	1	5.9	23	13.1	33	10.1	50	17.8	4	6.0	0	0.0
Polylobate	57	9.3	15	5.0	1	5.9	18	10.3	72	22.1	45	16.0	1	1.5	0	0.0
Crossbody	4	0.7	1	0.3	0	0.0	0	0.0	3	0.9	5	1.8	0	0.0	0	0.0
Flat Tower	2	0.3	3	1.0	1	5.9	2	1.1	1	0.3	2	0.7	1	1.5	0	0.0
Angle	14	2.3	0	0.0	0	0.0	1	0.6	7	2.1	3	1.1	0	0.0	0	0.0
Papillae	21	3.4	20	6.6	0	0.0	32	18.3	35	10.8	6	2.1	0	0.0	0	0.0
Non-Poaceae short cell																
Circular rugose	9	1.5	6	2.0	0	0.0	5	2.9	7	2.1	5	1.8	0	0.0	0	0.0
Corklike	7	1.1	1	0.3	0	0.0	3	1.7	2	0.6	4	1.4	1	1.5	0	0.0
trapezoid	2	0.3	0	0.0	0	0.0	5	2.9	1	0.3	0	0.0	0	0.0	0	0.0
Spherical with sockets	0	0.0	0	0.0	0	0.0	1	0.6	0	0.0	0	0.0	0	0.0		
Poaceae Long cell																
Sinuate long	0	0.0	0	0.0	0	0.0	0	0.0	0	0.0	0	0.0	0	0.0	0	0.0
Psilate long	0	0.0	0	0.0	1	5.9	2	1.1	1	0.3	1	0.4	0	0.0	0	0.0
Linearly articulated papillae	0	0.0	1	0.3	0	0.0	3	1.7	0	0.0	0	0.0	0	0.0	0	0.0
Elongated	118	19.3	15	5.0	3	17.6	19	10.9	16	4.9	32	11.4	20	29.9	0	0.0
Dendriform	32	5.2	73	24.2	2	11.8	5	2.9	8	2.5	5	1.8	4	6.0	0	0.0
Point shaped	70	11.5	37	12.3	1	5.9	7	4.0	11	3.4	21	7.5	5	7.5	0	0.0
Bulliform	7	1.1	7	2.3	0	0.0	0	0.0	1	0.3	5	1.8	2	3.0	0	0.0
Non-Poaceae long cell																
Stomata	6	1.0	0	0.0	0	0.0	0	0.0	0	0.0	1	0.4	0	0.0	0	0.0
Vascular	5	0.8	2	0.6	0	0.0	2	1.1	0	0.0	4	1.4	0	0.0	0	0.0
Ruminate long	0	0.0	0	0.0	0	0.0	0	0.0	0	0.0	0	0.0	0	0.0	0	0.0
Crenate epidermal	4	0.7	4	1.3	0	0.0	0	0.0	0	0.0	0	0.0	0	0.0	0	0.0
Rugulose epidermal	1	0.2	1	0.3	0	0.0	0	0.0	0	0.0	0	0.0	0	0.0	0	0.0
Castellated long	2	0.3	2	0.7	0	0.0	2	1.1	1	0.3	0	0.0	4	6.0	0	0.0

Table 8.5 (continued) Summary of phytolith analysis

	Ditch 460 57:607	%	Ditch 460 57:707	%	Ditch 460 56:711	%	Ditch 460 56:728	%	Ditch 574 58:861	%	Ditch 574 58:863	%	Ditch 574 59:864	%	Ditch 574 59:865	%
Hairs																
Uniform	7	1.1	12	4.0	2	11.8	2	1.1	0	0.0	3	1.1	0	0.0	0	0.0
Striated	1	0.2	0	0.0	0	0.0	0	0.0	0	0.0	0	0.0	0	0.0	0	0.0
Multicell hair base	0	0.0	3	1.0	0	0.0	0	0.0	0	0.0	0	0.0	0	0.0	0	0.0
Segmented	2	0.3	0	0.0	0	0.0	0	0.0	0	0.0	0	0.0	0	0.0	0	0.0
Others (Ignota)	19	3.1	4	1.3	1		4	2.3	25	7.7	15	5.3	0	0.0	0	0.0
Short cells	336	55.1	140	46.5	7		129	73.7	262	80.6	194	69.0	32	47.8	0	0.0
Long cells	245	40.2	142	47.2	7		40	22.9	38	11.7	69	24.6	35	52.2	0	0.0
Hairs	10	1.6	15	5.0	2		2	1.1	0	0.0	3	1.1	0	0.0	0	0.0
Totals	610		301		17		175		325		281		67		0	
Sum																
Poaceae short cell		52.0		44.2				66.3		77.5		65.8		46.3		0.0
Non-Poaceae short cell		2.9		2.3				8.0		3.1		3.2		1.5		0.0
Poaceae long cell		37.2		44.2				20.6		11.4		22.8		46.3		0.0
Non-Poaceae long cell		3.0		3.0				2.3		0.3		1.8		6.0		0.0
Hairs		1.6		5.0				1.1		0.0		1.1		0.0		0.0
Others		3.1		1.3				2.3		7.7		5.3		0.0		0.0

were mounted onto microscope slides using Canada Balsam and identified at x400 and x1000 magnifications using a Nikon Eclipse E400 light microscope.

Samples were compared with reference materials collected and processed by the author; reference keys including Cummings (1992), Mulholland and Rapp (1992), Piperno (1988) and Tubb et al. (1993) were also used. The phytolith sum varied between 175 to 610 and were counted and classified based on the modified Twiss et al. (1969). Table 8.5 shows some of the phytolith types identified.

All samples were dominated by phytoliths that fall into diagnostic categories:

- Short-cell Poaceae morphotypes
- Non-grass morphotypes mainly from ligneous dicotyledonous plants
- Long-cell morphotypes derived from Poaceae, these include dendritic forms which form in the inflorescences/panicles of grasses
- Other long cells that include vascular morphotypes and plant epidermal cell material
- Hairs
- Phytoliths classified as 'others' have sufficient diagnostic features to show only that they are from vascular plants

Results and discussion

Overall the level of phytolith preservation was good. Five samples yielded phytoliths in countable quantities (Table 8.5). Three samples contained few or no phytoliths, either due to post-depositional dissolution of the phytoliths or to the fact that the sediments at the time of deposition contained few or no phytoliths. These points will be discussed below.

The V-profiled ditch (574)

Two columns were recovered from the V-profiled ditch (574) for palynological investigation. All of the samples proved to be devoid of pollen in countable numbers. The lowest column (59) spans context 864 (cut 865, see Fig. 4.8, section 227) and the unnumbered deposits below, including the primary fill. The lower layers comprised brown fine sandy silt with flint pebbles and were totally devoid of phytoliths. Context 864 was characterised as a loose reddish-brown sandy gravel. This contained some phytoliths, oblong short cells, elongated long cells and some bilobate forms but not in sufficient quantities to give reliable statistical counts. These data support the notion that these two contexts represent material eroded and slumped from the side of the ditch and the adjacent upcast. The presence of some phytoliths at the top of the column perhaps relate to some sparse, grassy vegetation beginning to grow on the ditch interior.

Column 58 spans contexts 864, 863, 862 and 861 in the same section (Fig. 4.8, section 227). Contexts 863 and 861 were sampled for phytoliths. Both these contexts yielded phytoliths in countable numbers. Context 863 comprised a mid-brown gravel with a sand and silt matrix. This context yielded some degraded pollen grains, which included *Tilia, Pinus, Taxus, Calluna, Corylus, Quercus*, Cerealia, Poaceae, Chenopodiceae and Cyperaceae. These were found in insufficient quantities to produce a reliable count. The phytolith assemblage was dominated by short-cell Poaceae morphotypes (oblong, bilobate and poylobate forms). Long-cell elongated and point-shaped were also found in relatively high numbers. The presence of woody vegetation was suggested by the circular rugose morphotypes, which are found in ligneous dicotyledonous plants. Context 861 comprised reddish-brown gravelly sand. A similar phytolith signature to context 863 was found with a slightly higher short cell morphotypes component (80% of the sum).

Not surprisingly the phytoliths show a ditch that was initially unvegetated with the instability of the sides and adjacent upcast exacerbated by the coarse nature of these sediments. This would account for the total absence of phytoliths in context 865 and the slight increase in 864. With time the ditch would have become colonised, largely with grasses and eventually stabilised by context 861 (part of the standstill layer 1102). The fragmentary pollen evidence shows some open ground taxa, perhaps derived from the ditch and immediate surroundings with a background of oak, pine, hazel with some yew and lime present. Some evidence of sandy heathland is suggested by the presence of ling heather. This context is dated to 860-580 BC by modelling of the OSL dates, placing this context in the late Bronze Age or earliest Iron Age.

The U-profiled ditch (460)

Two columns were recovered from the U-profiled ditch (460). Column 56 spans contexts 728, 714 and 711 in cut 713 (see Fig. 5.2, section 219,), and is the lower of the two columns taken. These were the uppermost of the layers containing Iron Age finds 728 and 714) and the lowest containing Saxon material (711). Context 728 comprised gravelly sediment with a grey-brown matrix, and produced some phytoliths. Short cell morphotypes dominate the sample, however 10% of the total sum is derived from non-grass elements mainly from woody elements and also sedges. As grasses tend to be silica accumulators their presence is often over-represented when compared to woody taxa which do not accumulate silica into their tissues as readily. The woody elements are represented by the circular rugose forms derived from ligneous dicotyledonous plants. In addition, a single phytolith spherical with sockets form was identified. This would have been derived from a member of the Pinaceae family suggesting a presence of pine in the area. Sedges are represented by diagnostic trapezoid morphotypes. A few grains of Quercus and Poaceae pollen were also noted. Context 711 comprised a yellowish-brown sand and contained virtually no phytoliths at all.

Column 57 consisted of two contexts (707 and 607) forming the middle of the Saxon upper fills, both of which were analysed for their phytolith contents. Both samples yielded large quantities of phytoliths and both contained high proportions of long cell morphotypes. Of particular interest was the increased proportions of dendriforms (24% in context 707 and 5% in context 607). These are formed in the inflorescence bracts (glumes, paleas and lemmas) of mature Poaceae spikelets. The large size of many of these dendriforms suggest that they were derived from cereal chaff derived from the processing of cereals in the area. It is likely that the processing waste was cast into the ditch and incorporated in the sediment. In addition the presence of large inflorescence papillae was noted. Papilla phytoliths are cone hat-shaped and the number of pits in their bases varies between species. Rosen (1992) used papilla pit numbers and diameters to distinguish between wild and cultivated species of Poaceae. Tubb *et al.* (1993) investigated the diameter of inflorescence papillae and the number of pits in the base of the papilla of 45 accessions from the genera *Triticum, Hordeum,* and *Aegilops.* They found that there was a significant positive correlation between diameter and pit number when all the accessions were considered together. However, it was also found that there was little correlation between these variables when each genus was considered separately. Tubb *et al.* (1993) compared the mean overall pit number and papilla diameter for groups of accessions for these genera, giving a useful reference for identification of the papillae phytoliths found in this project. The papillae found in the samples from Taplow varied from 10 to 20 m in diameter. Mean diameters of papillae from barley are around 15μm with a pit number of approximately 8 (Tubb *et al.* 1993). The pit number of the papillae found at Taplow is between 8 and 10 indicating that they are most likely to be from barley (*Hordeum*), although the chance that they were derived from other grass types cannot be ruled out.

Conclusions

The virtual absence of pollen from both the ditch features sampled (574 and 460) was disappointing. However, the presence of phytoliths provides some insight into the local vegetation and land use at Taplow Court. The late Bronze Age ditch was initially unstable with rapid infill and the input of coarse sands and gravels into ditch 574. The ditch stabilised towards the end of the late Bronze Age and was vegetated with grasses. The sparse pollen points towards an open, grassy landscape with a local presence of heathland and background vegetation with some lime, oak, yew, pine and hazel elements present.

The later ditch (Iron Age to Saxon) comprised a grassy vegetation in context 728 dating to the Iron Age, with some woody elements present including pine. Context 707, dating from the Anglo-Saxon period contained phytoliths derived from cereal chaff, most probably from barley, which indicates the processing of cereals on the site. It was most likely to have been incorporated into the sediments as waste thrown in. Context 607 also dates from the Saxon period and shows a stable grassland in the vicinity of the ditch with some evidence for cereals.

Deposits and site formation processes
by M G Canti

Introduction

The main exposures in the 1999 excavation at Taplow Court were three roughly parallel, north-south aligned defences consisting of two ditches and a palisade trench. Various issues concerning the development of the ditch fills were discussed and some sampling carried out during two site visits in June 1999. This report provides the results of the analysis of those samples.

Dark feature fills and deposits (1100, 1120 and 1123)

On the western side of the site, the postholes were generally infilled with dark soil presumed to be occupation deposits. Only one larger feature (783) had this dark type of fill, layer (644), and this was one of the areas of burning in the rampart associated with the U-profiled ditch (460); (see Fig. 5.5 and Plate 8.1), leading to questions about its history and use. Similar material occurred in much of the western baulk, particularly in the northern half of the excavation. Towards the south a more complete soil profile appeared to be preserved around where the palisade trench (1106) went through the western baulk. It was decided to compare the topsoil of this profile (890, part of soil 1120 (see Fig. 4.9, section 229) buried below the rampart associated with the U-profiled ditch with some of the occupation-type material further north (889, part of the occupation layer (1123) within the hillfort) to see how these three deposits might have been related, and in particular whether one could be distinguished as the parent material for deposit 644. The comparison was carried out using particle size tests on the three materials.

The particle size analyses were carried out using analytical sieves for the coarse end of the spectrum and a Sedigraph 5100 for the <63 μm material. Further details of the method and interpretation can be found in Canti (1991).

Examination of the whole particle size spectrum for the three samples (Fig. 8.1) suggests consider-

Plate 8.1   The dark type fill (644)

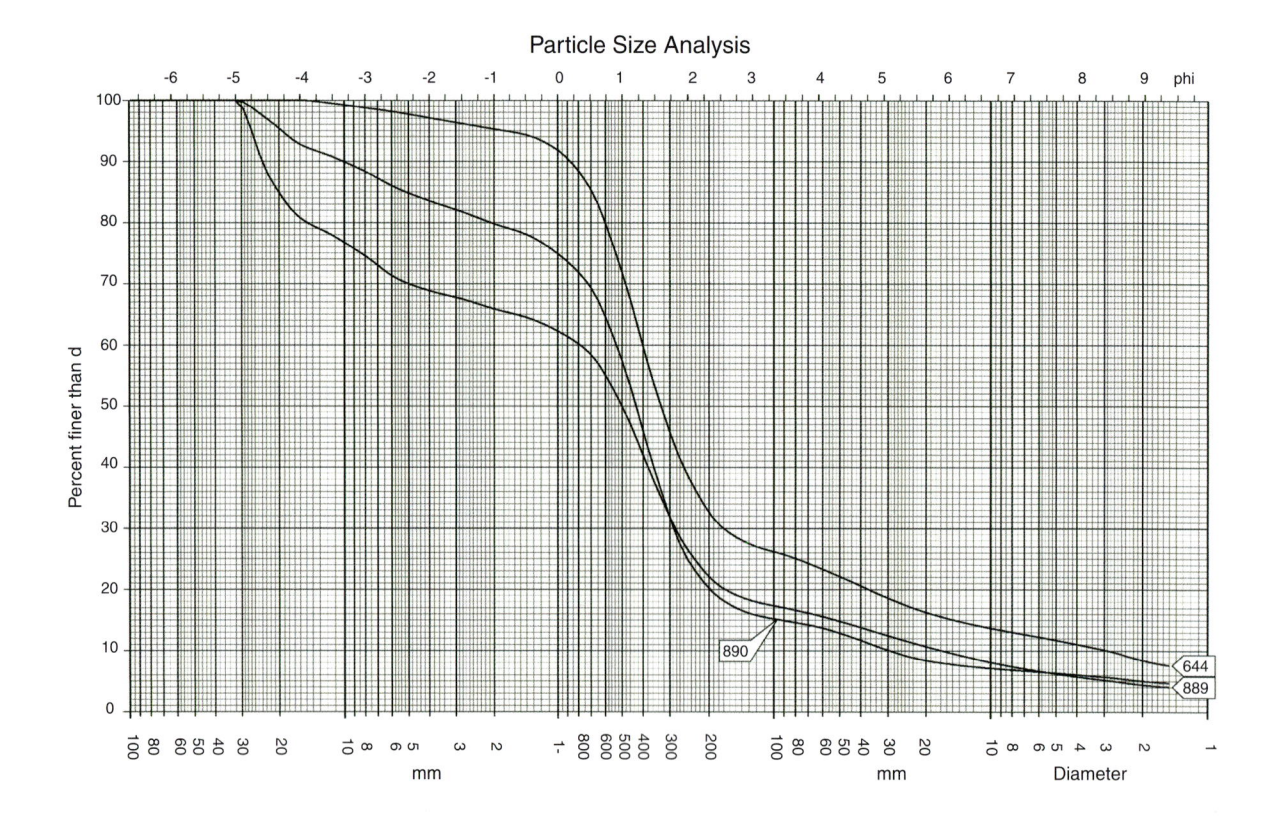

Fig. 8.1   Particle size analyses of the feature fill (644) and related deposits (889, 890) in the interior

Particle Size Analysis

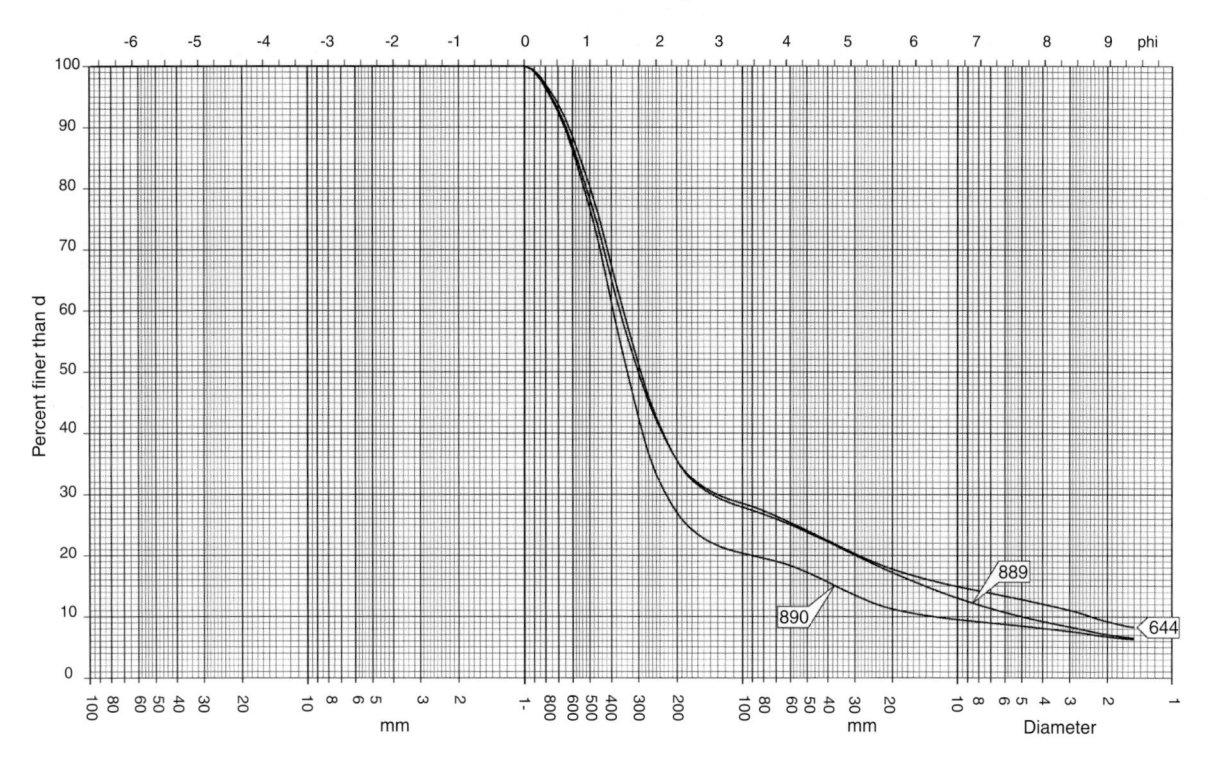

Fig. 8.2 Sub 1 mm particle size analyses of the feature fill (644) and related deposits (889 and 890) in the interior

able variation between them. Although they show broadly similar trends, coming as they do from the same gravel body, there is no consistent similarity between 644 and either of the two candidates for its origin (899 or 890). However, if we look only at the <1mm material (Fig. 8.2), a quite different picture emerges. 889 is almost identical to 644 down most of its length. This is likely to be the more reliable way of looking at the data, as the larger stones can be problematic for particle size analysis. A single large stone may be present or absent from the sample leading to unrepresentative results.

It is strongly suggested by this data, therefore, that the occupation-type material 889 either represents the source material of the fill (644), or they are both derived from another source from which they inherited the similar particle size characteristics. The most likely scenario is, perhaps, that the occupation layer (1123) of which 889 formed a part was the source of fill 644. This is consistent with the chronology outlined above (see above, Chapter 4) which suggests that 889 became differentiated from 890 in the late Bronze Age as a result of 890 being buried below the late Bronze Age rampart associated with the V-profiled ditch (574). The occupation deposits (889) were thus subject to anthropogenic and natural processes from which the buried soil (890) was protected. In the early-middle Iron Age it was the exposed cultural layer which become incorporated into the rampart as deposit 644, rather than the still buried soil (890).

Reddened fills (1100)

Large amounts of reddened gravel (1100; typically 2.5 YR 4/4 to 3/6) were present in the upper fill of the V-profiled ditch (574), often with the stains and remains of charred timber (1113) in or under it (Plate 8.2). The deposits were commonly 0.2 m thick and in places reached 0.7 m. Samples were taken at three places where the reddened sediment was most plentiful. These consisted simply of bulk samples of the reddened and surrounding un-reddened material. Starting with the northernmost feature and going south, the sample numbers of the reddened material (followed in brackets by the unreddened surrounding gravel number (1112), where available) were 645, 724 (725) and 616 (615).

The unreddened samples were heated on small trays to avoid the build-up of CO_2 that can occur in containers with any depth. The heating regimes were decided iteratively, starting at 500° C for 1 hour, followed by 400° C for 1 hour, both of which clearly reproduced the field reddening. 300° C was almost identical with the field deposits (slightly less red), and 250° C for 2 hours was significantly under reddened. Consequently, we can be confident that around 300–350° C for 1–2 hours is the minimum required to produce the reddening as found. Samples of the original contexts and furnace-reddened equivalents are shown in Plate 8.3.

This depth of heat-reddened gravel could not be generated by *in-situ* burning of surface fires. Ordinary surface fires will produce temperatures of

Plate 8.2 Reddened material (645) – one of the three samples tested

Plate 8.3 Reddening of the selected contexts at different temperatures and for different durations

300–350° C in the soil beneath them, but only to a few centimetres depth (Canti and Linford 2001). It is possible that vertical faces of the gravelly sediments at Taplow could be reddened by having fires lit up against them, or by the burning of supporting timbers associated with foundations or cellars. However, such vertical reddening would also only penetrate the sediment by a few centimetres, so, in disagreement with the excavators, it still seems likely that the deepest and thickest reddened layers would still need to be thickened by dumping.

Chapter 9 – Absolute dates

INTRODUCTION

A combination of techniques was used to assist in obtaining a dating sequence for the site. During the excavation, when it appeared that suitable organic remains might be lacking from some key features, the Research Laboratory for Archaeology was asked to take samples for Optically Stimulated Luminescence Dating. Subsequently, English Heritage agreed to undertake a programme of radiocarbon dating. The location of the samples taken for absolute dating is shown in Figure 9.1.

OPTICALLY STIMULATED LUMINESCENCE DATES
by Jean-Luc Schwenninger

Methodology

A series of five sediment samples, plus one of burnt flint and one of burnt stone were collected from the main excavation on the 23rd of June 1999 by Dr E J Rhodes for luminescence dating. The samples (Table 9.1) were obtained from the primary fill of the V-profiled ditch (574), the standstill layer (1102), the rampart (1112) associated with the U-profiled ditch and a slow-forming silt (712) in the upper part of the U-profiled ditch (460).

The age estimates presented in Table 9.1 are based on sand-sized quartz grains extracted from each sample. Dose rates were calculated by *in-situ* NaI gamma spectrometer measurements and using neutron activation analysis (NAA) for beta dose rates. The measurements reported here were made by Dr E J Rhodes in December 1999. Full details of the methodology are contained in the site archive.

Extremely low IRSL values were observed, suggesting good quartz separation had been achieved. A very low degree of variability between aliquots was observed for the sediment samples and no signs of incomplete zeroing were observed. The other observed luminescence characteristics, namely recycling values (means at 0.99 to 1.00) and low thermal transfer values (mean values below 5% of the natural OSL signal) strongly suggest that these age estimates are likely to be reliable.

The initial date obtained from the basal sediments of the V-profiled ditch (X074) was, however, higher than expected. It is possible that the initial infilling may have occurred relatively rapidly, involving lateral erosion of freshly removed sediments from the sides of the ditch. This could have resulted in the inclusion of a small amount of incompletely bleached grains, which in the case of conventional multigrain aliquots can lead to age overestimation. The latest developments in OSL dating enable the dating of individual grains and this sample was, therefore submitted for single grain analysis.

The revised single grain age estimate is presented in Table 9.1 and is based on four sand-sized quartz grains. A total of 800 single grain measurements were carried out but only six high quality grains passed the strict default acceptance criteria set by the analysis software.

Results

The results clearly indicate the presence of young modern contaminants (near zero palaeodose) and older grains, both potentially contributing to age-underestimation and age-overestimation (Figure 9.2). Several grains with a geological signal were also detected but are not featured on the frequency distribution diagram. The results suggest that the true palaeodose of the sample is likely to be around 1.8 Gy as opposed to 2.47 Gy previously derived from the multi-grain aliquots. This brings the age of the sample down from 3810 to 2770 years before present and provides a date in overall good agreement with the other OSL age estimates in the series.

The results obtained from the sample of burnt flint (X069) are inconclusive and the date must be considered as unreliable. Although a palaeodose of 1.68 Gy was obtained, the calculated age of 3.6 ka is clearly an overestimate. It is possible that the sample may not have been sufficiently heated to achieve full zeroing of the geological signal. Further investigations would be required to assess whether or not this sample is suitable for luminescence dating. These discouraging results also explain why no further work was undertaken on another sample of burnt stone (X070).

The sample from layer 712 in the U-profiled ditch (X071) produced a date (2060± 110) several centuries older than the radiocarbon date of 550-670 cal AD from articulating bones in the adjacent deposit 711 (OxA-14432;1451± 30 BP). Although this was a relatively slow-forming silt, and it is possible that the horse bones came from the top of the deposit, there is still a large discrepancy between the dates. It seems likely that sample (X071) included some older, incompletely bleached grains from the ditch sides.

Overall, the OSL dating appears to have worked relatively well at this site and confirms the possibility of dating ditch deposits at archaeological sites.

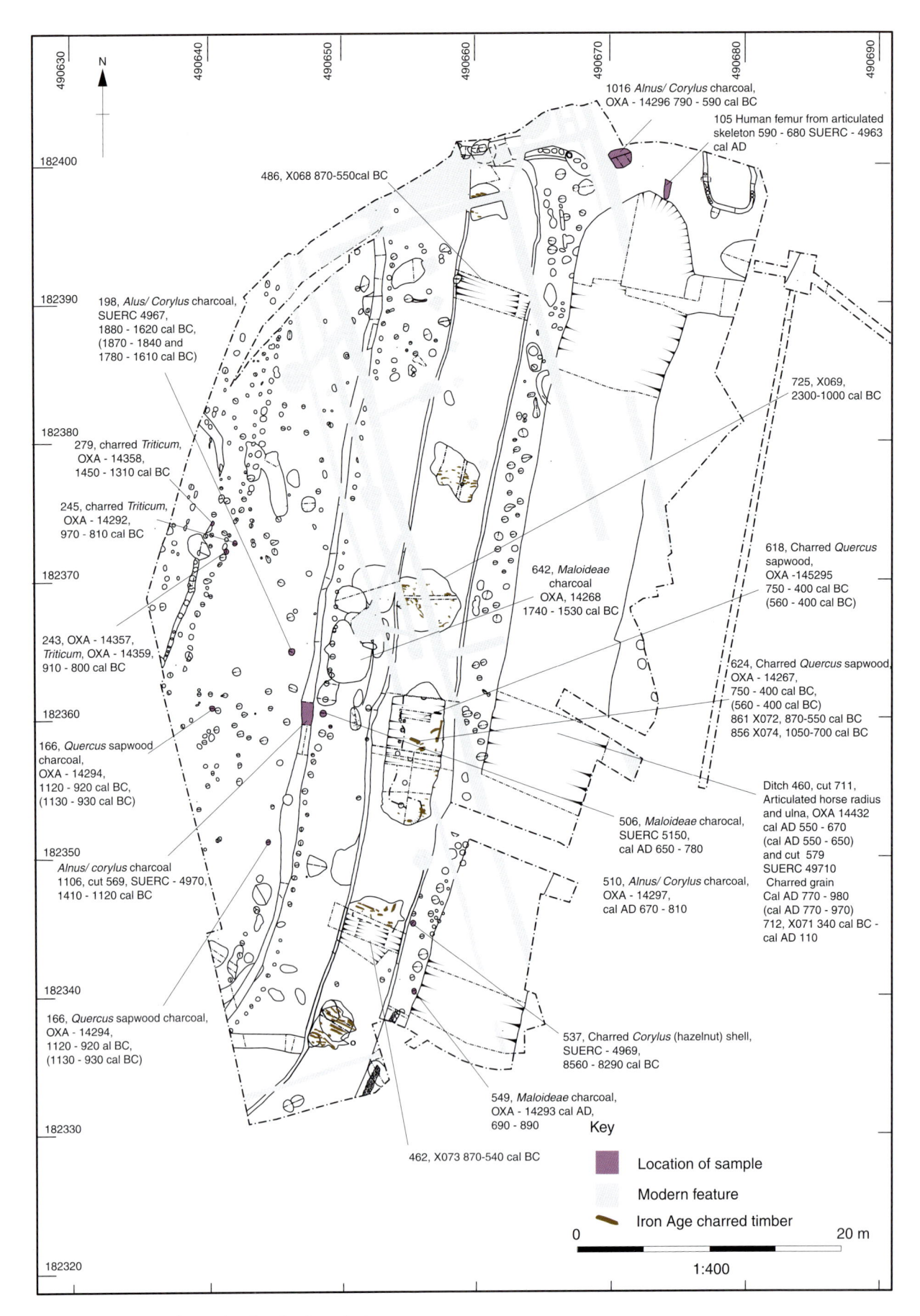

Fig. 9.1 Location of samples for absolute dating

Chapter 9

Table 9.1 Summary of OSL samples and dating results featuring the multi grain age estimates in addition to the revised single grain date for sample X074 (in bold characters). Gamma dose rates are based on in-situ gamma-ray spectroscopy measurements. Beta dose rate values were calculated using the concentrations of uranium, thorium and potassium as determined by neutron activation analysis (NAA). Corrections were made in the age calculation for the water content of the sediment samples using the correction factors of Aitken (1985). The contribution of cosmic radiation was calculated as a function of latitude, altitude, burial depth and average over-burden density according to the formulae of Prescott and Hutton (1994). Further details regarding individual samples may be found in the site archive.

Context	Feature	Group	Depth(cm)	Field code	Lab. code	Sample type and sedimentary unit	Palaeodose(Gy)	Dose rate(mGy/a)	Age(years BP) ± 1 sigma	Calendar date ranges (68% confidence)
primary fill	856	V-profiled ditch 574	250	THF99-07	X074	OSL tube sample	2.47 ± 0.15	0.65 ± 0.03	3810 ± 300	2110-1510 BC
primary fill	**856**	**V-profiled ditch 574**	**250**	**THF99-07**	**X074**	**OSL tube sample**	**1.80 ± 0.30**	**0.65 ± 0.03**	**2770 ± 480**	**1250-290 BC**
486	486	Standstill layer 1102	80	THF99-01	X068	OSL tube sample	2.24 ± 0.05	0.84 ± 0.04	2670 ± 150	820-520 BC
861	861	Standstill layer 1102	140	THF99-05	X072	OSL tube sample	2.29 ± 0.03	0.82 ± 0.04	2780 ± 150	930-630 BC
462	462	Standstill layer 1102	75	THF99-06	X073	OSL tube sample	2.39 ± 0.15	0.87 ± 0.04	2750 ± 230	980-520 BC
725	725	Rampart gravels 1112	80	THF99-02	X069	Bulk sample of burnt flint/burnt gravel deposit	1.68 ± 0.11	0.47 ± 0.02	(3600 ± 310)	1900-1290 BC
725	861	Standstill layer 1102	100	THF99-03	X070	Sample of burnt stone/ burnt gravel deposit [not dated]				
712	713	U-profiled ditch 460	150	THF99-04	X071	OSL tube sample - sandy silt (Anglo-Saxon deposits)	1.66 ± 0.03	0.81 ± 0.04	2060 ± 110	170 BC–AD50

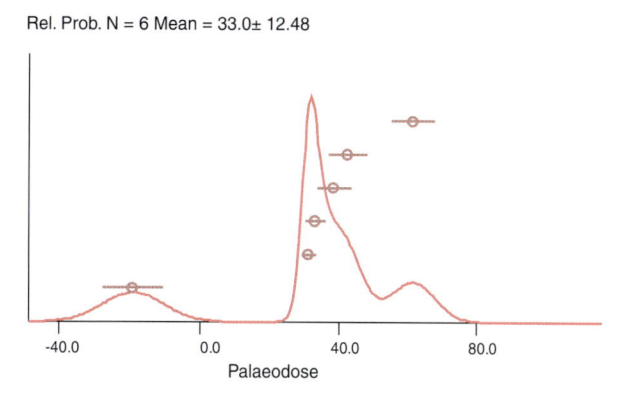

Fig. 9.2 Probability distribution of single grain data obtained for sample X074. The results clearly reveal the presence of one near zero outlier (to the left) and one substantially older grain or alternatively, a grain subjected to an enhanced dose rate perhaps due to microdosimetric effects (to the right). A palaeodose of 1.80±0.30 Gy was obtained from the four central grains (peak centered at circa 33 seconds of irradiation time). A total of 800 grains were measured but only 6 grains passed the acceptance criteria set for palaeodose calculation.

RADIOCARBON DATES AND BAYESIAN MODELLING

by P Marshall, D Hamilton, T Allen, C Bronk Ramsey, G Cook, J-L Schwenninger and C Hayden

Introduction

A total of 21 radiocarbon and five optically stimulated luminescence (OSL) measurements have been obtained on samples from Taplow Court.

Methodology

Eight samples were dated at the Scottish Universities Research and Reactor Centre in East Kilbride in 2004-2005. They were measured by Accelerator Mass Spectrometry at the Scottish Universities Environment Research Centre AMS Facility with sample preparation and measurement as outlined in Slota *et al.* (1987) and Freeman *et al.* (2004).

The twelve samples processed by the Oxford Radiocarbon Accelerator Unit in 2004 were prepared using the methods outlined in Bronk Ramsey *et al.* (2000) and Bronk Ramsey *et al.* (2004) and were measured using Accelerator Mass Spectrometry (Bronk Ramsey and Hedges 1997).

One sample was processed at the Poznan Radiocarbon Laboratory in 2005. The sample was prepared and measured by Accelerator Mass Spectrometry as desribed by Czernik and Goslar (2001).

All three laboratories maintain continual programmes of quality assurance procedures, in addition to participation in international intercomparisons (Scott 2003). These tests indicate no laboratory offsets and demonstrate the validity of the precision quoted.

Results

The radiocarbon results are given in Table 9.2, and are quoted in accordance with the international standard known as the Trondheim convention (Stuiver and Kra 1986). They are conventional radiocarbon ages (Stuiver and Polach 1977).

Calibration

The calibrations of the results, relating the radiocarbon measurements directly to calendar dates, are given in Table 9.2 and in outline in Figure 9.3. All have been calculated using the calibration curve of Reimer *et al.* (2004) and the computer program OxCal (v3.10) (Bronk Ramsey 1995; 1998; 2001). The calibrated date ranges cited in the text are those for 95% confidence. They are quoted in the form recommended by Mook (1986), with the end points rounded outwards to 10 years. The ranges quoted in italics are *posterior density estimates* derived from mathematical modelling of archaeological problems (see below). The ranges in plain type in Table 9.2 have been calculated according to the maximum intercept method (Stuiver and Reimer 1986). All other ranges are derived from the probability method (Stuiver and Reimer 1993).

Stable isotopes

The stable isotope values ($\delta^{13}C$ and $\delta^{15}N$, see Table 9.2) for the single human bone dated are consistent

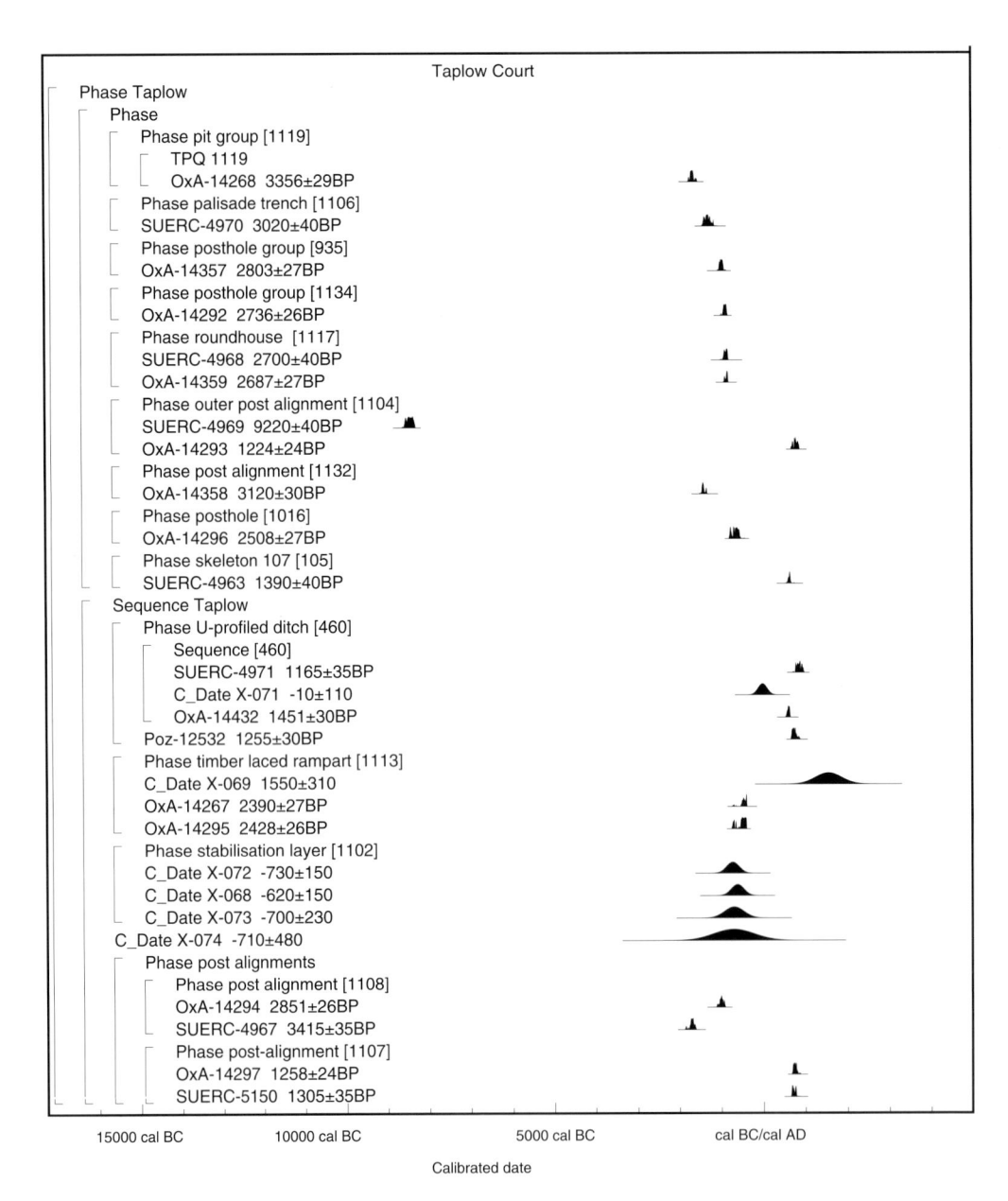

Fig. 9.3 Probability distributions of dates from Taplow Court. Each distribution represents the relative probability that an event occurred at a particular time. These distributions are the result of simple radiocarbon calibration (Stuiver and Reimer 1993).

with a very largely terrestrial diet and are not likely to have any effect on the radiocarbon dating (Chisholm *et al*.1982; Mays 2000). The C:N ratio suggest that bone preservation was sufficiently good to have confidence in the radiocarbon determination (Masters, 1987; Tuross *et al.* 1988).

Interpretative methodology
A Bayesian approach has been adopted for the interpretation of the chronology from this site (Buck *et al.* 1996). Although the simple calibrated dates are accurate estimates of the dates of the samples, this is usually not what archaeologists really wish to know. It is the dates of the archaeological events represented by those samples that are of interest. In the case of Taplow Court, it is the date of the palisades, enclosures and periods of abandonment that is under consideration, not the dates of single pieces of charcoal. The dates of this activity can be estimated not only using the absolute dating information from the radiocarbon and OSL measurements on the samples, but also by using the stratigraphic relationships between samples.

Fortunately, methodology is now available which allows the combination of these different types of information explicitly, to produce realistic estimates of the dates of archaeological interest. It should be emphasised that the *posterior density estimates* produced by this modelling are not absolute. They are interpretative *estimates*, which can and will change as further data become available and as other researchers choose to model the existing data from different perspectives.

The technique used is a form of Markov Chain Monte Carlo sampling, and has been applied using the program OxCal v3.10 (http://www.rlaha.ox.ac.uk/), which uses a mixture of the Metropolis-Hastings algorithm and the more specific Gibbs sampler (Gilks *et al.* 1996; Gelfand and Smith 1990). Details of the algorithms employed by this program are available from the on-line manual or in Bronk Ramsey (1995; 1998; 2001). The algorithm used in the models described below can be derived from the structures shown in Figure 9.4. The model uses the ranges quoted at 1 standard deviation (68.4% confidence).

The following section concentrates on describing the archaeological evidence, which has been incorporated into the chronological model, explaining the reasoning behind the interpretative choices made in producing the models presented. These archaeological decisions fundamentally underpin the choice of statistical model.

Objectives and sampling strategy
The radiocarbon programme was designed to achieve the following objectives:

- To date the first enclosure of the hilltop and clarify the sequence of defensive ditches and palisades

- Establish whether internal activity was related to the main sequence

- Provide a precise date for the Saxon activity

The first stage in sample selection was to identify short-lived material that was demonstrably not residual in the context from which it was recovered. The taphonomic relationship between a sample and its context is the most hazardous link in this process, since the mechanisms by which a sample came to be in its context are a matter of interpretative decision rather than certain knowledge. All samples consisted of single entities (Ashmore 1999). An attempt was made to select material only where there was evidence that a sample had been put fresh into its context. The main categories of material that met these taphonomic criteria were:

- Articulated animal bones. Articulated animal bone deposit must have been buried with tendons attached or they would not have remained in articulation, and so were almost certainly less than six months old when buried (Mant 1987)

- Human burials. Inhumations were almost certainly articulated when buried

- Concentrations of cereals that formed substantial and discrete deposits likely to represent a "single event"

- Sapwood from roundwood or split timbers found *in situ*. At Taplow, the ubiquity of oak charcoal in the rampart structure argues strongly that wood for the rampart was carefully selected. Even though the incorporation of stored or reused timber is possible, the relationship of the sapwood to the event to be dated is secure

Other samples with a less certain taphonomic origin submitted included material from the fill of postholes, interpreted as relating to the use of structures rather than its construction, as suggested by experimental archaeology (Reynolds 1995), and from the primary fill of pits. Where possible duplicate samples from these contexts were submitted to test the assumption that the material was of the same actual age.

Once suitable samples had been identified a model was devised, which incorporated the archaeological information along with simulated radiocarbon results. The radiocarbon results were simulated using the R_Simulate function in OxCal, with errors based on the material to be analysed and the type of measurement required (eg single run AMS/high precision). This was used to determine the number of samples that should be submitted in the dating programme.

Table 9.2 Summary of radiocarbon determinations

Lab Number	Context/sample Number	Material (identified by)
Residual Mesolithic date		
SUERC-4969	Sample 25, from fill 535 of posthole 537 part of posthole row 1104	Charcoal, hazelnut shell (D Challinor)
Early Bronze Age hollows 1119		
OxA-14268	Sample 35, from fill 553 of hollow 642 part of group 1119	Charcoal, Maloideae (D Challinor)
Residual Middle Bronze Age date		
OxA-14358	Sample 10, from fill 283 of posthole 279, part of posthole row 1132	Charred grain, *Triticum* sp (M Robinson)
SUERC-4970	Sample 30, from postpacking 571 within intervention 569 in palisade trench 1106	Charcoal, *Alnus/Corylus* (D Challinor)
Posthole row 1108		
OxA-14294	Sample 46, from postpipe fill 168 of posthole 166, part of posthole row 1108	Charcoal, *Quercus* sapwood (D Challinor & R Gale)
SUERC-4967	Sample 45, from postpipe fill 200 of posthole 198, part of posthole row 1108	Charcoal, *Alnus/Corylus* (D Challinor)
Posthole row 935		
OxA-14357	Sample 3, from fill 244 of posthole 244, part of posthole row 935	Charred grain, *T. dicoccum* or *Spelta* (M Robinson)
Posthole group 1132		
OxA-14292	Sample 4, from fill 246 of posthole 245 part of posthole group 1134	Charred grain, *Triticum* sp (M Robinson)
Posthole group 1117		
OxA-14359	Sample 49, fill 207 of posthole 206, part of posthole group 1117	Charred grain, *Spelta* wheat (M Robinson)
SUERC-4968	Sample 49, fill 207 of posthole 206, part of posthole group 1117	Charred grain, *Spelta* wheat (M Robinson)
Iron Age hillfort entrance		
OxA-14296	Sample 67, from fill 1018 of pit 1016	Charcoal, *Alnus/Corylus* (D Challinor)
Burnt rampart of Iron Age hillfort		
OxA-14267	Sample 41, charred timbers 624 part of rampart structure 1113	Charcoal, *Quercus* sapwood (D Challinor & R Gale)
OxA-14295	Sample 40, charred timbers 618 part of rampart structure 1113	Charcoal, *Quercus* sapwood (D Challinor & R Gale)
Saxon deposits in the U-profiled ditch (460)		
OxA-14432	Layer 711 upper fill of ditch 460	Animal bone, horse radius and ulna articulating (E-J Evans)
SUERC-4971	Sample 51, from upper fill 579 of ditch 460	Charred grain, *Secale cereale* (D Challinor)
Saxon deposits in the Outer ditch (3050)		
Poz-12532	From outer ditch 3050	
Anglo-Saxon inhumation 105		
SUERC-4963	Skeleton 107 from grave 105	Human bone, left femur from full articulated skeleton
Other Anglo-Saxon dates		
Posthole row 1107		
OxA-14297	Sample 21, from fill 511 of posthole 510, part of posthole row 1107	Charcoal, *Alnus/Corylus* (D Challinor)
SUERC-5150	Sample 23, from fill 507 of posthole 506, part of posthole row 1107	Charcoal, Maloideae (D Challinor)
Posthole row 1104		
OxA-14293	Sample 27, from fill 549 of posthole 548 part of posthole row 1104	Charcoal, Maloideae (D Challinor)
Failed date		
SUERC-4972	Sample 68, charred timbers 100 part of rampart structure {1113}	Charcoal, *Quercus* sapwood (D Challinor & R Gale)

Radiocarbon Age (BP)	δ¹³C (‰)	δ¹⁵N (‰)	C:N ratio	Calibrated date range (95% confidence)	Posterior Density Estimate (95% probability)
9220±40	-24.9			8560-8290 cal BC	-
3356±29	-23.4			1740-1530 cal BC	-
3120±30	-23.0			1450-1310 cal BC	
3020±40	-24.0			1410-1120 cal BC	-
2851±26	-22.7			1120-920 cal BC	1130-930 cal BC
3415±35	-25.7			1880-1620 cal BC	1870-1840 (2%) or 1780-1610 (93%) cal BC
2803±27	-21.7			1020-890 cal BC	
2736±26	-23.4			970-810 cal BC	-
2687±27	-23.0			910-800 cal BC	-
2700±40	-23.8			930-790 cal BC	-
2508±27	-26.9			790-520 cal BC	-
2390±27	-24.0			710-390 cal BC	520-390 cal BC
2428±26	-24.4			750-400 cal BC	560-400 cal BC
1451±30	-22.6			cal AD 550-670	cal AD 550-650
1165±35	-22.9			cal AD 770-980	cal AD 770-970
1255±30				cal AD 670-780	cal AD 670-870
1390±40	-20.3	9.9	3.4	cal AD 590-680	-
1258±24	-26.1			cal AD 670-810	-
1305±35	-24.4			cal AD 650-780	-
1224±24	-25.2			cal AD 690-890	-
Pmc 1.2073±0.0053	-25.2			-	-

The sequence

The earliest posthole rows were 1107 and 1108. The stratigraphic evidence relating to these posthole rows was not entirely consistent (see above, Chapter 4). However, the postholes in both rows lay below the soil (1120) which was either part of, or had been buried below the rampart associated with the V-profiled ditch (574). They therefore predate that ditch, and, stratigraphically, are the earliest posthole rows.

The two postholes at the centre of row 1107, from which charcoal suitable for radiocarbon analysis was identified, were not sealed by layer (1120) although as part of the same posthole row they should also therefore pre-date the formation of the soil. The measurements on charcoal from two

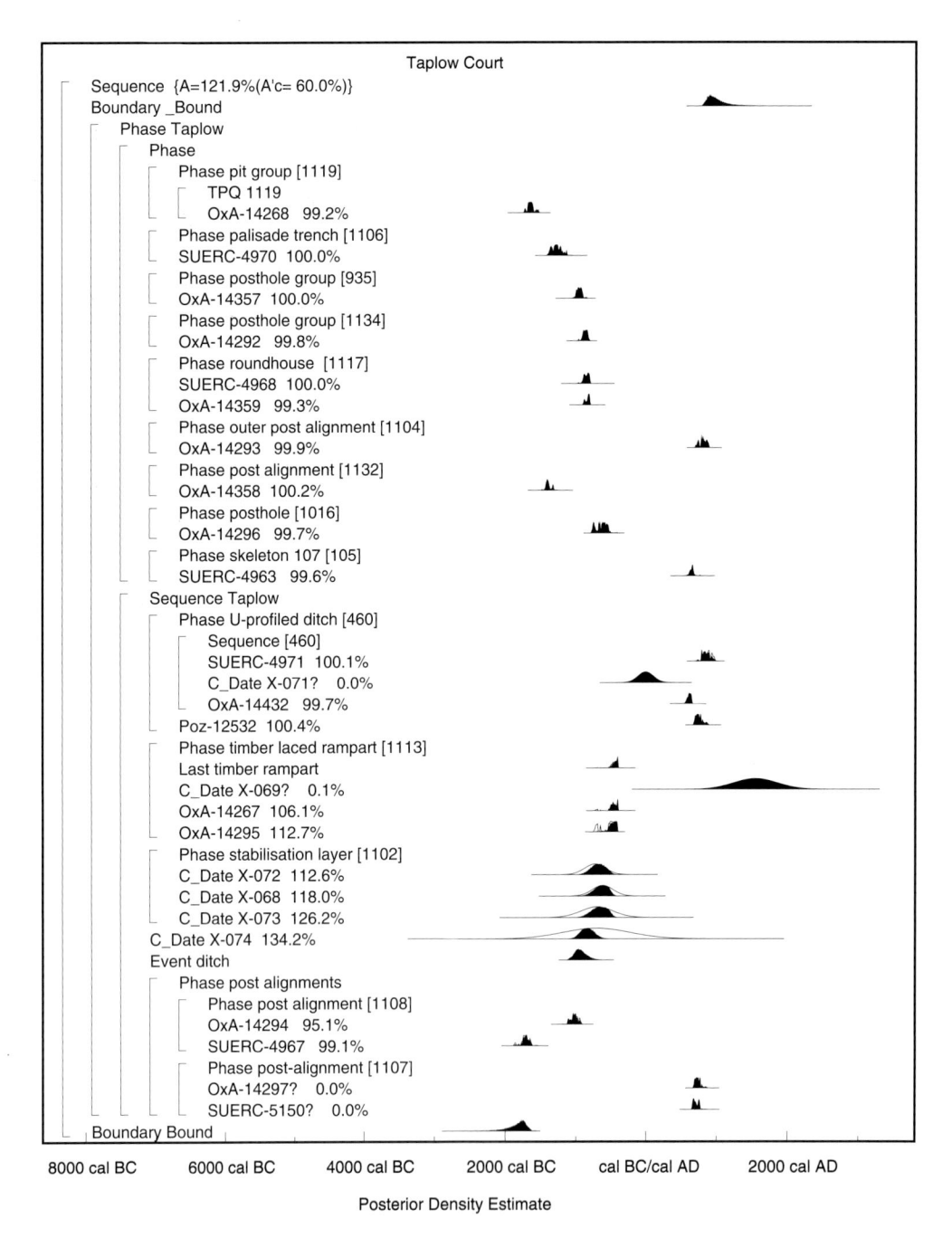

Fig. 9.4 Probability distributions of dates from Taplow Court: each distribution represents the relative probability that an event occurs at a particular time. For each of the radiocarbon/OSL dates two distributions have been plotted, one in outline, which is the result of simple calibration, and a solid one, which is based on the chronological model used. The other distributions correspond to aspects of the model. For example, the distribution 'event ditch' is the estimated date for the digging of ditch 574. A question mark (?) indicates that the result has been excluded from the model. The large square brackets down the left hand side along with the OxCal keywords define the model exactly.

different postholes (510 and 506) of this alignment (OxA-14297; 1258±24 BP and SUERC-5150; 1305±35 BP) are statistically consistent (T'=1.2; T'(5%)=3.8; v=1, Ward and Wilson 1978), but they are Anglo-Saxon in date. It is therefore suggested that the material is intrusive and originated from Saxon activity in the vicinity of the posthole row.

Measurements from two of the postholes belonging to posthole row 1108, posthole 166 (OxA-14294; 2851±26 BP) and posthole 198 (SUERC-4967; 3415±35 BP) are not statistically consistent (T'=170.5; T'(5%)=3.8; v=1, Ward and Wilson 1978) and therefore contain material of different ages. The material from posthole 198 may be residual, and that from posthole 166 may be intrusive, or conceivably both might be residual.

A series of intercutting hollows (1119) containing early Bronze Age Collared Urn pottery and coniferous wood were originally thought to cut posthole row 1107. However, further analysis suggests that it is more likely that the pit group predates the posthole row. It was originally agreed to submit the carbonised residue from one of the pieces of Collared Urn along with a piece of coniferous charcoal, as the presence of coniferous trees in the part of the landscape during the Bronze Age would be unusual. However, no further coniferous charcoal was found (see Gale, Chapter 8 above), and the sample submitted instead (OxA-14268; 3356±29 BP; Maloideae) had no direct functional relationship to the hollow (642), stratigraphically the latest in the group (1119) from which it was recovered and therefore only provides a *terminus post quem* for its context.

A single sample (SUERC-4970; 3020±40 BP) was submitted from palisade trench 1106. Palisade trench 1106 cuts, or is abutted by, the soil (1120) consisting of a mixed topsoil and rampart material associated with the V-profile ditch (574), and thus postdated posthole rows 1107 and 1108. Part of the buried soil (1120) was in turn overlain by the standstill layer (1102). The date is inconsistent with its stratigraphic position, and it seems likely that the *Alnus/Corylus* charcoal from which it was obtained was residual.

Ditch 574 cut ditch 1114 and was contemporary with soil 1120. The lower half of the V-profiled ditch was filled by a succession of gravelly silts that did not contain material suitable for radiocarbon analysis, but did provide an OSL sample from the primary silt (868; X-074; 2770±480 BP).

East of the V-profiled ditch (574) was a linear cluster of postholes (1104). The stratigraphic relationship between the postholes forming posthole row 1104 and the cutting of the ditch was unclear, although some were sealed by a distinct silt horizon (the standstill layer, 1102) which had formed towards the top of ditch (574). The posthole row may therefore represent a palisade preceding the V-profiled ditch 574, or may have been contemporary with it. None of the postholes containing material suitable for dating were sealed by the standstill layer. The two measurements from postholes belonging to posthole row 1104, posthole 537 (SUERC-4969; 9220±40 BP) and posthole 548 (OxA-14293; 1224±24 BP) are not statistically consistent (T'=170.5; T'(5%)=3.8; v=1, Ward and Wilson 1978) and therefore contain material of different ages. The hazelnut shell (SUERC-4969) in posthole 537 was clearly residual, while the fragment of Maloideae (OxA-14293) from posthole 548 is thought to have been intrusive.

Three distinct posthole rows were present in the interior of the hillfort. A single seed of carbonised grain (*Triticum* sp.) was submitted from posthole 279 in posthole row 1132 (OxA-14358; 3120±30 BP. Although running parallel to other post-built structures, 1132 had no direct relationship with any of the other alignments. A single carbonised grain (*T. dioccum* or *Spelta*; OxA-14357; 2803±27 BP) came from the fill of posthole 243, which was part of posthole row 935, and *Spelta* grains (OxA-14359; 2687±27 BP and SUERC-4968; 2700±40) from the fill

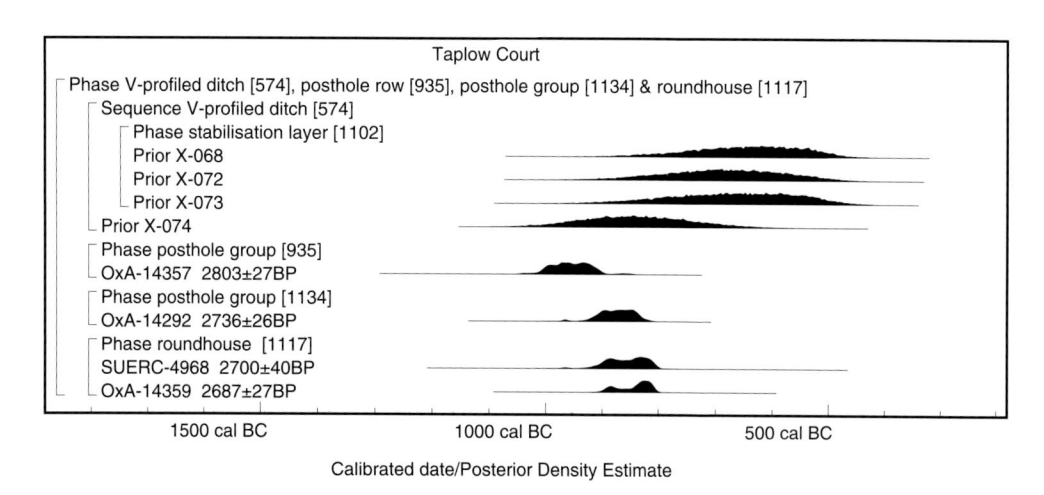

Fig. 9.5 Probability distributions of dates from Taplow Court: V-profiled ditch 574, posthole row 935, posthole group 1134 and roundhouse 1117. Each distribution represents the relative probability that an event occurred at a particular time.

of posthole 206, possibly belonging to four-post structures within posthole group 1117. *Triticum* from posthole 254, part of a further cluster of postholes (1134), provided a further determination (OxA-14292; 2736±26). This posthole may have belonged to four-post structures within the group.

The standstill layer (1102) sealing ditch 574 was up to 0.25 m in depth (Fig. 4.7). Three OSL samples were obtained from this layer: X-073 (2750±230 BP), X-072 (2780±150 BP) and X-068 (2670±150 BP). Cut into the standstill layer east of ditch 574 was another larger U-profiled ditch (460). Large quantities of gravel, probably thrown out in digging ditch 460, overlay the standstill layer (1102) and completely filled the top of the earlier ditch (574). This material was used to form a rampart. The rampart contained preserved *in situ* charred timbers (1113) that appeared to be the remains of a corduroy of timbers laid across the largely silted ditch. Three samples of oak sapwood were submitted from the charred timbers, two (OxA-14267; 2390±27 BP and OxA-14295; 2428±26 BP) produced statistically consistent radiocarbon measurements (T'=1.0; T'(5%)=3.8; v=1, Ward and Wilson 1978) and one (SUERC-4972) produced a modern result (from the 1950 levelling of the site).

At the northern end of the site (see Fig. 5.7) a pit or large posthole (1016) at the end of the U-profiled ditch (574) is interpreted as having been part of an entrance structure that was burnt along with the gravel rampart (1113). A single piece of charcoal (OxA-14296) was submitted from the fill of the posthole.

The U-profiled ditch (460) mainly silted up naturally. A single OSL sample (X-071; 2060±110 BP) was obtained from layer 712 abutting layer 711, a fill containing an articulating horse radius and ulna (OxA-14432; 1451±30 BP), and was overlain by a large grain assemblage associated with Saxon pottery and other finds (SUERC-4971; 1165±35 BP). An extended inhumation burial (107; SUERC-4963; 1390±40 BP) lay at the end of the ditch (460) but cannot be directly related to the deposits within it.

A further date (Poz-12532: 1255±30 BP) was obtained from layer (3004), a middle fill of the outer ditch (3050) that also contained charred grain and Anglo-Saxon pottery.

Results

The model shown in Figure 9.4 excludes those measurements that are clearly residual (SUERC-4969) and intrusive (SUERC-4972) into their respective contexts (see above). The model shows good agreement (Aoverall=121.9%) between the radiocarbon and OSL results and stratigraphic relationships where they exist as outlined in the previous section. (For a tabulated summary of the modelled dates see Table 9.3).

- The digging of ditch 574 is estimated to have taken place in *1100-750 cal BC (95% probability; Event ditch; Fig. 9.4)* and probably *1030-860 cal BC (68% probability)*.

- The standstill layer (1102) sealing ditch 574 formed in the first half of the first millennium BC.

- The best estimate for the construction of the second enclosure and the timber laced rampart is *510-390 cal BC 95% probability; Last timber rampart Fig. 9.4)* and probably *480-400 cal BC (68% probability)*

- The results suggest that ditch 460 may have taken more than a millennium to fill up and must have still been a visible feature in the landscape when the Taplow Mound was constructed.

- Internal activity, in the form of posthole row 1132, posthole row 935 and posthole groups 1134 and 1117, was probably contemporary with the first enclosure (see Fig. 9.5).

- Pit 1016 was earlier than the timbers of the burnt rampart (1113) (Fig. 9.6).

- A gap of *1-260 years (95% probability)* and probably *1-130 years (68% probability)* is estimated to have separated posthole row 1108 and the construction of the V-profiled ditch (574).

- The length of time between the primary fill of the V-profiled ditch 574 and the stabilisation layer (1102) higher up the same ditch is estimated at *1-250 years (95% probability)* and probably *1-120 years (68% probability)*.

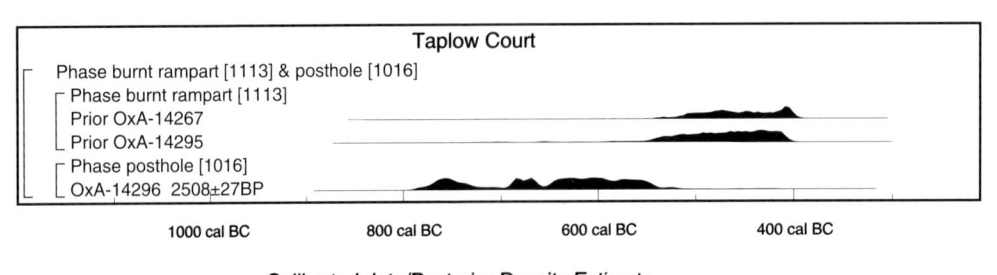

Fig. 9.6 Probability distributions of dates from Taplow Court: burnt rampart 1113 and pit 1016. Each distribution represents the relative probability that an event occurred at a particular time

- The length of time between the start of the formation of the stabilisation layer (1102) and its burial by the rampart that was subsequently burnt (1113) is estimated at *1-230 years (95% probability)* and probably *1-130 years (68% probability)*.

Conclusions

Absolute dating of a number of key features (eg posthole row 1104) has not been possible due to the submission of samples that were subsequently identified, on the basis of their radiocarbon ages, to be either intrusive of residual. However, the results have provided an estimate for the digging of the V-profiled ditch (574) of *1100-750 cal BC (95% probability)* and probably *1030-860 cal BC (68% probability)*, and helped to elucidate the sequence of activity on the site.

Discussion of the radiocarbon and OSL dates
by Chris Hayden

Of the total of 18 determinations (Table 9.2; Figs 9.1-5), six radiocarbon dates and six OSL dates can be related to the sequence of ditches and ramparts. The large errors associated with some of these dates, and in particular with the OSL dates, resulted in date ranges that were too wide, but on the basis of the stratigraphic evidence described above, they were refined by using a Bayesian model (Fig. 9.4). The modelled dates (to 1 and 2 standard deviations) are shown in stratigraphic sequence in Table 9.3, with the other dates in chronological sequence alongside.

The radiocarbon dates in this model include two from material associated with posthole row 1108 (OxA-14294 and SUERC-4967). The chronological evidence related to this posthole row is ambiguous, but some of the postholes belonging to it were clearly stratigraphically earlier than layers sealed by, or belonging to, the upcast from the V-profiled ditch (574), and it is on this basis that they are included in the model. The material available for radiocarbon dating was limited. With the exception of sapwood from the charred timbers (1113) within the rampart associated with the U-profiled ditch, none of the material that was radiocarbon dated could be related with certainty to the events that we were attempting to date. Many of the radiocarbon dates were obtained from small pieces of charcoal and charred plant remains, which had quite high chances of being residual or intrusive. Of the samples from the postholes, four were taken from post-pipes, and the material from the post-pipes may postdate the structures. The remaining sampled postholes contained only single undifferentiated fills, and the dated material might derive from post-packing containing material predating the structure, post-pipe material, if the post fitted tightly within the posthole, or a mixture of both. The single date from palisade trench 1106 came from the fill of the 'step' on the eastern edge (see below), whose stratigraphic equivalence is uncertain. As far as was possible, multiple samples were taken from the features or groups of features so that the results could be checked against each other.

The results clearly suggest that at least six of the 18 determinations were obtained from residual material. However, only one of the radiocarbon dates (SUERC-4967) from the stratified sequence of dates used in the model appears to have been derived from residual material.

Unlike the radiocarbon dates the OSL dates do not suffer from uncertain associations. They do, however, suffer from uncertainties concerning whether the material from which they were obtained had been exposed sufficiently to zero the geological signal. One of the OSL dates (X069) was rejected on these grounds, and is included in Figure 9.4 but does not form part of the model. One of the other OSL dates, on sand (X071), was too early given its stratigraphic relationships with two radiocarbon dates and has also been excluded from the model.

Overall, however, the absolute dates form a consistent sequence which agrees with the dates suggested on the basis of the pottery, and which helps to resolve some of the ambiguities in that evidence (and specifically the date of U-profiled ditch 460 and its rampart).

Chronological summary of late Bronze Age and Iron Age defences

Table 9.3 summarises the key dating evidence for all periods in relation to chronological schemes for the Bronze Age. The sequence seems to begin with posthole rows 1107 and 1108, probably dating from the 11th century BC (1120-980 cal BC at 68% confidence). These posthole rows may have been followed, or have been accompanied by, internal posthole rows 935, 1133 and 1132, probably in the 10th century BC (1005-910 cal BC at 68% confidence). At least some of the postholes in posthole row 1104 may also date from this phase. The palisade trench (1106) followed on from posthole rows 1107 and 1108, and was itself succeeded by the V-profiled ditch (574) and its bank, probably in the 10th or 9th century BC (980-800 cal BC at 68% confidence). Some of the internal groups of postholes and possible structures (eg. 1134) may have belonged to the same period. However, the pottery found within the hillfort, and especially in the occupation layer (1121) around posthole group 1117 is consistent with activity in that area beginning earlier in the late Bronze Age, contemporary with the earlier late Bronze Age palisades. The fills of the V-profiled ditch had stabilised by the 8th or 7th century BC (860-580 cal BC at 68% confidence), and this stabilisation phase (layer 1102) probably lasted for at least a further century before the U-profiled ditch (460) was cut in the 5th century BC (480-400 cal BC at 68% confidence). There is no stratigraphic or artefactual evidence for the chronological relationship of the U-profiled ditch (460) and the

Table 9.3 Summary of modelled absolute dates (dates given as minus are cal BC; others as cal AD)

Modelled Group	Lab no.	1 sd		2 sd	
1108	@OxA-14294	-1120	-980	-1130	-930
1108 - excluded	@SUERC-4967	-1750	-1640	-1870	-1610
@1108 to 574		1	130	1	260
574 primary fill	@X074	-980	-800	-1050	-700
@574 primary fill to standstill		1	120	1	250
Standstill layer	@X068	-790	-620	-870	-550
Standstill layer	@X072	-800	-620	-870	-550
Standstill layer	@X073	-790	-620	-870	-540
@standstill to rampart		1	130	1	230
Burnt rampart	@OxA-14267	-510	-400	-520	-390
Burnt rampart	@OxA-14295	-520	-410	-560	-400
excluded	@X069	-2000	-1300	-2300	-1000
U-profiled ditch Saxon deposits	@OxA-14432	590	650	550	650
U-profiled ditch Saxon deposits - excluded	@X071	-230	10	-340	110
U-profiled ditch Saxon deposits	@SUERC-4971	770	900	770	970

outer ditch (3050), although both were clearly open together into the Anglo-Saxon period, and were probably infilled at much the same time.

Durations and hiatuses

The Bayesian model which has been used to refine the radiocarbon and OSL dates on the basis of their stratigraphic relationships (see above) can also be used to answer questions concerning the spans of phases of activity and the intervals which may have intervened between them. The extent to which these questions can be answered by the absolute dates is limited by the fact that not all of the dates from the site were stratigraphically related to the others, and therefore cannot be included in the model. Without the constraints on the dates imposed by stratigraphic information the estimated ranges are usually too wide to be of interest. It thus needs to be borne in mind that not all of the activity on the site is represented in these models.

The interval between posthole row 1108 and the V-profiled ditch (574)

While the OSL date (X074) from the primary fill of the V-profiled ditch provides a securely associated estimate for the cutting of the ditch (assuming the primary fill was deposited soon after it was cut) the association between the construction of posthole row 1108 and the *Quercus* charcoal from posthole 166 used to estimate its date is less certain. The charcoal came from a post-pipe, and although it may well have belonged to the post itself, it is impossible to be certain that it was not residual.

The evidence reviewed above suggests that posthole row 1108 was stratigraphically earlier than the V-profiled ditch 574, and sufficient time must have elapsed between the two for either the postholes of row 1108 to have been obscured by reworking of the buried soil (1120), or at least for the posts to have been removed and the postholes infilled before the deposition of layer 1120 as part of the rampart associated with the V-profiled ditch. Palisade trench 1106 was also cut in this intervening period.

The results of the Bayesian model are consistent with this, suggesting that the interval between the construction of the posthole row (1108) and the V-profiled ditch (574) was less than 260 years (95.4% probability) and probably (68.2%) less than 130 years. Adding in palisade trench 1106, there may have been a relatively rapid sequence of construction, with each palisade lasting perhaps no more than 50 years. Estimates of the likely life span of

Unmodelled Group	Lab no.	1 sd		2 sd	
EBA hollows 1119	OxA-14268	-1690	-1610	-1740	-1530
MBA dates (posthole row 1132	OxA-14358	-1430	-1380	-1450	-1310
and palisade trench 1106)	SUERC-4970	-1380	-1210	-1410	-1120
Posthole row 935	OxA-14357	-1005	-910	-1020	-890
Posthole group 1134	OxA-14292	-910	-830	-970	-810
Posthole group 1117	OxA-14359	-840	-800	-910	-800
Posthole group 1117	SUERC-4968	-900	-800	-930	-790
Pit 1016 (hillfort entrance)	OxA-14296	-770	-540	-790	-520
Burial 105	SUERC-4963	630	670	590	680
Posthole row 1107	OxA-14297	680	780	670	810
Posthole row 1107	SUERC-5150	660	770	650	780
Posthole row 1104	OxA-14293	720	860	690	890
Outer ditch (3050) Saxon deposits	Poz-12532	680	780	670	870

timber structures are very varied (Brück 1999b), but it is possible that this replacement was motivated in part by the decay of the wood from which the palisades were constructed.

The period over which the V-profiled ditch (574) was filled and became stable

This period can be estimated using the OSL dates from the primary fill (X074) and those from the standstill layer (1102: X068, X072 and X073). Since these are all OSL dates the association between the date and the event that we wish to date is reasonably certain.

The model suggests that the filling of the ditch up to the development of the standstill layer spanned a period of less that 250 years (95.4%) and probably less that 120 years (68.2%). This is considerably longer than the periods observed at experimental earthworks; the fills of the ditch at the experimental earthwork on chalk at Overton Down had become almost stable after only a decade (Bell 1996, 236), while although the ditch at the Wareham earthwork, constructed on sand, had not stabilised after 30 years (ibid., 236), the report suggests that the fills had almost reached a stable state. It is of course possible that 'less than 120 years' could be as little as 30 years, but a longer period is at least as likely.

Several factors might have contributed to the possibly longer period of filling before stabilisation at Taplow Court. One is simply the fact that the ditch was larger (c 4.8 m wide by 2.2 m deep) than those at Wareham and Overton (3 m wide by 1.75 m deep). It is noticeable that the stabilisation layer in the V-profiled ditch has a very shallow profile, ie occurs only after a great depth of more rapid silting, in contrast to the stabilisation profiles of the experimental ditches. This may indicate that the rampart made a greater contribution to the filling of the ditch than was the case at the experimental earthworks. Material eroding from a bank or rampart may impede the growth of vegetation that stabilises the fills within the ditch. If deposition of material from the rampart is indicated by coarser, more gravelly soils, this seems to appear only some way up the sequence of fills within the V-profiled ditch, possibly just at the point when stabilisation would otherwise have begun. Against this, the spread of the standstill layer beyond the ditch edges (see Fig. 4.9, section 229; Fig. 4.11, section 230) may indicate that there had never been a bank within 1.5 m even of the eroded ditch edge, making erosion or slippage from the bank less likely. Deliberate slighting of a rampart remains a possibility, but this would have been a relatively quick process. The difference may simply be due to the different nature of the geology into which these several ditches were cut. It is also possible that the bank and ditch at Taplow were more subject to disturbance by animals and people than the experimental earthworks have been, although there is no positive evidence for this.

These figures support the absence of evidence from the ditch sections (eg recutting) for active maintainance over a long period. It should, however, be borne in mind not only that the state of the rampart may not have been reflected accurately by the fills of the ditch, but that it may have been the rampart, rather than the ditch, which was regarded as most important. A partially filled ditch need not have been seen as ineffective. Aside from the pottery in the standstill layer, however, there is relatively little indication of continuing activity in the area of the main excavation after the ditch had reached the standstill phase.

The interval between the stabilisation of the V-profiled ditch and the cutting of the U-profiled ditch

There is no solid evidence for further late Bronze Age defences once the V-profiled ditch had silted up, and the dates from the standstill layer (1102) provide the best point from which to estimate the duration of the possible hiatus between the late Bronze Age and the early-middle Iron Age defences (represented by the dates from the burnt timber in the early-middle Iron Age rampart). It should be recalled, however, that the digging of the outer ditch (3050) might fall into this period.

The model suggests that a period of less than 230 years (95.4%) and possibly less than 130 years (68.2%) elapsed between the start of the accumulation of the stabilisation layer within the V-profiled ditch (574) and the construction of the defences associated with the U-profiled ditch (460). The OSL dates themselves (at 68.2% probability) include one whose range is from 920 to 630 BC, and two others with ranges ending at 520 BC. Assuming that the range for the construction of the overlying rampart does begin at around 510 BC, this suggests that the stabilisation layer was accumulating for at least 120 years. Given the presence of early Iron Age pottery in the TCAST trenches down the slope to the south of the main excavation, it is possible that occupation in the vicinity of the site could have been almost continuous, even if the area of the main excavation was not always provided with defences.

Chapter 10 – Geophysical survey

INTRODUCTION

The post-excavation programme included a geophysical survey, of the open areas north of the Conference Hall and to the south within Taplow Court, in an attempt to trace the major defensive ditches and provide the wider context for the excavations. Funding for this was not forthcoming from English Heritage, so Tim Allen and Elias Kupfermann of the Taplow Court Archaeological Survey Team persuaded the Marlow Archaeological Society to volunteer their expertise to carry out a resistivity survey, and Roger Ainslie, an independent survey specialist, to undertake a complementary magnetometer survey, also free of charge.

Two phases of geophysical survey were carried out at Taplow Court (Fig. 10.1). The first survey, in 2005, consisted of a resistivity survey carried by the Marlow Archaeological Society, and a magnetometer survey by Roger Ainslie in three areas, (Kupfermann 2006).

The largest survey area lay to the north and west of the main excavation. Its aim was to trace the course of the three hillfort ditches corresponding to the late Bronze Age V-profiled ditch (574), the early-middle Iron Age U-profiled ditch (460) and the outer ditch (3050), and if possible, other features such as the late Bronze Age palisade trench (1106). It was hoped that the survey would define the northern extent of these defences.

The other two areas lay to the south of Taplow Court. The first was a square area within the disused churchyard associated with St Nicholas Church. Its aim was to define the plan of the church and to evaluate the evidence for an Anglo-Saxon church having existed on the site (Stocker *et al.* 1995). It was also hoped that it would provide evidence for the ditch which Rutland recorded in 1853 as running north-south below the church, and which he thought formed part of a hillfort within which the Taplow Mound lay (Scrimgeour and Farley 1987).

The second was an area to the south of the mound and church. It was hoped that this would provide further evidence which might be related to the earthworks recorded in the First and Second Edition 6" OS maps (1874 and 1899; SMR 1544) as running east-west in this area.

Following this first phase of survey, in 2006, the northern area was extended to the north and west, again in the hope of locating the hillfort ditches (Fig. 10.1).

More detailed reports on these surveys have been deposited at the Buckinghamshire SMR.

Methodology

All of the surveys were carried out in accordance with the guidelines set out by English Heritage (1995).

The resistivity survey (Figs 10.1-2) was carried out using a TRS Systems Resistance Meter with an automatic data logger. Meaurements were taken at 1 m intervals except in the area of the church where a more detailed survey, at 0.5 m intervals, was made. The images were plotted using AutoCad and Surfer 7 and 8 software (Kupfermann 2006).

The magnetometer survey (Fig. 10.3) was carried out using a Bartington Grad 601/2 magnetometer in gradiometer configuration. The transects were 1 m apart and readings were taken every 0.25 m. The data was processed using TR systems software and Archeosurveyor.

Results

The northern area

In general the results of the surveys were disappointing. In the northern area, despite their size, the hillfort ditches were not revealed very clearly. The surveys in this area were marred by the presence of recent features including a gravelled track that runs east-west through the survey area, turning to the south at the eastern edge, a modern water main running ESE-WNW near the northern edge, and a tennis court in the south-western corner. The magnetometer survey was also hindered by modern debris left immediately to the north and west of the Conference Hall where the construction compound had stood.

Nevertheless, some indications of what seem to be the late Bronze Age V-profiled ditch (574) and the early-middle Iron Age U-profiled ditch (460) can be made out running SE-NW and curving to the west near the middle of the survey area (Figs 10.2 and 3). At its southern end, where the anomaly representing the ditches is nearly 20 m wide, it is possible that two ditches are represented, but elsewhere only one can be made out. WA Trenches 3 and 4 suggest that the late Bronze Age ditch was not masked by gravel upcast at that point, so that both ditches were liable to be picked up by the survey, but if the late Bronze Age ditch was overlain by the upcast gravel from the U-profiled ditch further north, as it was in the main excavation area, this would effectively mask the ditch. Alternatively it is possible that the late Bronze Age and Iron Age ditches followed the same course in this area. The scant traces of the

From Bronze Age enclosure to Anglo-Saxon settlement

Fig. 10.1 The areas investigated by geophysical surveys

Chapter 10

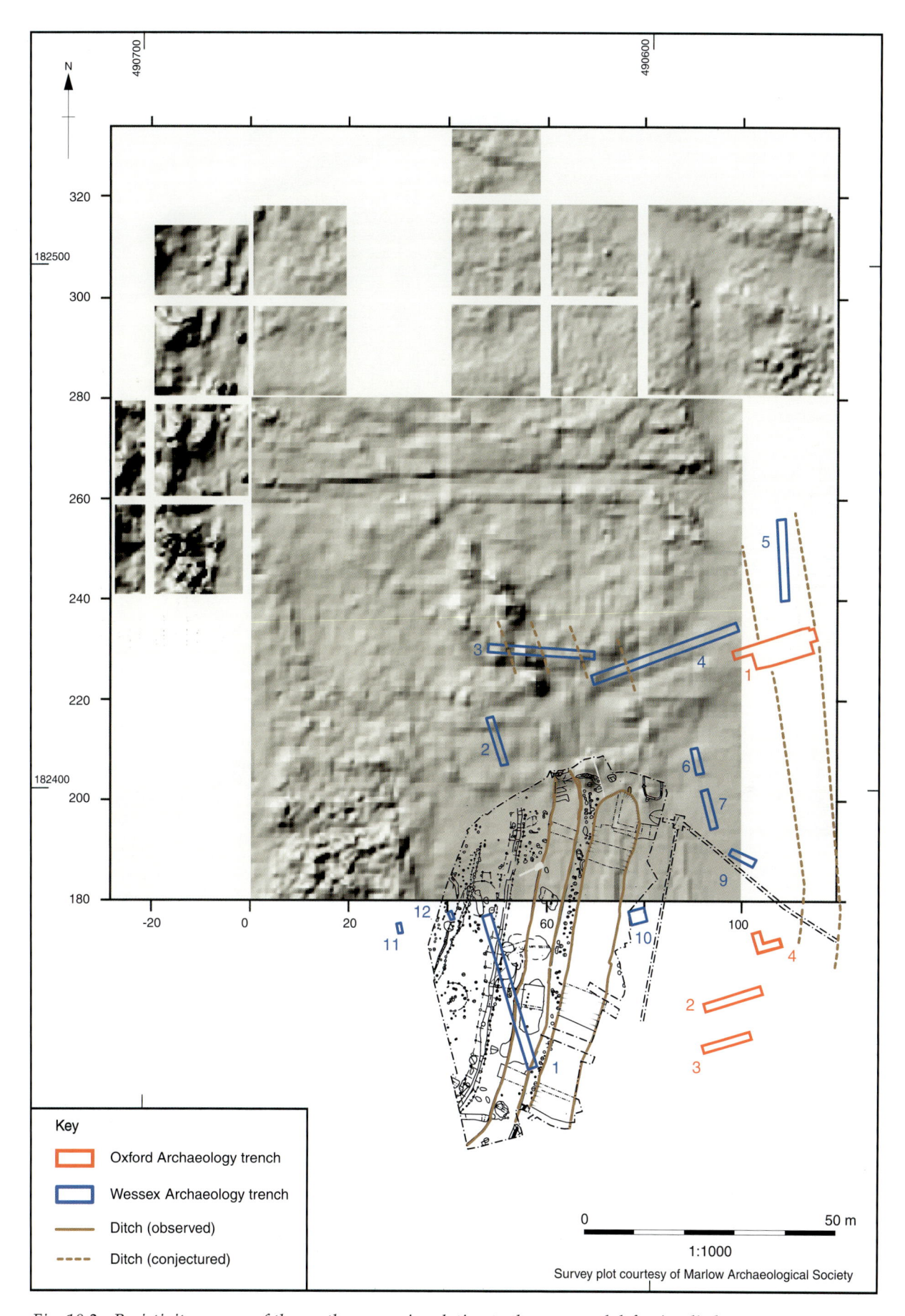

Fig. 10.2 Resistivity survey of the northern area in relation to the excavated defensive ditches

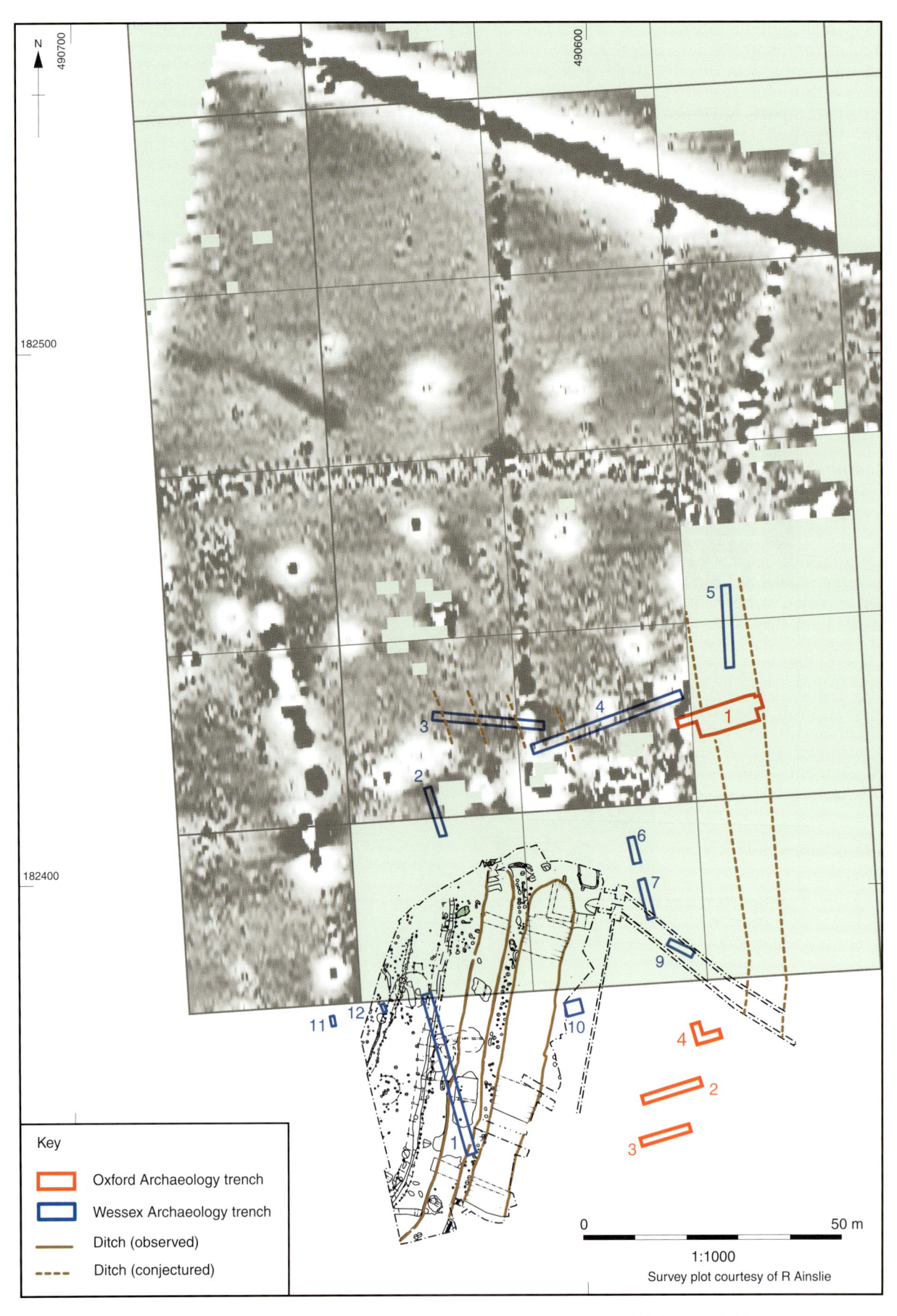

From Bronze Age enclosure to Anglo-Saxon settlement

Fig. 10.3 Magnetometer survey of the northern area in relation to the excavated defensive ditches

inner ditch and of the rampart of the U-profiled ditch in the magnetometer survey suggests either that the ramparts in this area were less affected by fire than those found within the main excavation, or that the ramparts have not been preserved in this area. Even within the excavation area the burnt areas were not evenly distributed along the ditch, and there were significant gaps.

No firm trace of the outer ditch (3050) has been identified, but the projected line of this ditch was crossed by a N-S water pipe, as well as by the track and the water main. It is possible that it runs to the east of the survey area or has been obscured by recent features along the eastern edge of the survey area.

Despite the lack of clarity, the combined surveys in this area indicate that the late Bronze Age V-profiled and early-middle Iron Age U-profiled ditches curved westwards almost to the terrace edge in this area.

The churchyard (Fig. 10.1)

The survey in the area of St Nicholas churchyard revealed quite clearly the plan of the church, which corresponds quite closely with that revealed as a parchmark in 1995 (Stocker *et al*. 1995). The plan of the remains of the church appears, in fact, to have been revealed rather more clearly by the parchmark survey than it was by the geophysical survey. No indications of the ditch observed by Rutland were found. However, given the relative lack of clarity with which the ditches were revealed in the northern area, and the number of later features in this area, this is hardly surprising. The report accompanying the survey of the churchyard (Kupfermann 2006) noted a lack of corroborating evidence for the Saxon church.

The southern area (Fig. 10.1)

The survey in the area to the south of the mound and church did not clearly reveal the presence of any features, but did not extend far enough to cross the earthworks marked on the 1899 OS map (see Fig. 11.1).

The extent of the hillfort defences

The full extent of the late Bronze Age (and the early-middle Iron Age) defences is unknown (see Fig. 11.1). However, to the north of the main excavation, ditches on a corresponding line to both the V- and the U-profiled ditches were found in WA Trenches 3 and 4 (Fig. 2.2). The resistivity survey carried out to the north of the main excavation revealed two large linear anomalies. One of these curved north-west across the whole width of the survey area, and appears to correspond to the early-middle Iron Age U-profiled ditch (460). Part of the line of this ditch was also very clear on the magnetometer survey. The other, less clear anomaly might correspond to the V-profiled ditch (574). This second anomaly runs parallel to the first, but appears to end half way across the survey area. Unless the hillfort remained unfinished, there seems no good reason (for example, in the local topography) for the ditch to end here, and it may be that the V-profiled ditch has been obscured by the Iron Age rampart, or that it followed the same line as the U-profiled ditch in this area.

At the south end of the main excavation the V-profiled ditch, posthole rows 1107, 1108 and palisade trench 1106 all turn westwards, suggesting that from this point the defences curve back south-westwards to the terrace edge.

Assuming that the V-profiled ditch turned to the west at the southern edge of the main excavation and ran to the terrace edge, and, to the north, followed the line suggested by the resistivity survey to the terrace edge, the late Bronze Age enclosure would have had an area in the order of 20,000 m^2 (estimated as a circle of radius 80 m or a rectangle 170 m by 130 m).

Whether the edge of the terrace scarp was defended is unknown. Although the scarp is certainly steep, possibly making defences on this side unnecessary, there is a distinct rise, dip and further rise across the Cedar Walk that runs along the edge of the escarpment, possibly indicating the presence of a former bank, ditch and perhaps an outer ditch. A detailed contour survey might assist in clarifying this.

Chapter 11 – Discussion

INTRODUCTION

The excavations at Taplow Court have revealed a long sequence of activity, punctuated by periods of abandonment, stretching from the Mesolithic to the Anglo-Saxon period. The evidence for the earlier periods is relatively slight: residual Mesolithic flint, a few possibly *in situ* assemblages of Mesolithic or earlier Neolithic worked flint in tree-throw holes, worked flint, sherds of Collared Urn and other finds in early Bronze Age hollows, and a sparse scatter of middle Bronze Age finds. According to the chronology outlined in the previous chapters, it was in the late Bronze Age, with the construction of the earliest enclosure, that the hilltop was first modified significantly.

Before discussing the implications of this preferred chronology, it must be admitted that other interpretations of the chronology remain possible. An earlier start to the sequence of post-rows could be argued from the stratigraphic evidence for 1107 predating the early Bronze Age pits, 1108 being dated by the early Bronze Age radiocarbon date, and a middle Bronze Age radiocarbon date for palisade 1106. The main reason for rejecting this is the long timespan involved between the different elements in the sequence of post-rows, palisade trench and ditch, given the very similar line taken by all of them.

Following the preferred chronology, then, during the late Bronze Age a complex sequence of defences – palisades and ditch and rampart – was built, apparently surrounding a late Bronze Age settlement. Although there may have been a gap in occupation in the early Iron Age following the silting up of the late Bronze Age defensive ditch, the remaining traces of the defences clearly influenced the location of the new hillfort defences constructed on the hilltop in the early-middle Iron Age. This phase of the hillfort may have been short-lived, its timber-laced rampart being fired soon after its construction, but the defences were supplemented, or possibly replaced, by an outer ditch, both ditches remaining open into the Anglo-Saxon period. The presence of these features is likely to have been a major factor influencing the selection of this location for the high status burial in the Taplow Mound and for the associated Saxon settlement, the debris from which was found in the upper fills of the hillfort ditches.

This long sequence of punctuated activity no doubt reflects the enduring significance of the Thames, as a trade route, a political boundary and as a symbolic resource. It also raises questions concerning the significance of the past in prehistoric and Anglo-Saxon society.

THE SITE CHRONOLOGY

The Mesolithic

The earliest activity at Taplow is Mesolithic flint, some of which may be early in that period, and a charred hazelnut shell from which a radiocarbon date of 8560-8290 cal BC (SUERC-4969: 9220±40 BP) was obtained. Although this hazelnut shell was not associated with any of the flint, it probably also derives from human activity. Two groups of flint found in tree-throw holes may have been Mesolithic, and the use of such naturally occurring hollows for the deposition of struck flint is also known locally at the Eton Rowing Course (Allen *et al.* 2004). All of the diagnostic pieces of flint – like the hazelnut shell – were residual, mixed with probably Neolithic and Bronze Age flint. Few useful inferences can, therefore, be made on the basis of this evidence, other than that activity involving the collection of wild resources (eg hazelnuts), hunting (indicated by the microliths) and a temporary encampment (the charring of the hazelnut in a fire and possibly clearance and the construction of shelters with the tranchet axe) took place in the 9th millennium BC. It has been argued that axes were used in flint procurement (Care 1982), and certainly the plateau gravels of the Taplow terrace might have been a source of flint, but there is no conclusive evidence from this site.

The archaeologically visible distribution of Mesolithic activity is subject to numerous biases (eg Richards 1978, 29-30), many of which have probably contributed to the apparent concentration of Mesolithic sites (as opposed to isolated finds) in river valleys (eg Ford 1987b; cf. Richards, 1978, 28; Holgate 1986, fig. 5; Ellaby 1987). Large early Mesolithic sites near to the Thames are known not far down-river at Holyport, Bray Wick and at the Eton Rowing Course (Ford 1987b, 59; Allen 1995, 29-31), the river being an attractive source of various resources (Fig. 1.3). Even though the known distribution is unlikely to provide an accurate representation of the actual distribution of activity (and the distribution of stray finds is much wider; Ford 1987b), the discovery of Mesolithic flint at Taplow close to the river is therefore unsurprising. Although within sight of the river, however, the top of the terrace at Taplow is not within easy reach, involving either a very steep descent and ascent down the escarpment to the west, or a gentler but much longer descent to the south.. This site itself is, therefore, unlikely to have been related to the immediate exploitation of riverine resources, although it might have been a temporary camp from which such resources were exploited. In a highly wooded environment, the views afforded at the edge of the high ground and overlooking the valley to the south and the river to the west may have been a significant factor in the choice of this location.

The Neolithic

A small number of assemblages of flint were found in tree-throw holes. Of these tree-throw holes, two contained probably earlier Neolithic assemblages, and a further two tree-throw holes contained smaller assemblages of either Mesolithic or earlier Neolithic flint. The only associated finds were charred hazelnut shells, which were found in just one of the tree-throw holes (497).

Several lines of evidence suggest that the flint in the tree-throw holes at Taplow Court was deliberately deposited. One is the fresh condition of the flint. However, as long as it had not been deposited long before the trees fell, it could be argued that flint would not have been much affected by redeposition into a tree-throw hole. The contrast found at sites such as Yarnton, Oxfordshire (Hey *et al.* in prep.) between abraded pottery and fresh flint suggests that the condition of flint does not necessarily provide a good indication of disturbance or its absence.

A more compelling argument for deliberate deposition in these features is the much greater density of flint in the tree-throw holes than the average of just over 1 piece of worked flint per m^2 across the site overall (Table 11.1; cf. Evans *et al.* 1999). A total of 61 and 20 pieces per m^2 came from tree-throw holes 497 and 816 respectively, and 11 pieces and 4 from tree-throw holes 813 and 914. It is, therefore, unlikely that the flint in the tree-throw holes derives from the low background scatter.

Table 11.1 Summary of the density of worked flint in tree-throw holes and on the site as a whole

	Area (m^2)	Total no. pieces of worked flint	Flint density (no. of pieces/m^2)
Site as a whole	2188	2601	1
497	1.2	74	62
816	4.65	96	21
813	1.19	13	11
914	0.82	3	4

A further argument against residuality is the distinctive character of the flint assemblages in the tree-throw holes compared to those from the rest of the site (Table 11.2). The assemblages from the tree-throw holes contain a higher proportion of blades, suggesting that they contain a distinctive earlier Neolithic element that is absent or is less marked elsewhere. The refitting pieces from different fills of tree-throw hole 816 suggest that the flint may have been deposited over quite a short period.

Assemblages of Neolithic finds in tree-throw holes are not unusual either in the Thames Valley or more widely. Numerous examples associated with Plain Bowl, others with Ebbsfleet Ware and chisel arrowheads, have been found, for example, at the Eton Rowing Course and at sites along the Jubilee river (Allen *et al.* 2004, 92). As has been pointed out by Evans *et al.* (1999) such deposits seem to be most common in the earlier Neolithic. Although there are sites where deposits in tree-throw holes were predominantly late Neolithic in date (eg Drayton; Barclay *et al.* 2003, 62-7; White Horse Stone; Hayden and Stafford 2006), in the area around Taplow most assemblages from tree-throw holes are indeed earlier Neolithic (Allen *et al.* 2004, 92; Lamdin-Whymark 2008, 93-6).

Table 11.2 Summary of the composition of worked flint from tree-throw holes, features and layers

	Flakes	Chips and waste flakes	Blades, bladelets and blade-like flakes	Cores	Retouched pieces, notches etc	Axes	Microliths and microburins	Other worked flint	Total	Burnt unworked
Number										
Features (postholes, pits, ditches, gullies)	1092	170	161	64	33	1	4	54	1579	245
Tree-throw holes	95	18	47	13	9	0	0	6	188	2
Layers (top, sub, and buried soils, including the stabilisation layer)	536	111	102	34	10	1	1	39	834	5
Percentage										
Features (postholes, pits, ditches, gullies)	69	11	10	4	2	0	0	3		13
Tree-throw holes	51	10	25	7	5	0	0	3		1
Layers (top, sub, and buried soils, including the stabilisation layer)	64	13	12	4	1	0	0	5		1

The predominance of earlier Neolithic assemblages is unlikely simply to indicate greater tree-cover in the earlier Neolithic, as clearance of the landscape appears to have been gradual, (Parker and Robinson 2003, 56; Allen *et al.* 2004, 92-3), with a continuing strong exploitation of forest resources (hazelnuts, crab apples, pigs and cattle) in the late Neolithic. The chronological pattern suggests that deposits in tree-throw holes were the product of more than just contingent and practical factors, and reflect a more specific aspect of earlier Neolithic life (Lamdin-Whymark 2008, 185-8).

Despite the deliberate choice of tree-throw holes for the deposition of struck flint, however, the finds from the Taplow tree-throw holes are far from exceptional, consisting of flakes, blades, a few retouched pieces and cores. They do not, however, contain much knapping waste, and there is thus no indication that knapping took place within the tree-throw holes themselves. The Taplow tree-throw holes therefore point to the deposition of material resulting from unremarkable 'everyday' activities in such contexts, a reminder that ritual may have been bound up with many aspects of Neolithic life, and that there may not have been a distinction between what we differentiate as secular and religious activities.

However, the regional context of the Taplow Court tree-throw holes is worth brief consideration (see Fig. 1.3) The excavations at the Eton Rowing Course found the remains of a wide variety of earlier Neolithic activity, ranging from extensive middens with high densities of artefacts representing both large-scale and long-term visitation of these sites, through occupation areas around hearths with evidence of varied activities and a duration of several days or weeks, to small flint scatters indicating single activities of short duration (Allen *et al.* 2004, 92-6 and fig. 9.11). Most of the latter occurred at some distance from the main activity areas, perhaps in wooded areas. Although we lack clear environmental evidence, it seems likely from the size of the lithic assemblages that the recovered Neolithic activity at Taplow Court was of the last kind, perhaps occurring in woodland, above the river. The relatively small quantities of Neolithic struck flint found nearby at the Taplow Mound, and to the east of the site, do not conflict with this.

The significance of the limited evidence from the high ground at Taplow Court could be interpreted in a number of ways. Evans *et al.* (1999) have drawn attention to the possible significance of woodland – and its contrast with cleared land – within earlier Neolithic cosmologies. Such environmental contrasts are often related to other aspects of cosmologies. Some societies have more or less elaborate restrictions on movement between such environments (eg Douglas 1954). In the later early Neolithic, and in the middle Neolithic, much activity in the river valley below took place between one causewayed enclosure at Eton Wick only 4 km downriver (Ford 1993), and another known only from cropmarks at Dorney Reach only 2 km from Taplow (Carstairs 1986 Site D; Dyer 1996). Middle Neolithic settlement was even closer to Taplow at Lake End Road West and at Taplow Mill Lane Site 1 just south of the site (Allen *et al.* 2004, 92). There were also pits at Cippenham (Ford 2003, 153-5). The Neolithic landscape was partly cleared, and extensively, though probably not permanently settled, during this time. From the excavated site at Taplow this activity would have been invisible, but the end of the promontory just a few hundred metres to the south would have commanded a fine view of the landscape below.

The early Bronze Age

The early Bronze Age finds from the site consist primarily of sherds of Collared Urns, worked flint, fired clay, charcoal from a wide range of species, and charred wheat and barley, all recovered from a group of intercutting shallow hollows. Although limited in quantity, this evidence is valuable, since non-funerary evidence from this period remains relatively scarce (Brück 1999a).

The fact that some of the hollows from which the finds were recovered were cut into others suggests that the activity was spread over a period of some duration. The only evidence to suggest that it might have been continuous – rather than having consisted of repeated episodes – is the similarity of the finds from different hollows, though this could be due to the deliberate selection of similar materials. The struck flint from all of the hollows suggested a similar range of activities, the predominance of scrapers and the presence of an awl suggesting that hide preparation may have been carried out. The other retouched flakes and the notched flake have less specific uses. Knapping was clearly occurring, but this has the character of opportunistic tool-production as needed for other tasks.

Other aspects of the evidence consistent with longer-term occupation may include the presence of fired clay, although only one fragment had any identifiable features. It may have been part of a made hearth or oven. The presence of pottery itself might support prolonged occupation. Collared Urns have now been found in non-funerary contexts on a number of sites (eg Allen *et al.* 2004, 98), perhaps sufficiently frequently to suggest that their apparently exclusive association with funerary contexts was more the product of biases in preservation and recovery than of an original functional exclusivity (Tomalin 1995; Longworth 1984).

The final strand which could be related to more prolonged occupation is the presence of charred hulled wheat, possibly emmer wheat, and six-row hulled barley, albeit in very small quantities. Such evidence is not common in the early Bronze Age. This does not necessarily indicate that the cereals were grown near the site, nor is there any indication that cereals were processed or stored on the site, although both are possible.

The only other environmental evidence from this period is charcoal. Alongside charcoal from oak, field maple and ash, which suggests woodland existed not far away, the presence of some shrubby species – blackthorn and hawthorn/*Sorbus* – which grow at the forest edge or in more open areas suggests the existence of clearings. This is consistent with the evidence from the Eton Rowing Course, which suggests increased clearance in the early Bronze Age (Parker and Robinson 2003, 56). This evidence could be related to the presence of charred cereals.

Overall, then the early Bronze Age finds could be seen as reflecting more clearly domestic activity, of longer duration, than had occurred in the earlier Neolithic. The overall quantity of evidence was small, but many examples of prehistoric house-like structures (eg Hayden and Stafford 2006) are associated with only very small quantities of artefacts. The small quantity of finds is not, therefore, necessarily a good indicator of the absence of domestic occupation.

The use of the hollows is uncertain. They are far too shallow to have been used for storage, and this same shallowness makes it unlikely that that they were cut to obtain sand and gravel or for flint, although it is possible that they were daub pits. The largest of the hollows (642), which was subrectangular and measured approaching 3 m by 4 m, could conceivably have been a domestic structure of some sort. There was a layer containing charcoal in the base of the pit at the north end (553), but there was no evidence of burning *in situ* (though a hearth could have lain in the destroyed north-east corner), and a similarly charcoal-rich fill was found in the adjacent earlier pit (703). No evidence of structural supports was found. It is alternatively possible that the hollows represent a continuation of the late Neolithic and Beaker tradition of pit digging, where pits may have been dug specifically for groups of carefully selected artefacts (possibly representative of the activities that had recently taken place) rather than for other 'practical' purposes. This interpretation might explain the dark soils (interpreted on site as possible 'midden' deposits) and the varied contents of the pits including pottery and charred cereals.

The early Bronze Age evidence at Taplow is quite similar to that found on the plain below at the Eton Rowing Course . As well as being found in funerary contexts, sherds of Collared Urn were found mixed with lithic scatters and associated with hearths. Little evidence for early Bronze Age activity was, however, found nearer to Taplow along the route of the Jubilee river, and what was found was funerary, including a cremation deposit at Marsh Lane East (Site 2) associated with a ring ditch (Foreman 1998,

28), and other, unexcavated ring ditches around Dorney (eg. Carstairs 1986, fig. 2 Site E).

About 1 km to the east (Fig. 11.1) excavations along the Taplow to Dorney pipeline in 2006 recovered two sherds of grog-tempered pottery attributed to the early/middle Bronze Age (McSloy in Hart and Mudd forthcoming). However, as the middle Bronze Age assemblages from the neighbouring sites at the Eton Rowing Course, the Jubilee River and from Cippenham do not include grog-tempered fabrics (Barclay in Allen *et al.* in prep. b; Raymond in Ford 2003), it seems likely that these sherds belong to the early Bronze Age. Another 40 sherds of early Bronze Age pottery were recovered from the limited trenching around the Taplow Mound to the south of Taplow Court, indicating either another focus of domestic activity, or possibly a funerary site associated with the settlement activity on this site. The excavators of the trenches around the Taplow Mound believed that they had found a barrow ditch, although the scale of excavation, and the uncertainty of the stratigraphic record, make it impossible to confirm this. A possible small ring ditch has, however, been recorded as a cropmark some 2 km north-east of Taplow (SMR 4552), and the local absence of burial evidence at Taplow does not necessarily mark a distinction between differing kinds of landscape.

Overall, the early Bronze Age evidence in the local area consists of a dispersed pattern of comparable, small, possibly domestic sites (hollows, hearths and scatters) interspersed with funerary sites, which on present evidence, and *pace* Brück (1999), appear in this area to maintain a distinction between 'domestic' and funerary activity, based primarily upon the presence or absence of human remains.

The middle Bronze Age

The only indications of activity in the middle Bronze Age were a few pottery sherds, fragments of cylindrical loomweights and two radiocarbon dates, one on charred wheat, the other on *Alnus/Corylus* charcoal. This collection of finds – pottery, possibly weaving equipment, charred grain and charcoal – could be interpreted as a typically domestic assemblage, but issues similar to those discussed above in relation to the early Bronze Age finds arise here, and the quantities of finds are very small. In addition, the finds were residual, and it is unclear whether they were associated with one another.

It has also been suggested that even such a slight scatter of finds might reflect the proximity of a focus of middle Bronze Age settlement, and that such scatters might be a product of dispersed settlement

Fig. 11.1 (facing page) Plan showing conjectural extents of the late Bronze Age hilltop enclosure and of the early-middle and later Iron Age hillforts in relation to local archaeological discoveries, together with an extract from the 2nd edn 6" OS map of 1899 showing the supposed southern banks

Chapter 11

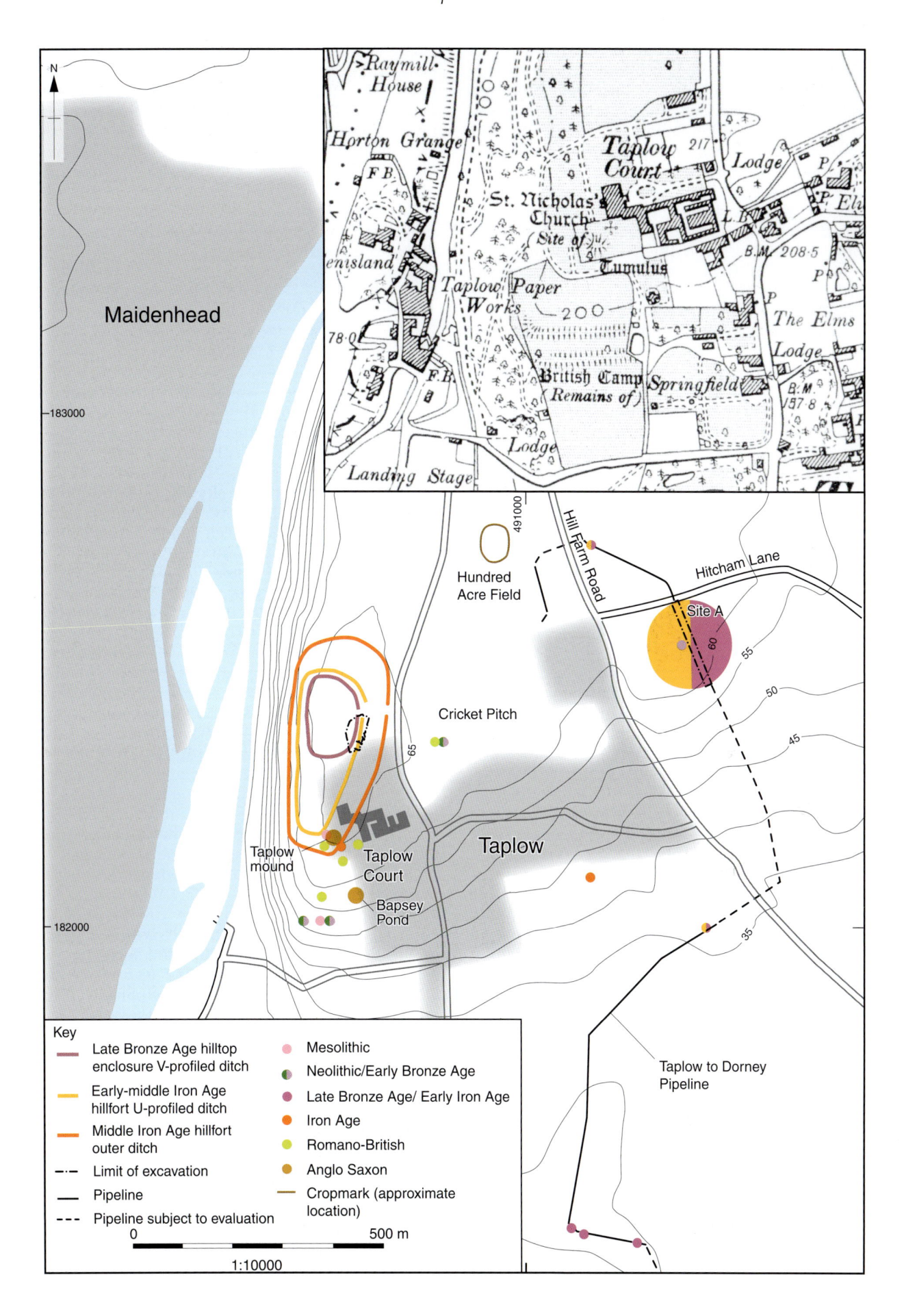

pattern, such as has been found upstream at Yarnton (Hey *et al.* in prep.) and downstream at Perry Oaks (Framework Archaeology 2006). As argued above, the two sherds of grog-tempered pottery found on the Taplow to Dorney pipeline were attributed to the middle Bronze Age (McSloy in Hart and Mudd forthcoming), but were probably early Bronze Age. The middle Bronze Age structures at Yarnton were not associated with field systems, while those at Perry Oaks were, the houses being scattered between different landholdings. The significance of field systems will be discussed further below. They are not known in the immediate vicinity of Taplow Court (unless the short length of straight ditch at the south end of the excavation area is of this date), but were laid out in the river valley below in the middle Bronze Age. Extensive areas were enclosed at the Eton Rowing Course, with smaller systems at Weir Bank Stud Farm, Bray and at Marsh Lane East (Site 1) (Allen and Mitchell 2001, 26-8; Barnes *et al.* 1995; Foreman 1998, 28)

Perhaps the most important question, however, is whether the middle Bronze Age activity at Taplow Court had any connection to the late Bronze Age occupation, particularly as the radiocarbon dates from Rams Hill allow the possibility that the hilltop enclosure there was constructed as early as the 13th century BC. At the nearby Eton Rowing Course, Deverel-Rimbury (ie middle Bronze Age) cremations have radiocarbon dates strongly suggesting that this pottery tradition continued after 1300 BC, and possibly into the 12th century BC (Allen *et al.* 2000, 76-7). There need not, therefore, have been any long gap between the middle Bronze Age activity and the late Bronze Age enclosure of the hilltop. However, the radiocarbon date on the charred cereal grain at Taplow indicated activity before 1300 BC, and while the other middle Bronze Age date from Taplow has a wider range, there is no positive evidence of later middle Bronze Age activity.

The low numbers of middle Bronze Age artefacts, and the likelihood that the middle Bronze Age radiocarbon dates obtained from the palisade trench and one of the internal post-rows are both residual, leave no significant chronological overlap between the main period of settlement within the major field systems on the gravel terrace below Taplow and the construction of the hilltop enclosure. The dates for the enclosure lie beyond the latest radiocarbon dates for both the field systems and the ring ditches and associated cremations at the Eton Rowing Course. In addition the rather more fragmentary field systems discovered along the Jubilee River also appear to be dated to the middle Bronze Age rather than later (Foreman 1998, 28; Allen *et al.* in prep. b). This pattern is also common at other sites where middle Bronze Age field systems and large Bronze Age enclosures are in close proximity, as for instance at Mucking, where both the North and South Rings cut across the ditches of middle Bronze Age field systems (Bond 1988). A late Bronze Age ringwork set within a contemporary settlement and field system was found at South Hornchurch in Essex (Guttmann and Last 2000), but here the ringwork was very much smaller and less substantial. The system of organisation and possibly increased production indicated by the field systems below Taplow may ultimately have given rise to the wealth that allowed the emergence of such high status (or at least, high investment) sites, but this was a long drawn-out process.

The late Bronze Age

Recurrence without transmission

Enclosed sites provide good examples of what anthropologists have called 'recurrence without transmission' (Boyer 1997), enclosures occurring because the circumstances which lead to their construction are widely distributed both in time and space (whether these circumstances are the psychological propensities stressed by some anthropologists or more mundane practicalities), rather than because they have been 'copied' from others. The widespread distribution of defensive enclosures, for example, must in part reflect the widespread occurrence of warfare, theft, or other forms of violence. The recurrence of enclosed settlements more generally must in part reflect conceptual distinctions between settlements or other kinds of sites and their surroundings, which exist whether or not they are marked by palisades or ditches. Such boundaries mark the distinction between spaces in which different kinds of behaviour are expected, and these expectations in turn give meaning to behaviour (especially if it deviates from expectations). The construction of such physical boundary features makes the conceptual boundary visible and affects its physical properties. They thus produce differentiation and protection. The significance of such boundaries is, of course, dependent upon wider classifications.

The fact that enclosed sites can be seen as examples of recurrence without transmission has implications for how we understand such sites. To compare the details of defensive features in the hope of defining traditions overlooks a prior question concerning how the knowledge and techniques involved were transmitted. If, for example, such enclosures were political centres of potentially conflicting groups it is unlikely that detailed knowledge of such sites would be shared (unless they were built by itinerant specialists). The existence of such a social situation would, however, provide conditions that would encourage the construction of such sites, and thus could lead to their replication. This view also has implications for how the relationship between late Bronze Age enclosures such as Taplow Court and their possible middle Bronze Age precursors is understood.

Possible middle Bronze Age precursors

Small numbers of houses in later Bronze Age settlements in Sussex that predate, but also probably chronologically overlap with, the earliest defences at Taplow, were enclosed by banks, ditches and palisades (Drewett *et al.* 1988). Slightly larger enclosures of various kinds, again enclosed with banks, ditches and palisades are known in Wessex (eg Barrett *et al.* 1991). Few enclosed middle Bronze Age sites are known closer to Taplow, and none in the immediate area, where settlement is either unenclosed or within systems of fields or enclosures. In the Upper Thames Valley, however, Corporation Farm, Abingdon (Barclay *et al.* 2003; Lambrick with Robinson 2009) was a middle Bronze Age enclosed settlement with a ditch and palisade. Downstream, at Muckhatch Farm, Thorpe (Needham 1987), a small middle Bronze Age settlement seems to have been enclosed within a circular palisade. These sites indicate that Taplow falls within the overall distribution of enclosed middle Bronze Age sites, although none of these middle Bronze Age sites had boundaries that were particularly substantial.

In his discussion of the hilltop enclosure at Rams Hill, Bradley placed the late Bronze Age enclosure at a point of transition, marking the change from ritual to agricultural or defensive functions (Bradley and Ellison 1975). Although the subsequent redating of Rams Hill to the late 2nd millennium BC (Needham and Ambers 1994) means that parts of Bradley's discussion have lost their salience, Rams Hill and Taplow Court can still be seen as lying at a significant point of transition (Thomas 1997), between middle Bronze Age enclosed settlements related to agriculture and pastoralism, and late Bronze Age hilltop enclosures intended to be defensive. The contrast could, therefore be seen as marking a transition from economics to politics.

In a broad context, then, the first palisade at Taplow should not be seen as something entirely new, but the contrast in scale between sites such as Taplow Court and these earlier enclosed sites remains, and the presence of superficial similarities such as palisades does not explain the transition between the two kinds of sites.

Taplow in relation to other late Bronze Age enclosures

The evidence suggests that the Taplow Court Bronze Age enclosure was established in the 11th century BC, and continued through several phases of defensive barrier to the 9th (or 8th) century BC (see Fig. 4.4). It shares both substantial defences (palisades, ditches and ramparts) and its substantial size with a group of other late Bronze Age enclosed sites, a selection of which is illustrated in Figure 11.2. They enclose areas ranging between 9000 and 16000 m^2, and the suggested area of 1.2 ha for the Taplow Court enclosure lies within this, and very close to the area of Rams Hill and Castle Hill, the others closest in form to Taplow. All three sites lie within the Upper and Middle Thames, and their locations are shown in Figure 11.3, together with the other major defended and riverine late Bronze Age sites in this area. The earliest of these sites may have been Rams Hill, which could have been constructed as early as the 13th century BC, although the radiocarbon dates leave open the possibility that it was not really much earlier than Taplow Court (Bradley and Ellison 1975; Needham and Ambers 1994). Two other sites have radiocarbon dates with ranges spanning the 13th-11th centuries: Camp Gardens, Stow-on-the-Wold – 1400-990 BC (Parry 1999) and Fairfield, Stotfold – 1250-1000 BC (Webley *et al.* 2007). The dates for Castle Hill span the 11th-9th centuries (Allen *et al.* 2006), and dates from Thrapston (Hull 2000) and the unusual site at Wolstonbury are 10th century or later (Hamilton and Manley 1997).

On the basis of size the incompletely investigated enclosure at Carshalton (Adkins and Needham 1985; Groves and Lovell 2002) may well also belong to this group, although probably dating from the later part of this period (10th century BC). It also shares the elevated position of the enclosure at Taplow overlooking a river, as does the enclosure at Little Wittenham. This site is usually related to the ring works of eastern England, although as only the southern half of the circuit was seen, it could instead have shared the sub-rectangular or D-shape of the other enclosures illustrated (see Fig. 11.2).

A number of other sites, including Highdown Hill, Sussex (Hamilton and Manley 1997; Wilson 1940 and 1950), North Fitzwarren, Somerset (Ellis 1993), Hog Cliff Castle, Dorset (Ellison and Rahtz 1987), and Thundersbarrow Hill, Sussex (Hamilton and Manley 1997) have been cited as early enclosures, but there are doubts about the association between the dating evidence and the enclosure features at some of these sites (Ambers and Needham 1994). According to the dating evidence, the *floruit* for such sites seems to have begun, as it probably did at Taplow, *c* 1100 BC and continued to around 900 or 800 BC.

The ringworks or ringforts of eastern England have been discussed in relation to hilltop enclosures by Needham (1993). The largest certain example of these, covering just over 1 ha at Thwing (Manby 1980), has recently been reconsidered by Manby, and the outer ditch of the ringfort with its inner ditch dated to the 10th – 8th centuries BC (Manby 2007), similar to those at Mucking (Jones and Bond 1980), Springfield Lyons (Buckley and Hedges 1987), South Hornchurch (Guttmann and Last 2000) and Mill Hill (Champion 1980). These are therefore contemporary with the later phases of Taplow Court, and most of them (with the exception of Thwing and Carshalton) are considerably smaller than Taplow Court, Rams Hill and Castle Hill. Recent discoveries are making it clear, however, that there is a much wider spectrum of size and shape of enclosures of the late Bronze Age in South-East England, including smaller oval or sub-rectangular

From Bronze Age enclosure to Anglo-Saxon settlement

Rams Hill

Fairfield Park, Stotfold

Carshalton

Castle Hill

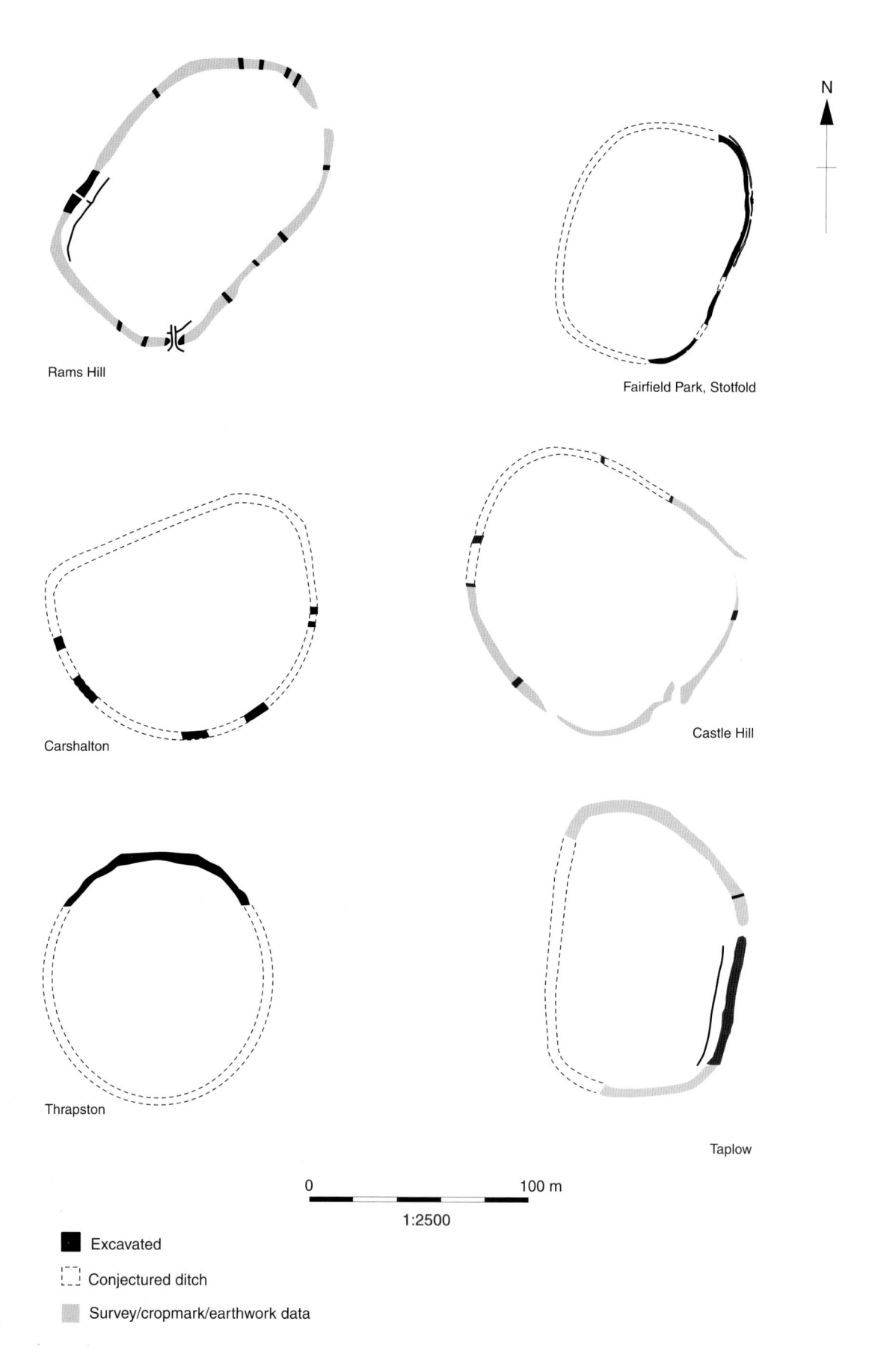

Thrapston

Taplow

0 — 100 m
1:2500

■ Excavated
⸭ Conjectured ditch
▨ Survey/cropmark/earthwork data

Fig. 11.2 Plans of comparative Late Bronze Age hilltop enclosures in Southern England

enclosures such as Highstead and Ramsgate in Kent (Champion 2007, fig. 4.25) and rectangular enclosures like Lofts Farm in Essex (Brown 1988). The functions and status of these are likely to have been just as varied.

As Manby has recently observed, a number of these sites occupy hilltop or hillslope locations, which together with their size suggest that the sites were intended to be defensive. They may, therefore, be marking the beginning of the development of hillforts. Like Taplow Court, several of these sites were later the location of Iron Age hillforts, for instance Rams Hill, Berkshire (Bradley and Ellison 1975) and Castle Hill, Little Wittenham, Oxfordshire (Allen *et al.* 2006), although the sequence of development appears often to be discontinuous.

Rather larger sites which have been recognised as early hillforts, such as the Breidden (Musson 1991), Dinorben (Savory 1971) and Grimthorpe (Stead 1968), Beeston Castle (Ellis 1993) Balksbury Camp (Ellis and Rawlings 2001) and other sites (Cunliffe 1990 and 2004; Osgood 1998), seem to belong to a slightly later period, the earliest perhaps in the 10th century BC, but most in the 9th century, and thus precede the more widespread construction of hillforts from the 8th century.

A number of other defended sites with some evidence for late Bronze Age activity have been noted in the Thames Valley, including Mayfield Farm, Marshall's Hill, Burroway, Chastelton Camp, Lyneham, and Bozedown Camp (Lambrick with Robinson 2009). Most of these sites have not been investigated in detail, however, and their precise chronology – and the relationship of the late Bronze Age finds to their enclosure features – remains to be established. The double-ditched cropmark enclosure at Mayfield Farm in particular has been argued to be a henge monument rather than a late Bronze Age ringwork (Needham 1993; Lewis 2000, 69 and 71).

Overall, then, Taplow Court can be placed within a group of hilltop enclosures most of which began to be constructed from the 11th century. These sites can be distinguished from a slightly later group of larger hillforts, most of which were constructed in the 9th century or later, and from a group of smaller ring works with a generally eastern distribution, most of which were constructed from the 10th century BC, and not all of which were necessarily defensive (Bradley 1984; see also Guttmann and Last 2000). In the case of the hilltop enclosures such as Taplow, however, the size of the palisades, ditches and ramparts, suggests that they were intended to be defensive.

The chronological evidence for the sequence of defensive features – palisades and ramparts – of at least three, and possibly as many as six, phases of activity, is set out in Chapter 4. The earliest of these phases seems to have been related to posthole rows 1107 and 1108, probably constructed in the 11th century BC (1120-980 cal BC). These may have belonged to two successive simple palisades, but the layout of the posts in these rows could also represent a composite structure consisting of a timber palisade and raised walkway that did not retain a bank. The postholes of neither row at Taplow are particularly substantial (only *c* 0.5 m deep to the top of buried soils 1105, and possibly 0.6 m if part of soil 1120 is included, although some postholes further north were deeper). Mercer (1981) suggested that the height of the posts above ground could be calculated using a ratio of 3:1 or 3.5: 1 in relation to the original depth of the posthole. More recently Gibson has revisited these figures, and suggested that a ratio of 4:1 is commonly used in practice today (Gibson 1998, 106-7). Even using Gibson's ratio, however, the Taplow structure is unlikely to have been more than 2-2.4 m tall, and the raised walkway perhaps only 1 m off the ground (see Fig. 4.4A).

There are several other examples of this type of construction at others of the late Bronze Age enclosures. At Thwing, where the bank survived, two lines of paired postholes 1.8-2.0 m apart were found, the outer line 5.5 m from the surrounding ditch, with posts spaced 0.6 m apart, and have been reconstructed as a raised walkway behind the bank (Manby 2007, fig. 36.3). A similar construction was found at Springfield Lyons in Essex, where two lines of postholes varying from 1.5 – 3 m apart was found, the front row 6 m inside the ditch, and with postholes at intervals of 1.4 m to 1.7 m. The postholes in the two rows generally corresponded, but were not always exactly in line, just as at Taplow. This double line was also interpreted as forming a contemporary revetment and raised walkway behind the bank (Buckley and Hedges 1987, 5-5 and fig. 5). At Rams Hill the continuous palisade inside the ditch had a line of widely spaced postholes 2.5-3.2 m behind it, but this was interpreted as belonging to an earlier phase, forming an internal revetment to stone-faced rampart, the palisade succeeding it (Bradley and Ellison 1975, 34-5). Manby has recently suggested that the two lines might instead have been associated in yet another of these raised walkways (Manby 2007, 409). In a later phase, a double palisade was constructed in the top of the infilled ditch at Rams Hill, and the two lines of this lay 2.5-3.5 m apart, and did not enclose a rampart (ibid., 35-6). This may also have been another example of this type of defensive structure.

The examples at Thwing and Springfield Lyons formed a rear revetment to the upcast bank, interpreted at Thwing by Manby as a glacis-style rampart (Manby 2007, 407-9). At Taplow Court, however, such a timber defence would probably have preceded the digging of the V-profiled ditch, standing alone. The same might have occurred at Springfield Lyons, and this possibility was not discussed by Manby for Thwing.

As reconstructed, this composite palisade and walkway does not appear very effective as a defence, and would seem (to a modern eye) to represent a disproportionate amount of effort for

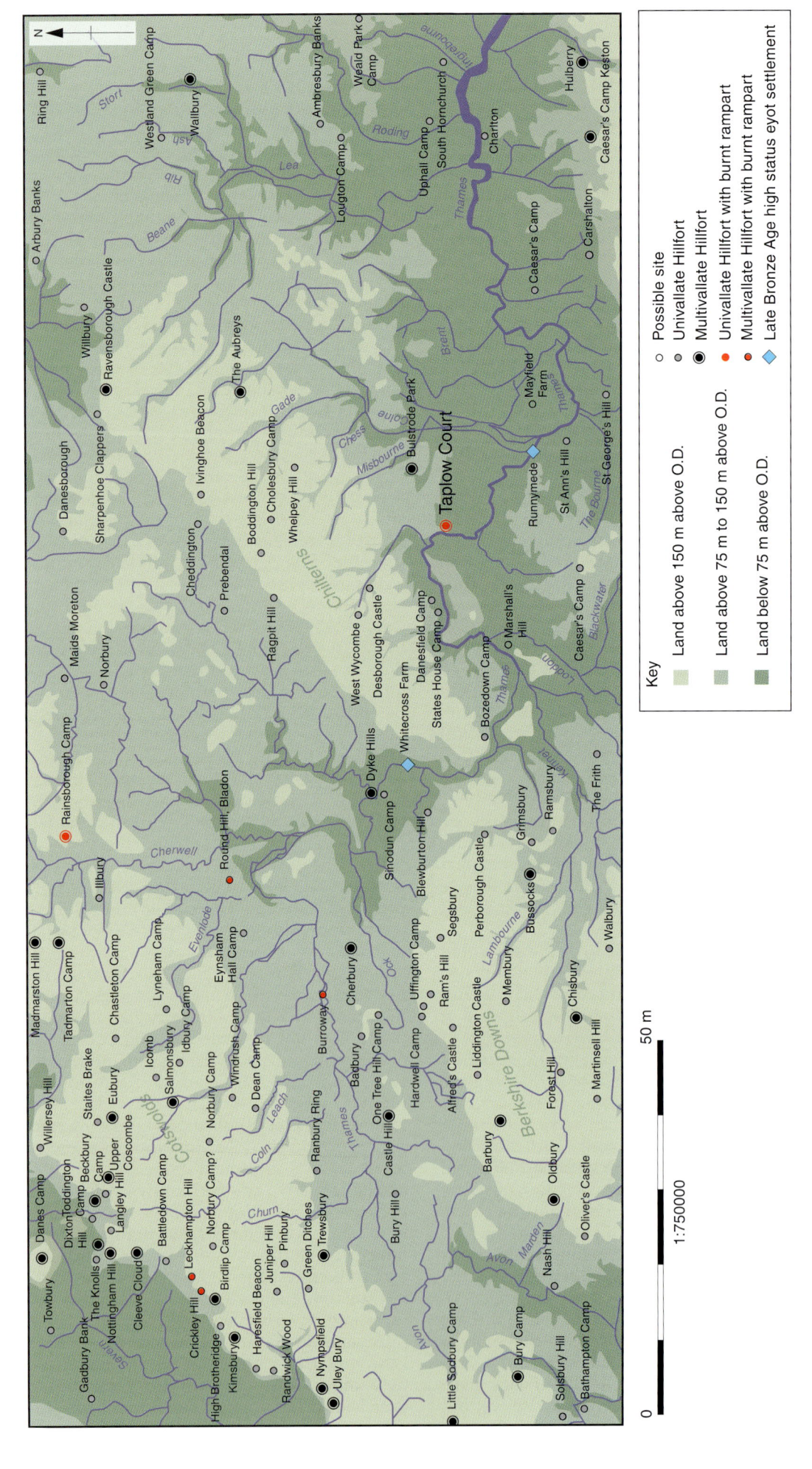

Fig. 11.3 *Map of major Bronze Age and Iron Age defended and riverine sites in the Upper and Middle Thames valley.*

what was actually achieved. We should however beware of interpreting these enclosures in purely defensive terms, or indeed using modern preconceptions of any kind. There is a long tradition of monument construction antedating this enclosure in which enormous effort was expended, and it may be that the intention of a raised walkway was for procession or display, not for defence. The deeper postholes found along part of the length of row 1107, and for that matter the continuous palisade trench that succeeded it, may have served a similar, purpose, the line of posts varying in height around the perimeter, rather than being of uniform length. The post-circles of pre-Roman Dacia, for instance, have been interpreted in just such a manner.

The replacement of post-built structure 1107/8 with a continuous palisade at Taplow Court is paralleled by the preferred sequence at Rams Hill, where the continuous palisade was seen as belonging to a second phase, replacing a stone-faced rampart (Bradley and Ellison 1975, 32-7). None of the other sites illustrated, or of the ringworks, has a similar palisade, though a late Bronze Age date has been claimed for primary palisades at hillforts such as Blewburton Hill, Oxfordshire (Collins 1947; Collins 1953). The palisade trench at Taplow, which was up to 0.8 m deep where best-preserved, would have allowed free-standing uprights between 2.4 m and 3.2 m high above ground (see Fig. 4.4B). For the palisade to have formed an impassable barrier further timbers would have had to have been added, probably in the form of horizontal planking pegged into the uprights, or possibly as additional shorter verticals placed within the gaps and held in place by horizontal timbers at intervals pegged to the earthfast uprights on the inside.

As already suggested, however, the palisade may have been intended for display, and to bound a special area, rather than as a physical defence. The variation in depth of the palisade trench, whose deepest section corresponded to the deepest postholes of the earlier post-row 1107, has already been mentioned. The posts of 1107 were deepest on the east, tailing off towards the north-east and south-east, and it is possible that some connection with the rising sun, or perhaps some other astronomical phenomenon, was intended. Palisade 1106 was superseded by the bank associated with the V-profiled ditch.

The ditch at Rams Hill and at Castle Hill was U-profiled, and in this respect Taplow Court has more in common with the enclosures further east, Carshalton and Springfield Lyons also having V-profiled ditches. The local geology (both Rams Hill and Castle Hill are on chalk) may explain the difference, although the succeeding Iron Age hillfort ditch at Taplow was U-profiled, and did not erode significantly. Much more spoil is created by a U-profiled ditch, and a combination of the labour required and the size of bank required may have influenced the shape of ditch to be dug. At Taplow, where the ditch may have been fronted by another post-row (see below), such a large bank may not have been needed. The investigation of the V-profiled ditch was limited, but there was certainly no indication of cleaning out or recutting from the sections examined, unlike Rams Hill.

As argued in Chapter 4, it would have been possible to construct a bank some 2 m high without the need for revetment in the 7.5 m band between the ditch and the occupation soil found within the interior, or, providing that the front and back of the rampart was revetted with turf, a narrower and higher bank with a berm up to 2 m wide between the ditch and bank. The late Bronze Age hilltop enclosure at Castle Hill also appears to have had either a simple dump rampart or one revetted only with turf (Allen et al. 2006, 20-21).

A series of simple fences involving posthole rows 935, 1132 and 1132 were also constructed in the late Bronze Age, which may indicate yet another defensive line, but more likely belong to internal divisions within the enclosure. Posthole row 1104 is the most difficult to interpret. The only secure stratigraphic evidence suggests that it predated the U-profiled ditch and the standstill layer in the top of the V-profiled ditch, and so belongs in the late Bronze Age phase. The irregularity of the row, containing postholes two or three deep along most of its length, but without clear alignments or matching pairs of posts, has led to the suggestion that its postholes in fact derive from more than one phase. Almost all of the postholes were however filled with very similar soils, and the evidence of the internal post-rows 935 and 1133 provides other examples of irregular post-rows of the late Bronze Age on this site.

It might be possible to reconstruct the internal post-rows as paired rows forming lines of uprights between which horizontal logs or timbers were piled up to make a crude timber barricade without the need for jointing or otherwise attaching the timbers together (see Fig. 4.4D). Although there are also short stretches of post-row 1104, particularly in the northern half of the excavations, where this might have worked, there are other lengths where the posts were too close together to make this likely. While the possibility remains that post-row 1104 represents another separate phase (or phases) of hilltop palisade, it lies east of the V-profiled ditch, palisade 1106 and the adjacent post-rows 1107-8, and its very irregularity may be the key to its role as an element of the late Bronze Age defences contemporary with the other palisades, and possibly even with ditch 574. A number of examples of chevaux-de-frise, irregular rows of stones placed outside the main defences to hinder men and horses, are known in Wales and the north of England, and it is possible that post-row 1104, with its substantial postholes, represents an example of the same type constructed in wood (cf. Harbison 1971). Equitation in Britain is now known to have begun in the later Bronze Age, based on the evidence of bone and bronze horse-harness from Runnymede, Isleham and elsewhere (Longley and Needham 1980, 29; Cunliffe 1991, 54-5) and more importantly on evidence of bitting wear on horse bones at Runnymede (Bendrey 2007, 234). Chevaux-de-frise usually cover a wider band than post-row 1104, sometimes as much as 10 m, and in this case further postholes may have been removed by the digging of the U-profiled ditch 460 (see Fig. 4.4C).

The precise extent of these defences is unknown, but what evidence there is suggests that they enclosed an area of around 1.2 ha on the highest point of the end of the Burnham plateau, which was bordered to the west by the precipitous terrace edge overlooking the river.

Activity within the enclosure

Although the extent of the excavation within the enclosure was limited, the evidence includes postholes that might indicate the presence of roundhouses, and of a number of four-post structures. The possible roundhouses were quite small, with diameters of only 5 or 6 m, but those at Rams Hill had comparable diameters (5 to 7 m), and the roundhouses at many of the ring works were also of comparable dimensions (North Ring, Mucking, 7 m across; Springfield Lyons, 5 to 7 m across; Jones and Bond 1980; Buckley and Hedges 1987), although the central annular ditch at the South Ring, Mucking, was around 11 m across, and the majority of suggested roundhouses at South Hornchurch were 10-12.5 m in diameter (Guttmann and Last 2000). The four-post structures were mostly quite small, and several were trapezoidal rather than square or rectangular, but the four-post structures at South Hornchurch were all well under 2 m square (Guttmann and Last 2000, fig. 10), and both of these characteristics are also common at Rams Hill (Bradley and Ellison 1975, fig. 2.26). Six or eight-post structures are less common, but although not discussed in detail in the report on South Hornchurch, several possible six or eight-post structures are shown on plan, and one arrangement of eight posts is interpreted either as 2 four-post structures or one eight-post one (ibid., 331 and fig. 10).

The internal fence lines are not easy to interpret from the limited area of the interior that lay within the excavation. They seem unlikely to have co-existed alongside the more northerly roundhouse, but could have fenced off an area containing a number of storage structures, although there is little evidence of order in the arrangement of the putative four-post structures. Internal posthole rows running almost parallel to the defences are known from Thwing (Manby 2007), but their precise chronological relationship to the various phases of the ditches is not described, and here too excavation was only partial. What seems clear at Taplow is that a south-east to north-west division of long standing existed, as shown by the turn of posthole row 1132, the line of posthole row 1108a and of posthole row 1108b, running approximately at right angles to the axis of the north-east entrance to the enclosure. This may have been similar to the line of postholes found within some of the ringworks at right angles to the entrance, as at Mucking North Ring and at Highstead in Kent (Jones and Bond 1980; Champion 2007, fig. 4.25). Much more of the interior would need to be exposed at Taplow to clarify this, however.

The artefactual evidence is similar to that found on many late Bronze Age settlements: pottery, charred cereals, a few domestic animal bones, a little fired clay and worked stone, but also part of a decorated bronze bracelet. Evidence for metalwork and metalworking has been found at Mucking (Jones and Bond 1980), Thwing (Manby 1980), Springfield Lyons (Buckley and Hedges 1987) and South Hornchurch (Guttmann and Last 2000, 344). No comparable evidence for metalworking has been found at Taplow Court or Rams Hill (although the extent of excavation at both has been limited in comparison to that at these ringworks). It is, however, perhaps worth noting that a crucible and small bronze fragments, reportedly of Bronze Age date, were found just 0.5 km m to the south-east of Taplow Court (NMR NatInv-251821). However, this evidence might be entirely unrelated to the hilltop enclosure.

Most of the finds at Taplow came from the general occupation layers 1121 and 1123, only loosely related to the archaeological features, but a large proportion of the pottery from both the occupation layer and from postholes in the interior was in late Bronze Age flint-tempered fabrics, suggesting that the enclosure and settlement were established at roughly the same time (rather than an open settlement having been enclosed or a settlement having been created within an enclosure). The presence of flint and sand-, sand and flint- and a little sand-tempered pottery suggests that activity within the hillfort continued throughout the whole sequence of defences. Indeed, the presence of significant quantities of late Bronze Age-early Iron Age pottery in the standstill layer (1102) filling the top of the V-profiled ditch suggests that occupation may have continued even when the ditch had fallen into disuse, the bank continuing to provide an adequate barrier for the purposes of the enclosure.

Because of the limited extent of the excavation at Taplow and at some other sites, it is difficult to establish and compare the character of the activity within these enclosures. In contrast to Taplow and Rams Hill, the excavated areas within Castle Hill, Little Wittenham and Fairfield are devoid of features (Allen *et al.* 2006; Webley *et al.* 2007), though this may in part be due to the level of truncation on these latter sites. The density of internal activity at Taplow certainly appears to be high, and it is possible that both the Rams Hill and Taplow Court enclosures contained larger settlements than the ringworks, which extensive excavation has shown generally contain between one and three roundhouses, often centrally-placed. In the case of the ringworks, the boundaries may have enclosed a single household or extended household group, whereas at Rams Hill and Taplow Court the enclosure may have been placed around a wider community.

At South Hornchurch a substantial number of possible roundhouses were found in the enclosures or fields around the ringwork, perhaps indicating a different social arrangement (Guttmann and Last 2000). The ringworks could be seen as aggrandising a single high status residence, and thus could have been related in a quite straightforward way to status (as an expression of wealth, for example), while the situation at Taplow Court and Ram's Hill may indicate that any relationship between the enclosure and status was mediated by a communal model of authority (that is, a model upon which status was related to duties to and power over a community).

Taplow Court in relation to boundaries in other contexts: field systems and territorial boundaries

Excavations in the river valley to the south have shown that, beginning in the middle Bronze Age, the lower ground below the hilltop enclosure was divided up by ditches into field systems. These were presumably used to manage the movement of animals, to provide them and perhaps also crops, with some protection, and to define property rights (Yates 1999, 2001 and 2007). Barrett (1994) has also noted how such boundaries would have affected the movement of people. In general, the middle and late Bronze Age was a time when physical boundaries were imposed on a wider scale than before, marking them in ways that were permanent, physically and visually effective, and which controlled movement and made claims to control. In this rather abstract way, the late Bronze Age hilltop enclosure at Taplow Court could be seen as part of a wider pattern.

There may also be relationships, perhaps related primarily to political authority, between hilltop enclosures and territorial boundaries, examples of which in Berkshire Ford (1982) has argued date from the late Bronze Age. However, no such boundaries are known in the immediate vicinity of Taplow Court. The river Thames itself could have formed a significant boundary in this period, although there is insufficient evidence to suggest any cultural differences in this stretch of the Thames, and the presence of field systems either side probably indicates that the Thames was most significant as an artery of communication and exchange, hence the location of Taplow (and other enclosures such as Castle Hill, Little Wittenham, South Hornchurch and Mucking North and South Rings) alongside it.

Both kinds of boundaries might have been linked to changes in the significance of wealth, and in particular an increasing emphasis on the significance of livestock, agricultural produce and land as forms of wealth (Thomas 1997). The construction of field boundaries could be seen as implying an increase in the value of animals and crops, and the increasingly widespread adoption of new forms of storage such a four-post structures might have been related to similar developments (cf. Bradley 1984, 118-19). The development of defended settlements might be seen as a further consequence of these developments, providing not only a secure storage place but also, perhaps, being related to a centralised political authority which could provide wider protection.

Yates (1999 and 2007) has made a close link between the development of field systems and the emergence of `aggrandised enclosures', of which Taplow Court is one. Although, as argued above, there is no obvious chronological overlap between the initial use of these field systems and the construction of the Taplow Court enclosure, there is some evidence for the continued use of the middle Bronze Age field system in association with a late Bronze Age house at Weir Bank Stud Farm, Bray (Barnes and Cleal 1995), and possible evidence of continuity into the Iron Age at the Eton Rowing Course (Allen *et al.* forthcoming b). A link between secondary use of some of these field systems and the central site at Taplow Court is therefore still possible, but by no means proven. Yates has recently argued that the field systems could be seen as ideal or model landscapes that were intended to be viewed from the aggrandised enclosures, including Taplow (Yates 2007, 134-5). The enclosure at Taplow was not however located to look out over the valley. It also raises the question as to whether visibility was actually desired when constructing the enclosure.

The discovery of the late Bronze Age enclosure at Taplow Court does not fit the more or less regular pattern of such centres along the river which Yates had envisaged (Yates 2001), although in his most recent publication (Yates 2007) this has been modified. The date and character of a number of other centres he proposed – Marshall's Hill near Reading and Burroway in West Oxfordshire, for example – still appear on his maps, but have also been questioned (Lambrick with Robinson 2009). While Yates' broad thesis is argued very persuasively, the patterns he suggests are often based upon inaccurate data, and do not take sufficient account of the variability of the evidence.

Taplow Court in relation to other late Bronze Age settlements: longevity

The relationship between the Taplow Court late Bronze Age enclosure and surrounding settlement is unclear due to the lack of detail about other late Bronze Age sites. Despite this, the quantities of pottery recovered from the TCAST trenches some 200 m distant at the south end of the ridge suggest that a contemporary settlement lay close by. There is no evidence at present that this was enclosed. This juxtaposition, which is similar to that at Castle Hill,

Little Wittenham, Oxfordshire, where late Bronze Age occupation lies less than 200 m outside a defensible enclosure (Hingley 1980; Allen and Lamdin-Whymark 2005, 77; Allen *et al.* 2006), might be interpreted in several ways. It might indicate satellite settlement of lower status outside the defended enclosure, or complementary areas used by a single group for different activities, or possibly merely an emphasis on activites of different types in the two areas. At South Hornchurch, the landscape around the ringwork consisted of a number of enclosed fields in which a number of broadly contemporary houses and other structures were found (Guttmann and Last 2000), while at Little Wittenham, late Bronze Age pottery was found both in pits and postholes below and within a midden only a few hundred metres outside the ditched enclosure (Allen and Lamdin-Whymark 2005, 77; Allen *et al.* 2006). At present the limited excavation both in the interior of the enclosure and of the external activity makes this impossible to clarify.

The defences at Taplow were long-lived; occupation seems to have lasted from at least the 11th century BC to the 9th century, and the palisades were renewed in the same location, albeit in different forms. Occupation of the enclosure thus appears to have lasted longer than at many other late Bronze Age settlements.

One effect of the permanence of the hilltop enclosure – paralleled by the field boundaries – may have been to change the relationship between social structure and space. Social hierarchy, even hierarchy linked to martial symbolism, was not new in the late Bronze Age, but in the early and middle Bronze Age such hierarchies are reflected primarily in burials. If, in the late Bronze Age, hilltop enclosures were related to political, and especially military power, sites such as Taplow Court would have created an enduring relationship between a particular location and that power. Current evidence does not allow such an assumption about the role of the site, but the effort required to construct and maintain the defences shows that it was important to the local community over a long period of time, so that whatever the basis of this significance, the link between place and significance would have grown.

Taplow Court in relation to weapons and warfare: defence

While recent scholarship has stressed that the significance of hillfort defences went beyond defence, it is still worth examining the significance of defence itself.

One obvious reason for the increased scale of the defences associated with late Bronze Age hilltop enclosures would be an increase in the scale of the perceived threat.

There is no clear indication that this was related to the development of new types of weaponry. On the basis of skeletal evidence with wounds (and ignoring questions concerning the likely origins of those wounds – which might be the result of rituals or brawling as much as the results of warfare), spears were the most commonly used weapons (Osgood 1998). There were gradual changes in the design of spears through the late Bronze Age as well as changes in sword design (Ehrenberg 1977; Burgess and Colquhoun 1988). The development of shields (Osgood 1998) in the late Bronze Age suggests that these changes in weaponry were associated with the development of methods of defence. However, none of these developments seem to mark a change radical enough to explain the development of hillforts. Slingshots seem to have been one of the main weapons used to attack hillforts in the Iron Age, but are not found in late Bronze Age sites.

One very significant introduction of the middle and late Bronze Age, however, was the use of horses, for which both bones of the animals themselves, and horsegear, first appear in significant numbers at this time (eg. Longley 1980, 29; Levitan 1992). Their occurrence on middle Bronze Age sites is patchy, but becomes increasingly common in the late Bronze Age. The introduction of mounted warriors will have made a significant difference to warfare that required new and better defences ie wider and deeper ditches, higher banks and palisades. The increased speed available to raiders may also have been a factor in the development of large enclosures into which livestock could be herded for protection.

It is also possible that the perception of an increased threat was related to changes in the organisation of warfare or raiding, as well as, perhaps, in its 'social position'. The construction of defences such as those at Taplow Court might in part have been motivated by the organisation of larger forces, and the organisation of such forces is likely to have been related to a new understanding of the place of warfare in social life.

Violence and cosmology

Various anthropologists have examined the place of warfare and other, smaller-scale forms of violence in social life. Bloch (1992), for example, has suggested that the final phases of ritual sequences, such as rites of passages, often involve violence directed outwards towards some 'other'. More generally, Leach (2000) has argued that warfare is always, in some way, ritualised. In many societies the commencement of warfare was marked by particular rituals and was associated with restrictions on behaviour of various kinds (eg Beard *et al.* 1998; Douglas 1954). Warfare thus constituted not just physical violence but formed a particular social state, associated with particular forms of social relationships and practices, marked off in time from the everyday (cf. Mauss 2004). The defences at Taplow Court could thus also be seen as having been related to, or potentially related to, a particular social state, associated with warfare, and marked off from contrasting social states. It should be stressed, however, that this may have been related to the defences themselves and not to the settlement within. Indeed, the defences and the interior may have been of opposed kinds. Such associations may be complex. The Pomerium of Rome, for example, was a (barely marked) boundary beyond which soldiers could not pass (except during rites of inversion) but which was quite distinct from the defensive walls of the city (Beard *et al.* 1998).

There is some evidence to suggest that the context of warfare was restricted in the later Bronze Age. The clearest evidence for this is the distinction between defended sites, such as Taplow Court, and other late Bronze Age settlements in the Thames Valley, most of which consist of rather dispersed, unenclosed scatters of roundhouses and other structures (eg Reading Business Park; Shorncote; Cassington; Moore and Jennings 1992; Hearne and Adam 1999; Hey *et al.* in prep.). Near to Taplow, the sites at Widbrook Common (Allen *et al.* in prep. b) and at Furze Platt, Maidenhead (Rutland and Greenaway 1970, 56), appear to be of this kind. Limited excavation at a late Bronze Age site at Eton Wick (Ford 1993) revealed ditches that Ford interpreted as representing a substantial enclosure, although these were not on the scale of those at Taplow, and may instead have been field boundaries. At Perry Oaks (Framework Archaeology 2006), late Bronze Age settlement seems to have been more nucleated than that of the middle Bronze Age, but still falls short of concentrations of houses that might be described as villages. Even in the early Iron Age, most settlements seem to have consisted of only small numbers of houses, usually unenclosed (eg Lambrick and Allen 2004). Not only do they lack boundary defences, but the houses themselves were not clustered so as to provide mutual protection. There are exceptions, such as the dense settlements on riverine islands, sometimes perhaps associated with palisades (eg Runnymede and Wallingford; Longley and Needham 1980; Needham 1991; Needham and Spence 1996; Cromarty *et al.* 2006), but these were exceptional sites probably central to exchange along the river and with the Continent.

The implication of this is that if the defences of sites such as Taplow Court were associated with real violence, it occurred within a constrained context, and thus suggests that, although the details elude us, warfare in the late Bronze Age occupied a particular 'social position'. The fact that violence was directed at a specific context also suggests that political authority was to some degree centralised. An attack on a political body could thus have been effectively directed at its symbolic head.

Taplow Court in relation to other late Bronze Age settlements: similarities and differences

As well as providing evidence for the restricted context of warfare in the late Bronze Age and its association with sites such as Taplow Court, the contrasts between hilltop enclosures such as Taplow Court and the more widely occurring open settlements highlight further effects of the creation of the enclosures. One of these effects was to create social distance between the hilltop enclosures and open settlements. This is not just a matter of marking a difference between the two kinds of sites. The boundaries of the hilltop enclosures also insulate them from the world around, the physical boundary corresponding to a social distinction. At the same time, however, the defences at Taplow Court can also be seen as projecting an image outwards to outsiders of the power implicit in the labour necessary to construct the defences.

The enclosure need not however have been built primarily for defence and for warfare. Similar expenditure of communal effort had been seen in the enclosures of the late Neolithic, which are not interpreted as primarily concerned with warfare, and the general similarity of the finds from the Taplow Court enclosure and from the surrounding unenclosed settlements (as at Rams Hill) may indicate that there was no significant social difference between the occupants of the enclosure and those in the surrounding territory. We do not know that the enclosure was permanently occupied, and it may instead have been used by the surrounding inhabitants on occasions, perhaps seasonally or for particular ceremonies and gatherings. The feature types, such as roundhouses and four-posters, also occur at both kinds of sites. Very few pits were found at Taplow, but this may well simply reflect the limited extent of the excavation; pits have been found within and outside late Bronze Age enclosures elsewhere (eg Carshalton, Groves and Lovell 2002 and Thrapston, Hull 2000). Apart from exceptional midden sites (eg Potterne; Lawson 2000) late Bronze Age settlements are usually not associated with large quantities of finds. At Taplow Court only the bronze bracelet might be considered out of the ordinary.

Taplow Court in relation to the Thames: metalwork and human remains

The social position of the hilltop enclosure at Taplow Court may also be reflected in its relationship with metalwork and human remains recovered from the Thames. It has been suggested that there might be a relationship between hilltop enclosures and the deposition of metalwork in the river (Yates 1999).

Considerable quantities of late Bronze Age metalwork have been recovered from the Thames near Taplow. York (2002) lists 25 items from Taplow and 6 from Maidenhead, making this the largest concentration in her survey. This metalwork consists of primarily of weapons, and spears in particular, as does most of the metalwork from this stretch of the Thames (York 2002; Ford 1987b). Numerous factors influence the evidence from the river, however, and the location of find spots must be regarded as

From Bronze Age enclosure to Anglo-Saxon settlement

Plate 11.1 Taplow Court from the south, across the recently cut Jubilee River

approximate. What indications there are concerning the find spots of this metalwork (in the SMR) shows that only a few finds come from the stretch directly adjacent to the hilltop enclosure around Boulter's Lock, and none from the Cliveden Reach immediately upriver. Most of the nearest finds appear to come from a stretch just downriver, around Maidenhead Bridge. The stretch or river below this also contained quite high number of finds of similar types.

There are other possible explanations for the presence of the metalwork in the river. Several human skulls from the river, not far away at the Eton Rowing Course, have been radiocarbon dated to the late Bronze Age (Allen *et al.* 2000, Bradley and Gordon 1988), and it is possible that the deposition of the metalwork was linked to the deposition of these human remains, ie as grave goods, although no metalwork has been recovered in association with any of the human bones. York (2002) notes that the proportion of deliberately broken or 'killed' weapons in the river near Taplow was particularly high. The settlement of the living in the hilltop enclosure (just as much as in other settlements) might therefore have been seem as contrasting with the river as a place in some way associated with the dead. The ritual 'killing' of weapons may have been related to 'burying the hatchet' in North American Indian societies, representing agreements made between different groups at the boundary between them. In this case the river as boundary may have been the important location for deposition. Despite the extended distribution of these river finds, however, the correspondence of this concentration to the Taplow enclosure, a focal point for the local community, seems unlikely to have been coincidental.

The abandonment of the late Bronze Age enclosure

The only evidence from the site that may have been related to the reasons for its abandonment was provided by the pollen from the standstill layer (1102). This suggests the presence of ling heather and hence the development of heathland in the surrounding area. The environmental degradation this suggests might have provided one reason for abandonment. It is, however, likely that this was only part of the story. It may, however, also have been linked to a decline in the trade in bronze metalwork and no doubt other items along the Thames. The concentration of Bronze Age metalwork from the river near Taplow is not matched by metalwork of Iron Age date.

The early-middle Iron Age

The early-middle Iron Age evidence was almost entirely related to the hillfort defences. These were represented by two large ditches – the inner, U-profiled ditch (460, 6 m wide by 3 m deep) and the outer ditch (3050, 10 m wide by 3 m deep) – as well as by the remains of the burnt timber-laced rampart associated with the U-profiled ditch and some features related to the hillfort entrance, most of which had also been burnt. Although the precise course of these defences is unknown, what evidence there is suggests that they enclosed an area of 3-4 ha, at the end of the Burnham plateau (see Fig. 11.1). The extension of the defences south of the late Bronze Age enclosure brought the hillfort to the edge of the plateau, making them much more visible than those of the preceding phase, and giving the hillfort a commanding position over the river valley to the south (Plate 11.1). The Iron Age hillfort was therefore a much more obvious symbol of power than its predecessor, and may have had different roles in contemporary society.

The defences

The most securely dated of these features were the U-profiled ditch (460) and its associated rampart and entrance features, which were constructed during the period 510-390 BC (and probably some time between 480-400 BC). On the basis of indications from the ditch fills, it seems that the rampart was burnt quite soon after its construction.

The overall chronology of the hillfort remains ambiguous because no clear evidence for the date of the outer ditch (3050) was recovered. Anglo-Saxon finds were recovered from a depth of 2.25 m in the outer ditch, and at least 1.65 m in the U-profiled ditch, showing that both ditches survived as appreciable features into the Saxon period. There are several possibilities; while sequences of development at other hillforts suggest that where sequences of development are apparent sites were often enlarged in their later phases, there are also more complex sequences that involved contractions in size (Ralston 2006).

One possibility is that both V-profiled ditches were contemporary, making this a late Bronze Age double-ditched enclosure perhaps similar to Thwing or Mucking South Rings (Cunliffe 1991, fig. 3.6), although Thwing has recently been reinterpreted (Manby 2007). In this case, the inner V-profiled ditch would have been replaced by a more substantial U-profiled ditch at the end of the early Iron Age. Such a double ditch would make Taplow much larger than most of the other ringworks, although the possible site at Mayfield Farm, some 160 m in diameter, would have been comparable, if it was indeed late Bronze Age (Lewis 2000). There are however no traces of palisades or other postholes associated with the outer ditch, as there were at Thwing, instead there are several inside the inner V-profiled ditch. While the area east of the U-profiled ditch may have been truncated to a greater degree than the area to the west, a small pit survived in this area, and the deeper postholes and the palisade found west of the inner V-profiled ditch should have survived as well. This suggests that the inner ditch formed the sole defensive line. It is also unclear why, if the outer ditch was already in existence before the U-profiled ditch was dug, the replacement inner U-profiled ditch should have been burnt, when there is no trace of such burning associated with the (admittedly limited) sections into the outer ditch. Even if the outer ditch had a dump rampart that could not have been burnt (and Cunliffe (1991) quotes examples of early dump ramparts as early as the 8th-6th century at sites such as Balksbury, Hants), there is no evidence that the outer defences were slighted. On present evidence the outer ditch does not appear to have been infilled until the early medieval period.

A second possibility, that the U-profiled ditch and the outer ditch were dug contemporarily, seems less likely. The outer ditch is V-profiled whereas the early Iron Age ditch is U-profiled, and the U-profiled ditch was accompanied by a timber-framed rampart of sorts, of which there is no trace next to the outer ditch, so the two are unlikely to have been dug contemporarily. The same objection regarding the burning of the rampart of the U-profiled ditch and the absence of similar burning, or slighting of the rampart, in the outer ditch is relevant here as in the previous sequence.

It thus seems more likely that the outer ditch was dug later than the U-profiled ditch (460), and would thus date to the 4th century BC or later. The most common style of ditch and rampart in the later part of the Iron Age was the glacis style, in which the ditch and bank formed one continuous slope, and the rampart was not revetted, although it may well have been topped by a palisade. This may well explain the wider ditch, the absence of any revetment alongside the outer ditch, and also the paucity of archaeological features found between the U-profiled and the outer ditch, as much of this area would have been taken up with the rampart.

This interpretation fits with the Anglo-Saxon finds, which show that the U-profiled ditch and much of its rampart survived as visible features within the outer defences. It is possible that the burning of the timber-laced rampart did not constitute the end of use of the U-profiled ditch as a defence, in which case the hillfort would have been multivallate (see Fig. 5.6C). Multivallation is generally a later feature usually dating from the 1st century BC (Cunliffe 1991), although there are exceptions which could be earlier (eg Rainsborough, Avery *et al.* 1967).

The early Iron Age hiatus

The available absolute dates suggest that the formation of the standstill layer (1102) in the top of the late Bronze Age V-profiled ditch (574) may have taken as much as 230 years, though more likely 130 years. There is very little evidence from the interior of the hillfort for activity in this period, which spans much of the early Iron Age, though only a small part of the interior lay within the excavated area. Rather more early Iron Age pottery was found in the TCAST trenches to the south of the main excavation, but there is no indication of significant early Iron Age settlement in the immediate vicinity. About 1 km to the east of the site, however, excavations along the Taplow to Dorney pipeline have uncovered a large pit cluster settlement (see Fig. 11.1), possibly bounded by ditches, that appears to date from the very late Bronze Age and early Iron Age (Coleman and Collard 2006; Hart and Mudd forthcoming). This settlement, which may have been enclosed, is unusual for the area, and its scale (at least 100 m long) may indicate some element of centralised storage, although in the Upper Thames valley large numbers of storage pits can be found on settlements such as Gravelly Guy, Stanton Harcourt, Oxfordshire that were occupied by relatively small groups (Lambrick and Allen 2004). Otherwise evidence for early Iron Age activity in the local area is small-scale. Most of the Iron Age settlement activity found at the Eton Rowing Course, at Cippenham (Ford 2003) and at Agars Plough east of Eton (Catherall and Foreman 2000, 21-2) dates from the middle and late Iron Age, although a group of early Iron Age pits was found at Lake End Road West (Foreman 1998, 29), possibly accompanied by a group of ditched fields, and an unenclosed settlement within the Rowing Course was of early-middle Iron Age date. Wooden bridges, pottery and human bones were also found in a palaeochannel of the Thames at the Eton Rowing Course (Allen and Welsh 1997, 31-4; Allen and Welsh 1998, 80-83). It is tempting to relate this to the environmental evidence suggesting the formation of heathland discussed above. Although this likely to have affected only a small part of the available land, a decline in agricultural productivity at the margin may have had wider consequences.

Despite the large amount of archaeological work in this area in recent years, however, this is still too little to generalise about any phase of later prehistory with any confidence. On the basis of the excavated sample of the local area, continuity of settlement during the millennium from the middle Bronze Age to the middle Iron Age, whether from the middle to late Bronze Age, late Bronze Age to early Iron Age or early to middle Iron Age, is very patchy. Only one likely example of a settlement of the late Bronze Age succeeding one of the middle Bronze Age, that at Weir Bank Stud Farm south of the river at Bray, has been demonstrated (Barnes *et al.* 1995); the significant middle Bronze Age activity at the Eton Rowing Course, at Marsh Lane East and West and at Cippenham, is not followed by similar levels of activity in the late Bronze Age, while new late Bronze Age foci emerge at Lot's Hole, at Widbrook Common (Barclay *et al.* forthcoming), and at Eton Wick (Ford 1993). None of these sites shows significant early Iron Age activity, although low-level activity of the early Iron Age is present at Lake End Road West (Foreman 1998, 29), and a new early Iron Age focus emerges east of Taplow on the Taplow to Dorney pipeline (Hart and Mudd forthcoming). There is little evidence of middle Iron Age activity at Lake End Road West following the early Iron Age (Foreman 1998, 29), and the middle-late Iron Age enclosed settlements at Eton Rowing Course, Cippenham and Agars Plough do not appear to have significant early Iron Age antecedents. The evidence therefore appears to indicate a tendency for settlements to shift over time within the local area (although some elements of the landscape such as fields may remain unchanged), but not necessarily any significant discontinuity in population numbers.

The significance of re-use

Given the apparent hiatus in the early Iron Age, should the Iron Age hillfort be seen as the elaboration of an existing defensive enclosure or as a new foundation? The late Bronze Age V-profiled ditch (574) had largely filled before the Iron Age defences were constructed. The extent of the standstill layer, which ran beyond the sloping edge of the ditch on both sides, suggests that when this layer formed there was only a very shallow hollow in the ditch top, otherwise the layer would not have accumulated beyond the slope of the ditch. The corduroy of timbers laid along the base of the rampart upon the standstill layer also implies that the standstill layer did not dip far into the underlying ditch, or these would not have formed a suitable foundation for the rampart. It is likely that the weight of the rampart of the U-profiled ditch subsequently compacted the fills of the V-profiled ditch below, causing the standstill layer to slump into the ditch.

Despite the almost complete disappearance of the late Bronze Age defensive ditch, however, the line of the former ditch would still have been very visible, forming a broad if shallow clayey silt band that would have held water whenever it rained, becoming wet and treacherous. As discussed above, calculation of the width of the berm between the V-profiled ditch and its rampart makes it unlikely that a large proportion of the rampart had slipped back into the ditch, and even though there was gravel in some of the upper fills of the ditch, the proportion of gravel was not sufficient to indicate slighted rampart material. It is therefore plausible that much of the rampart remained intact behind the silt-filled hollow, a visual reminder of the former defences. It is also possible that one or more lines of posts remained outside the V-profiled ditch and beyond the standstill layer, though these may all have rotted by the early Iron Age.

Most compelling, however, is the fact that the line of the U-profiled ditch ran parallel to that of the V-profiled ditch, and that its rampart overlay the earlier ditch line, all along the east side of the hillfort, and that the entrance into both was at the same point on the east side. The most plausible explanation for this is that the new defences, which were more substantial than those of the late Bronze Age, took advantage of the existing rampart by digging the new ditch just outside the old line, piling the upcast as a rampart on top, and using the old rampart to retain the new upcast at the back. This would also have done away with the need for revetting timbers at the rear of the rampart. It is possible that some of the earlier rampart was spread when constructing the new one, thus explaining the residual late Bronze Age pottery within the later rampart.

This is not to imply that the early Iron Age hillfort enclosed exactly the same area as the late Bronze Age hilltop enclosure, as we only have evidence for the line of the former ditch along the east and northeast sides of the late Bronze Age enclosure, and it is uncertain whether the early Iron Age ditch continued south beyond the south-eastern corner of the earlier enclosure. The broader evidence for the reuse of late Bronze Age hilltop enclosures in the Iron Age varies. Some, such as Rams Hill and Castle Hill, Little Wittenham, Oxfordshire, were on sites that did become Iron Age hillforts (Bradley and Ellison 1975; Allen *et al.* in prep. b), although in both cases there is evidence for a probable hiatus, while others (eg Fairfield and Carshalton; Webley *et al.* forthcoming; Adkins and Needham 1985) were not. The sequence of development may therefore have depended upon local factors.

The extent of the Iron Age hillfort

To the north, two ditches likely to represent the continuations of the V-profiled and U-profiled ditches were found in WA Trenches 3 and 4 (see Fig. 2.2). These suggest that that the U-profiled ditch and its bank continued to follow closely the line of the preceding Bronze Age ditch for some distance north of the entrance, and were turning back north-westwards towards the edge of the escarpment. The magnetometer survey suggests that the U-profiled ditch curves gradually north-west towards the terrace edge (Chapter 10, Fig. 10.3). To the south, the 1st and 2nd edition Ordnance Survey maps (1874 and 1899) show two linear earthworks running east-west to the south of the Taplow mound, and turning to the north at their western end. It seems unlikely that these earthworks were related to the V- or U-profiled ditches since the earthworks seem to extend too far to the east, and, the survey to the south of Taplow Court did not indicate the ditch below the church continuing southwards (see Chapter 10). The earthworks recorded on the OS maps may have been much later, more superficial features.

A more likely match is provided by the north-south aligned ditch which Rutland observed in 1853 running below the church (BRO D/X/748/9; VCH Bucks 1, 199; cited in Scrimgeour and Farley 1987, 5). This ditch is likely to be a continuation of the Iron Age defences, although whether it was a continuation of the U-profiled or the outer ditch is unclear. Based on the limited information available, suggested lines for the Bronze Age and Iron Age ditch circuits are given on Fig. 11.1, but plainly these can do no more than suggest an order of magnitude.

The increase in the extent of the hillfort indicated by the large ditch found under the Norman church may belong either with the U-profiled ditch or with the outer V-profiled ditch circuit.

Taplow Court and other local hillforts

The hillfort at Taplow Court is one of a row of hillforts running along the southern edge of the Chilterns, consisting of Bulstrode Park, 10 km to the east, Danesfield Camp and States House Camp around 10 km to the west, and Bozedown a further 20 km west, to the south of the Goring Gap (Fig. 11.3; Hogg 1979 and Ordnance Survey 1962). These sites could be seen as forming a group comparable to that running along the northern edge of the Berkshire Downs (eg Blewburton, Segsbury, Rams Hill, Uffington and Alfred's Castle: Miles *et al.* 2003). None of the hillforts near to Taplow Court has been excavated on any scale, and their chronology is virtually unknown. It is, therefore, impossible to compare the sequence of development of these hillforts with each other and with those elsewhere. The dates for the U-profiled ditch at Taplow Court suggest that it was established later than most of the Berkshire Downs hillforts (Miles *et al.* 2003), at a time when the distribution of hillforts in Wessex, more generally, was beginning to become consolidated into a smaller number of larger sites (Cunliffe 1991). The use of a timber-laced rampart at Taplow Court may also have been among the later occurrences of such ramparts, yet still predates the widespread construction of dump ramparts beginning in the 4th century BC (Avery 1993; Cunliffe 1991).

Internal features

The difficulties of relating features within the hillforts to the defences have already been discussed above. There it was suggested that much of the activity within the hillfort seemed to belong to the late Bronze Age. The proportion of the pottery from within the hillfort that can be dated to the Iron Age is small, and only a few postholes can be confidently assigned to the Iron Age, although these may also indicate that one roundhouse is Iron Age in date. What evidence there is nevertheless appears to suggest that activity within the hillfort in the Iron Age was limited. Elsewhere along the Thames Valley both hillforts with evidence for dense occupation and others with little evidence for internal activity in the Iron Age are known (eg Cherbury Camp; Bradford 1940 or Rams Hill and White Horse Hill; Bradley and Ellison 1975, Miles *et al.* 2003), and there is no reason to make assumptions about the expected level of activity within the hillfort. The presence of a large settlement on the Taplow pipeline, with evidence of occupation in both the early and middle Iron Age, may indicate that, as at Castle Hill, Little Wittenham (Allen *et al.* 2006, 259-60), settlement lay close to, but largely outside the hillfort. Given the small proportion of the enlarged Iron Age defended area that has been examined, however, it is difficult to draw any firm conclusions from this regarding the use of its interior or its role in the surrounding region.

Taplow Court in relation to local Iron Age settlement

The evidence for Iron Age settlement found in other local excavations, on the Taplow to Dorney pipeline, at Cippenham, along the Jubilee River and at the Eton Rowing Course, is now considerable, although only a small fraction of the surrounding area has been examined (see Fig. 11.3). While continuity between late Bronze Age and early Iron Age activity is not general, evidence from the Eton Rowing Course and from Lake End Road West suggests that field systems continued in use (Allen *et al.* in prep. b). The more extensive early-middle Iron Age evidence consists of field systems, scattered round-houses, four-posters and pits (at Lake End Road West and Area 15 at the Eton Rowing Course) and suggests a pattern of occupation not very different from that in the late Bronze Age. Towards the end of the middle Iron Age enclosed settlements were established at both Cippenham and the Eton Rowing Course (Ford 2003; Allen *et al.* 1997), with group of enclosures or fields of late Iron Age and Roman date at Lake End Road West (Foreman 1998, 29) and Agars Plough ((Catherall and Foreman 2000). At Perry Oaks, however, a nucleated middle Iron Age settlement was established, mirroring the development of more nucleated and more stable settlements in the Iron Age in the Upper Thames Valley.

The sequence of development at the hillfort seems generally to correspond to shifts in the wider settlement pattern in the area around Taplow, the end of the earlier defences corresponding to one shift in settlement, and the refortification of the hilltop corresponding to another in the early-middle Iron Age, perhaps following a phase of nucleation at the extended pit settlement east of Taplow. Whether the Thames formed a significant boundary in the earlier Iron Age, and how this might have affected the defensive sequence, is unclear. The distribution of late Iron Age coins (Sellwood 1984) suggests that by the late Iron Age the Thames did form a boundary (the area around Taplow lying roughly at the boundary of the distribution of Atrebatic and Cunobelin coins).

In discussing the late Bronze Age settlement it was suggested that the construction of the hilltop defences was related to changes in the organisation of warfare. Such changes are likely to have been related to wider changes in society. The development of more stable patterns of settlement and political geographies may well have increased the potential to organise large military forces. There is, however, little evidence that Iron Age sites other than hillforts were attacked, and it thus seems that, as in the late Bronze Age, the context of warfare was constrained, and perhaps focused upon significant centres. In this context it is striking that the rampart associated with the U-profiled ditch was burnt.

The burnt rampart and entrance features

The burning of the rampart led to the preservation of details of its timber-laced construction that have been discussed above. The issue of whether the burnt gravel deposits surrounding the charred timbers have remained *in situ* has already been discussed. The burnt deposits and charred timbers provide evidence for what seems to have been the deliberate destruction of at least parts of the rampart. Recent scholarship has tended to downplay the role of defence in the interpretation of hillforts, and has stressed the wider potential significance of their boundary features (Hingley 1990; Bowden and McOmish 1985; 1989; Hamilton and Manley 2001). However, the discovery of the burnt rampart at Taplow Court could be seen as underlining the reality of their defensive role – that hillforts were attacked and destroyed- and that defence must have been a highly significant influence upon the design and location (Avery 1986; 1993).

A case could be made for the suggestion that the rampart was burnt not as the result of an attack but for other, perhaps ritual reasons (Bowden and McOmish 1985; Cunliffe 2004, 96). Fires may, for example, be used as a means of purification (Hubert and Mauss 1964; Hocart 1970). One more prosaic possibility is that the timber-laced rampart was fired because it had begun to collapse. In support of this it could be pointed out that there is no other evidence – such as slingstones or other weapons – to suggest that the hillfort had been attacked, although this is not conclusive. However, the burning of the entrance would seem unnecessary even if the rampart was being remodelled, unless this was a necessary part of the purification of the site beforehand.

The firing of ramparts was at one time associated with the `vitrified' forts of Scotland and others in Northern England. More recently, a number of other burnt ramparts have been found along the Thames Valley and in neighbouring areas, occurring at, for example, Burroway (Lambrick with Robinson 2009), Bladon Round Hill (Ainslie 1988), Leckhampton (Champion 1976), Crickley Hill (Dixon 1994) and Rainsborough (Avery 1986; see also Avery 1993, 43 for further examples). At all of these sites the burning was widespread and extensive, at Crickley Hill turning the limestone rampart core into a `meringue' (Dixon 1994). It may not be coincidental that all of these other sites (other than Bladon, where only an exposed section was seen) are also forts where a corduroy of timbers was used at the base of the rampart (Lambrick 1984; Avery 1993, 44; Lambrick with Robinson 2009). Only particular arrangements of timber would have allowed the generation of the necessary temperatures for this to occur. The frequency of such finds does not prove either way whether the fires resulted from attacks or ritual. However, at Crickley Hill, the interior buildings were also burnt, and it seems easiest to view attack as the most likely cause in this and the other cases.

Multivallation

The evidence for the survival of both the inner and outer Iron Age defensive ditches to a depth of nearly 2 m, plus the fact that rampart material was still eroding into the inner ditch during the Saxon occupation, strongly suggests that the inner ditch and its rampart remained substantial defences throughout the middle to late Iron Age and Roman periods, and that Taplow had been a multivallate hillfort (see Fig. 5.9). Due to the fairly level ground upon which the hillfort was built, using all of the spoil to make the highest bank possible would have made the outer bank slightly higher than the inner one, which is defensively less advantageous. It is alternatively possible that the upcast from the outer ditch was spread over most of the area between the inner and outer ditch, creating a lower bank, or that some of the spoil was added to the bank of the inner ditch, although the distribution of Saxon material from the interior of the hillfort makes this last suggestion less likely.

Multivallate forts are rare in the middle Thames valley, although the nearest neighbour, Bulstrode Park, is also multivallate (Fig. 11.3). Due to the absence of further dating or detail for either site, nothing more can be said at present.

The Anglo-Saxon period

The Anglo-Saxon evidence from these excavations, although scant, has a special significance because of its local context, both in that it occurred within the still visible ditches of the Iron Age hillfort, and in relation to the princely burial under the Taplow Mound, and also in the wider context in relation to the exceptional sites found along the Jubilee river (Foreman *et al.* 2002).

The Taplow Mound

The Taplow mound, reconstituted after its excavation, stands 4 m tall and 21 m wide (Stocker *et al.* 1995, 441), and lies 160 m south of the excavations. Excavations of the mound in 1882 (Rutland 1885; Geake 1997, 146; Stocker *et al.* 1995) revealed a poorly preserved skeleton associated with an extremely rich assemblage of grave goods: clothing represented by gold braid, a large gold buckle and two clasps; weaponry consisting of two shields, a sword and three spearheads; a varied collection of vessels and cups, including a 'Coptic' bowl, a bronze cauldron in which two large decorated drinking horns were found – two further horns was found elsewhere – two bronze and iron-bound buckets, four glass claw-beakers and the silver rims of two wooden cups; as well as a lyre and gaming pieces. The burial dates from the late 6th century or the first half of the 7th and was thus probably roughly contemporary with the inhumation burial (105) found during the recent excavations, and with the earliest phases of Anglo-Saxon deposition in the old hillfort ditches.

Status and occupation: the finds from the hillfort ditches

Certain aspects of the debris found in the hillfort ditches hint at high status occupation which would fit with the burial: the high proportion of deer bones, the bronze pin (although this may have derived from a disturbed burial), and most noticeably a sherd possibly imported from the eastern Mediterranean. In general, however, the finds consist of the everyday debris that could be found on both high status and more lowly sites. They include not only an assortment of animal bones, but also crop processing waste and charcoal. The crop processing debris includes weeds that suggest the crops derive from a wide area including wet ground, perhaps below the hillfort nearer to the river. The charcoal also includes a range of species including beech and oak, but also possibly coppiced hazel and willow or poplar, again suggesting exploitation of a wide area including the riverside.

Overall, this evidence suggests that the debris derives from domestic occupation, even though no direct evidence for any structures was found. It also seems likely, however, that the site drew in resources from a quite wide area, extending beyond the immediate surroundings. It is, of course, impossible to determine whether this represents production based at the site itself or tributes extracted from other sites.

A small number of artefacts provide further evidence for wider links, and underline the possible significance of the river as a trade route. These finds include the lava quern fragments which are also common at Lake End Road West close to the river (Roe 2002, 37-39). The most striking import, however, is the possibly eastern Mediterranean sherd.

The eastern Mediterranean sherd and connections with Kent

The presence of eastern Mediterranean pottery is most often associated with late Celtic settlements in south-western Britain (Thomas 1988; Fulford 1989; Campbell 1996; Harris 2003) as is the re-use of hillforts (Burrow 1981; Dark 1994). Such pottery, and the re-use of hillforts, is rare elsewhere (Huggett 1988; Harris 2003; Halsall 1989; Fowler 1971; Williams 1997 and 1998). These two features thus seem to relate Taplow Court to the British south-west, and perhaps suggest lingering British influence in an area which may have remained British territory till a late date (Hawkes 1986, 73). In fact, however, there are reasons to doubt the significance of these possible relationships. The re-use of the hillfort is discussed further below. Here it is worth noting that what evidence there is for the date of the eastern Mediterranean sherd suggests that it was later in date than the imports found in the south-west. The eastern Mediterranean pottery imported into the south-west seems to belong to a quite restricted period, c AD 475 – 550 (Campbell 1996; Thomas 1988; Fulford 1989). The sherd at Taplow Court cannot be accurately dated (although the class 44 amphorae to which it was initially compared are dated by Peacock and Williams (1986) to a period extending from the early 5th century to the mid 7th century). However, wheat from the same context gave a date of AD 670-870, and thus suggests that the deposition, at least, of the sherd occurred some time after the main period of imports into the south-west.

Although the single sherd at Taplow Court seems insignificant in relation to the much larger quantities found in the south-west, it can be related to wider patterns of exchange. The sherd can be matched in the Taplow Mound by the eastern Mediterranean 'Coptic' bowl in the burial. This bowl (Harris 2003), as well as the distribution of other categories of imports from the eastern Mediterranean not represented at Taplow (Huggett 1988), suggest connections with Kent. Many of the remaining grave goods from the mound can also be traced back to Kent. The sherd thus lends further weight to the connections to the south-east (rather than the south-west) suggested by the grave goods. It is these finds which provide the basis for seeing 'Taeppa', or whoever was buried at Taplow, as a Kentish prince or an ally of the Kentish king (Hawkes 1986, 85).

Anglo-Saxon re-use of the hillfort

The suggestion of a Kentish prince or ally, ruling a small local territory, also provides a significant context in which to understand the re-use of the hillfort. It is clear from the distribution of Anglo-Saxon finds in the Iron Age hillfort ditches that the ditches survived as features up to 2 m deep in the Anglo-Saxon period. The condition of the associated ramparts is uncertain, but it is nonetheless clear that the ditches were still significant features that would have impeded movement around the site.

No evidence for Anglo-Saxon structures was found. A few postholes within the post-rows contained charcoal that gave Anglo-Saxon radiocarbon date, but the material is believed to be intrusive. The only other candidate is the undated foundation trench 846 (see Fig. 6.3). Although post-in-trench construction is a known Saxon building technique, the small size and rhomboidal shape of this structure are difficult to parallel. It is possible that the trench originally lay around the edge of a sunken-floored building that had been truncated; examples of such trenches are known from the early Saxon period (Chapelot and Fossier 1985). Even then, however, the structure has an irregular shape. Alternatively this could have been a later structure, perhaps similar to medieval structure 9160 found south-west of Great Barford, Bedfordshire (Timby *et al.* 2007, 175-6 and fig. 6.11). This was a continuous wall-trench forming a structure 6 m wide but with rounded ends like those of structure 846, and was interpeted as an agricultural structure, perhaps a sheep pen (ibid., 207). The position of structure 846 at Taplow across the entrance to the hillfort might support such a date, after the ditches had finally been infilled.

The high frequency with which Anglo-Saxon sites – and in particular burial sites – re-use prehistoric monuments has been widely noted (Williams 1997; 1998). Most of these prehistoric monuments were barrows. Re-use of hillforts seems to have been rare (Williams 1997). The closest parallel for Taplow Court is at Blewburton Hill (Collins 1947; 1953; Collins and Collins 1959; Harding 1976) where 18 Anglo-Saxon inhumations and 2 cremation burials were found – all positioned, as the inhumation at Taplow was, within the entrance to the hillfort. Anglo-Saxon burials, probably slightly earlier in date (late 5th-6th century AD) seem also to have been placed on the side of the Lyneham Camp hillfort (Dickinson 1976).

In contrast to the situation in the south-west, none of these hillforts appears to have been renovated in the Anglo-Saxon period. The only features found at Taplow that might have been associated with an attempt at renovation were a pit (796) and a posthole (719) at the entrance. Although these features appear to post-date the burning of the Iron Age rampart associated the U-profiled ditch, there is no other indication of their date, and they may be related to a rebuilding of the Iron Age defences, rather than with a Saxon refortification of the hillfort.

The fact that the ditches were used to deposit rubbish may indicate that maintenance of the ditches was not a high priority, although insufficient of the outer ditch has been examined to generalise about it, and the gradual infilling of the inner ditch may not have mattered as long as the outer ditch remained open. The presence of a small sherd of Cotswold-type ware in one of the lower Saxon fills in one section of the U-profiled ditch may indicate that some of the Anglo-Saxon debris was redeposited in the ditches at a late phase of the occupation, implying that the ditches had remained quite conspicuous throughout much of the Anglo-Saxon occupation. It is however also possible that this sherd came from the edge of this layer high up in the ditch, and was intrusive. Nevertheless, given the presence of a burial in the entrance (cf. Blewburton Hill, Oxfordshire), it is possible that the re-use of the hillfort was related more directly to the burials than to settlement. The mound itself probably stood near to the southern edge of the hillfort defences.

There may have been a connection between the re-use of a prehistoric site for burial and the exotic grave goods in the mound. Both imply a relationship with an 'other': the imported artefacts with an 'other', far away place, and the hillfort to an 'other' far away time. It is perhaps easiest to think of the re-use of prehistoric barrows and other sites as an attempt to legitimate authority or territorial claims by creating genealogical links to past generations. The connection need not, however, have been so simple. Sahlins (1985, chap. 3) has suggested that in many societies political power is viewed as being imposed from the outside. Kings are thus seen, in origin, as foreigners who usurp indigenous authority. The deposition of exotic grave goods with high status individuals could thus be seen as reflecting (and creating) an association with a far away place which was viewed as a source of political power. The use of barrows, if it was seen as related to barrows in the Anglo-Saxon homelands, might have had a similar significance. It is also possible, however, that the re-use of prehistoric monuments expressed the replacement or usurpation of local power.

Whatever the case, it seems that Anglo-Saxon burials were used for political purposes (Lucy 1992). Furthermore, especially in the 7th century, they were placed at boundaries (Goodier 1984). Along the Middle and Upper Thames Valley it is worth noting that the richest burials – Asthall, Cuddesdon and Taplow – were placed near to rivers (Booth *et al.* 2007). This may have been related to the importance of the Thames as a political boundary and as a trade route. In the case of Taplow, the burial and settlement may, therefore, have been deliberately placed near to what may have been a disputed boundary between the *Cilternsæte* and the *Sunningas* (Foreman *et al.* 2002; Bailey 1989; Blair 1989).

Taplow and the wider Anglo-Saxon context

The political significance of this area is also highlighted by the discoveries made along the Jubilee River (Foreman *et al.* 2002). At Lake End Road West there was no evidence for structures, but a number of large pits were found that – alongside more prosaic debris such as chaff-tempered pottery, animal bones and charred plant remains – contained imported pottery including North French wares, Tating ware and Ipswich ware, fragments of Anglo-Saxon glass, a large assemblage of Niedermendig lava fragments and some other imported stone, and evidence for metalworking. The character of activity at this site was interpreted as the site of a temporary meeting place, market or fair. The possible date range of the finds stretches from the 7th to the 9th centuries AD, although the authors of the report suggest that the finds could derive from a much shorter period of activity in the 8th century, and possibly the mid-8th century. The activity thus probably post-dates the burial in the Taplow mound but would have been contemporary with the later Anglo-Saxon occupation of the Taplow Court hillfort. An association can now be suggested between the location of this trading place and the high status residence adjacent to the princely burial mound, reinforcing the links between the Saxon settlement within the former hillfort and the lower-lying ground close to the Thames indicated by the environmental evidence. The later medieval parish of Taplow, like most along the southern edge of the Chilterns, was one of a series of long narrow north-south strips including both the plateau and the lower-lying gravel terraces below, and stretched alongside the Thames almost to the site of the `fair' (Foreman *et al.* 2002, fig. 2.3). This pattern of land-use is likely to have originated during the Saxon period.

There is a broad parallel between developments at this site and those at Sutton Courtenay, discussed by Hamerow (Hamerow *et al.* 2007). At Sutton Courtenay the evidence of sunken-featured buildings suggests that settlement began in the 6th century and continued into the 7th, during which large timber halls were constructed. The evidence of fine metalwork suggests that high status burials took place in the area at the end of 6th or early in the 7th century. Finds of coins suggest that the site was used a market or meeting place early in the 8th century. Although the kinds of evidence at Taplow are in some respects quite different from that at Sutton Courtenay, the overall sequence is similar. The hillfort seems to have been occupied as a settlement in the 6th century and was the location of high status burial late in the 6th or early in the 7th century. To this, the evidence from the Jubilee River adds indications of a market or meeting place in the 8th century.

Bibliography

Adkins, L, and Needham, S, 1985 New research on a late Bronze Age enclosure at Queen Mary's Hospital, Carshalton, *Surrey Archaeol Collect* **76**, 11-50

Ainslie, R, 1988 Bladon Round Castle 1987, *South Midlands Archaeology* **18**, 94

Aitken, M J, 1985 Thermoluminescence Dating, *Studies in Archaeological Science* London

Allen, T, 1995 Dorney, Eton College Rowing Lake: 1994 evaluation, *South Midlands Archaeol* **25**, 29-31

Allen, T, 2000 Dorney, Eton Rowing Lake: Fourth Interim Report, *South Midlands Archaeol* **30**, 21

Allen, T G, Anderson, L, Barclay, A, Parker, A G, Robinson, M A, in prep. a) *Opening the wood, making the land: the archaeology of a Middle Thames landscape, Mesolithic to early Bronze Age*, Oxford Archaeology Thames Valley Landscapes Monograph

Allen, T, Barclay, A, and Lamdin-Whymark, H, 2004 Opening the wood, making the land: the study of a Neolithic landscape in the Dorney area of the Middle Thames Valley, in J Cotton and D Field (eds),*Towards a New Stone Age: aspects of the Neolithic in south-east England*, CBA Res. Rep. **137**, 82-98

Allen, T G, Bradley, P, Cromarty, A-M, Parker, A G, and Robinson, M A, in prep. b) Bridging the river, dividing the land: *the archaeology of a Middle Thames landscape, Middle Bronze Age to Roman*, Oxford Archaeology Thames Valley Landscapes Monograph

Allen, T, Cramp, K, Lamdin-Whymark, H, and Webley, L, 2006 Castle Hill and its landscape, Little Wittenham, Oxfordshire. Report upon the archaeological investigations 2002-2006, unpublished client report for the Northmoor Trust, Little Wittenham

Allen, T, Hacking, P, and Boyle, A, 2000 Eton rowing course at Dorney Lake: the burial traditions, *Tarmac Papers* **4**, 65-106

Allen, T G, and Lamdin-Whymark, H, 2000 The rediscovery of Taplow Hillfort, *South Midlands Archaeol* **30**, 22-28

Allen, T, and Lamdin-Whymark, H, 2005 Little Wittenham, Excavations at and around Castle Hill, *South Midlands Archaeol* **35**, 69-82

Allen, T, Lamdin-Whymark, H, and Maricevic, D, 2006 Taplow, Taplow Court (Phase 2), Cliveden Road, *South Midlands Archaeol* **36**, 19-21

Allen, T, and Mitchell, N, 2001 Dorney, Eton Rowing Lake: Fifth Interim Report, *South Midlands Archaeol* **31**, 26-30

Allen, T, and Welsh, K, 1997 Eton Rowing Lake, Dorney, Buckinghamshire. Second Interim Report, *South Midlands Archaeol* **27**, 25-34

Allen, T, and Welsh, K, 1998 Eton Rowing Lake, Dorney, Buckinghamshire. Third Interim Report, *South Midlands Archaeol* **28**, 75-84

Ashmore, P, 1999 Radiocarbon dating: avoiding errors by avoiding mixed samples, *Antiquity* **73**, 124–30

Avery, M, 1986 'Stoning and fire' at hillfort entrances of southern Britain, *World Archaeology* **18/2**, 216-30

Avery, M, 1993 *Hillfort defences of southern Britain*, BAR Brit Ser **231**, Oxford

Avery, M, Sutton, J E G, and Banks, J W, 1967 Rainsborough, Northants, England: excavations 1961-5, *Proc Prehist Soc* **33**, 207-306

Bailey, K, 1989 The middle Saxons, in *The origins of Anglo-Saxon kingdoms* (S Basset ed.), Leicester, 108-22

Ball, T B, Gardner, J S, and Anderson, N, 1999, Identifying inflorescence phytoliths from selected species of wheat (*Triticum monococcum, T. dicoccum, T. aestivum*) and barley (*Hordeum vulgare* and *H. spontaneum*) (Gramineae), *American Journal of Botany* **86**, 1615-23

Bamford, H M, 1985 *Briar Hill excavation 1974-1978*, Northampton Development Corporation Archaeol Mono **3**, Northampton

Barber, M, 2003 *Bronze and the Bronze Age*, Stroud

Barclay, A, and Halpin, C, 1999 *Excavations at Barrow Hills, Radley, Oxfordshire: Volume 1 The Neolithic and Bronze Age Monument Complex* Thames Valley Landscapes Monograph **11**, Oxford

Barclay, A, Lambrick, G, Moore, J, and Robinson, M, 2003 *Lines in the landscape: cursus monuments in the Upper Thames Valley – excavations at the Drayton and Lechlade cursuses*, Thames Valley Landscapes **15**, Oxford

Barker, G, 1985 *Prehistoric Farming in Europe* Cambridge

Barnes, I, and Cleale, R M J, 1995 pottery in Barnes et al.1995

Barnes, I, Boismier, W A, Cleale, R M J, Fitzpatrick, Roberts, M R, 1995 *Early settlement in Berkshire: Mesolithic-Roman occupation in the Thames and Kennet Valleys*, Wessex Archaeology Report **6**, Salisbury

Barrett, J, 1980 The pottery of the later Bronze Age in lowland England. In *Proc Prehist Soc* **46**, 297-320

Barrett, J C, 1994 *Fragments from antiquity: an archaeology of social life in Britain, 2900-1200 BC*, Oxford

Barrett, J, and Bradley, R (eds), 1980 *Settlement and society in the British later Bronze Age*, BAR Brit Ser **83**, Oxford

Barrett, J, Bradley, R, and Green, M, 1991 *Landscape, monuments and society: the prehistory of Cranborne Chase*, Cambridge

Bates, W E, and Stanley, C C, 1985 Excavations at the Late Roman and Early Saxon site at Bray, Berkshire, 1969-71, unpublished manuscript

Beard, M, North, J, and Price, S, 1998 *Religions of Rome*, Cambridge

Bell, M, Fowler, P J, and Hillson, S W, (eds) 1996 *The experimental earthwork project, 1960-1992*, CBA Res Rep **100**, London

Bendrey, R, 2007 The development of new methodologies for studying the horse: case studies from prehistoric southern England, Unpublished PhD thesis, University of Southampton

Biddulph, E, unpubl. Ceramic material from Field 4, report prepared for the Datchet Village Society

Bird, J, and Bird, D G (eds), 1987 *The archaeology of Surrey to 1540*, Guildford

Blackmore, L, 1988 The Anglo-Saxon Pottery in R L Whytehead and R Cowie with L Blackmore Two Middle Saxon Occupation Sites: Excavations at Jubilee Hall and 21-22 Maiden Lane *Trans London Middlesex Archaeol Soc* **39**, 81-110

Blackmore, L, 1989 The Anglo-Saxon Pottery in R L Whytehead and R Cowie with L Blackmore Excavations at the Peabody site, Chandos Place and the National Gallery *Trans London Middlesex Archaeol Soc* **40**, 71-107

Blair, J, 1989 Frithuwold's kingdom and the origins of Surrey, in *The origins of Anglo-Saxon kingdoms* (S Basset ed), Leicester, 97-107

Blinkhorn, P W, 2002 The Anglo-Saxon Pottery in S Foreman, J Hiller and D Petts *Gathering the People, settling the land. The Archaeology of a Middle Thames Landscape*, Oxford Archaeology Thames Valley Landscapes Monograph **14**, 35 and CD-ROM

Blinkhorn, P W, 2007 The Anglo-Saxon Pottery in R Chambers and E McAdam *Excavation at Barrow Hills, Radley, Oxon. Volume 2: The Romano-British cemetery and Anglo-Saxon Settlement*, Oxford Archaeology Thames Valley Landscapes Monograph **25**, 229-48

Blinkhorn, P W, forthcoming The post-Roman pottery in D Stansbie, R Brown, T Allen and A Hardy, The excavation of Iron Age ditches and a medieval farmstead at Allcourt Farm, Little London, Lechlade, 1999, *Trans Bristol Gloucestershire Archaeol Soc*

Bloch, M, 1992 *Prey into hunter: the politics of religious experience*, Cambridge

Boessneck, J, 1969 Osteological Differences in Sheep (*Ovis aries* Linné) and Goat (*Capra hircus* Linné), in D Brothwell and E Higgs (eds), *Science in Archaeology*, London, 331-358

Boessneck, J, and von den Driesch, A, 1974 Kritische Anmerkingen zur Widerristhöhenberechnung aus Längenmassen vor und frühgeschichtlicher Tierknochen, *Saugetierkdl Mitt* **22**(4), 325-48

Boismier, W A, 1995 An analysis of worked flint concentrations from Maidenhead Thicket, Maidenhead, in I Barnes *et. al. Early Settlement in Berkshire; Mesolithic – Roman occupation in the Thames and Kennet Valleys*. Wessex Archaeology Report No. **6** Wessex Archaeology

Bond, D, 1988 *Excavation at the North Ring, Mucking, Essex*, Chelmsford, E. Anglian Archaeol **43**

Booth, P, 1995 Iron Age and Roman pottery, in *Early settlement in Berkshire: Mesolithic-Roman occupation sites in the Thames and Kennet Valleys* (I Barnes, W A Boismier, R M J Cleal, A P Fitzpatrick, and M R Roberts), Wessex Archaeology Report **6**, Salisbury, 106-117

Booth, P, Dodd, A, Robinson, M, and Smith, A, 2007 *The Thames through time: the archaeology of the gravel terraces of the Upper and Middle Thames*, **3**, *The early historical period: Rome and the Anglo-Saxons in the Thames Valley, AD 1-1000*, Thames Valley Landscapes, Oxford

Booth, P, nd Oxford Archaeology Roman pottery recording system: an introduction, Oxford Archaeology, unpublished

Bowden, M, and McOmish D, 1985 The required barrier, *Scottish Archaeological Review* **4**, 78-84

Bowden, M, and McOmish D, 1989 Little boxes: more about hillforts, *Scottish Archaeological Review* **6**, 12-16

Boyer, P, 1997 Recurrence without transmission: the intuitive background of religious traditions, in *Present is past: some uses of tradition in native societies* (ed. M Mauze), Lanham

Bradford, J S P, 1940 The excavations of Cherbury Camp, *Oxoniensia* **5**, 13-20

Bradley, R, 1984 *The social foundations of prehistoric Britain*, Harlow

Bradley, R, and Ellison, A, 1975 *Rams Hill: a Bronze Age defended enclosure and its landscape*, BAR Brit Ser **19**, Oxford

Bradley, R, and Gordon, K, 1988 Human skulls from the river Thames: their dating and significance, *Antiquity* **62**, 503-9

Bradley, R, Lobb, S, Richard, J, and Robinson, M, 1980 Two Late Bronze Age settlements on the Kennet gravels: excavations at Aldermaston Wharf and Knight's Farm, Burghfield, Berkshire, *Proc Prehist Soc* **46**, 217-296

Bronk Ramsey, C, 1995 Radiocarbon calibration and analysis of stratigraphy, *Radiocarbon* **36**, 425–30

Bronk Ramsey, C, 1998 Probability and dating, *Radiocarbon* **40**, 461–74

Bronk Ramsey, C, 2001, Development of the Radiocarbon Program OxCal, *Radiocarbon*, **43** (2A) 355–363

Bronk Ramsey, C, and Hedges, R E M, 1997 Hybrid ion sources: radiocarbon measurements from microgram to milligram, *Nuclear*

Instruments and Methods in Physics Research B **123**, 539–45

Bronk Ramsey, C, Higham, T F G, Bowles, A, and Hedges, R E M, 2004 Improvements to the pretreatment of bone at Oxford, *Radiocarbon* **46**, 155–63

Bronk Ramsey, C, Pettitt, P B, Hedges, R E M, Hodgins, G W L, and Owen, D C, 2000 Radiocarbon dates from the Oxford AMS system: Archaeometry datelist 30, *Archaeometry* **42**, 259–79

Brossler, A, Early, R, and Allen, C, 2004 *Green Park (Reading Business Park). Phase 2 Excavations 1995 – Neolithic and Bronze Age Sites*, Thames Valley Landscapes Monograph **19**, Oxford

Brown, N, 1988 A late Bronze Age enclosure at Lofts Farm, Essex, *Proc Prehist Soc* **54**, 249-302

Brück, J, 1999a What's in a settlement? Domestic practice and residential mobility in early Bronze Age southern England, *Making places in the prehistoric world* (eds J Brück and M Goodman), London, 52-75

Brück, J, 1999b Houses, lifecycles and deposition on middle Bronze Age settlements in Southern England, *Proc Prehist Soc* **65**, 145-166

Buck, C E, Cavanagh, W G, and Litton, C D, 1996 *Bayesian Approach to Interpreting Archaeological Data*. Chichester

Buckley, D G, and Hedges J D, 1987 *The Bronze Age and Saxon settlements at Springfield Lyons, Essex: an interim report*, Essex County Council Occasional Paper **5**, Chelmsford

Burgess, C, 1986 `Urnes of no small variety': Collared Urns reviewed, *Proc Prehist Soc* **52**, 339-51

Burgess, C B, and Colquhoun, I, 1988 *The swords of Britain*, Prähistorische Bronzefunde **4/5**, Munich

Burrow, I, 1981 *Hillfort and hill-top settlement in Somerset in the first to eighth centuries AD*, BAR Brit Ser **91**, Oxford

Campbell, E, 1996 The archaeological evidence for external contacts: imports, trade and economy in Celtic Britain, in K R Dark (ed.) *External contacts and the economy of late Roman and post-Roman Britain*, Woodbridge

Canti, M, 1991 *Soil particle size analysis: a revised interpretative guide for excavators*. English Heritage Ancient Monuments Laboratory Reports, **1/91**

Canti, M G, and Linford, N, 2001 The effects of fire on archaeological soils and sediments: temperature and colour relationships *Proc Prehist Soc* **66**, 385-395

Care, V, 1982 The collection and distribution of lithic materials during the Mesolithic and Neolithic periods in southern England, *Oxford J Archaeol* **1**, 269-85

Carstairs, P, 1986 An archaeological study of the Dorney area, *Rec Buckinghamshire* **28**, 163-8

Case, H, Bayne, N, Steele, S, Avery, G, and Sutermeister, H, 1964/5 Excavations at City Farm, Hanborough, Oxon, *Oxoniensia* **29/30**, 1-98

Catherall, P, and Foreman, S, 2000 The Maidenhead, Windsor and Eton Flood Alleviation Scheme: Agars Plough excavation, *South Midlands Archaeol* **30**, 21-2

Challinor, D, 2004 Environmental remains – charcoal, in Taplow Court, Buckinghamshire: Post-Excavation Assessment and Updated Project Design, Oxford Archaeology, Appendix 12, 125-127

Champion, S, 1976 Leckhampton Hill, Gloucestershire, 1925 and 1970, in D W Harding (ed.) *Hillforts: later prehistoric earthworks in Britain and Ireland*, London, 171-81

Champion, T C, 1980 Settlement and environment in later Bronze Age Kent, in Barrett and Bradley (eds) 1980, 223-46

Champion, T C, 2007 Prehistoric Kent, in Williams, J (ed.) *The Archaeology of Kent to AD 800*, Kent History Project **8**, Kent County Council, 67-132

Chapelot, J, and Fossier, R, (trans. H Cleere) 1985 *The village and house in the Middle Ages*, London

Childe, V G, and Thorneycroft, W, 1937 The experimental production of the phenomena distinctive of vitrified forts, *Proc Soc Antiq Scot* **72**, 44-55

Chisholm, B S, Nelson, D E, and Schwarcz, H P 1982 Stable carbon isotope ratios as a measure of marine versus terrestrial protein in ancient diets, *Science,* **216**, 1131–32

Clapham, A R, Tutin, T G, and Moore, D M, 1987 *Flora of the British Isles* (3rd edition) Cambridge

Clutton-Brock, J, 1976 The Animal Resources, in D Wilson, *The Archaeology of Anglo-Saxon England*, Cambridge

Coleman, L, and Collard, M, 2005 Taplow to Dorney pipeline, Taplow, Buckinghamshire: Post-excavation assessment and updated project design, unpublished client report prepared for Thames Water Utilities Ltd by Cotswold Archaeology

Collins, A E P, and Collins F J, 1959 Excavations on Blewburton Hill, 1953, *Berkshire Archaeol J* **59**, 52–73

Collins, A E P, 1947 Excavations on Blewburton Hill, 1947, *Berkshire Archaeol J* **50**, 4–29

Collins, A E P, 1953 Excavations on Blewburton Hill, 1948 and 1949, *Berkshire Archaeol J* **56**, 21–59

Cotterell, B, and Kamminga, J, 1987 The formation of flakes, *American Antiquity* **52**, 675-708

Cotton, M A, and Frere, S S, 1968 Ivinghoe Beacon excavations, 1963-5, *Records of Bucks* **18**, 187-260

Cromarty, A M, Barclay, A, Lambrick, G, and Robinson, M, 2006 *Late Bronze Age ritual and habitation on a Thames eyot at Whitecross Farm, Wallingford: the archaeology of the Wallingford bypass, 1986-92*, Thames Valley Landscapes **22**, Oxford

Cummings, L S, 1992 Illustrated phytoliths from assorted food plants, in G Rapp Jr. and S C Mulholland (eds) *Phytolith Systematics- Emerging Issues*, New York, 175-192

Cunliffe, B, 1990 Before hillforts, *Oxford Journal of Archaeology* **9/3**, 323-36

Cunliffe, B, 1991 *Iron Age communities in Britain*, London

Cunliffe, B, 2004 *Iron Age Britain*, London

Czernik, J, and Goslar, T, 2001 Preparation of graphite targets in the Gliwice Radiocarbon Laboratory for AMS 14C dating, *Radiocarbon*, **43** (2A) 282–91

Dark, K R, 1994 *Civitas to kingdom: British political continuity, 300-800*, Leicester

Davies, B, Richardson, B, and Tomber, R, 1994 *A dated corpus of early Roman pottery from the City of London*, CBA Res Rep **98**, London

Dickinson, T M, 1976 The Anglo-Saxon burial sites of the Upper Thames region, and their bearing on the history of Wessex, c AD 400-700, unpubl. DPhil thesis, University of Oxford

Dixon, P, 1994 *Crickley Hill*, **1**, *The hillfort defences*, Nottingham

Douglas, M, 1954 The Lele of Kasai, in *African minds: studies in the cosmological ideas and social values of African peoples* (ed D Forde) Oxford, 1-26

Drennan, R D, 1997 *Statistics for Archaeologists*, New York

Drewett, P, Rudling, D, and Gardiner, M, 1988 *The south-east to AD 1000*, London

Durden, T, and Lamdin-Whymark, H, The flint, in Allen *et al.* in prep a)

Dyer, C, 1996 A possible Neolithic causewayed enclosure at Dorney, Buckinghamshire, in Industry and Enclosure in the Neolithic, unpublished Aerial Photographic Transcription and Analysis

Edwards, E, and Barclay, A, Early prehistoric pottery, in Hey *et al.* in prep.

Ehrenberg, M R, 1977 *Bronze Age spearheads from Berkshire, Buckinghamshire and Oxfordshire*, BAR Brit. Ser **34**, Oxford

Ellaby, R, 1987 The Upper Palaeolithic and Mesolithic in Surrey, in Bird and Bird (eds), 53-70

Ellis, C J, and Rawlings, M, 2001 Excavations at Balksbury Camp, Andover 1995-97, *Proc Hants Field Club Archaeol Soc* **56**, 21-94

Ellis, P, 1993 *Beeston Castle, Cheshire: a report on the excavations 1968-85 by Laurence Keen and Peter Hough*, English Heritage Archaeological Report **23**, London

Ellison, A, and Rahtz, P, 1987 Excavations at Hog Cliff Castle, Maiden Newton, Dorset, *Proc Prehist Soc* **53**, 223-69

English Heritage, 1995 *Geophysical survey in archaeological field excavation*, London

Evans, J G, and Limbrey, S, 1974 The experimental earthwork on Morden Bog, Wareham, Dorset, England, *Proc Prehist Soc* **40**, 170-202

Evans, C, Pollard, J, and Knight, M, 1999 Life in woods: tree-throws, 'settlement' and forest cognition, *Oxford J of Archaeol* **18/3**, 241-254

Fairclough, G, 2001 A report on the prehistoric, Romano British and Saxon ceramics excavated from Taplow Court, Taplow, Bucks, by the Taplow Court Archaeological Survey Team, unpublished manuscript

Fairclough, G, 2003 Taplow Court, South terrace, 1998/1999. Report on the excavations by the Taplow Court Archaeological Survey Team, Trenches 3, 4 and 5, unpublished manuscript

Fairclough, G, and Kupfermann, E, 2003 A report on the research and excavation fieldwork, Taplow Court Archaeological Survey Team, 1995-1999. Part 1: Trenches 1 and 2, unpublished manuscript

Fock, J, 1966, *Metrische Untersuchungen an Metapodien einiger europäischer Rinderrassen*, Munich

Ford, S, 1982 Linear earthworks on the Berkshire Downs, *Berkshire Archaeological Journal* **71**, 21-32

Ford, S, 1987a Chronological and functional aspects of flint assemblages, in A G Brown, and M R Edmonds (eds), *Lithic analysis and later British prehistory*, BAR Brit Ser **162**, Oxford, 67-81

Ford, S, 1987b *East Berkshire archaeological survey*, Department of Highways and Planning, Berkshire County Council Occasional Paper **1**

Ford, S, 1991-3 Excavations at Eton Wick, *Berkshire Archaeol J* **74**, 27-36

Ford, S, 2003 *Excavations at Cippenham, Slough, Berkshire 1995-7*, TVAS Monograph **3**, Reading

Foreman, S, 1998 Excavations in advance of the Environment Agency Maidenhead, Windsor and Eton Flood Alleviation Scheme, *South Midlands Archaeology* **28**, 26-31

Foreman, S, Hiller, J, and Petts, D, 2002 *Gathering the people, settling the land: the archaeology of a Middle Thames Landscape, Anglo-Saxon to post-medieval*, Thames Valley Landscapes **14**, Oxford

Fowler, P J, 1971 Hillforts, AD 300-700, in M Jesson and D Hill (eds) *The Iron Age and its hillforts*, Southampton, 203-13

Framework Archaeology, 2006 *Landscape evolution in the Middle Thames Valley: Heathrow Terminal 5 excavations*, 1, *Perry Oaks*, Framework Archaeology Monograph **1**, Oxford and Salisbury

Fredlund, G G, and Tieszan, L T, 1994 Modern phytolith assemblages from the North American great Plains. *Journal of Biogeography* **21**, 321-335

Freeman, S, Bishop, P, Bryant, C, Cook, G, Fallick, A, Harkness, D, Metcalfe, S, Scott, M, Scott, R, and Summerfield, M, 2004 A new environmental sciences AMS laboratory in Scotland, *Nuclear Instruments and Methods in Physics Research B*, **223-4**, 31–4

Fulford, M, 1989 Byzantium and Britain: a Mediterranean perspective on post-Roman imports in western Britain and Ireland, *Medieval Archaeol* **33**, 1-6

Gale, R, and Cutler, D, 2000 *Plants in Archaeology*, London

Geake, H, 1997 *The use of grave-goods in conversion-period England, c 600-c 850*, BAR Brit Ser **261**, Oxford

Gelfand, A E, and Smith, A F M, 1990 Sampling approaches to calculating marginal densities, *J Amer Stat Assoc*, **85**, 398–409

Gibson, A, 1998 *Stonehenge and timber circles*, Stroud

Gilks, W R, Richardson, S, and Spiegelhalther, D J, 1996 *Markov Chain Monte Carlo in practice*, London

Gingell, C J, and Morris, E L, 2000 Pottery, in A J Lawson *Potterne 1982-5: animal husbandry in later prehistoric Wiltshire*, Wessex Archaeology Report **17**, Salisbury

Godwin, H, 1956 *The History of the British Flora*, Cambridge

Goodier, A, 1984 The formation of boundaries in Anglo-Saxon England: a statistical study, *Medieval Archaeol* **28**, 1-12

Grant, A, 1982 The Use of Tooth Wear as a Guide to the Age of Domestic Ungulates, in Wilson *et al.* 1982, 91-108

Greig, J R A, 1991 The botanical remains, in S P Needham *Excavation and salvage at Runnymede Bridge, 1978: the late Bronze Age waterfront site*, London, 234-61

Groves, J, and Lovell, J, 2002 Excavations within and close to the late Bronze Age enclosure at the former Queen Mary's Hospital, Carshalton, 1999, *London Archaeol* **10**, 13-19

Guttman, E B A, and Last, J, 2000 A Late Bronze Age Landscape at South Hornchurch, Essex, *Proc Prehist Soc* **66**, 319-59

Halsall, G, 1989 Anthropology and the study of pre-conquest warfare and society: the ritual war in Anglo-Saxon England, in S C Hawkes (ed.) *Weapons and warfare in Anglo-Saxon England*, Oxford

Halstead, P, 1985 A Study of Mandibular Teeth from Romano-British Contexts at Maxey, in F Pryor, *Archaeology and Environment in the Lower Welland Valley*, East Anglian Archaeol Rep **27**, 219-224

Hamerow, H, 1993 *Excavations at Mucking Volume 2: The Anglo-Saxon settlement*. English Heritage Archaeological Report No. **21**, London

Hamerow, H, Hayden, C, and Hey, G, 2007 Anglo-Saxon and earlier settlement near Drayton Road, Sutton Courtenay, Berkshire, *Archaeological J* **164**, 109-96

Hamilton, S, and Manley, J 2001 Hillforts, monumentality and place: a chronological and topographic review of first millennium BC hillforts in south-east England, *European Journal of Archaeology* **4/1**, 7-42

Hamilton, S, and Manley, J, 1997 Points of view: prominent enclosures in 1st millennium BC Sussex, *Sussex Archaeological Collections* **135**, 93–112

Harbison, P, 1971 Wooden and stone chevaux-de-frise in central and western Europe, *Proc Prehist Soc* **37**, 195-225

Harding, D W, 1976 Blewburton Hill: re-excavation and reappraisal, in D W Harding (ed) *Hillforts: later prehistoric earthworks in Britain and Ireland*, London

Harding, P, 1990 The worked flint in J Richards *The Stonehenge environs project*, English Heritage Archaeol Rep **16**, London

Harris, A, 2003 *Byzantium, Britain and the west: the archaeology of cultural identity*, Stroud

Hart, J, and Mudd, A, forthcoming, A late prehistoric hilltop settlement and other excavations along the Taplow to Dorney Water Pipeline, 2003–4, Cotswold Archaeology Report

Hawkes, S C, 1986 The early Saxon period, in G Briggs, J Cook, T Rowley (eds) *The Archaeology of the Oxford Region*, Oxford, 64-108

Hayden, C, and Stafford, E, 2006 The Prehistoric Landscape at White Horse Stone, Boxley, Kent, *CTRL Integrated Site Report Series*, Archaeology Data Service [http://ads.ahds.ac.uk/]

Hayden, C, 2006 The Prehistoric Landscape at Eyhorne Street, Hollingbourne, Kent, *CTRL Integrated Site Report Series*, Archaeology Data Service [http://ads.ahds.ac.uk/]

Healy, F, 1988 *The Anglo-Saxon cemetery at Spong Hill, North Elmham, part VI: occupation during the seventh to second millennia BC*, E Anglian Archaeol **39**, Gressenhall

Healy, F, 1995 Ceramics and settlement in East Anglia, in Kinnes, I, & Varndell, G, (eds) *'Unbaked Urns of a Rudley Shape'. Essays on British and Irish Pottery for Ian Longworth*, Oxbow Monograph **55**, Oxford

Healy, F, Heaton, M J' and Lobb, S J, 1992 Excavations of a Mesolithic site at Thatcham, Berkshire, *Proc Prehist Soc* **58**, 41-76

Hearne, C M, and Adam, N, 1999 Excavation of an extensive late Bronze Age settlement at Shorncote Quarry near Cirencester, 1995-6, *Trans Bristol and Gloucestershire Archaeol Soc* **117**, 35-73

Hey, G, Dennis, C, and Bell, C, in prep. *Yarnton: Neolithic and Bronze Age settlement and landscape*, Thames Valley Landscapes Monograph, Oxford

Hingley, R, 1979-80 Excavations by R A Rutland on an Iron Age site at Wittenham Clumps, *Berkshire Archaeol J* **70**, 21-55

Hingley, R, 1990 Boundaries surrounding Iron Age and Romano-British settlements, *Scottish Archaeological Review* **7**, 96-103

Hinton, D A, 1996 *The Gold, Silver and other non-ferrous alloy objects from Hamwic, and the non Ferrous metalworking evidence*, Southampton Archaeological Monographs **6**, Southampton

Hinton, D A, and Parsons, A L, 1996, Pins, in Hinton 1996, 14-37

Hocart, A M, 1970 Baptism by fire, in *The life-giving myth and other essays* (eds Lord Raglan and R Needham), London

Hodson, M J, 2002 Phytoliths, in S Foreman et al. 2002 (CD Rom)

Hogg, A H A, 1979 *British hill-forts: an index*, BAR Brit Ser **62**, Occasional papers of the Hill-fort Studies Group **1**, Oxford

Holgate, R, 1986 Mesolithic, Neolithic and earlier Bronze Age settlement patterns south-west of Oxford, *Oxoniensia* **51**, 1-14

Hubert, H, and Mauss, M, 1964 *Sacrifice: its nature and functions*, (trans. W D Halls), Chicago

Huggett, J, 1988 Imported grave goods and the early Anglo-Saxon economy, *Medieval Archaeol* **32**, 63-96

Hugh-Jones, S, and Laidlaw, J, (eds) 2000 *The essential Edmund Leach*, **1**, *Anthropology and society*, New Haven

Hull, G, 2000 A late Bronze Age ringwork, pits and later features at Thrapston, Northamptonshire, *Northamptonshire Archaeol* **29**, 73-92

Inizan M-L, Roche H, Tixier J, 1992 *The Technology of Knapped Stone*, Meudon : Cercle de Recherches et d'etudes prehistoriques

Ishida, S, Parker, A.G, Kennet, D, and Hodson, M J, 2003 Phytolith analysis from the archaeological site of Kush, Ras al-Khaimah, United Arab Emirates *Quaternary Research* **59**, 310-321

Jacobi, R, 1978 The Mesolithic of Sussex, in P L Drewett (ed) *Archaeology in Sussex to AD 1500* CBA Res Rep **29**, 15-22

Johnston, J, and Bowden, M, 1985 Excavations at Pingewood, *Berks. Archaeol J* **72**, 17-52

Jones, M U, and Bond, D, 1980 Later Bronze Age settlement at Mucking, Essex, in Barrett and Bradley (eds), 471-82

Kidd, A M, 2004 Hillforts and Churches: a coincidence of locations? *Rec Buckinghamshire* **44**, 105-110

Kupfermann, E, 2006 Geophysical Survey at the Old Churchyard, Taplow, Buckinghamshire, unpublished report on geophysical survey at Taplow Court produced for English Heritage

Lambrick, G, 1984 Clanfield Burroway, *South Midlands Archaeol* **14**, 104-5

Lambrick, G, and Allen, T, 2004 *Gravelly Guy, Stanton Harcourt, Oxfordshire: the development of a prehistoric and Romano-British community*, Thames Valley Landscapes **21**, Oxford

Lambrick, G, with Robinson, M, 2009 *The Thames through Time: The Archaeology of the Gravel Terraces of the Upper and Middle Thames, Volume 2: The Thames Valley in Late Prehistory: 1500 BC–AD 50* Thames Valley Landscapes Monograph **29**, Oxford

Lamdin-Whymark, H, 2008 *The residue of ritualised action: Neolithic deposition practices in the Middle Thames Valley*, BAR Brit Ser **466**, Oxford

Lawson, A J, 2000 *Potterne, 1982-5: animal husbandry in later prehistoric Wiltshire*, Wessex Archaeology Report **17**, Salisbury

Leach, E R, 2000 The nature of war, in Hugh-Jones and Laidlaw (eds), 343-56

Levine, M A, 1982 The Use of Crown Height Measurements and Eruption-Wear Sequences to Age Horse Teeth, in Wilson *et al.* 1982, 223-250

Levitan, B, 1992 Vertebrate remains, in Moore and Jennings 1992, 98-103

Lewis, J, 2000 The Neolithic Period, in *The Archaeology of Greater London*, Museum of London, 63-80

Longley, D, and Needham, S, 1980 *Runnymede Bridge 1976: Excavations on the site of a Late Bronze Age Settlement*, Research Volume of the Surrey Archaeological Society, **6**. Surrey Archaeological Society

Longworth, I H, 1984 *Collared Urns of the Bronze Age in Britain and Ireland*, Cambridge

Lucy, S, 1992 The significance of mortuary ritual in the political manipulation of the landscape, *Archaeological Review from Cambridge* **11/2**, 93-105

Lyman, R L, 1996 *Vertebrate Taphonomy*, Cambridge Manuals in Archaeology, Cambridge

Manby, T G, 1980 Bronze Age settlement in eastern Yorkshire, in Barrett and Bradley (eds) 1980, 307-70

Manby, T G, 2007 Continuity of monumental traditions into the late Bronze Age? Henges to ring forts, and shrines, in C Burgess, P Topping and F Lynch (eds) *Beyond Stonehenge. Essays on the Bronze Age in honour of Colin Burgess*, Oxford, 403-424

Mant, A K, 1987 Knowledge acquired from post-war exhumations, in A Boddington, A N Garland, and R C Janaway (eds), *Death, decay, and reconstruction : approaches to archaeology and forensic science*, Manchester 65-80

Marren, P, 1992 *The Wild Woods: a Regional Guide to Britain's Ancient Woodland*, Newton Abbott

Martin, E, and Murphy, P, 1988 West Row Fen, Suffolk; a Bronze Age fen-edge settlement site *Antiquity* **62**, 353-358

Masters, P M, 1987 Preferential preservation of non-collagenous protein during bone diagenesis: implications for chronometric and stable isotope measurements, *Geochimica et Cosmochimica Acta*, **51**, 3209–14

Mauss, M, 2004 *Seasonal variations of the Eskimo: a study in social morphology* (trans. J Fox), London

Mays, S, 2000 New directions in the analysis of stable isotopes in excavated bones and teeth, in M Cox and S Mays (eds) *Human osteology in archaeology and forensic science*, London, 425-38

McHardy, A, 1906 On vitrified forts, with results of experiments as to the probable manner in which their vitrification may have been produced, *Proc Soc Antiq Scot* **40**, 136-50

McSloy, E, The pottery, in Hart and Mudd forthcoming

Mellor, M, 1994 Oxford Pottery: A Synthesis of middle and late Saxon, medieval and early post-medieval pottery in the Oxford Region, *Oxoniensia* **59**, 17-217

Mercer, R J, 1981 The excavation of a late Neolithic henge-type enclosure at Balfarg, Markinch, Fife, Scotland, 1977-8 *Proc Soc Antiq Scot* **111**, 63-17

Miles, D, Palmer, S, Lock, G, Gosden, C, and Cromarty, A M, 2003 *Uffington White Horse and its landscape: investigations at White Horse Hill, Uffington, 1989-95 and Tower Hill, Ashbury, 1993-4* Thames Valley Landscapes **18**, Oxford

Mitchell, A, 1974 *A Field Guide to the Trees of Britain and Northern Europe*, London

Mook, W G, 1986 Business Meeting: recommendations/resolutions adopted by the twelfth international radiocarbon conference, *Radiocarbon* **28**, 799

Moore, J, and Jennings, D, 1992 *Reading Business Park: a Bronze Age Landscape*. Oxford Archaeology Thames Valley Landscapes **3**, Oxford

Morris, E, 2004 Later prehistoric pottery, in *Green Park (Reading Business Park). Phase 2 Excavations 1995 – Neolithic and Bronze Age sites*, Oxford Archaeology Thames Valley Landscapes Monograph **19**, Oxford, 58-90

MPRG, 1998 *Guide to the Classification of Medieval Ceramic Forms*, MPRG Occasional Paper **1**

MPRG, 2001 *Minimum Standards for the Processing, Recording, Analysis and Publication of post-roman Ceramics*, Medieval Pottery Res Group Occ Paper **2**

Mulholland, S C, and Rapp, G Jr., 1992 Phytolith Systematics: An Introduction, in Rapp and Mulholland (eds) 1992, 65-89

Musson, C R, 1991 *The Breiddin hillfort: a later prehistoric settlement in the Welsh Marches*, CBA Res Rep **76**, London

Needham, S, 1987 The Bronze Age, in Bird and Bird (eds) 1987, 97-138

Needham S, *Excavation and salvage at Runnymede Bridge, 1978: the Late Bronze Age waterfront site*, London

Needham, S, 1993 The structure of settlement and ritual in the late Bronze Age of south-east Britain, in C Mordant and A Richard (eds) *L'habitat et l'occupation du sol a l'Age du Bronze en Europe*, Documents Prehistoriques **4**, Paris, 46-69

Needham, S. 1996. Chronology and Peridisation in the British Bronze Age. In *Acta Archaeologica*, **67**, 121-140

Needham, S, and Ambers, J, 1994 Redating Rams Hill and reconsidering Bronze Age enclosure, *Proc Prehist Soc* **60**, 225-44

Needham, S, and Spence, T, 1996 *Refuse and disposal at Area 16 east, Runnymede*, Runnymede Bridge research excavations Vol. **2**, London

Newcomer, M H, and Karlin, C, 1987 Flint chips from Pincevent, in G de G Sieveking and M H Newcomer (eds) *The human uses of flint and chert: papers from the fourth international flint symposium*, Cambridge, 33-6

O'Connell, M, 1986 *Petters Sports Field, Egham. Excavation of a late Bronze Age/Early Iron Age Site*, Research Volume of the Surrey Archaeological society, **10**

Onhuma, K, and Bergman, C, 1982 Experimental studies in the determination of flake mode, *Bulletin of the Institute of Archaeology, London* **19**, 161-71

Ordnance Survey, 1962 *Map of southern Britain in the Iron Age*, Chessington

Orton, C, 1998-99 Minimum Standards in Statistics and Sampling, *Medieval Ceramics* **22-23**, 135-8

Osgood, R, 1998 *Warfare in the late Bronze Age of North Europe*, BAR Int Ser **694**, Oxford

Over, L J, 1973 A Belgic occupation site at Knowl Hill, Berks, *Berkshire Archaeol J* **67**, 63-70

Oxford Archaeology (OA), 2002 Taplow Court: project design, unpublished report for English Heritage

Oxford Archaeology (OA), 2007 Lift-pit excavation, Taplow Court, Taplow, Buckinghamshire. Archaeological Investigation Report, unpublished report prepared for SGI-UK by Oxford Archaeology

Page, W, 1925 *Victoria county history of Buckinghamshire*, **3**, London

Parker, A, and Robinson, M, 2003 Palaeoenvironmental investigations on the middle Thames at Dorney, UK, in A J Howard, M G Macklin and D G Passmore (eds) *Alluvial archaeology in Europe : proceedings of the Alluvial archaeology of North-West Europe and Mediteranian, 18-19 December 2000, Leeds, UK* Lisse

Parker, A G, Eckersley, L, Goudie, A S, Stokes, S, White, K, and Hodson, M J, (subm.) Holocene vegetation dynamics in the eastern Rub al Khali desert, Arabian Peninsula: a phytolith and carbon isotope study, *Journal of Quaternary Science* **19/7**, 665-76

Parry, C, 1999 Excavations at Camp Gardens, Stow-on-the-Wold, Gloucestershire, *Trans Bristol Gloucestershire Archaeol Soc* **117**, 75-87

Peacock, D P S, 1986 Iron Age and Roman Quern Production at Lodsworth, West Sussex. *Antiq J* **67**, 61-85

Peacock, D P, and Williams, D F, 1986 *Amphorae and the Roman economy: an introductory guide*, London

Pearsall, D M, 2000 *Paleoethnobotany: A Handbook of Procedures* (2nd edition), San Diego

Pelling, R, 2002 The charred plant remains in Foreman *et al.* 2002, 97

Pelling, R, and Robinson, M A, 2000 Saxon Emmer wheat from the Upper and Middle Thames Valley, England. *Environmental Archaeology* **5**, 117-19

Piperno, D R, 1988 *Phytolith Analysis: An Archaeological and Geological Perspective*, San Diego

Poole, C, 1991 Objects of baked clay, in Cunliffe, B, and Poole, C, 1991 *Danebury: an Iron Age hillfort in Hampshire*, **5**, *The excavation, 1979-88: the finds*, CBA Res Rep **73b**

Powers-Jones, A, 1984 The use of phytolith analysis in the interpretation of archaeological deposits: an Outer Hebridean example, in R Luff and P Rowley-Conwy (eds) *Whither Environmental Archaeology?* Oxford, 41-50

Prescott, J R, and Hutton, J T, 1994 Cosmic ray contributions to dose rates for luminescence and ESR dating: large depths and long term time variations, *Radiation Measurements* **23**, 497-500

Prior, J, and Alvin, K L, 1983 Structural changes on charring woods of *Dichostachys* and *Salix* from Southern Africa, *Internat. Ass. of Wood Anatomists Bulletin*, n.s.**4 (4)**, 197-206

Prummel, W, and Frisch, H-J, 1986 A Guide for the distinction of species, sex and body size in bones of sheep and goat, *Journal of Archaeological Science* **13**, 567–577

Rackham, O, 1986 *The History of the Countryside.* London

Ralston, I, 2006 *Celtic fortifications*, Stroud

Rapp Jr, G, and. Mulholland S C (eds), 1992 *Phytolith Systematics- Emerging Issues*, New York

Reimer, P J, Baillie, M G L, Bard, E, Bayliss, A, Beck, J W, Bertrand, C J H, Blackwell, P G, Buck, C E, Burr, G S, Cutler, K B, Damon, P E, Edwards, R L, Fairbanks, R G, Friedrich, M, Guilderson, T P, Hogg, A G, Hughen, K A, Kromer, B, McCormac, G, Manning, S, Bronk Ramsey, C, Reimer, R W, Remmele, S, Southon, J R, Stuiver, M, Talamo, S, Taylor, F W, van der Plicht, J, and Weyhenmeyer, C E, 2004 IntCal04 Terrestrial radiocarbon age calibration, 0–26 Cal Kyr BP, *Radiocarbon* **46**, 1029–58

Rayner, D H, 1981 *The stratigraphy of the British Isles* Cambridge

Reynolds, P, 1995 The life and death of a post-hole, *Interpreting Stratigraphy*, **5**, 21–5

Richards, J C, 1978 *The archaeology of the Berkshire Downs: an introductory survey*, Berkshire Archaeological Committee Publication **3**, Reading

Robertson-Mackay, R, 1987: The Neolithic Causewayed Enclosure at Staines, Surrey: Excavations 1961-63, *Proc Prehist Soc* **53**, 23-128

Robinson, M, 2004 Environmental remains – charred plant remains, in Taplow Court, Buckinghamshire: Post-Excavation Assessment and Updated Project Design, Oxford Archaeology, Appendix 11, 118-124

Robinson, M, and Wilson, B, 1987 A survey of environmental archaeology in the South Midlands, in H C M Keeley, *Environmental Archaeology: a Regional Review*, Historic Buildings and Monuments Commission for England, Occasional Paper No.**1**, 16-100

Roe, F, 2002 The Worked Stone, in Foreman *et al.* 2002, 37-39

Roe, F, The Worked Stone, in Allen *et al.* in prep. b)

Rosen, A M, 1992 Preliminary identification of silica skeletons from near eastern archaeological sites: an anatomical approach, in Rapp Jr. and Mulholland (eds) 1992, 129-147

Runge, F, 1999 The opal phytolith inventory of soils in central Africa – quantities, shapes, classification, and spectra. *Review of Palaeobotany and Palynology* **107**, 23-53

Rutland, J, 1885 Proceedings, *Proc Soc Antiq* **2nd ser, 10**, 19-20

Rutland, R A, and Greenaway, J A, 1970 Archaeological Notes from Reading Museum, *Berkshire Archaeol J* **65**, 53-60

Sahlins, M, 1985 *Islands of history*, Chicago

Saville, A, 1980 On the measurement of struck flakes and flake tools, *Lithics* **1**, 16-20

Saville, A, 1981 *Grimes Graves, Norfolk. Excavations 1971-72. Vol. 2: the flint assemblage.* London. HMSO

Savory, N H, 1971 A Welsh Bronze Age hillfort, *Antiquity* **45**, 251-61

Scott, E M, 2003 The third international radiocarbon intercomparison (TIRI) and the fourth international radiocarbon intercomparison (FIRI) 1990 – 2002: results, analyses, and conclusions, *Radiocarbon*, **45**, 135-408

Scrimgeour, G E, and Farley, M, 1987 Taplow and its setting, unpubl. report, Buckinghamshire SMR

Sellwood, L, 1984 Tribal boundaries viewed from the perspective of numismatic evidence, in B Cunliffe and D Miles (eds) *Aspects of the Iron Age in central southern Britain*, Oxford University Committee for Archaeology Monograph **2**, Oxford

Serjeantson, D, 1996 The Animal Bones, in Needham and Spence (eds), 1996

Shepherd, W, 1972 *Flint: its origin, properties and uses*, London

Silver, I A, 1969 The Ageing of Domestic Animals, in D Brothwell and E S Higgs, *Science in Archaeology*, Thames and Hudson

Slota Jr, P J, Jull A J T, Linick T W, and Toolin, L J, 1987 Preparation of small samples for 14C accelerator targets by catalytic reduction of CO, *Radiocarbon*, **29(2)**, 303–6

Stanley, C, 1972 Bray Roman cemetery, Berkshire, *CBA Group 9 Newsletter* **2**, 12-13

Stead, I M, 1968 An Iron Age hillfort at Grimthorpe, Yorkshire, England *Proc Prehist Soc* **4**, 148-90

Stocker, D, Went, D, and Farley, M, 1995 The evidence for a pre-Viking church adjacent to the Anglo-Saxon barrow at Taplow, Buckinghamshire, *Archaeol J* **152**, 441-54

Stuiver, M, and Kra, R S, 1986 Editorial comment, *Radiocarbon*, **28(2B)**, ii

Stuiver, M, and Polach, H J, 1977 Discussion: reporting of 14C data, *Radiocarbon*, **19**, 355–63

Stuiver, M, and Reimer, P J, 1986 A computer program for radiocarbon age calculation, *Radiocarbon* **28**, 1022–30

Stuiver, M, and Reimer, P J, 1993 Extended 14C

data base and revised CALIB 3.0 14C age calibration program, *Radiocarbon* **35**, 215–30

Theunissen, J D, 1994 A method for isolating and preparing silica bodies in grasses for scanning electron microscopy. *Biotechnic and Histochemistry* **69**, 291-294

Thomas, C, 1988 The context of Tintagel: a new model for the diffusion of post-Roman Mediterranean imports, *Cornish Archaeology* **27**, 7-25

Thomas, R, 1997 Land, kinship relations and the rise of enclosed settlements in first millennium BC Britain, *Oxford J Archaeol* **16/2**, 211-18

Timby, J, Brown, R, Hardy, A, Leech, S, Poole, C, and Webley, L, 2007 *Settlement on the Bedfordshire Claylands; archaeology along the A421 Great Barford Bypass* Bedfordshire Archaeology Monograph **8**, Oxford

Tipper, J, 2004 *The Grubenhaus in Anglo-Saxon England: an analysis and interpretation of the evidence from a most distinctive building type*, Yedingham

Tixier, J, Inizan, M-L and Roche, H, 1980 *Préhistoire de la pierre taillée. I. Terminologie et téchnologie*, Valbonne, Association pour la Promotion et la Diffusion des Connaissances Archéologiques

Tomalin, D, 1995 Cognition, ethnicity and linguistics of 'Collared Urn Art', in I Kinnes and G Varndell (eds) *'Unbaked Urns of a Rudley Shape'. Essays on British and Irish Pottery for Ian Longworth*, Oxbow Monograph **55**, Oxford

Tomber, R, and Dore, J, 1998 *The National Roman Fabric Reference Collection: a handbook,* MoLAS monograph **2**, London

Tubb, H J, Hodson, M J, and Hodson, G C, 1993 The inflorescence papillae of the Triticeae: a new tool for taxonomic and archaeological research, *Annals of Botany* **72**, 537-45

Tuross, N, Fogel, M L, and Hare, P E, 1988 Variability in the preservation of the isotopic composition of collagen from fossil bone, *Geochimica Cosmochimica Acta*, **52**, 929–35

Tutin, T G, Heywood, V H, and Burges, A (eds), 1964-80 *Flora Europaea*, 1-5, Cambridge

Twiss, P C, Suess, E, and Smith, R M, 1969 Morphological classification of grass phytoliths, *Soil Science Society of America: Proceedings* **33**, 109-115

von den Driesch, A, 1976 *A Guide to the Measurement of Animal Bones from Archaeological Sites*, Peabody Museum

Ward, G K, and Wilson, S R, 1978 Procedures for comparing and combining radiocarbon age determinations: a critique, *Archaeometery* **20**, 19–31

Webley, L, Timby, J, and Wilson, M, 2007 *Fairfield Park, Stotfold, Bedfordshire: later prehistoric settlement in the eastern Chilterns*, Bedfordshire Archaeology Monograph **7**, Oxford

Welch, M, 1992 *Anglo-Saxon England*, London

Wessex Archaeology, 1998 Taplow Court, Taplow, Buckinghamshire: Archaeological Evaluation, unpublished report, Wessex Archaeology, Salisbury

Williams, H, 1997 Ancient landscapes and the dead: the re-use of prehistoric and Roman monuments as early Anglo-Saxon burial sites, *Medieval Archaeol* **41**, 1-32

Williams, H, 1998 Monuments and the past in early Anglo-Saxon England, *World Archaeology* **30/1**, 90-108

Wilkinson, D W (ed), 1992 The Oxford Archaeological Unit Field Manual

Wilson, A E, 1940 Report on the excavations at Highdown Hill, Sussex, August 1939, *Sussex Archaeol Collect* **81**, 173-203

Wilson, A E, 1950 Excavations at Highdown Hill, Sussex, 1947, *Sussex Archaeological Collections* **89**, 163-78

Wilson, B, Grigson, C, and Payne, S, *Ageing and Sexing Animal Bones from Archaeological Sites*, BAR British Series **109**, Oxford

Workshop of European Anthropologists, 1980 Recommendations for age and sex diagnoses of skeletons, *J Human Evolution* **9**, 517-49

Wright, K, 1991 The Origins and Development of Ground Stone assemblages in Late Pleistocene Southwest Asia, *Paléorient* **17/1**, 19-45

Yates, D T, 1999 Bronze Age field systems in the Thames Valley, *Oxford Journal of Archaeology* **18/2**, 157-70

Yates, D T, 2001 Bronze Age agricultural intensification in the Thames Valley and estuary, in J Brück (ed), *Bronze Age landscapes: tradition and transformation* Oxford, 65-82

Yates, D T, 2007 *Land, Power and Prestige. Bronze Age field systems in Southern England*, Oxford

York, J, 2002 The life cycle of Bronze Age metalwork from the Thames, *Oxford J Archaeol* **21/1**, 77-92

Index

Created by Tim Allen and Paul Backhouse

11th century 104-5, 137, 141, 175, 191, 193, 198

activity, domestic 145, 188
Aerial photograph 4, 11-12
aerial reconnaissance, military 11
Agars Plough, Berkshire 5, 202-4
Aldermaston, Berkshire 126, 134, 145
amphora *see* pottery, Roman, Amphora
Anglo-Saxon 7-8, 15, 89, 91, 95, 99, 101, 103-5, 107, 119, 137-9, 141-2, 147-51, 185, 201-2, 205-7
  cemeteries 141-2
  church 7, 12, 179
  deposits 86, 88, 97, 105, 149, 154-5, 167
  occupation 101, 103, 151, 207-8
  pottery – *see pottery, Anglo Saxon*
  settlement 2, 4, 8, 10, 12, 16, 18, 20, 24, 26, 28, 30, 32, 36, 101-2, 104-6
  sites 149, 207
  structures 206
animal bones 27, 49, 55, 61, 65-6, 69, 91, 104-5, 147-9, 169-70, 206-7
AOC Archaeology 1
awl 110-11, 115-17, 187
Axe, flint – *see flint, axe*

Bapsey Pond, Berkshire 8
barley 27, 31-2, 65, 105, 150, 152, 159, 187
  hulled 150-2, 187
barrow 1, 7, 33, 130, 137, 188, 207
  prehistoric 207
Barrow Hills, Radley, Oxfordshire 130
beech 97, 151, 153-5, 206
Blewburton Hill, Oxfordshire 56, 195, 207
Bozedown Camp, Oxfordshire 193
Bronze Age
  bracelet 63, 65-6, 140-2, 196, 199
  defences, late 23, 35, 70, 178, 195
  enclosure 2, 4, 6, 8, 10, 12, 16, 18, 20, 24, 26, 35-6, 78, 182-3, 190-3, 196-204
  field systems, middle 190, 197
  flint – *see flint, Bronze Age*
  hillfort, late 35, 58
  hilltop enclosures, late 188, 191-2, 195, 197-8, 203
  occupation 91, 123, 190, 198
  pits, late 5, 70
  ringwork, late 33, 190, 193
  sites 33, 145, 191, 197-9
brooch, Hod Hill-type bronze 7
buckets, iron-bound 7, 206
Buckinghamshire County Council 10
Buckinghamshire SMR 5, 7, 179
building
  Anglo-Saxon 101, 107
  manorial 8

  sunken-featured 105, 208
burial 1, 5, 7-8, 11, 19, 56, 91, 101, 103-4, 142, 147, 169-70, 174-5, 198-9, 201-2, 205-8
  adult male 101
  Anglo-Saxon 101, 107, 147, 207
  cemetery, Late Roman 7-8
  cremations 5, 128, 145, 190, 207
  female 8
  grave 101, 103, 142, 147, 170
  grave goods 7, 201, 205-7
  high status 185, 208
burial monuments 128
burial mound 7, 208
Burnham plateau 1, 196, 201
Burroway, Oxfordshire 193, 205

Cambridge University Collection 11-12
Carshalton, Surrey 33, 191, 199, 203
Castle Hill, Oxfordshire 191, 193, 195-7, 203-4
cattle 27, 61-2, 65, 88-91, 94, 105, 148-9, 187
cauldron, bronze 7, 205
cereals
  chaff 151-2, 159
  grain 65, 88, 150, 152-3
    charred 29, 33, 63, 70, 150, 154, 170, 174, 188, 190
chalk 1, 78, 80, 90, 92, 177, 195
  blocks 71
  fragments 80, 94
  kerb 78, 80, 83, 85, 89-90, 95
Chastelton Camp, Gloucestershire 193
chevauxde-frise 195
Chilterns, hills 154-5, 204, 208
church 5, 7-8, 179, 183, 203
  Norman 204
churchyard 7-8, 12, 183
Cippenham, Berkshire 5, 7, 134, 187-8, 202, 204
Conference Hall excavation 1, 10-11, 119, 127, 179
Coptic bowl 7, 205-6
cosmologies 187, 198
Crickley Hill, Gloucestershire 83, 205
cropmarks 11, 187-8
  rectilinear 7

deer 149
  red 88, 148-9
  roe 88, 90-1, 105, 148-9
defences 42, 49, 58, 62, 87, 91, 98-9, 104, 178-9, 183, 185, 191, 193, 195-6, 198-9, 201-5
  early-middle Iron Age 58, 154, 178
  hilltop 35, 204
  Iron Age multivallate 98
defensive barrier 35
  ditches 119, 151, 169, 179, 181-2, 185, 203, 205
  features 87, 190, 193

ditch
  early Iron Age 5, 19, 202-3
  inner 5, 183, 191, 201, 205, 207
  late Bronze Age 75, 154, 179, 202-3
  outer 19, 70, 87, 95-7, 99, 101, 103-5, 134, 136, 139, 170, 176-9, 183, 201-3, 205, 207
  post-medieval 8, 10
dog 88, 90, 105, 148-9
Domesday 8, 155
Dorney, Berkshire 7-8, 146, 151, 188
Dorney Court, Berkshire 5
Dorney Reach, Berkshire 7, 187

earthworks 11, 103, 179, 183, 203
  experimental 50, 73, 89, 177-8
  linear 5, 203
enclosures 1, 5, 35, 49, 62, 169, 174, 190-1, 193, 195-9, 203-4
  aggrandised 197
  defensive 190, 203
  early Iron Age 4
English Heritage 4, 165, 179
Eton Flood Alleviation Scheme 5, 134, 137, 146
Eton Rowing Course, Berkshire 5, 7-8, 123, 134, 150, 185-8, 190, 197, 201-4
Eton Wick, Berkshire 5, 187, 199, 202
evaluation trenches 8, 10-11, 15, 70, 95, 107
Ewart Park phase 19, 65, 141

field systems 190, 197, 204
fired clay 28, 31, 46, 54-5, 65-6, 88-9, 105, 118, 143-5, 187, 196
flint
  axe 23, 32, 55, 109-11, 115, 118, 185
    tranchet 109-10, 118, 185
  earlier Neolithic 23, 49, 186
  Bronze Age 28, 29, 31-33, 35, 41, 73, 110, 115-118, 187, 188, 196
  knapping 27, 109, 113, 115, 118, 187
  Mesolithic 5, 23, 28, 49, 109, 111-113, 115, 185
  Neolithic 5, 23, 27-8, 49, 109, 111, 113-115, 123, 186-7, 185-187
fork, post-medieval 141-2
fowl, domestic 88-9, 105, 148-9

gaming pieces 7, 206
gate 95
glass, claw-beakers 7, 206
grange, medieval 8
graveyard 1, 5, 7
Green Park, Reading, Berkshire 126

Hammerstone 40, 110, 116-17, 145-6
hazelnut shell 23, 49, 61-2, 111, 150-1, 154, 170, 173, 185
hearth 65, 105, 118, 143, 145, 187-8
hillfort
  defences 1, 35, 85, 103, 183, 185, 198, 201, 207
  ditches 8, 15, 21, 103-4, 119, 151, 179, 185, 206
  early-middle Iron Age 73, 93-4, 99, 103, 107, 122, 147
  middle Iron Age 101
  prehistoric 8
  re-use of 206
hillfort entrance, early-middle Iron Age 94
hilltop enclosures 190-3, 196-9, 201
hoards 141
hollows 27-9, 31-2, 35, 41, 63, 71, 75, 83, 87, 109, 115, 123, 145-6, 153, 173, 187-8
  Bronze Age, early 23, 28-32, 35, 39, 41, 111, 119, 123, 143-4, 150-1, 153-4, 185
horns, drinking 7, 206
hornwork 92, 94-5, 107
horses 55, 88-9, 105, 148-9, 195, 198
houses 8, 191, 199

Isleham 196

Jubilee River 5, 186, 188, 190, 200, 204-5, 207-8

Kentish king 7, 206
knife 8, 88, 141-2
  iron 8
  whittle tang 101, 142
Knight's Farm, Berkshire 134

Lake End Road West, Buckinghamshire 5, 7-8, 146, 151, 187, 202-4, 206-7
lead objects 141-2
Little Wittenham, Oxfordshire 69, 191, 193, 197-8, 203-4
London, England 1, 137
Long Wittenham, Oxfordshire 130
looms 145
loomweight 23, 33, 65-6, 105, 143-5, 188
  Anglo-Saxon 144
  cylindrical 23, 33, 65, 143-4, 188
  pyramidal 143-4
Lord Desborough 7
Lot's Hole, Buckinghamshire 5, 119, 122, 146, 202
Lyneham 193
lyre 7, 206

Maidenhead 5, 7, 111, 134, 137, 199
  Windsor and Eton Flood Alleviation scheme 5, 122, 134, 137, 146
Marlow Archaeological Society 4, 8, 12, 179
Marsh Lane East, Buckinghamshire 5, 146, 188, 190, 202
Marshall's Hill, Berkshire 193, 197
Mayfield Farm, Middlesex 193, 201
medieval 8
  early 137, 202
medieval pottery 10
Mesolithic 4-5, 8, 15, 19, 23-4, 27-9, 49, 62-3, 109, 111, 113, 115, 118, 150-1, 170, 185-6
  early 23, 62, 111, 118, 150
Mesolithic flint *see flint, Mesolithic*
metalwork 15, 19, 140-1, 196, 199, 201, 208
  Bronze Age 5, 141, 199, 201
  copper alloy 141-2
  iron 141-2
midden 67, 124, 187, 198
military forces 204

Index

monastic grange 8
Mucking, Sussex 124, 145, 190-1, 196
Mucking South Rings, Sussex 201
musket ball 141-2

Neolithic 5, 15, 19, 23, 27, 111, 115, 118, 150-1, 186-7
  activity 4, 150, 187
  early 23, 27, 29, 109, 111, 115, 118, 150-1, 185-8
  industries, early 111, 113
neutron activation analysis (NAA) 165, 167

oak 31, 55, 80, 86, 90-2, 94, 97, 151, 153-4, 158-9, 188, 206
  charcoal 27, 40-1, 46, 86, 90, 94, 154, 169
OSL (Optical Stimulated Luminescence) 13, 15, 54, 56, 71, 158, 167, 173-8
oven 65, 105, 143, 145, 187
Oxford, Oxfordshire 11, 137, 145

Palaeolithic 5
palisade 10-11, 23, 27-9, 32-3, 41, 43-7, 49-50, 56-7, 80, 94, 143-4, 169-70, 175-7, 190-1, 193, 195
  continuous 193, 195
  double 107, 193
  foundation trench 41, 92, 94, 101, 104-5, 107
  slot 10-11, 45, 47, 49, 80
  trench 11, 28-9, 33, 41, 43-6, 56-7, 94, 99, 110-11, 119-20, 125-6, 143-4, 159, 173, 175-7, 195
Park Farm, Binfield 135
passageway, timber-lined 92, 95
Perry Oaks, Heathrow, Middlesex 190, 199, 204
Petters Sports Field, Surrey 122, 124-6, 134, 145
pig 88-91, 97, 105, 148-9, 187
pin, spiral-headed 88, 101, 141-2
post-medieval 5, 8, 39, 141-2
post-pipes 32-3, 39, 41, 44-5, 47, 61, 78, 80, 92, 94, 105, 175-6
posthole circle 49, 63, 65, 67, 69-70, 99, 148
  rows 15, 19, 32-3, 35, 39-41, 44-7, 49-50, 58, 60-3, 69-70, 82-3, 125-7, 150-4, 170, 172-7, 195-6
Potterne, Wiltshire 124, 145, 199
Pottery
  Anglo-Saxon 105, 136-9, 174
  beakers 5, 135-6
    poppy-headed 135-6
  Belgic-type ware 134
  biconical bowl 19, 54, 122-4, 126
  biconical urn 120, 123, 128
  black-burnished 135
  bowls 123-4, 135, 206
  Bronze Age 8, 27-9, 32, 35, 58, 65, 70, 120, 129, 132, 145, 188, 198, 203
    early 27-9, 32, 35, 63, 120, 123-4, 126, 128, 145, 188
    collared urn 173
    middle 120, 124, 126
    late -early Iron Age 56, 196
    late 8, 49, 58, 63, 65, 70, 90, 120, 124, 126-7, 129, 145, 198, 203
  Bronze Age cordon 124
  carinated 124-6
  collared urn 23, 28-9, 32, 109, 115, 118, 123, 128, 144-5, 173, 185, 187-8
  collared urn, non-funerary 128
  decorated 54, 105, 119, 121, 123-6, 136, 138-9
  fabrics, sand-tempered 46, 63, 90, 92, 94, 99, 119, 122, 124
  flagon 139
  flint-tempered pottery 35, 39, 63, 83, 95
  grog 120-1, 124-5, 127, 135, 188, 190
  Ipswich ware 137, 207
  Iron Age 5, 35, 49, 56, 63, 90-1, 99, 120, 122-3, 126, 130-1, 133, 178, 196, 202
    early 90, 126, 130, 133, 178, 202
  jars, carinated 127
    ovoid 124, 126-7
    storage 135
    tripartite 122-6
  Mediterranean, eastern 101, 105, 134, 139, 206
  Neolithic, Peterborough ware 5
  North French wares 207
  post medieval 145
  prehistoric 21, 88-91, 97, 119
  Late Vessel Forms 123
  rims 119, 122-8, 130, 135-6, 138-9
    cabled 123-5
  Roman 101, 120, 134, 136
    Amphora 139, 206
    late 97, 105, 134, 139
  samian ware
    central Gaulish 135
    South Gaulish 134
  Saxon 121, 145, 174
    Ipswich Ware 137
    Early/middle 139
    Saxon, late 136
  Tating ware 207
  urn, biconical 120, 123, 128
  vessels 119-20, 123-8, 130, 134-5, 137, 205
  wares
    Cotswolds-type 103-4, 137
    grey 134-6
    oxidised 134-5
    reduced 135
    white 134-5

Quern
  saddle 145-6
  rotary 88-91, 97, 104, 145-6

radiocarbon date 13, 32-3, 39, 46-7, 49, 58, 62-3, 70, 103, 120, 136-9, 150, 153-4, 175-6, 185, 190-1
rampart
  box 41, 56, 85
  Bronze Age 65, 83, 161
  burnt 78, 81, 85, 87, 89-90, 109, 145, 154, 174, 176, 205
    gravel 82
  construction 75
  deposits 32, 38-9, 56, 83, 85-7, 89, 91, 122
  early-middle Iron Age 50, 61, 85, 94, 151, 154, 178
  gravel 17, 83, 87, 90-1, 109, 120, 122, 125, 143-5, 154-5, 174

Iron Age 50, 61, 71, 85, 94, 151, 154, 170, 178, 183, 207
  material 57, 173, 205
  soil 44-5
  stone-faced 193, 195
  structure 154, 169-70
  surviving 75, 82-3, 85, 87, 99, 104
  timber-laced 80, 85, 201-2, 204-5
  timbers, burnt 155
Rams Hill, Oxfordshire 63, 190-1, 193, 195-6, 199, 204
Reading Business Park, Berkshire 124, 126, 134, 145, 199
ringworks 190-1, 195-8, 201
Roman 4-5, 7-8, 10, 97, 101, 204
  conquest 136
  periods 5, 101, 205
  settlement 7, 101, 136
roundhouse 19, 38, 40, 49, 63-5, 67, 69-70, 99, 118-20, 122-3, 126-8, 149-53, 173, 196-7, 199, 204
  Iron Age 49
  late Bronze Age 151
Runnymede Bridge, Surrey 119, 122, 124-6, 134, 145-6, 151, 196, 199
Rutland, James 5

Saxon 1, 5, 8, 10, 19, 39, 90, 136-7, 139, 141-2, 145-6, 159, 169-70, 173, 201, 208
  early 8, 136-8, 152-3, 207
  early-middle 35, 62, 88-9, 91, 97, 136-7
  burial *see* burial, Anglo-Saxon
  finds 8, 89, 91, 95, 99, 101, 103-5, 201-2, 206
  postholes 62
  settlement 33, 101, 104, 118, 136, 142, 150, 190-1, 196, 199, 201-4, 207-8
    Bronze Age 5, 23, 128, 151, 185, 188, 191, 196-9, 204
    Iron Age 5, 202-204
settlements
sheep/goat 47, 105, 147, 149
shields 7, 198, 205
South Hornchurch, Essex 190-1, 196-8
spearheads 7, 205
spindlewhorls 5
St Nicholas Church, Taplow 1, 7-8, 179, 183
structure 4, 13, 41, 49, 63, 67, 69-70, 83, 92, 95, 107, 154, 169, 175, 198-9, 206-7
  eight-post 69, 196
  entrance 58, 67, 92, 95, 174
  four-post 19, 49, 63-4, 67, 69-70, 150, 174, 196-7
  oak 155
  semicircular post-built 63
  single 35, 41
  timber 5, 154, 177
survey
  geophysical 1, 4, 7-8, 12-13, 179-80, 183
  magnetometer 4, 12, 179, 182-3, 203
  resistivity 4, 12, 179, 181, 183
Sutton Courtenay, Berkshire 208
swords 7, 205

Taplow Court 1, 4-5, 7-8, 11-12, 118-19, 122, 145, 159, 167-9, 172-4, 179, 185-8, 190-1, 193, 195-200, 203-8
Taplow Court Archaeological Survey Team *see* TCAST
Taplow Court Estate 1
Taplow hilltop enclosure 130
Taplow Manor 8
Taplow Mill Site 5, 118, 187
Taplow Mound 1, 5, 7-8, 12, 101, 174, 179, 185, 187-8, 205-6
Taplow to Dorney pipeline 130, 188, 190, 202, 204
Taplow village 1
TCAST (Taplow Court Archaeological Survey Team) 8, 119, 126, 134, 139, 179, 202
TCAST trenches 32, 35, 101, 105, 119, 122, 126-8, 130, 132-4, 136, 138-9, 178, 197
Ten Acre Field, Taplow 5, 7
Thames, River 1, 5, 21, 75, 185, 191, 194, 197, 199, 201-2, 204, 207-8
Thwing, Yorkshire 191, 193, 196, 201
timber 10-11, 45-6, 71, 75, 80-3, 85-7, 90, 94, 154-5, 163, 169-70, 174-5, 195, 203, 205
  burnt 87
  carbonised 87
  charred 10-11, 71, 75, 80-3, 85, 90, 154, 161, 170, 174-5, 205
  horizontal 45, 83, 195
  lacing 55, 75, 78, 83, 85-7
  longitudinal 82
  rampart 80, 87, 174
  roundwood posts 45, 154-5, 169
  supporting 163
  transverse 82-3, 86
  uprights 45
  vertical 80, 82-3
tree-throw 5, 10, 19, 23, 27-9, 32, 47, 49, 63, 99, 104-5, 109-11, 113-16, 118-19, 150-3, 185-7
turf 56, 83, 85, 195
  revetment 80
  walls, low 57

violence 190, 198-9

walkway 83, 95, 193
  raised 41, 193, 195
warfare 190, 198-9, 205
watching brief 1, 10-11, 15, 32, 50, 63, 78, 95, 110
weapons 5, 7, 87, 198-9, 201, 205
weaving equipment 33, 188
Weir Bank Stud Farm 5, 190, 197
Wessex Archaeology 1, 8, 23
Wessex Archaeology Trench 8, 105-6
Weybridge, Surrey 124, 126
wheat 47, 49, 69-70, 105, 139, 150-2, 206
  bread 150-2
  emmer 150-2, 187
  hulled 150-1
Widbrook Common 5, 199, 202
Wilburton period 65, 141

Yarnton, Oxfordshire 123, 127, 186, 190